Ubuntu Server Cookbook

Arm yourself to make the most of the versatile, powerful
Ubuntu Server with over 100 hands-on recipes

Uday R. Sawant

BIRMINGHAM - MUMBAI

Ubuntu Server Cookbook

First published: June 2016

Production reference: 1270616

Published by Packt Publishing Ltd.
Livery Place
35 Livery Street
Birmingham B3 2PB, UK.

ISBN 978-1-78588-306-4

www.packtpub.com

Credits

Author

Uday R. Sawant

Reviewer

Dominik Jakub Szynk

Commissioning Editor

Neil Alexander

Acquisition Editor

Divya Poojari

Content Development Editor

Deepti Thore

Technical Editor

Devesh Chugh

Copy Editor

Safis Editing

Project Coordinator

Shweta H Birwatkar

Proofreader

Safis Editing

Indexer

Monica Ajmera Mehta

Graphics

Kirk D'Penha

Production Coordinator

Shantanu N. Zagade

Cover Work

Shantanu N. Zagade

About the Author

Uday R. Sawant has completed his master's in computer applications from Mumbai University. He is skilled with more than four years of experience in software development and operations field.

He is an expert with the LAMP stack, JavaScript, and cloud infrastructure. Before starting as a software developer, he worked extensively with server hardware and has more than two years of experience as system administrator.

Currently, he is working as a software scientist in a Mumbai-based start-up called Sweet Couch. His responsibilities include developing backend services, setting up real-time communication server, and automating various daily tasks. With immense interest in machine learning, he likes to spend his spare time exploring this subject. His first book was *Instant Building Multi-Page Forms with Yii How-To* published by *Packt Publishing*.

I would like to thank Packt Publishing for giving me another opportunity to work with them and write my second book. A big thanks goes to my parents for their support throughout the time of writing this book. Also, I would like to thank my team at Sweet Couch as without their support, it would have not been possible to write a full length book. A special thanks to Mr. Mitul Thakkar who always encouraged me to keep on writing. Finally, thanks to Preeti Singh, an editor for this book, for keeping things on track.

www.PacktPub.com

eBooks, discount offers, and more

Did you know that Packt offers eBook versions of every book published, with PDF and ePub files available? You can upgrade to the eBook version at www.PacktPub.com and as a print book customer, you are entitled to a discount on the eBook copy. Get in touch with us at customercare@packtpub.com for more details.

At www.PacktPub.com, you can also read a collection of free technical articles, sign up for a range of free newsletters and receive exclusive discounts and offers on Packt books and eBooks.

https://www2.packtpub.com/books/subscription/packtlib

Do you need instant solutions to your IT questions? PacktLib is Packt's online digital book library. Here, you can search, access, and read Packt's entire library of books.

Why Subscribe?

- Fully searchable across every book published by Packt
- Copy and paste, print, and bookmark content
- On demand and accessible via a web browser

Table of Contents

Preface

Welcome to *Ubuntu Server Cookbook*, a step-by-step guide to your own Ubuntu server.

Ubuntu is an open source operating system, or rather, I should say that Ubuntu is a mission to provide quality software to everybody without any cost. As mentioned on the official site, the meaning of the word Ubuntu is *I am, cause we are* and Ubuntu is working hard towards their mission by being more than just a free operating system.

Ubuntu is based on Debian, a well-established Linux distribution. However, Debian is kind of limited to geeks. Ubuntu added an easy user interface named Unity that made it popular with various desktop users. One answer on Ask Ubuntu compares Ubuntu and Debian to a local restaurant and a farmer, respectively. Ubuntu carefully selects the best things from Debian and adds its own flavors to make it easy and more enjoyable for the end users. It's still Debian at base, but it more easier to use and more stable with frequent updates and a definite release cycle.

Users can choose an Ubuntu operating system from nine different flavors, starting with lightweight desktop to a fully loaded multimedia editing system. In addition to desktop systems, Ubuntu provides separate editions for various server platforms, cloud systems, mobile devices, and tablets. The new versions are released every six months with a major release in April and updates in October. All security updates are released throughout the year, as and when necessary. Every new version released in an even year (2014, 2016, and so on) are tagged for Long Term Support (LTS). These versions receive extended support period of five years and are generally used in production environments.

At the time of writing, Ubuntu has already taken a major share in the server market and has already become a default choice of millions of cloud users. According to an article by Dustin Kirkland, a member of the product team at Canonical, "November 2015 has seen over 2 million cloud instances being launched with Ubuntu Server. That's nearly one instance per second" and these are just the numbers from cloud services. Ubuntu is being used in Desktop systems, laptops, mobiles, routers, and even to control your cars, drones, and countless Internet of Things (IoT) devices. Docker hub, a popular container repository reports more than 40 million pulls of official Ubuntu image.

The purpose of this book is to provide step-by-step solutions using the Ubuntu server. We will focus on common, server-related tasks such as user management, installing various packages for web servers, database, some low hanging fruits in performance and security, and many more. The book also covers the latest development in the container world with LXD and Docker. All recipes are based on the Ubuntu server, Xenial Xerus (version 16.04), the latest LTS release of Ubuntu.

What this book covers

The book is divided into multiple chapters, covering details of specific tasks.

Chapter 1, Managing Users and Groups, covers common user management tasks such as adding or removing user accounts, creating separate groups, assigning access rights, and setting user-level resource limits.

Chapter 2, Networking, explore the various network management functions, including network configuration, setting up DNS and DHCP servers, installing network proxy, and VPN setup. It also includes performance tuning tips and firewall setup.

Chapter 3, Working with Web Servers, provides a detailed configuration of web servers. This chapter covers both Apache and Nginx. You will also find some advance topics such as reverse proxy and load balancing using Nginx.

Chapter 4, Working with Mail Servers, explains the installation and configuration of your e-mail server.

Chapter 5, Handling Databases, discusses the popular relational database server, MySQL. It also covers MongoDB as a NoSQL database system, which is quite a hot technology in recent days.

Chapter 6, Network Storage, explains how to set up the good old Samba server along with FTP and Rsync details. Additionally, it includes the basics of NFS.

Chapter 7, Cloud Computing, includes details on virtualization with the Ubuntu server and some advance tools from Ubuntu to set up your own cloud system with OpenStack and Juju.

Chapter 8, Working with Containers, introduces Linux containers (LXC) and a container management tool by Ubuntu, LXD. This chapter also covers another hot topic, Docker.

Chapter 9, Streaming with Ampache, helps you to set up your own streaming server. We will take a quick look at Ampache, an open source web application for media streaming.

Chapter 10, Communication Server with XMPP, covers the installation of XMPP-based chat server, Ejabberd.

Chapter 11, Git Hosting, covers basic work flow of version control system Git and an open source web-based repository management tool GitLab.

Chapter 12, Collaboration Tools, explores more open source tools for your team and also covers the various tools to help your team stay connected.

Chapter 13, Performance Monitoring, introduces various monitoring tools that can help you optimize the performance of your Ubuntu server.

Chapter 14, Centralized Authentication Service, saves some efforts by introducing LDAP. This chapter covers the LDAP-based centralized authentication and authorization.

What you need for this book

The book is written with the help of Ubuntu server 16.04 and few virtual machines with VirtualBox. The recipes should work fine with Ubuntu version 14.04 and higher. For most of the recipes, a minimum hardware configuration of 512 MB memory with single CPU is enough. However, a few recipes such as OpenStack installation require additional hardware resources. The specific requirements are given in the respective recipes, if any.

Feel free to use any virtualization tool of your choice. Also, you can skip the local set up and use cloud servers. Many cloud providers give free introductory service for limited period. You can use these services to test your setup.

Who this book is for

Ubuntu Server Cookbook is intended for system administrators with a basic understanding of Linux operating system. If you are a software developer or a newbie system administrator and want to setup your own servers, this book is an ideal guide for you. You are not required to have an in-depth knowledge or hands-on experience with Ubuntu, but you should know the basic commands for directory navigation, file management, and file editing tool. An understanding of computer networks and Internet is advisable.

Sections

In this book, you will find several headings that appear frequently (Getting ready, How to do it..., How it works..., There's more..., and See also).

To give clear instructions on how to complete a recipe, we use these sections as follows:

Getting ready

This section tells you what to expect in the recipe, and describes how to set up any software or any preliminary settings required for the recipe.

How to do it...

This section contains the steps required to follow the recipe.

How it works...

This section usually consists of a detailed explanation of what happened in the previous section.

There's more...

This section consists of additional information about the recipe in order to make the reader more knowledgeable about the recipe.

See also

This section provides helpful links to other useful information for the recipe.

Conventions

In this book, you will find a number of text styles that distinguish between different kinds of information. Here are some examples of these styles and an explanation of their meaning.

Code words in text, database table names, folder names, filenames, file extensions, pathnames, dummy URLs, user input, and Twitter handles are shown as follows: "You can check other log files like `/var/log/mail.err` and `/var/log/upstart/dovecot.log`"

A block of code is set as follows:

```
disable_plaintext_auth = yes
```

Any command-line input or output is written as follows:

```
$ sudo adduser bob
```

New terms and **important words** are shown in bold. Words that you see on the screen, for example, in menus or dialog boxes, appear in the text like this: "You can access the **Inbox** panel on port 7071."

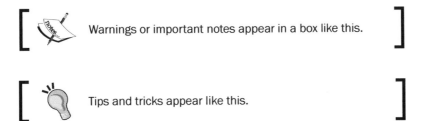

Warnings or important notes appear in a box like this.

Tips and tricks appear like this.

Reader feedback

Feedback from our readers is always welcome. Let us know what you think about this book—what you liked or disliked. Reader feedback is important for us as it helps us develop titles that you will really get the most out of.

To send us general feedback, simply e-mail feedback@packtpub.com, and mention the book's title in the subject of your message.

If there is a topic that you have expertise in and you are interested in either writing or contributing to a book, see our author guide at www.packtpub.com/authors.

Customer support

Now that you are the proud owner of a Packt book, we have a number of things to help you to get the most from your purchase.

Downloading the example code

You can download the example code files for this book from your account at http://www.packtpub.com. If you purchased this book elsewhere, you can visit http://www.packtpub.com/support and register to have the files e-mailed directly to you.

You can download the code files by following these steps:

1. Log in or register to our website using your e-mail address and password.
2. Hover the mouse pointer on the **SUPPORT** tab at the top.
3. Click on **Code Downloads & Errata**.

4. Enter the name of the book in the **Search** box.

5. Select the book for which you're looking to download the code files.

6. Choose from the drop-down menu where you purchased this book from.

7. Click on **Code Download**.

You can also download the code files by clicking on the **Code Files** button on the book's webpage at the Packt Publishing website. This page can be accessed by entering the book's name in the **Search** box. Please note that you need to be logged in to your Packt account.

Once the file is downloaded, please make sure that you unzip or extract the folder using the latest version of:

- ▶ WinRAR / 7-Zip for Windows
- ▶ Zipeg / iZip / UnRarX for Mac
- ▶ 7-Zip / PeaZip for Linux

The code bundle for the book is also hosted on GitHub at `https://github.com/PacktPublishing/Ubuntu-Server-Cookbook`. We also have other code bundles from our rich catalog of books and videos available at `https://github.com/PacktPublishing/`. Check them out!

Downloading the color images of this book

We also provide you with a PDF file that has color images of the screenshots/diagrams used in this book. The color images will help you better understand the changes in the output. You can download this file from: `http://www.packtpub.com/sites/default/files/downloads/UbuntuServerCookbook_ColorImages.pdf`.

Errata

Although we have taken every care to ensure the accuracy of our content, mistakes do happen. If you find a mistake in one of our books—maybe a mistake in the text or the code—we would be grateful if you could report this to us. By doing so, you can save other readers from frustration and help us improve subsequent versions of this book. If you find any errata, please report them by visiting `http://www.packtpub.com/submit-errata`, selecting your book, clicking on the **Errata Submission Form** link, and entering the details of your errata. Once your errata are verified, your submission will be accepted and the errata will be uploaded to our website or added to any list of existing errata under the Errata section of that title.

To view the previously submitted errata, go to `https://www.packtpub.com/books/content/support` and enter the name of the book in the search field. The required information will appear under the **Errata** section.

Piracy

Piracy of copyrighted material on the Internet is an ongoing problem across all media. At Packt, we take the protection of our copyright and licenses very seriously. If you come across any illegal copies of our works in any form on the Internet, please provide us with the location address or website name immediately so that we can pursue a remedy.

Please contact us at copyright@packtpub.com with a link to the suspected pirated material.

We appreciate your help in protecting our authors and our ability to bring you valuable content.

Questions

If you have a problem with any aspect of this book, you can contact us at questions@packtpub.com, and we will do our best to address the problem.

1
Managing Users and Groups

In this chapter, we will cover the following recipes:

- ▶ Creating a user account
- ▶ Creating user accounts in batch mode
- ▶ Creating a group
- ▶ Adding group members
- ▶ Deleting a user account
- ▶ Managing file permissions
- ▶ Getting root privileges with sudo
- ▶ Setting resource limits with limits.conf
- ▶ Setting up public key authentication
- ▶ Securing user accounts

Introduction

In this chapter, you will see how to add new users to the Ubuntu server, update existing users, and set permissions for users. You will get to know the default setting for new users and how to change them. Also, you will take a look at secure shell (SSH) access and securing user profiles.

Creating a user account

While installing Ubuntu, we add a primary user account on the server; if you are using the cloud image, it comes preinstalled with the default user. This single user is enough to get all tasks done in Ubuntu. There are times when you need to create more restrictive user accounts. This recipe shows how to add a new user to the Ubuntu server.

Getting ready

You will need super user or root privileges to add a new user to the Ubuntu server.

How to do it...

Follow these steps to create the new user account:

1. To add a new user in Ubuntu, enter following command in your shell:

    ```
    $ sudo adduser bob
    ```

2. Enter your password to complete the command with `sudo` privileges:

3. Now enter a password for the new user:

```
ubuntu@ubuntu:~$
ubuntu@ubuntu:~$ sudo adduser bob
[sudo] password for ubuntu:
Adding user `bob' ...
Adding new group `bob' (1009) ...
Adding new user `bob' (1006) with group `bob' ...
Creating home directory `/home/bob' ...
Copying files from `/etc/skel' ...
Enter new UNIX password:
```

4. Confirm the password for the new user:

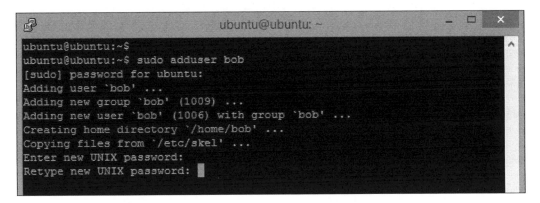

5. Enter the full name and other information about the new user; you can skip this part by pressing the *Enter* key.

6. Enter Y to confirm that information is correct:

```
ubuntu@ubuntu: ~
ubuntu@ubuntu:~$
ubuntu@ubuntu:~$ sudo adduser bob
[sudo] password for ubuntu:
Adding user `bob' ...
Adding new group `bob' (1009) ...
Adding new user `bob' (1006) with group `bob' ...
Creating home directory `/home/bob' ...
Copying files from `/etc/skel' ...
Enter new UNIX password:
Retype new UNIX password:
passwd: password updated successfully
Changing the user information for bob
Enter the new value, or press ENTER for the default
        Full Name []: Bob
        Room Number []:
        Work Phone []:
        Home Phone []:
        Other []:
Is the information correct? [Y/n]
```

7. This should have added new user to the system. You can confirm this by viewing the file /etc/passwd:

```
ubuntu@ubuntu: ~                                    _  □  ×
ubuntu@ubuntu:~$ tail -n 2 /etc/passwd
user2:x:1005:1007:user2,,,:/home/user2:/bin/bash
bob:x:1006:1009:Bob,,,:/home/bob:/bin/bash
ubuntu@ubuntu:~$
```

How it works...

In Linux systems, the adduser command is higher level command to quickly add a new user to the system. Since adduser requires root privileges, we need to use sudo along with the command, adduser completes following operations:

1. Adds a new user.
2. Adds a new default group with the same name as the user.
3. Chooses **UID (user ID)** and **GID (group ID)** conforming to the Debian policy.
4. Creates a home directory with skeletal configuration (template) from /etc/skel.
5. Creates a password for the new user.
6. Runs the user script, if any.

If you want to skip the password prompt and finger information while adding the new user, use the following command:

```
$ sudo adduser --disabled-password --gecos "" username
```

Alternatively, you can use the useradd command as follows:

```
$ sudo useradd -s <SHELL> -m -d <HomeDir> -g <Group> UserName
```

Where:

▶ -s specifies default login shell for the user

▶ -d sets the home directory for the user

▶ -m creates a home directory if one does not already exist

▶ -g specifies the default group name for the user

Creating a user with the command useradd does not set password for the user account. You can set or change the user password with the following command:

```
$sudo passwd bob
```

This will change the password for the user account bob.

 Note that if you skip the username part from the above command you will end up changing the password of the root account.

There's more...

With adduser, you can do five different tasks:

- Add a normal user
- Add a system user with system option
- Add user group with the --group option and without the --system option
- Add a system group when called with the --system option
- Add an existing user to existing group when called with two non-option arguments

Check out the manual page man adduser to get more details.

You can also configure various default settings for the adduser command. A configuration file /etc/adduser.conf can be used to set the default values to be used by the adduser, addgroup, and deluser commands. A key value pair of configuration can set various default values, including the home directory location, directory structure skel to be used, default groups for new users, and so on. Check the manual page for more details on adduser.conf with following command:

```
$ man adduser.conf
```

See also

- Check out the command useradd, a low level command to add new user to system
- Check out the command usermod, a command to modify a user account
- See why every user has his own group at http://unix.stackexchange.com/questions/153390/why-does-every-user-have-his-own-group

Creating user accounts in batch mode

In this recipe, you will see how to create multiple user accounts in batch mode without using any external tool.

Getting ready

You will need a user account with root or root privileges.

How to do it...

Follow these steps to create a user account in batch mode:

1. Create a new text file `users.txt` with the following command:

   ```
   $ touch users.txt
   ```

2. Change file permissions with the following command:

   ```
   $ chmod 600 users.txt
   ```

3. Open `users.txt` with **GNU nano** and add user account details:

   ```
   $ nano users.txt
   ```

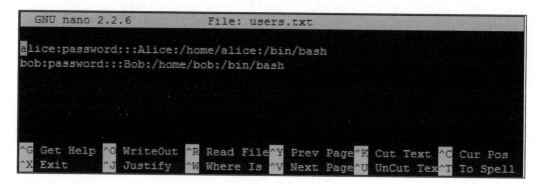

```
  GNU nano 2.2.6                    File: users.txt

alice:password:::Alice:/home/alice:/bin/bash
bob:password:::Bob:/home/bob:/bin/bash




^G Get Help  ^O WriteOut  ^R Read File ^Y Prev Page ^K Cut Text  ^C Cur Pos
^X Exit      ^J Justify   ^W Where Is  ^V Next Page ^U UnCut Tex ^T To Spell
```

4. Press *Ctrl + O* to save the changes.
5. Press *Ctrl + X* to exit **GNU nano**.
6. Enter `$ sudo newusers users.txt` to import all users listed in `users.txt` file.
7. Check `/etc/passwd` to confirm that users are created:

```
ubuntu@ubuntu:~$ tail -n 4 /etc/passwd
user1:x:1004:1006:user1,,,:/home/user1:/bin/bash
user2:x:1005:1007:user2,,,:/home/user2:/bin/bash
alice:x:1006:1009:Alice:/home/alice:/bin/bash
bob:x:1007:1010:Bob:/home/bob:/bin/bash
ubuntu@ubuntu:~$
```

How it works...

We created a database of user details listed in same format as the `passwd` file. The default format for each row is as follows:

```
username:passwd:uid:gid:full name:home_dir:shell
```

Where:

- ▶ `username`: This is the login name of the user. If a user exists, information for user will be changed; otherwise, a new user will be created.
- ▶ `password`: This is the password of the user.
- ▶ `uid`: This is the `uid` of the user. If empty, a new `uid` will be assigned to this user.
- ▶ `gid`: This is the `gid` for the default group of user. If empty, a new group will be created with the same name as the username.
- ▶ `full name`: This information will be copied to the `gecos` field.
- ▶ `home_dir`: This defines the `home` directory of the user. If empty, a new `home` directory will be created with ownership set to new or existing user.
- ▶ `shell`: This is the default login `shell` for the user.

The new user command reads each row and updates the user information if the user already exists, or it creates a new user.

We made the `users.txt` file accessible to owner only. This is to protect this file, as it contains the user's login name and password in unencrypted format.

Creating a group

Group is a way to organize and administer user accounts in Linux. Groups are used to collectively assign rights and permissions to multiple user accounts.

Getting ready

You will need super user or root privileges to add a group to the Ubuntu server.

How to do it...

Follow these steps to create a group:

1. Enter the following command to add a new group:

   ```
   $ sudo addgroup guest
   ```

2. Enter your password to complete addgroup with root privileges.

How it works...

Here, we are simply adding a new group guest to the server. As addgroup needs root privileges, we need to use sudo along with the command. After creating a new group, addgroup displays the GID of the new group.

There's more...

Similar to adduser, you can use addgroup in different modes:

- Add a normal group when used without any options
- Add a system group with the --system option
- Add an existing user to an existing group when called with two non-option arguments

Check out the manual page for the addgroup(man addgroup) to get more details.

See also

- Check out groupadd, a low level utility to add new group to the server

Adding group members

Once you have groups in place, you can add existing users as well as new users to that group. All access rights and permissions assigned to the group will be automatically available to all the members of the group.

Getting ready

You will need super user or root privileges to add a group member to the Ubuntu server.

How to do it...

Follow these steps to add group members:

1. Here, you can use `adduser` command with two non-option arguments:

   ```
   $ sudo adduser john guest
   ```

2. Enter your password to complete `addgroup` with root privileges.

How it works...

As mentioned previously, you can use the `adduser` command to add an existing user to an existing group. Here, we have passed two non-option arguments:

   ▸   `john`: This is the name of the user to be added to the group
   ▸   `guest`: This is the name of the group

There's more...

Alternatively, you can use the command `usermod` to modify the group assigned to the user:

```
$ sudo usermod -g <group> <username>
```

To add a user to multiple groups, use the following command:

```
$ sudo usermod -a -G <group1>,<group2>,<group3> <username>
```

This will add `<username>` to `<group1>`, `<group2>`, and `<group3>`. Without flag `-a`, any previously assigned groups will be replaced with new groups.

Deleting a user account

If you no longer need a user account, it is good idea to delete that account.

Getting ready

You will need super user or root privileges to delete a group from the Ubuntu server.

How to do it...

Follow these steps to delete the user account:

1. Enter the following command to delete a user account:

   ```
   $ sudo deluser --remove-home john
   ```

2. Enter your password to complete `addgroup` with root privileges:

```
ubuntu@ubuntu:~$ sudo deluser --remove-home bob
[sudo] password for ubuntu:
Looking for files to backup/remove ...
Removing files ...
Removing user `bob' ...
Warning: group `bob' has no more members.
Done.
ubuntu@ubuntu:~$ 
```

How it works...

Here, we used the `deluser` command with the option `--remove-home`. This will delete the user account named `john` and also remove the `home` and `mail spool` directories associated with `john`. By default, the `deluser` command will delete the user without deleting the `home` directory.

It is a good idea to keep a backup of user files before removing the `home` directory and any other files. This can be done with an additional flag along with the `deluser` command:

```
$ deluser --backup --remove-home john
```

This will create a backup file with the name `john.tar.gz` in the current working directory, and then the user account and the `home` directory will removed.

There's more...

When called with the `--group` option, the `deluser` command will remove the group. Similarly, when called with two non-option arguments, the `deluser` command will try to remove a user from a specific group:

```
$ deluser john guest # this will remove user john from group guest
$ deluser --group guest # this will remove a group
```

If you want to disable the user account rather than delete it, you can do it with the following commands:

```
$ sudo usermod --expiredate 1 john # disable the user account john
$ sudo usermod --expiredate "" john # re-enable user account john
$ sudo usermod -e YYYY-MM-DD john # specify expiry date
```

See also

  ▶ Refer to the manual page for `deluser` with `man deluser`

Managing file permissions

We have created users and groups. In this recipe, you will work with default file permissions for users and groups, as well as see how to modify those permissions.

Getting ready

Create two users, `user1` and `user2`. Create new group `editor` and add `user1` and `user2` as members.

How to do it...

Follow these steps to manage file permissions, follow these steps:

1. To change groups for files and directories:

    1. Log in with `user1`.

    2. Create a new directory `documents` under `home`:

        ```
        user1@ubuntu:~$ mkdir documents
        ```

    3. Create a text file under `documents`:

        ```
        user1@ubuntu:~$ echo "hello world"> documents/file.txt
        ```

    4. Now log in with `user2`:

        ```
        user1@ubuntu:~$ su user2
        ```

5. Try to edit the same text file. It should say `Permission denied`:

   `user2@ubuntu:/home/user1$ echo "hello again">`
   `documents/file.txt`

```
user2@ubuntu:/home/user1$
user2@ubuntu:/home/user1$ echo "hello again" > documents/file.txt
bash: documents/file.txt: Permission denied
user2@ubuntu:/home/user1$
```

6. log in as `user1` and change the group of `documents` to `editor`:

   `user1@ubuntu:~$ chgrp -R editor documents`

```
user1@ubuntu:~$ chgrp -R editor documents/
user1@ubuntu:~$ ls -l
total 4
drwxrwxr-x 2 user1 editor 4096 Jun 26 15:36 documents
user1@ubuntu:~$
```

7. Switch to `user2` and try editing the same file. Now it should work:

```
user1@ubuntu:~$ su user2
Password:
user2@ubuntu:/home/user1$ echo "hello again" > documents/file.txt
user2@ubuntu:/home/user1$
```

2. To set permissions with `chmod`, follow these steps:

   1. Create simple shell script with the following command:

      `$ echo 'echo "Hello World!!"'> hello.sh`

   2. Execute a shell script with the following command:

      `$ ./hello.sh`

```
user1@ubuntu:~$ echo 'echo "hello world!!!"' > hello.sh
user1@ubuntu:~$ ls -l
total 8
drwxrwxr-x 2 user1 editor 4096 Jun 26 15:36 documents
-rw-rw-r-- 1 user1 user1    22 Jun 26 15:59 hello.sh
user1@ubuntu:~$ ./hello.sh
bash: ./hello.sh: Permission denied
```

   3. Set executable permission to `hello.sh` with the following command:

      `$ chmod u+x hello.sh`

4. Check new permission with the following command:

   ```
   $ ls -l
   ```

```
user1@ubuntu:~$ chmod u+x hello.sh
user1@ubuntu:~$ ls -l
total 8
drwxrwxr-x 2 user1 editor 4096 Jun 26 15:36 documents
-rwxrw-r-- 1 user1 user1    23 Jun 26 15:54 hello.sh
user1@ubuntu:~$
```

5. Execute `hello.sh` again:

```
user1@ubuntu:~$ ./hello.sh
hello world!!!
user1@ubuntu:~$
```

3. To protect shared files with sticky bit, follow these steps:

   1. Log in as `user1` and set sticky bit for directory `documents`:

      ```
      user1@ubuntu:~$ chmod +t documents
      ```

   2. Log in as `user2` and create a new file.

   3. Try to delete any file under `documents`. It should fail:

```
user1@ubuntu:~$ chmod +t documents/
user1@ubuntu:~$ ls -l
total 4
drwxrwxr-t 2 user1 editor 4096 Jun 26 15:36 documents
user1@ubuntu:~$ su user2
Password:
user2@ubuntu:/home/user1$ rm documents/file.txt
rm: cannot remove 'documents/file.txt': Operation not permitted
user2@ubuntu:/home/user1$
```

How it works...

When you create a new file or directory in Ubuntu, the default permissions for files are read and write access to owner and owner's private group, along with read, write, and execute access for directories. You can check the default setting with `umask -S`.

In our example, we have `user1` and `user2`. Both of them are members of the `editor` group. When `user1` creates a file, the default permissions are limited to `user1` and its private group (user1) named after the user account. This is the reason `user2` sees `Permission denied` on editing file. By changing the group of `documents` to `editor` we allow all members of `editor` to read and write to files in `documents`.

With the `chmod` command, we can set permissions at a more granular level. In our example of `hello.sh`, we have set the executable permission for `hello.sh`. Similarly, we can set read permission as follows:

```
$chmod +r filename
```

To set write permission, use the following command:

```
$chmod +w filename
```

You can set more selective permissions with additional parameters before mode expression as follows:

```
$chmod ugo+x filename
```

Here, `u` sets the permission for user, `g` for group, and `o` for all others.

To remove permissions, replace + with -. For example, `$chmod o-w filename`. Alternatively, you can use the Octal format to specify permissions:

```
$chmod 777 filename
```

This gives read, write, and execute permission to user group and others, whereas the command `$chmod 600 filename` gives set, read, and write permissions for owner and no permission to groups and others. In Octal format [777], the first bit is used for the user or owner of the file, the second bit is for group, and the third bit is for everyone else. Check out the following table for more information:

Notation	Octal value	Permissions
-|—|—|—	0|000|000|000	Regular files, no permissions
d|r–|r–|r–	d|400|400|400	Directory, read permission to owner, group, and others
-|rw-|r–|r–	-|644|644|644	Regular file, read and write permission to owner and read permission to group or others
-|rwx|rwx|rwx	-|777|777|777	Regular file, all permissions to everyone

Finally, when you share files within a group of users, there are chances that someone deletes the file that is required by other users. Sticky bit can protect these file from deletion. When sticky bit is set, only the owner or a user with root privileges can delete a file.

You can set sticky bit with the command `chmod` as `$chmod +t directoryName`. Sticky bit is shown in long listing (`ls -l`) with symbol `t` or `T`. Additionally, sticky bit works only with directories and is ignored on ordinary files.

There's more...

Many times when working as a root user, all files and directories created are owned by root. A non-root user can't write to these directories or files. You can use the command `chown` to change the ownership of such files and assign them to respective users.

To change ownership of a file, use the following command:

```
$chown newuser filename
```

To change the owner as well as the group of file, use the following command:

```
$chown newuser:newgroup filename
```

You can skip changing owner and change only the group with the following command:

```
$chown :newgroup filename
```

Note that the `chown` command can only be used by users with root privileges.

Getting root privileges with sudo

When you create a new Ubuntu server in the cloud, by default you get the root account. This account has full system access with no restrictions at all and should only be used for administrative tasks. You can always create a new user account with fewer privileges. But there are times when you need extra root privileges to add a new user or change some system setting. You can use the `sudo` command to temporarily get extra privileges for a single command. In this recipe, you will see how to grant `sudo` privileges to a newly created user.

Getting ready

You will need a root account or an account with root privileges.

How to do it...

Follow these steps to get the root privileges with `sudo`:

1. Add new user if required:

   ```
   $sudo adduser john
   ```

2. Make `john` a member of `sudo` group with the following command:

   ```
   $sudo adduser username sudo
   ```

How it works...

All `sudo` access rules are configured in a file located at `/etc/sudoers`. This file contains a list of users and groups that are allowed to use the `sudo` command:

```
alan ALL=(ALL:ALL)ALL // allow sudo access to user alan
%sudo  ALL=(ALL)  ALL // allow sudo access to members of sudo
```

The line `alan  ALL=(ALL:ALL)  ALL` specifies that the user `alan` can run any command as any user and optionally set any group (taken from `man` pages for sudoers: `man sudoers`).

The entry `%sudo ALL=(ALL)  ALL` specifies that any member of system group `sudo` can run any command as any user.

All we have to do is add a new user to the group `sudo` and that user will automatically get `sudo` privileges. After getting the membership of the `sudo` group, user needs to log out and log back in for the changes to take effect. Basically, the user shell needs to be restarted with new privileges. Optionally, you can always go and change the `sudoers` file for a specific condition.

[Make sure that you use the `visudo` tool to make any changes to sudoers file.]

There's more...

Here, we will discuss how to set a password-less `sudo` and some additional benefits of `sudo`.

Setting password less sudo

`sudo` is a useful and handy tool for temporary root privileges, but you need to enter your password every time. This creates problems especially for users with no password set. This problem can be solved by setting the `NOPASSWD` flag in the `sudoers` file. Make sure you use the `visudo` tool to edit the `sudoers` file:

1. Open the `sudoers` file with the `visudo` command:

   `$sudo visudo`

2. Select the line for user or group you want to allow password-less `sudo` access.

3. Add `NOPASSWD` after closing the bracket:

   `%sudo    ALL=(ALL:ALL) NOPASSWD: ALL`

4. Press *Ctrl + O* and then confirm with the *Enter* key to save the changes.

5. Press *Ctrl + X* to exit `visudo`.

Now, the users of the group `sudo` should be able to use the `sudo` command without providing a password. Alternatively, you can add a separate entry to limit password-less access to a specific user.

Note that the `sudoers` program performs cache authentication for a small time (default is 15 minutes). When repeated within timeout, you may notice password-less `sudo` without setting the `NOPASSWD` flag.

Other uses of sudo

In addition to running a single command with `sudo`, you might want to execute a list of commands with the `sudo` privileges. Then, you can open a shell with root access (`# prompt`) with the command `$sudo -s`. The shell environment remains same as original user, but now you can execute commands as a root user.

Alternatively, you can switch user to root with the command `$sudo su -`. This command will open a new shell as a root user.

See also

- Check manual pages for `sudo` with `$man sudo`
- For more details on `adduser`, check the *Creating user account* recipe

Setting resource limits with limits.conf

Ubuntu is a multiuser and multi-process operating system. If a single user or process is consuming too many resources, other processes might not be able to use the system. In this recipe, you will see how to set resource limits to avoid such problems.

Getting ready

User account with root privileges is required.

How to do it...

Following are the steps to set the resource limits:

1. Check the CPU use limit with `$ulimit -t`.
2. To set new limit, open `limits.conf` with the following command:

   ```
   $sudo nano /etc/security/limits.conf
   ```

3. Scroll to the end of the file and add following lines:

```
username   soft   cpu   0   # max cpu time in minutes
username   hard   cpu   1000 # max cpu time in minutes
```

4. Enter *Ctrl + O* to save the changes.

5. Enter *Ctrl + X* to exit **GNU nano** editor.

How it works...

PAM stands for pluggable authentication module. The PAM module `pam_limits.so` provides functionality to set a cap on resource utilization. The command `ulimit` can be used to view current limits as well as set new limits for a session. The default values used by `pam_limits.so` can be set in `/etc/security/limits.conf`.

In this recipe, we are updating `limits.conf` to set a limit on CPU uses by user `username`. Limits set by the `ulimit` command are limited to that session. To set the limits permanently, we need to set them in the `limits.conf` file.

The syntax of the `limits.conf` file is as follows:

```
<domain> <type> <item> <value>
```

Here, `<domain>` can be a username, a group name, or a wildcard entry.

`<type>` denotes the type of the limit and it can have the following values:

► `soft`: This is a soft limit which can be changed by user

► `hard`: This is a cap on soft limit set by super user and enforced by kernel

`<item>` is the resource to set the limit for. You can get a list of all items with `$ulimit -a`:

```
user2@ubuntu:/home/user1$ ulimit -a
core file size          (blocks, -c) 0
data seg size           (kbytes, -d) unlimited
scheduling priority             (-e) 0
file size               (blocks, -f) unlimited
pending signals                 (-i) 3887
max locked memory       (kbytes, -l) 64
max memory size         (kbytes, -m) unlimited
open files                      (-n) 1024
pipe size            (512 bytes, -p) 8
POSIX message queues     (bytes, -q) 819200
real-time priority              (-r) 0
stack size              (kbytes, -s) 8192
cpu time               (seconds, -t) unlimited
max user processes              (-u) 3887
virtual memory          (kbytes, -v) unlimited
file locks                      (-x) unlimited
```

In our example, we have set `soft` limit on CPU uses to `0` minutes and `hard` limit to `1000` minutes. You can changes soft limit values with the `ulimit` command. To view existing limits on open files, use the command `$ulimit -n`. To change limits on open files, pass the new limit as follows:

```
$ulimit -n 4096
```

An unprivileged process can only set its `soft` limit value between `0` and `hard` limit, and it can irreversibly lower `hard` limit. A privileged process can change either limit values.

There's more...

The command `ulimit` can be used to set limits on per process basis. You can't use the `ulimit` command to limit resources at the user level. You can use `cgroups` to set a cap on resource use.

Setting up public key authentication

In this recipe, you will see how to set up secure public key authentication.

Getting ready

You might need root privileges for certain tasks.

How to do it...

Follow these steps to set up public key authentication:

1. Add a new user. You can skip this step if you have already created a user:

   ```
   $sudo adduser john
   ```

2. Log in as `john` and change to the `home` directory with `cd ~/`:

3. Create a `.ssh` directory if it doesn't already exist:

   ```
   $ mkdir .ssh
   ```

4. Create a file named `authorized_keys` under the `.ssh` directory:

   ```
   $ touch .ssh/authorized_keys
   ```

5. Set permissions on the `.ssh` directory to `700`:

   ```
   $chmod 700 .ssh
   ```

6. Set permissions for `authorized_keys` to `600`:

   ```
   $ chmod 600 .ssh/authorized_keys
   ```

7. Generate public key pair on your local system with the following command:

   ```
   $ ssh-keygen
   ```

8. Copy the generated public key from the `.ssh/id_rsa.pub` file to the `authorized_keys` file on the server.

9. Now, open an `ssh` connection from local to server with the following command:

   ```
   $ ssh john@server
   ```

10. If asked for confirmation, type `yes` and press the *Enter* key to continue:

```
user1@ubuntu:~$ ssh localhost
The authenticity of host 'localhost (::1)' can't be established.
ECDSA key fingerprint is c7:1c:46:a4:1a:9f:4a:3b:81:df:a8:3c:ef:89:a1:59.
Are you sure you want to continue connecting (yes/no)?
```

How it works...

Logging in with SSH supports different authentication methods. Public key authentication and password-based authentication are two common methods. To log in with public key authentication, we need a public private key pair. We generate this key pair with the `ssh-keygen` command. This command creates two files under the `.ssh` directory in the user's home:

- `id_rsa`: This is the private key file
- `id_rsa.pub`: This is the public key file

You can view the contents of the files with `$cat id_rsa.pub`. It should start with something like `ssh-rsa AAAA...`(except for the trailing dots).

```
ubuntu@ubuntu:~$ cat .ssh/id_rsa.pub
ssh-rsa AAAAB3NzaC1yc2EAAAADAQABAAABAQDJEAOwVaT0mhE+PTjEON1YAs3QG0UdyKdT8vNwMhVT
3fAHYwq5ka3Lo5d59tHcio6kWINrbyjD3cBoAnCwcvGOY3YDB1Lf4IAm3Re10g/MvJECcd99WuAvNCk0
knnqJ/LVJk6W7YSOHAV1X+Q8HaVbLijWYBjNnZNdSYAFM4Hh91PMCn4FpuqfLW+EzXO3xDoiGdqcHGuc
stuSkpaej+ZDteVX4s4hMr/X1Df38y7rDzdy9EzI2iDA9AMohxWEKM2rpcLhP3YAuNi4m+Ueef+wzlCx
YJMfOsQuP1B95/1931Ne/UnOESHINqlHadmaPbreVGF9JSJv4Fj0btUBPEAH ubuntu@ubuntu
```

We then copy the contents of public key to the server's `authorized_keys` file. Ensure that all contents are listed on single line in the `authorized_keys` file.

Also, ensure the permissions are properly set for the `.ssh` directory, and ensure that the `authorized_keys` file and directory are owned by the user. The permissions for the `.ssh` directory limits read, write, and execute permissions to the owner of the file. Similarly, for `authorized_keys` file, permissions are limited to read and write for owner only. This ensures that no other user can modify the data in the `.ssh` directory. If these permissions are not properly set, the SSH daemon will raise the warning `Permission denied`?.

Working of SSH authentication

When the SSH client initiates a connection with the server, the server sends public key identification of server to client. If a client is connecting to the server for the first time, it shows a warning and asks for user confirmation to store the server key in the `known_hosts` file under the `.shh` directory. After receiving the identity, the client authenticates server to ensure that it is really the intended server.

After server authentication, the server sends a list of possible authentication methods. The client selects the authentication method and selection to the server. After receiving the authentication method, the server sends a challenge string encrypted with client's private key. The client has to decrypt this string and send it back to server along with previously shared session key. If the response from the client matches the response generated by the server, then client authentication succeeds.

There's more...

You might be searching for a secure option to install key on server. Here's one way!

If your local system has the `ssh-copy-id` tool installed, you can directly add your public key to the server's `authorized_keys` file with a single command:

```
$ ssh-copy-id john@serverdomain
```

After providing the password, your local public key will be added to the `authorized_keys` file under the `.ssh` directory of the user `john`.

Troubleshooting SSH connections

Most of the connection issues are related with configuration problems. If you happen to face any such issue, read the error message in detail. It is descriptive enough to understand the mistake. You can also go through following checklist:

- Check if the SSH daemon is running. Check the port in use and port conflicts, if any
- Check whether the firewall configuration allows SSH ports
- Check the list of configuration methods that are enabled

- ▸ Check permissions for your private keys on your local system
- ▸ Check `authorized_keys` file for your public key on the server
- ▸ Check for any entry with the old address of the server in `known_hosts` on the local system

Additionally, you can use the verbose flag (`-v` or `-vvv`) with the `ssh` command to get details of every step taken by the SSH client. Also, check SSH daemon logs on server.

SSH tools for the Windows platform

If your local system runs Windows, then you can use tools provided by puTTYto generate new keys and connect to the server:

- ▸ `putty.exe`: This is the SSH client on Windows
- ▸ `puttygen.exe`: This tool generates public or private keys
- ▸ `pscp.exe`: This is the SCP client for secure file transfer

When using public key generated by the `puttygen.exe` tool, make sure that you convert the key to OpenSSH key format. Remove all comments and prepend `ssh-rsa`. Additionally, the entire key should be listed on a single line.

Another easy option is to use `puttygen.exe`. Load your private key in PuTTYgen and then copy the public key from the **Key** section of the PuTTYgen window.

See also

- ▸ For more information on the full working of SSH authentication, visit `http://www.slashroot.in/secure-shell-how-does-ssh-work`

Securing user accounts

In this recipe, we will look at ways to make user profiles more secure.

How to do it...

Follow these steps to secure the user account:

1. Set a strong password policy with the following steps:

   - ❑ Open the `/etc/pam.d/common-password` file with **GNU nano**:

     ```
     $ sudo nano /etc/pam.d/common-password
     ```

   - ❑ Find the line similar to this:

     ```
     password      [success=1 default=ignore]   pam_unix.so obscure
     sha512
     ```

- ❏ Add `minlen` to the end of this line:

  ```
  password      [success=1 default=ignore]  pam_unix.so obscure
  sha512 minlen=8
  ```

- ❏ Add this line to enforce alphanumeric passwords:

  ```
  password requisite pam_cracklib.so ucredit=-1 lcredit=-1
  dcredit=-1  ocredit=-1
  ```

- ❏ Save changes and exit **GNU nano** editor.

- ❏ Press *Ctrl + O* to save changes.

- ❏ Press *Ctrl + X* to exit **GNU nano** editor.

2. Secure the `home` directory with the following steps:

   - ❏ Check `home` directory permissions with the following command:

     ```
     $ ls -ld /home/username
     ```

   - ❏ Restrict permissions to user and group with the following command:

     ```
     $ chmod 750 /home/username
     ```

   - ❏ Change `adduser` default permissions by editing `/etc/adduser.conf`. Find `DIR_MODE=0755` and change it to `DIR_MODE=0750`.

3. Disable SSH access to root user with the following step:

   - ❏ Open `/etc/ssh/sshd_config` and add or edit `PermitRootLogin` to `PermitRootLogin no`

4. Disable password authentication with the following step:

   - ❏ Open `/etc/ssh/sshd_config` and add or edit `PasswordAuthentication no`

5. Install `fail2ban` with `sudo apt-get install fail2ban`.

How it works...

This recipe discussed a few important steps to make user accounts more secure.

A password is the most important aspect in securing user accounts. A weak password can be easily broken with brute force attacks and dictionary attacks. It is always a good idea to avoid password-based authentication, but if you are still using it, then make sure you enforce a strong password policy.

Password authentication is controlled by the PAM module `pam_unix`, and all settings associated with login are listed at `/etc/pam.d/login`. An additional configuration file `/etc/pam.d/common-password` includes values that control password checks.

The following line in the primary block of `common-password` file defines the rules for password complexity:

```
password [success=1 default=ignore] pam_unix.so obscure sha512
```

The default setting already defines some basic rules on passwords. The parameter `obscure` defines some extra checks on password strength. It includes the following:

- ▸ Palindrome check
- ▸ Case change only
- ▸ Similar check
- ▸ Rotated check

The other parameter, `sha512`, states that the new password will be encrypted with the `sha512` algorithm. We have set another option, `minlen=8`, on the same line, adding minimum length complexity to passwords.

[💡 For all settings of the `pam_unix` module, refer to the manual pages
       with the command `man pam_unix`.]

Additionally, we have set alphanumeric checks for new passwords with the PAM module `pam_cracklib`:

```
password requisite pam_cracklib.so ucredit=-1 lcredit=-1 dcredit=-
1  ocredit=-1
```

The preceding line adds requirement of one uppercase letter, one lowercase letter, one digit (`dcredit`), and one special character (`ocredit`)

There are other PAM modules available, and you can search them with the following command:

```
$ apt-cache search limpam-
```

You might also want to secure the `home` directory of users. The default permissions on Ubuntu allow read and execute access to everyone. You can limit the access on the `home` directory by changing permission on the `home` directory as required. In the preceding example, we changed permissions to `750`. This allows full access to the user, and allows read and execute access to the user's primary group.

You can also change the default permissions on the user's `home` directory by changing settings for the `adduser` command. These values are located at `/etc/adduser.conf`. We have changed default permissions to `750`, which limits access to the user and the group only.

Additionally, you can disable remote login for the root account as well as disable password-based authentication. Public key authentication is always more secure than passwords, unless you can secure your private keys. Before disabling password authentication, ensure that you have properly enabled public key authentication and you are able to log in with your keys. Otherwise, you will lock yourself out of the server.

You might want to install a tool like `fail2ban` to watch and block repeated failed actions. It scans through access logs and automatically blocks repeated failed login attempts. This can be a handy tool to provide a security against brute force attacks.

2
Networking

In this chapter, we will cover the following recipes:

- ▸ Connecting to a network with a static IP
- ▸ Installing the DHCP server
- ▸ Installing the DNS server
- ▸ Hiding behind the proxy with squid
- ▸ Being on time with NTP
- ▸ Discussing load balancing with HAProxy
- ▸ Tuning the TCP stack
- ▸ Troubleshooting network connectivity
- ▸ Securing remote access with OpenVPN
- ▸ Securing a network with uncomplicated firewall
- ▸ Securing against brute force attacks
- ▸ Discussing Ubuntu security best practices

Introduction

When we are talking about server systems, networking is the first and most important factor. If you are using an Ubuntu server in a cloud or virtual machine, you generally don't notice the network settings, as they are already configured with various network protocols. However, as your infrastructure grows, managing and securing the network becomes the priority.

Networking can be thought of as an umbrella term for various activities that include network configurations, file sharing and network time management, firewall settings and network proxies, and many others. In this chapter, we will take a closer look at the various networking services that help us set up and effectively manage our networks, be it in the cloud or a local network in your office.

Connecting to a network with a static IP

When you install Ubuntu server, its network setting defaults to dynamic IP addressing, that is, the network management daemon in Ubuntu searches for a DHCP server on the connected network and configures the network with the IP address assigned by DHCP. Even when you start an instance in the cloud, the network is configured with dynamic addressing using the DHCP server setup by the cloud service provider. In this chapter, you will learn how to configure the network interface with static IP assignment.

Getting ready

You will need an Ubuntu server with access to the root account or an account with `sudo` privileges. If network configuration is a new thing for you, then it is recommended to try this on a local or virtual machine.

How to do it...

Follow these steps to connect to the network with a static IP:

1. Get a list of available Ethernet interfaces using the following command:

    ```
    $ ifconfig -a | grep eth
    ```

```
ubuntu@ubuntu:~$ ifconfig -a | grep eth
eth0      Link encap:Ethernet   HWaddr 08:00:27:bb:a6:03
ubuntu@ubuntu:~$
```

2. Open `/etc/network/interfaces` and find the following lines:

   ```
   auto eth0
   iface eth0 inet dhcp
   ```

```
# The loopback network interface
auto lo
iface lo inet loopback

# The primary network interface
auto eth0
iface eth0 inet dhcp
```

3. Change the preceding lines to add an IP address, net mask, and default gateway (replace samples with the respective values):

   ```
   auto eth0
   iface eth0 inet static
       address 192.168.1.100
       netmask 255.255.255.0
       gateway 192.168.1.1
       dns-nameservers 192.168.1.45 192.168.1.46
   ```

4. Restart the network service for the changes to take effect:

   ```
   $ sudo /etc/init.d/networking restart
   ```

5. Try to ping a remote host to test the network connection:

   ```
   $ ping www.google.com
   ```

```
                                ubuntu@ubuntu: ~                        _ □ ×
ubuntu@ubuntu:~$ ping -c 3 www.google.com
PING www.google.com (216.58.220.4) 56(84) bytes of data.
64 bytes from bom05s05-in-f4.1e100.net (216.58.220.4): icmp_seq=1 ttl=56 time=12.3 ms
64 bytes from bom05s05-in-f4.1e100.net (216.58.220.4): icmp_seq=2 ttl=56 time=5.59 ms
64 bytes from bom05s05-in-f4.1e100.net (216.58.220.4): icmp_seq=3 ttl=56 time=5.75 ms

--- www.google.com ping statistics ---
3 packets transmitted, 3 received, 0% packet loss, time 2004ms
rtt min/avg/max/mdev = 5.597/7.912/12.386/3.164 ms
ubuntu@ubuntu:~$ []
```

How it works...

In this recipe, we have modified the network configuration from dynamic IP assignment to static assignment.

First, we got a list of all the available network interfaces with `ifconfig -a`. The `-a` option of `ifconfig` returns all the available network interfaces, even if they are disabled. With the help of the pipe (|) symbol, we have directed the output of `ifconfig` to the `grep` command. For now, we are interested with Ethernet ports only. The `grep` command will filter the received data and return only the lines that contain the `eth` character sequence:

```
ubuntu@ubuntu:~$ ifconfig -a | grep eth
eth0        Link encap:Ethernet   HWaddr 08:00:27:bb:a6:03
```

Here, `eth0` means first Ethernet interface available on the server. After getting the name of the interface to configure, we will change the network settings for `eth0` in interfaces file at `/etc/network/interfaces`. By default, `eth0` is configured to query the DHCP server for an IP assignment. The `eth0` line `auto` is used to automatically configure the `eth0` interface at server startup. Without this line, you will need to enable the network interface after each reboot. You can enable the `eth0` interface with the following command:

```
$ sudo ifup eth0
```

Similarly, to disable a network interface, use the following command:

```
$ sudo ifdown eth0
```

The second `iface eth0 inet static` line sets the network configuration to static assignment. After this line, we will add network settings, such as IP address, netmask, default gateway, and DNS servers.

After saving the changes, we need to restart the networking service for the changes to take effect. Alternatively, you can simply disable the network interface and enable it with `ifdown` and `ifup` commands.

There's more...

The steps in this recipe are used to configure the network changes permanently. If you need to change your network parameters temporarily, you can use the `ifconfig` and `route` commands as follows:

1. Change the IP address and netmask, as follows:

```
$ sudo ifconfig eth0 192.168.1.100 netmask 255.255.255.0
```

2. Set the default gateway:

   ```
   $ sudo route add default gw 192.168.1.1 eth0
   ```

3. Edit /etc/resolv.conf to add temporary name servers (DNS):

   ```
   nameserver 192.168.1.45
   nameserver 192.168.1.46
   ```

4. To verify the changes, use the following command:

   ```
   $ ifconfig eth0
   $ route -n
   ```

5. When you no longer need this configuration, you can easily reset it with the following command:

   ```
   $ ip addr flush eth0
   ```

6. Alternatively, you can reboot your server to reset the temporary configuration.

IPv6 configuration

You may need to configure your Ubuntu server for IPv6 IP address. Version six IP addresses use a 128-bit address space and include hexadecimal characters. They are different from simple version four IP addresses that use a 32-bit addressing space. Ubuntu supports IPv6 addressing and can be easily configured with either DHCP or a static address. The following is an example of static configuration for IPv6:

```
iface eth0 inet6 static
address 2001:db8::xxxx:yyyy
gateway your_ipv6_gateway
```

See also

You can find more details about network configuration in the Ubuntu server guide:

- ► https://help.ubuntu.com/lts/serverguide/network-configuration.html
- ► Checkout the Ubuntu wiki page on IP version 6 - https://wiki.ubuntu.com/IPv6

Installing the DHCP server

DHCP is a service used to automatically assign network configuration to client systems. DHCP can be used as a handy tool when you have a large pool of systems that needs to be configured for network settings. Plus, when you need to change the network configuration, say to update a DNS server, all you need to do is update the DHCP server and all the connected hosts will be reconfigured with new settings. Also, you get reliable IP address configuration that minimizes configuration errors and address conflicts. You can easily add a new host to the network without spending time on network planning.

DHCP is most commonly used to provide IP configuration settings, such as IP address, net mask, default gateway, and DNS servers. However, it can also be set to configure the time server and hostname on the client.

DHCP can be configured to use the following configuration methods:

> ▸ **Manual allocation**: Here, the configuration settings are tied with the MAC address of the client's network card. The same settings are supplied each time the client makes a request with the same network card.

> ▸ **Dynamic allocation**: This method specifies a range of IP addresses to be assigned to the clients. The server can dynamically assign IP configuration to the client on first come, first served basis. These settings are allocated for a specified time period called **lease**; after this period, the client needs to renegotiate with the server to keep using the same address. If the client leaves the network for a specified time, the configuration gets expired and returns to pool where it can be assigned to other clients. Lease time is a configurable option and it can be set to infinite.

Ubuntu comes pre-installed with the DHCP client, `dhclient`. The DHCP `dhcpd` server daemon can be installed while setting up an Ubuntu server or separately with the `apt-get` command.

Getting ready

Make sure that your DHCP host is configured with static IP address.

You will need an access to the root account or an account with `sudo` privileges.

How to do it...

Follow these steps to install a DHCP server:

1. Install a DHCP server:

```
$ sudo apt-get install isc-dhcp-server
```

2. Open the DHCP configuration file:

    ```
    $ sudo nano -w /etc/dhcp/dhcpd.conf
    ```

3. Change the default and max lease time if necessary:

    ```
    default-lease-time 600;
    max-lease-time 7200;
    ```

4. Add the following lines at the end of the file (replace the IP address to match your network):

    ```
    subnet 192.168.1.0 netmask 255.255.255.0 {
        range 192.168.1.150 192.168.1.200;
        option routers 192.168.1.1;
        option domain-name-servers 192.168.1.2, 192.168.1.3;
        option domain-name "example.com";
    }
    ```

5. Save the configuration file and exit with *Ctrl + O* and *Ctrl + X*.

6. After changing the configuration file, restart dhcpd:

    ```
    $ sudo service isc-dhcp-server restart
    ```

How it works...

Here, we have installed the DHCP server with the isc-dhcp-server package. It is open source software that implements the DHCP protocol. **ISC-DHCP** supports both IPv4 and IPv6.

After the installation, we need to set the basic configuration to match our network settings. All dhcpd settings are listed in the /etc/dhcp/dhcpd.conf configuration file. In the sample settings listed earlier, we have configured a new network, 192.168.1.0. This will result in IP addresses ranging from 192.168.1.150 to 192.168.1.200 to be assigned to clients. The default lease time is set to 600 seconds with maximum bound of 7200 seconds. A client can ask for a specific time to a maximum lease period of 7200 seconds. Additionally, the DHCP server will provide a default gateway (routers) as well as default DNS servers.

If you have multiple network interfaces, you may need to change the interface that dhcpd should listen to. These settings are listed in /etc/default/isc-dhcp-server. You can set multiple interfaces to listen to; just specify the interface names, separated by a space, for example, INTERFACES="wlan0 eth0".

There's more...

You can reserve an IP address to be assigned to a specific device on network. Reservation ensures that a specified device is always assigned to the same IP address. To create a reservation, add the following lines to `dhcpd.conf`. It will assign IP `192.168.1.201` to the client with the `08:D2:1F:50:F0:6F` MAC ID:

```
host Server1 {
  hardware ethernet 08:D2:1F:50:F0:6F;
  fixed-address 192.168.1.201;
}
```

Installing the DNS server

DNS, also known as name server, is a service on the Internet that provides mapping between IP addresses and domain names and vice versa. DNS maintains a database of names and related IP addresses. When an application queries with a domain name, DNS responds with a mapped IP address. Applications can also ask for a domain name by providing an IP address.

DNS is quite a big topic, and an entire chapter can be written just on the DNS setup. This recipe assumes some basic understanding of the working of the DNS protocol. We will cover the installation of BIND, installation of DNS server application, configuration of BIND as a caching DNS, and setup of Primary Master and Secondary Master. We will also cover some best practices to secure your DNS server.

Getting ready

In this recipe, I will be using four servers. You can create virtual machines if you want to simply test the setup:

1. `ns1`: Name server one/Primary Master
2. `ns2`: Name server two/Secondary Master
3. `host1`: Host system one
4. `host2`: Host system two, optional

    ❑   All servers should be configured in a private network. I have used the `10.0.2.0/24` network

    ❑   We need root privileges on all servers

How to do it...

Install BIND and set up a caching name server through the following steps:

1. On `ns1`, install BIND and `dnsutils` with the following command:

   ```
   $ sudo apt-get update
   $ sudo apt-get install bind9 dnsutils
   ```

2. Open `/etc/bind/named.conf.optoins`, enable the `forwarders` section, and add your preferred DNS servers:

   ```
   forwarders {
        8.8.8.8;
        8.8.4.4;
   };
   ```

3. Now restart BIND to apply a new configuration:

   ```
   $ sudo service bind9 restart
   ```

4. Check whether the BIND server is up and running:

   ```
   $ dig -x 127.0.0.1
   ```

5. You should get an output similar to the following code:

   ```
   ;; Query time: 1 msec
   ;; SERVER: 10.0.2.53#53(10.0.2.53)
   ```

6. Use `dig` to external domain and check the query time:

   ```
   ;; Query time: 268 msec
   ;; SERVER: 10.0.2.53#53(10.0.2.53)
   ;; WHEN: Tue Jul 28 10:17:10 IST 2015
   ;; MSG SIZE  rcvd: 270
   ```

7. Dig the same domain again and cross check the query time. It should be less than the first query:

   ```
   ;; Query time: 29 msec
   ;; SERVER: 10.0.2.53#53(10.0.2.53)
   ;; WHEN: Tue Jul 28 10:20:11 IST 2015
   ;; MSG SIZE  rcvd: 270
   ```

Set up Primary Master through the following steps:

1. On the `ns1` server, edit `/etc/bind/named.conf.options` and add the `acl` block above the `options` block:

```
acl "local" {
       10.0.2.0/24;  # local network
};
```

2. Add the following lines under the `options` block:

```
recursion yes;
allow-recursion { local; };
listen-on { 10.0.2.53; };  # ns1 IP address
allow-transfer { none; };
```

3. Open the `/etc/bind/named.conf.local` file to add forward and reverse zones:

```
$ sudo nano /etc/bind/named.conf.local
```

4. Add the forward `zone`:

```
zone "example.com" {
       type master;
       file "/etc/bind/zones/db.example.com";
};
```

5. Add the reverse `zone`:

```
zone "2.0.10.in-addr.arpa" {
       type master;
       file "/etc/bind/zones/db.10";
};
```

6. Create the `zones` directory under `/etc/bind/`:

```
$ sudo mkdir /etc/bind/zones
```

7. Create the forward `zone` file using the existing zone file, `db.local`, as a template:

```
$ cd /etc/bind/
$ sudo cp db.local  zones/db.example.com
```

8. The default file should look similar to the following image:

```
ubuntu@ns1:~$ cat /etc/bind/db.local
;
; BIND data file for local loopback interface
;
$TTL    604800
@       IN      SOA     localhost. root.localhost. (
                                2         ; Serial
                          604800          ; Refresh
                           86400          ; Retry
                         2419200          ; Expire
                          604800 )        ; Negative Cache TTL
;
@       IN      NS      localhost.
@       IN      A       127.0.0.1
@       IN      AAAA    ::1
```

9. Edit the `SOA` entry and replace `localhost` with FQDN of your server.

10. Increment the serial number (you can use the current date time as the serial number, `201507071100`)

11. Remove entries for `localhost`, `127.0.0.1` and `::1`.

12. Add new records:

    ```
    ; name server - NS records
    @  IN  NS  ns.exmple.com
    ; name server A records
    ns  IN  A 10.0.2.53
    ; local - A records
    host1  IN A  10.0.2.58
    ```

13. Save the changes and exit the nano editor. The final file should look similar to the following image:

```
ubuntu@ns1:~$ cat /etc/bind/zones/db.example.com
;
; BIND data file for local loopback interface
;
$TTL    604800
@       IN      SOA     example.com. root.example.com. (
                                3         ; Serial
                          604800          ; Refresh
                           86400          ; Retry
                         2419200          ; Expire
                          604800 )        ; Negative Cache TTL
;
@       IN      NS      ns.example.com.
@       IN      A       10.0.2.53
@       IN      AAAA    ::1
NS      IN      A       10.0.2.53
host1   IN      A       10.0.2.58
host2   IN      A       10.0.2.55
```

14. Now create the reverse `zone` file using `/etc/bind/db.127` as a template:

    ```
    $ sudo cp db.127 zones/db.10
    ```

15. The default file should look similar to the following screenshot:

```
ubuntu@ns1:~$ cat /etc/bind/db.127
;
; BIND reverse data file for local loopback interface
;
$TTL    604800
@       IN      SOA     localhost. root.localhost. (
                              1         ; Serial
                         604800         ; Refresh
                          86400         ; Retry
                        2419200         ; Expire
                         604800 )       ; Negative Cache TTL
;
@       IN      NS      localhost.
1.0.0   IN      PTR     localhost.
```

16. Change the `SOA` record and increment the serial number.

17. Remove `NS` and `PTR` records for `localhost`.

18. Add `NS`, `PTR`, and `host records`:

    ```
    ; NS records
    @   IN   NS   ns.example.com
    ; PTR records
    53   IN   PTR   ns.example.com
    ; host records
    58   IN   PTR   host1.example.com
    ```

19. Save the changes. The final file should look similar to the following image:

```
ubuntu@ns1:~$ cat /etc/bind/zones/db.10
;
; BIND reverse data file for local loopback interface
;
$TTL    604800
@       IN      SOA     ns.example.com. root.ns.example.com. (
                              2         ; Serial
                         604800         ; Refresh
                          86400         ; Retry
                        2419200         ; Expire
                         604800 )       ; Negative Cache TTL
;
@       IN      NS      ns.
53      IN      PTR     ns.example.com.
58      IN      PTR     host1.example.com.
55      IN      PTR     host2.example.com.
```

20. Check the configuration files for syntax errors. It should end with no output:

    ```
    $ sudo named-checkconf
    ```

21. Check zone files for syntax errors:

    ```
    $ sudo named-checkzone example.com
    /etc/bind/zones/db.example.com
    ```

22. If there are no errors, you should see an output similar to the following:

    ```
    zone example.com/IN: loaded serial 3
    OK
    ```

23. Check the reverse zone file, zones/db.10:

    ```
    $ sudo named-checkzone example.com /etc/bind/zones/db.10
    ```

24. If there are no errors, you should see output similar to the following:

    ```
    zone example.com/IN: loaded serial 3
    OK
    ```

25. Now restart the DNS server bind:

    ```
    $ sudo service bind9 restart
    ```

26. Log in to host2 and configure it to use ns.example.com as a DNS server. Add ns.example.com to /etc/resolve.conf on host2.

27. Test forward lookup with the nslookup command:

    ```
    $ nslookup host1.example.com
    ```

28. You should see an output similar to following:

    ```
    $ nslookup host1.example.com
    Server: 10.0.2.53
    Address: 10.0.2.53#53
    Name: host1.example.com
    Address: 10.0.2.58
    ```

29. Now test the reverse lookup:

    ```
    $ nslookup 10.0.2.58
    ```

30. It should output something similar to the following:

    ```
    $ nslookup 10.0.2.58
    Server: 10.0.2.53
    Address: 10.0.2.53#53
    58.2.0.10.in-addr.arpa      name = host1.example.com
    ```

Set up Secondary Master through the following steps:

1. First, allow zone transfer on Primary Master by setting the `allow-transfer` option in `/etc/bind/named.conf.local`:

    ```
    zone "example.com" {
        type master;
        file "/etc/bind/zones/db.example.com";
        allow-transfer { 10.0.2.54; };
    };
    zone "2.0.10.in-addr.arpa" {
        type master;
        file "/etc/bind/zones/db.10";
        allow-transfer { 10.0.2.54; };
    };
    ```

     A syntax check will throw errors if you miss semicolons.

2. Restart BIND9 on Primary Master:

    ```
    $ sudo service bind9 restart
    ```

3. On Secondary Master (`ns2`), install the BIND package.

4. Edit `/etc/bind/named.conf.local` to add `zone` declarations as follows:

    ```
    zone "example.com" {
        type slave;
        file "db.example.com";
        masters { 10.0.2.53; };
    };
    zone "2.0.10.in-addr.arpa" {
        type slave;
        file "db.10";
        masters { 10.0.2.53; };
    };
    ```

5. Save the changes made to `named.conf.local`.

6. Restart the BIND server on Secondary Master:

    ```
    $ sudo service bind9 restart
    ```

7. This will initiate the transfer of all zones configured on Primary Master. You can check the logs on Secondary Master at `/var/log/syslog` to verify the zone transfer.

 A zone is transferred only if the serial number under the SOA section on Primary Master is greater than that of Secondary Master. Make sure that you increment the serial number after every change to the zone file.

How it works...

In the first section, we have installed the BIND server and enabled a simple caching DNS server. A caching server helps to reduce bandwidth and latency in name resolution. The server will try to resolve queries locally from the cache. If the entry is not available in the cache, the query will be forwarded to external DNS servers and the result will be cached.

In the second and third sections, we have set Primary Master and Secondary Master respectively. Primary Master is the first DNS server. Secondary Master will be used as an alternate server in case the Primary server becomes unavailable.

Under Primary Master, we have declared a forward zone and reverse zone for the `example.com` domain. The forward zone is declared with domain name as the identifier and contains the type and filename for the database file. On Primary Master, we have set `type` to `master`. The reverse zone is declared with similar attributes and uses part of an IP address as an identifier. As we are using a 24-bit network address (`10.0.2.0/24`), we have included the first three octets of the IP address in reverse order (`2.0.10`) for the reverse zone name.

Lastly, we have created zone files by using existing files as templates. Zone files are the actual database that contains records of the IP address mapped to FQDN and vice versa. It contains SOA record, A records, and NS records. An SOA record defines the domain for this zone; A records and AAAA records are used to map the hostname to the IP address.

When the DNS server receives a query for the `example.com` domain, it checks for zone files for that domain. After finding the zone file, the host part from the query will be used to find the actual IP address to be returned as a result for query. Similarly, when a query with an IP address is received, the DNS server will look for a reverse zone file matching with the queried IP address.

See also

▸ Checkout the DNS configuration guide in the Ubuntu server guide at `https://help.ubuntu.com/lts/serverguide/dns-configuration.html`

▸ For an introduction to DNS concepts, check out this tutorial by the DigitalOcean community at `https://www.digitalocean.com/community/tutorials/an-introduction-to-dns-terminology-components-and-concepts`

- ▸ Get manual pages for BIND9 at `http://www.bind9.net/manuals`
- ▸ Find manual pages for named with the following command:

  ```
  $ man named
  ```

Hiding behind the proxy with squid

In this recipe, we will install and configure the squid proxy and caching server. The term **proxy** is generally combined with two different terms: one is forward proxy and the other is reverse proxy.

When we say proxy, it generally refers to forward proxy. A forward proxy acts as a gateway between a client's browser and the Internet, requesting the content on behalf of the client. This protects intranet clients by exposing the proxy as the only requester. A proxy can also be used as a filtering agent, imposing organizational policies. As all Internet requests go through the proxy server, the proxy can cache the response and return cached content when a similar request is found, thus saving bandwidth and time.

A reverse proxy is the exact opposite of a forward proxy. It protects internal servers from the outside world. A reverse proxy accepts requests from external clients and routes them to servers behind the proxy. External clients can see a single entity serving requests, but internally, it can be multiple servers working behind the proxy and sharing the load. More details about reverse proxies are covered in *Chapter 3, Working with Web Servers*.

In this recipe, we will discuss how to install a squid server. Squid is a well-known application in the forward proxy world and works well as a caching proxy. It supports HTTP, HTTPS, FTP, and other popular network protocols.

Getting ready

As always, you will need access to a root account or an account with `sudo` privileges.

How to do it...

Following are the steps to setup and configure Squid proxy:

1. Squid is quite an old, mature, and commonly used piece of software. It is generally shipped as a default package with various Linux distributions. The Ubuntu package repository contains the necessary pre-compiled binaries, so the installation is as easy as two commands.

2. First, update the `apt` cache and then install squid as follows:

   ```
   $ sudo apt-get update
   $ sudo apt-get install squid3
   ```

3. Edit the `/etc/squid3/squid.conf` file:

   ```
   $ sudo nano /etc/squid3/squid.conf
   ```

4. Ensure that the `cache_dir` directive is not commented out:

   ```
   cache_dir ufs /var/spool/squid3 100 16 256
   ```

5. Optionally, change the `http_port` directive to your desired TCP port:

   ```
   http_port 8080
   ```

6. Optionally, change the squid hostname:

   ```
   visible_hostname proxy1
   ```

7. Save changes with *Ctrl + O* and exit with *Ctrl + X*.

8. Restart the squid server:

   ```
   $ sudo service squid3 restart
   ```

9. Make sure that you have allowed the selected `http_port` on firewall.

10. Next, configure your browser using the squid server as the `http/https` proxy.

How it works...

Squid is available as a package in the Ubuntu repository, so you can directly install it with the `apt-get install squid` command. After installing squid, we need to edit the `squid.conf` file for some basic settings. The `squid.conf` file is quite a big file and you can find a large number of directives listed with their explanation. It is recommended to create a copy of the original configuration file as a reference before you do any modifications.

In our example, we are changing the port squid listens on. The default port is `3128`. This is just a security precaution and it's fine if you want to run squid on the default port. Secondly, we have changed the hostname for squid.

Other important directive to look at is `cache_dir`. Make sure that this directive is enabled, and also set the cache size. The following example sets `cache_dir` to `/var/spool/suid3` with the size set to `100MB`:

```
cache_dir ufs /var/spool/squid3 100  16  256
```

To check the cache utilization, use the following command:

```
$ sudo du /var/spool/squid3
```

There's more...

Squid provides lot more features than a simple proxy server. Following is a quick list of some important features:

Access control list

With squid ACLs, you can set the list of IP addresses allowed to use squid. Add the following line at the bottom of the `acl` section of `/etc/squid3/squid.conf`:

```
acl developers   src 192.168.2.0/24
```

Then, add the following line at the top of the `http_access` section in the same file:

```
http_access allow developers
```

Set cache refresh rules

You can change squid's caching behavior depending on the file types. Add the following line to cache all image files to be cached—the minimum time is an hour and the maximum is a day:

```
refresh_pattern -i \.(gif|png|jpg|jpeg|ico)$  3600    90%    86400
```

This line uses a regular expression to find the file names that end with any of the listed file extensions (`gif`, `png`, and `etc`)

Sarg – tool to analyze squid logs

Squid Analysis Report Generator is an open source tool to monitor the squid server usages. It parses the logs generated by Squid and converts them to easy-to-digest HTML-based reports. You can track various metrics such as bandwidth used per user, top sites, downloads, and so on. Sarg can be quickly installed with the following command:

```
$ sudo apt-get install sarg
```

The configuration file for Sarg is located at `/etc/squid/sarg.conf`. Once installed, set the `output_dir` path and run `sarg`. You can also set cron jobs to execute `sarg` periodically. The generated reports are stored in `output_dir` and can be accessed with the help of a web server.

Squid guard

Squid guard is another useful plugin for squid server. It is generally used to block a list of websites so that these sites are inaccessible from the internal network. As always, it can also be installed with a single command, as follows:

```
$ sudo apt-get install squidguard
```

The configuration file is located at `/etc/squid/squidGuard.conf`.

See also

▸ Check out the squid manual pages with the `man squid` command

▸ Check out the Ubuntu community page for squid guard at
`https://help.ubuntu.com/community/SquidGuard`

Being on time with NTP

Network Time Protocol (**NTP**) is a TCP/IP protocol for synchronizing time over a network. Although Ubuntu has a built-in clock that is helpful for keeping track of local events, it may create issues when the server is connected over a network and provides time-critical services to the clients. This problem can be solved with the help of NTP time synchronization. NTP works by synchronizing time across all servers on the Internet.

NTP uses hierarchies of servers with top-level servers synchronizing time with atomic clocks. This hierarchy levels are known as **stratum**, and the level can range between 1 and 15, both inclusive. The highest stratum level is 1 and is determined by the accuracy of the clock the server synchronizes with. If a server synchronizes with other NTP server with stratum level 3, then the stratum level for this server is automatically set to 4.

Another time synchronization tool provided by Ubuntu is `ntpdate`, which comes preinstalled with Ubuntu. It executes once at boot time and synchronizes the local time with Ubuntu's NTP servers. The problem with `ntpdate` is that it matches server time with central time without considering the big drifts in local time, whereas the NTP daemon `ntpd` continuously adjusts the server time to match it with the reference clock. As mentioned in the `ntpdate` manual pages (`man ntpdate`), you can use `ntpdate` multiple times throughout a day to keep time drifts low and get more accurate results, but it does not match the accuracy and reliability provided by ntpd.

In this recipe, we will set up a standalone time server for an internal network. Our time server will synchronize its time with public time servers and provide a time service to internal NTP clients.

How to do it...

Following are the steps to install and configure NTP daemon:

1. First, synchronize the server's time with any Internet time server using the `ntpdate` command:

   ```
   $ ntpdate -s ntp.ubuntu.com
   ```

2. To install ntpd, enter the following command in the terminal:

   ```
   $ sudo apt-get install ntp
   ```

3. Edit the `/etc/ntp.conf` NTP configuration file to add/remove external NTP servers:

```
$ sudo nano /etc/ntp.conf
```

4. Set a fallback NTP server:

```
server ntp.ubuntu.com
```

5. Block any external access to the server, comment the first `restrict` line, and add the following command:

```
restrict default noquery notrust nomodify
```

6. Allow the clients on local network to use the NTP service:

```
restrict 192.168.1.0 mask 255.255.255.0
```

7. Save changes with *Ctrl + O* and exit nano with *Ctrl + X*.

8. Reload the NTP daemon with the following command:

```
$ sudo service ntp restart
```

How it works...

Sometimes, the NTP daemon refuses to work if the time difference between local time and central time is too big. To avoid this problem, we have synchronized the local time and central time before installing ntpd. As ntpd and ntpdate both use the same UDP port, 123, the `ntpdate` command will not work when the ntpd service is in use.

Make sure that you have opened UDP port 123 on the firewall.

After installing the NTP server, you may want to set time servers to be used. The default configuration file contains time servers provided by Ubuntu. You can use the same default servers or simply comment the lines by adding # at the start of each line and add the servers of your choice. You can dig into `http://www.pool.ntp.org` to find time servers for your specific region. It is a good idea to provide multiple reference servers, as NTP can provide more accurate results after querying each of them.

You can control polling intervals for each server with the `minpoll` and `maxpoll` parameters. The value is set in seconds to the power of two. `minpoll` defaults to 6 (2^6 = 64 sec) and `maxpoll` defaults to 10 (2^10 = 1024 sec).

Additionally, we have set a fallback server that can be used in case of network outage or any other problems when our server cannot communicate with external reference servers. You can also use a system clock as a fallback, which can be accessed at `127.127.1.0`. Simply replace the fallback server with the following line to use a system clock as a fallback:

```
server 127.127.0.1
```

Lastly, we have set access control parameters to protect our server from external access. The default configuration is to allow anyone to use the time service from this server. By changing the first `restrict` line, we blocked all external access to the server. The configuration already contains the exception to local NTP service indicated by the following:

```
restrict 127.0.0.1
```

We created another exception by adding a separate line to allow access to the clients on local network (remember to replace the IP range with your network details):

```
restrict 192.168.1.0 mask 255.255.255.0
```

There's more...

A central DHCP server can be configured to provide NTP settings to all DHCP clients. For this to work, your clients should also be configured to query NTP details from DHCP. A DHCP client configuration on Ubuntu already contains the query for network time servers.

Add the following line to your DHCP configuration to provide NTP details to the clients:

```
subnet 192.168.1.0 netmask 255.255.255.0 {

    ...

    option ntp-servers  your_ntp_host;
}
```

On the clientside, make sure that your `dhclient.conf` contains `ntp-servers` in its default `request`:

```
request subnet-mask, broadcast-address, time-offset, routers,

    ...

        rfc3442-classless-static-routes, ntp-servers,
```

See also

- Check the default `/etc/ntp.conf` configuration file. It contains a short explanation for each setting.
- Check the manual pages for ntpd with `man ntpd`.

Discussing load balancing with HAProxy

When an application becomes popular, it sends an increased number of requests to the application server. A single application server may not be able to handle the entire load alone. We can always scale up the underlying hardware, that is, add more memory and more powerful CUPs to increase the server capacity; but these improvements do not always scale linearly. To solve this problem, multiple replicas of the application server are created and the load is distributed among these replicas. Load balancing can be implemented at OSI Layer 4, that is, at TCP or UDP protocol levels, or at Layer 7, that is, application level with HTTP, SMTP, and DNS protocols.

In this recipe, we will install a popular load balancing or load distributing service, HAProxy. HAProxy receives all the requests from clients and directs them to the actual application server for processing. Application server directly returns the final results to the client. We will be setting HAProxy to load balance TCP connections.

Getting ready

You will need two or more application servers and one server for HAProxy:

> You will need the root access on the server where you want to install HAProxy

> It is assumed that your application servers are properly installed and working

How to do it...

Follow these steps to discus load balancing with HAProxy:

1. Install HAProxy:

   ```
   $ sudo apt-get update
   $ sudo apt-get install haproxy
   ```

2. Enable the HAProxy `init` script to automatically start HAProxy on system boot. Open /etc/default/haproxy and set ENABLE to 1:

```
ubuntu: ~ $ cat /etc/default/haproxy
# Set ENABLED to 1 if you want the init script to start haproxy.
ENABLED=1
# Add extra flags here.
#EXTRAOPTS="-de -m 16"
ubuntu: ~ $
```

3. Now, edit the HAProxy `/etc/haproxy/haproxy.cfg` configuration file. You may want to create a copy of this file before editing:

```
$ cd /etc/haproxy
$ sudo cp haproxy.cfg haproxy.cfg.copy
$ sudo nano haproxy.cfg
```

4. Find the `defaults` section and change the `mode` and `option` parameters to match the following:

```
mode    tcp
option  tcplog
```

```
defaults
        log      global
        mode     tcp
        option   tcplog
        option   dontlognull
        contimeout 5000
```

5. Next, define `frontend`, which will receive all requests:

```
frontend www
    bind 57.105.2.204:80      # haproxy public IP
    default_backend as-backend     # backend used
```

6. Define `backend` application servers:

```
backend as-backend
    balance leastconn
    mode tcp
    server as1 10.0.2.71:80 check      # application srv 1
    server as2 10.0.2.72:80 check      # application srv 2
```

7. Save and quit the HAProxy configuration file.

8. We need to set `rsyslog` to accept HAProxy logs. Open the `rsyslog.conf` file, `/etc/rsyslog.conf`, and uncomment following parameters:

```
$ModLoad imudp
$UDPServerRun 514
```

```
# provides UDP syslog reception
$ModLoad imudp
$UDPServerRun 514
```

9. Next, create a new file under `/etc/rsyslog.d` to specify the HAProxy log location:

```
$ sudo nano /etc/rsyslog.d/haproxy.conf
```

10. Add the following line to the newly created file:

```
local2.*   /var/log/haproxy.log
```

11. Save the changes and exit the new file.

12. Restart the `rsyslog` service:

```
$ sudo service rsyslog restart
```

13. Restart HAProxy:

```
$ sudo service haproxy restart
```

14. Now, you should be able to access your backend with the HAProxy IP address.

How it works...

Here, we have configured HAProxy as a frontend for a cluster of application servers. Under the `frontend` section, we have configured HAProxy to listen on the public IP of the HAProxy server. We also specified a backend for this frontend. Under the `backend` section, we have set a private IP address of the application servers. HAProxy will communicate with the application servers through a private network interface. This will help to keep the internal network latency to a minimum.

HAProxy supports various load balancing algorithms. Some of them are as follows:

- **Round-robin** distributes the load in a round robin fashion. This is the default algorithm used.
- **leastconn** selects the backend server with fewest connections.
- **source** uses the hash of the client's IP address and maps it to the backend. This ensures that requests from a single user are served by the same backend server.

We have selected the **leastconn** algorithm, which is mentioned under the `backend` section with the `balance leastconn` line. The selection of a load balancing algorithm will depend on the type of application and length of connections.

Lastly, we configured `rsyslog` to accept logs over UDP. HAProxy does not provide separate logging system and passes logs to the system log daemon, `rsyslog`, over the UDP stream.

There's more ...

Depending on your Ubuntu version, you may not get the latest version of HAProxy from the default `apt` repository. Use the following repository to install the latest release:

```
$ sudo apt-get install software-properties-common
$ sudo add-apt-repository ppa:vbernat/haproxy-1.6  # replace 1.6 with
required version
$ sudo apt-get update && apt-get install haproxy
```

See also

> ▸ An introduction to load balancing the HAProxy concepts at `https://www.digitalocean.com/community/tutorials/an-introduction-to-haproxy-and-load-balancing-concepts`

Tuning the TCP stack

Transmission Control Protocol and **Internet Protocol** (**TCP/IP**) is a standard set of protocols used by every network-enabled device. TCP/IP defines the standards to communicate over a network. TCP/IP is a set of protocols and is divided in two parts: TCP and IP. IP defines the rules for IP addressing and routing packets over network and provides an identity IP address to each host on the network. TCP deals with the interconnection between two hosts and enables them to exchange data over network. TCP is a connection-oriented protocol and controls the ordering of packets, retransmission, error detection, and other reliability tasks.

TCP stack is designed to be very general in nature so that it can be used by anyone for any network conditions. Servers use the same TCP/IP stack as used by their clients. For this reason, the default values are configured for general uses and not optimized for high-load server environments. New Linux kernel provides a tool called `sysctl` that can be used to modify kernel parameters at runtime without recompiling the entire kernel. We can use `sysctl` to modify and TCP/IP parameters to match our needs.

In this recipe, we will look at various kernel parameters that control the network. It is not required to modify all parameters listed here. You can choose ones that are required and suitable for your system and network environment.

It is advisable to test these modifications on local systems before doing any changes on live environment. A lot of these parameters directly deal with network connections and related CPU and memory uses. This can result in connection drops and/or sudden increases in resource use. Make sure that you have read the documentation for the parameter before you change anything.

Also, it is a good idea to set benchmarks before and after making any changes to `sysctl` parameters. This will give you a base to compare improvements, if any. Again, benchmarks may not reveal all the effects of parameter changes. Make sure that you have read the respective documentation.

Getting ready...

You will need root access.

Note down basic performance metrics with the tool of your choice.

How to do it...

Follow these steps to tune the TCP stack:

1. Set the maximum open files limit:

```
$ ulimit -n    # check existing limits for logged in user
# ulimit -n 65535    # root change values above hard limits
```

2. To permanently set limits for a user, open `/etc/security/limits.conf` and add the following lines at end of the file. Make sure to replace values in brackets, <>:

```
<username>  soft  nofile  <value>    # soft limits
<username>  hard  nofile  <value>    # hard limits
```

3. Save `limits.conf` and exit. Then restart the user session.

4. View all available parameters:

```
# sysctl -a
```

5. Set the TCP default read-write buffer:

```
# echo 'net.core.rmem_default=65536' >> /etc/sysctl.conf
# echo 'net.core.wmem_default=65536' >> /etc/sysctl.conf
```

6. Set the TCP read and write buffers to 8 MB:

```
# echo 'net.core.rmem_max=8388608' >> /etc/sysctl.conf
# echo 'net.core.wmem_max=8388608' >> /etc/sysctl.conf
```

7. Increase the maximum TCP orphans:

```
# echo 'net.ipv4.tcp_max_orphans=4096' >> /etc/sysctl.conf
```

8. Disable slow start after being idle:

```
# echo 'net.ipv4.tcp_slow_start_after_idle=0' >>
/etc/sysctl.conf
```

9. Minimize TCP connection retries:

```
# echo 'net.ipv4.tcp_synack_retries=3' >> /etc/sysctl.conf

# echo 'net.ipv4.tcp_syn_retries =3' >> /etc/sysctl.conf
```

10. Set the TCP window scaling:

    ```
    # echo 'net.ipv4.tcp_window_scaling=1' >> /etc/sysctl.conf
    ```

11. Enable timestamps:

    ```
    # echo 'net.ipv4.tcp_timestamp=1' >> /etc/sysctl.conf
    ```

12. Enable selective acknowledgements:

    ```
    # echo 'net.ipv4.tcp_sack=0' >> /etc/sysctl.conf
    ```

13. Set the maximum number of times the IPV4 packet can be reordered in the TCP packet stream:

    ```
    # echo 'net.ipv4.tcp_reordering=3' >> /etc/sysctl.conf
    ```

14. Send data in the opening SYN packet:

    ```
    # echo 'net.ipv4.tcp_fastopen=1'  >> /etc/sysctl.conf
    ```

15. Set the number of opened connections to be remembered before receiving acknowledgement:

    ```
    # echo 'tcp_max_syn_backlog=1500' >> /etc/sysctl.conf
    ```

16. Set the number of TCP keep-alive probes to send before deciding the connection is broken:

    ```
    # echo 'tcp_keepalive_probes=5' >> /etc/sysctl.conf
    ```

17. Set the keep-alive time, which is a timeout value after the broken connection is killed:

    ```
    # echo 'tcp_keepalive_time=1800' >> /etc/sysctl.conf
    ```

18. Set intervals to send keep-alive packets:

    ```
    # echo 'tcp_keepalive_intvl=60' >> /etc/sysctl.conf
    ```

19. Set to reuse or recycle connections in the wait state:

    ```
    # echo 'net.ipv4.tcp_tw_reuse=1' >> /etc/sysctl.conf
    # echo 'net.ipv4.tcp_tw_recycle=1' >> /etc/sysctl.conf
    ```

20. Increase the maximum number of connections:

    ```
    # echo 'net.ipv4.ip_local_port_range=32768 65535' >> /etc/sysctl.conf
    ```

21. Set TCP FIN timeout:

    ```
    # echo 'tcp_fin_timeout=60' >> /etc/sysctl.conf
    ```

How it works...

The behavior of Linux kernel can be fine tuned with the help of various Linux kernel parameters. These are the options passed to the kernel in order to control various aspects of the system. These parameters can be passed while compiling the kernel, at boot time, or at runtime using the /proc filesystem and tools such as sysctl.

In this recipe, we have used sysctl to configure network-related kernel parameters to fine tune network settings. Again, you need to cross check each configuration to see if it's working as expected.

Along with network parameters, tons of other kernel parameters can be configured with the sysctl command. The -a flag to sysctl will list all the available parameters:

```
$ sysctl -a
```

All these configurations are stored in a filesystem at the /proc directory, grouped in their respective categories. You can directly read/write these files or use the sysctl command:

```
ubuntu@ubuntu:~$ sysctl fs.file-max
fs.file-max = 98869
ubuntu@ubuntu:~$ cat /proc/sys/fs/file-max
98869
```

See also

Find the explanation of various kernel parameters at the following websites:

▶ http://www.cyberciti.biz/files/linux-kernel/Documentation/networking/ip-sysctl.txt

▶ https://www.kernel.org/doc/Documentation/networking/ip-sysctl.txt

Troubleshooting network connectivity

Networking consists of various components and services working together to enable systems to communicate with each other. A lot of times it happens that everything seems good, but we are not able to access other servers or the Internet. In this recipe, we will look at some tools provided by Ubuntu to troubleshoot the network connectivity issues.

Getting ready

As you are reading this recipe, I am assuming that you are facing a networking issue. Also, I am assuming that the problems are with a primary network adapter, eth0.

You may need access to root account or account with similar privileges.

How to do it...

Follow these steps to troubleshoot network connectivity:

1. Let's start with checking the network card. If it is working properly and is detected by Ubuntu. Check boot time logs and search for lines related to Ethernet, `eth`:

   ```
   $ dmesg | grep eth
   ```

   ```
   ubuntu@ubuntu:~$ dmesg | grep eth
   [    2.667415] e1000 0000:00:03.0 eth0: (PCI:33MHz:32-bit) 08:00:27:bb:a6:03
   [    2.672249] e1000 0000:00:03.0 eth0: Intel(R) PRO/1000 Network Connection
   [   12.592892] IPv6: ADDRCONF(NETDEV_UP): eth0: link is not ready
   [   12.593695] e1000: eth0 NIC Link is Up 1000 Mbps Full Duplex, Flow Control: R
   X
   [   12.605255] IPv6: ADDRCONF(NETDEV_CHANGE): eth0: link becomes ready
   ```

2. If you don't find anything in the boot logs, then most probably, your network hardware is faulty or unsupported by Ubuntu.

3. Next, check whether the network cable is plugged in and is working properly. You can simply check the LED indicators on the network card or use the following command:

   ```
   $ sudo mii-tool
   ```

   ```
   ubuntu@ubuntu:~$ sudo mii-tool
   [sudo] password for ubuntu:
   eth0: no autonegotiation, 1000baseT-FD flow-control, link ok
   ubuntu@ubuntu:~$
   ```

4. If you can see a line with `link ok`, then you have a working Ethernet connection.

5. Next, check whether a proper IP address is assigned to the `eth0` Ethernet port:

   ```
   $ ifconfig eth0
   ```

   ```
   ubuntu@ubuntu:~$ ifconfig eth0
   eth0      Link encap:Ethernet  HWaddr 08:00:27:bb:a6:03
             inet addr:10.0.2.15  Bcast:10.0.2.255  Mask:255.255.255.0
             inet6 addr: fe80::a00:27ff:febb:a603/64 Scope:Link
             UP BROADCAST RUNNING MULTICAST  MTU:1500  Metric:1
   ```

6. Check whether you can find a line that starts with `inet addr`. If you cannot find this line or it is listed as inet addr 169.254, then you don't have an IP address assigned.

7. Even if you see a line stating the IP address, make sure that it is valid for network that you are connected to.

8. Now assuming that you have not assigned an IP address, let's try to get dynamic IP address from the DHCP server. Make sure that `eth0` is set for dynamic configuration. You should see line similar to `iface eth0 inet dhcp`:

   `$ cat /etc/network/interfaces`

```
ubuntu@ubuntu:~$ cat /etc/network/interfaces
# The loopback network interface
auto lo
iface lo inet loopback

# The primary network interface
auto eth0
iface eth0 inet dhcp
```

9. Execute the `dhclient` command to query the local DHCP server:

   `$ sudo dhclient -v`

```
ubuntu@ubuntu:~$ sudo dhclient -v
Internet Systems Consortium DHCP Client 4.2.4
Copyright 2004-2012 Internet Systems Consortium.
All rights reserved.
For info, please visit https://www.isc.org/software/dhcp/

Listening on LPF/eth0/08:00:27:bb:a6:03
Sending on   LPF/eth0/08:00:27:bb:a6:03
Sending on   Socket/fallback
DHCPDISCOVER on eth0 to 255.255.255.255 port 67 interval 3 (xid=0x408c0d92)
DHCPREQUEST of 10.0.2.15 on eth0 to 255.255.255.255 port 67 (xid=0x408c0d92)
DHCPOFFER of 10.0.2.15 from 10.0.2.2
DHCPACK of 10.0.2.15 from 10.0.2.2
RTNETLINK answers: File exists
bound to 10.0.2.15 -- renewal in 40826 seconds.
```

10. If you can see a line similar to `bound to 10.0.2.15`, then you are assigned with a new IP address. If you keep getting `DHCPDISCOVER` messages, this means that your DHCP server is not accessible or not assigning an IP address to this client.

11. Now, if you check the IP address again, you should see a newly IP address listed:

    ```
    $ ifconfig eth0
    ```

12. Assuming that you have received a proper IP address, let's move on to the default gateway:

    ```
    $ ip route
    ```

```
ubuntu@ubuntu:~$ route -n
Kernel IP routing table
Destination     Gateway         Genmask         Flags Metric Ref    Use Iface
0.0.0.0         10.0.2.2        0.0.0.0         UG    0      0        0 eth0
10.0.2.0        0.0.0.0         255.255.255.0   U     0      0        0 eth0
```

13. The preceding command lists our default route. In my case, it is `10.0.2.2`. Let's try to ping the default gateway:

    ```
    $ ping -c 5 10.0.2.2
    ```

14. If you get a response from the gateway, this means that your local network is working properly. If you do not get a response from gateway, you may want to check your local firewall.

15. Check the firewall status:

    ```
    $ sudo ufw status
    ```

16. Check the rules or temporarily disable the firewall and retry reaching your gateway:

    ```
    $ sudo ufw disable
    ```

17. Next, check whether we can go beyond our gateway. Try to ping an external server. I am trying to ping a public DNS server by Google:

    ```
    $ ping -c 5 8.8.8.8
    ```

18. If you successfully receive a response, then you have a working network connection. If this does not work, then you can check the problem with the `mtr` command. This command will display each router between your server and the destination server:

```
$ mtr -r -c 1 8.8.8.8
```

```
ubuntu@ubuntu:~$ mtr -r -c 1 8.8.8.8
Start: Tue Jul 28 11:57:48 2015
HOST: ubuntu                        Loss%   Snt   Last    Avg  Best  Wrst StDev
  1. |-- 10.0.2.2                    0.0%     1    0.6    0.6   0.6   0.6   0.0
  2. |-- 192.168.0.1                 0.0%     1   10.0   10.0  10.0  10.0   0.0
  3. |-- 78-212-119-111.mysipl.com   0.0%     1    5.0    5.0   5.0   5.0   0.0
  4. |-- 77-212-119-111.mysipl.com   0.0%     1    6.4    6.4   6.4   6.4   0.0
  5. |-- 157-134.87.183.mysipl.com   0.0%     1    7.9    7.9   7.9   7.9   0.0
  6. |-- 72.14.196.213               0.0%     1    5.7    5.7   5.7   5.7   0.0
  7. |-- 209.85.142.228              0.0%     1    6.1    6.1   6.1   6.1   0.0
  8. |-- 66.249.94.39                0.0%     1   34.1   34.1  34.1  34.1   0.0
  9. |-- 216.239.48.227              0.0%     1   58.7   58.7  58.7  58.7   0.0
 10. |-- 209.85.246.37               0.0%     1   67.5   67.5  67.5  67.5   0.0
 11. |-- ???                       100.0%     1    0.0    0.0   0.0   0.0   0.0
 12. |-- google-public-dns-a.googl   0.0%     1   60.4   60.4  60.4  60.4   0.0
```

19. Next, we need to check DNS servers:

```
$ nslookup www.ubuntu.com
```

```
ubuntu@ubuntu:~$ nslookup www.ubuntu.com
Server:         192.168.0.1
Address:        192.168.0.1#53

Non-authoritative answer:
Name:   www.ubuntu.com
Address: 91.189.89.103
```

20. If you received an IP address for Ubuntu servers, then the DNS connection is working properly. If it's not, you can try changing the DNS servers temporarily. Add the `nameserver` entry to `/etc/resolve.conf` above other `nameserver`, if any:

```
nameserver 8.8.8.8
```

21. At this point, you should be able to access the Internet. Try to ping an external server by its name:

```
$ ping -c 3 www.ubuntu.com
```

```
ubuntu@ubuntu:~$ ping -c 2 www.ubuntu.com
PING www.ubuntu.com (91.189.89.103) 56(84) bytes of data.
64 bytes from www-ubuntu-com.privet.canonical.com (91.189.89.103): icmp_seq=1 tt
l=47 time=125 ms
64 bytes from www-ubuntu-com.privet.canonical.com (91.189.89.103): icmp_seq=2 tt
l=47 time=128 ms

--- www.ubuntu.com ping statistics ---
2 packets transmitted, 2 received, 0% packet loss, time 1003ms
rtt min/avg/max/mdev = 125.001/126.741/128.481/1.740 ms
```

There's more...

The following are some additional commands that may come handy while working with a network:

- lspci lists all pci devices. Combine it with grep to search for specific device.

- Lsmod shows the status of modules in Linux kernels.

- ip link lists all the available network devices with status and configuration parameters.

- ip addr shows the IP addresses assigned for each device.

- ip route displays routing table entries.

- tracepath/traceroute lists all the routers (path) between local and remote hosts.

- iptables is an administration tool for packet filtering and NAT.

- dig is a DNS lookup utility.

- ethtool queries and controls network drivers and hardware settings.

- route views or edits the IP routing table.

- telnet was the interface for telnet protocol. Now it is a simple tool to quickly check remote working ports.

- Nmap is a powerful network mapping tool.

- netstat displays network connections, routing tables, interface stats, and more.

- ifdown and ifup start or stop the network interface. They are similar to ifconfig down or ifconfig up.

Securing remote access with OpenVPN

VPN enables two or more systems to communicate privately and securely over the public network or Internet. The network traffic is routed through the Internet, but is encrypted. You can use VPN to set up a secure connection between two datacenters or to access office resources from the leisure of your home. The VPN service is also used to protect your online activities, access location restricted contents, and bypass restrictions imposed by your ISP.

VPN services are implemented with a number of different protocols, such as **Point-to-Point Tunneling Protocol** (**PPTP**), **Layer two tunneling protocol** (**L2TP**), IPSec, and SSL. In this recipe, we will set up a free VPN server, OpenVPN. OpenVPN is an open source SSL VPN solution and provides a wide range of configurations. OpenVPN can be configured to use either TCP or UDP protocols. In this recipe, we will set up OpenVPN with its default UDP port 1194.

Getting ready...

You will need one server and one client system and root or equivalent access to both systems.

How to do it...

1. Install OpenVPN with the following command:

    ```
    $ sudo apt-get update
    $ sudo apt-get install openvpn easy-rsa
    ```

2. Now, set up your own certification authority and generate certificate and keys for the OpenVPN server.

3. Next, we need to edit the OpenVPN files that are owned by the root user, and the `build-ca` script needs root access while writing new keys. Temporarily, change to root account using `sudo su`:

    ```
    $ sudo su
    ```

    Copy the Easy-RSA directory to `/etc/openvpn`:

    ```
    # cp -r /usr/share/easy-rsa  /etc/openvpn/
    ```

4. Now edit `/etc/openvpn/easy-rsa/vars` and change the variables to match your environment:

    ```
    export KEY_COUNTRY="US"
    export KEY_PROVINCE="ca"
    export KEY_CITY="your city"
    export KEY_ORG="your Company"
    ```

```
export KEY_EMAIL="you@company.com"

export KEY_CN="MyVPN"

export KEY_NAME="MyVPN"

export KEY_OU="MyVPN"
```

5. Generate a Master certificate with the following commands:

```
# cd /etc/openvpn/easy-vars

# source vars

# ./clean-all

# ./build-ca
```

6. Next, generate a certificate and private key for the server. Replace the server name with the name of your server:

```
# ./build-key-server servername
```

7. Press the *Enter* key when prompted for the password and company name.

8. When asked for signing the certificate, enter y and then press the *Enter* key.

9. Build **Diffie Hellman** parameters for the OpenVPN server:

```
# ./build-dh
```

10. Copy all the generated keys and certificates to /etc/openvpn:

```
# cp /etc/openvpn/easy-rsa/keys/{servername.crt,
servername.key, ca.crt, dh2048.pem}  /etc/openvpn
```

11. Next, generate a certificate for the client with the following commands:

```
# cd /etc/openvpn/easy-rsa

# source vars

# ./build-key clientname
```

12. Copy the generated key, certificate, and server certificate to the client system. Use a secure transfer mechanism such as SCP:

```
/etc/openvpn/ca.crt

/etc/openvpn/easy-rsa/keys/clientname.crt

/etc/openvpn/easy-rsa/keys/clientname.key
```

13. Now, configure the OpenVPN server. Use the sample configuration files provided by OpenVPN:

```
$ gunzip -c /usr/share/doc/openvpn/examples/sample-config-
files/server.conf.gz > /etc/openvpn/server.conf
```

14. Open `server.conf` in your favorite editor:

    ```
    # nano /etc/openvpn/server.conf
    ```

15. Make sure that the certificate and key path are properly set:

    ```
    ca ca.crt
    cert servername.crt
    key servername.key
    dh dh2048.pen
    ```

16. Enable clients to redirect their web traffic through a VPN server. Uncomment the following line:

    ```
    push "redirect-gateway def1 bypass-dhcp"
    ```

17. To protect against DNS leaks, push DNS settings to VPN clients and uncomment the following lines:

    ```
    push "dhcp-option DNS 208.67.222.222"
    push "dhcp-option DNS 208.67.220.220"
    ```

18. The preceding lines point to OpenDNS servers. You can set them to any DNS server of your choice.

19. Lastly, set OpenVPN to run with unprivileged `user` and `group` and uncomment the following lines:

    ```
    user nobody
    group nogroup
    ```

20. Optionally, you can enable compression on the VPN link. Search and uncomment the following line:

    ```
    comp-lzo
    ```

21. Save the changes and exit the editor.

22. Next, edit `/etc/sysctl` to enable IP forwarding. Find and uncomment the following line by removing the hash, #, in front of it:

    ```
    #net.ipv4.ip_forward=1
    ```

23. Update `sysctl` settings with the following command:

    ```
    # sysctl -p
    ```

24. Now start the server. You should see an output similar to the following:

    ```
    # service openvpn start
     * Starting virtual private network daemon(s)
     *     Autostarting VPN 'server'
    ```

25. When it starts successfully, OpenVPN creates a new network interface named `tun0`. This can be checked with the `ifconfig` command:

```
# ifconfig tun0

tun0      Link encap:UNSPEC  HWaddr 00-00-00-00-00-00-00-
00-00-00-00-00-00-00-00-00

          inet addr:10.8.0.1  P-t-P:10.8.0.2
Mask:255.255.255.255
```

26. If the server does not start normally, you can check the logs at `/var/log/syslog`. It should list all the steps completed by the OpenVPN service.

How it works...

OpenVPN is the open source VPN solution. It is a traffic-tunneling protocol that works in client-server mode. You might already know that VPN is widely used to create a private and secure network connection between two endpoints. It is generally used to access your servers or access office systems from your home. The other popular use of VPN servers is to protect your privacy by routing your traffic through a VPN server. OpenVPN needs two primary components, namely a server and a client. The preceding recipe installs the server component. When the OpenVPN service is started on the OpenVPN host, it creates a new virtual network interface, a tun device named `tun0`. On the client side, OpenVPN provides the client with tools that configure the client with a similar setup by creating a tap device on the client's system.

Once the client is configured with a server hostname or IP address, a server certificate, and client keys, the client initiates a virtual network connection using a tap device on client to a tun device on the server. The provided keys and certificate are used to cross-check server authenticity and then authenticate itself. As the session is established, all network traffic on the client system is routed or tunneled via a tap network interface. All the external services that are accessed by the OpenVPN client, and you get to see the requests as if they are originated from the OpenVPN server and not from the client. Additionally, the traffic between the server and client is encrypted to provide additional security.

There's more...

In this recipe we have installed and configured OpenVPN server. To use the VPN service from your local system you will need a VPN client tool.

Following are the steps to install and configure VPN client on Ubuntu systems:

1. Install the **OpenVPN** client with a similar command the one we used to install the server:

```
$ sudo apt-get update
$ sudo apt-get install openvpn
```

2. Copy the sample `client.conf` configuration file:

```
$ sudo cp /usr/share/doc/openvpn/examples/sample-config-
files/client.conf /etc/openvpn/
```

3. Copy the certificates and keys generated for this client:

```
$ scp user@yourvpnserver:/etc/openvpn/easy-
rsa/keys/client1.key /etc/openvpn
```

4. You can use other tools such as **SFTP** or **WinSCP** on the Windows systems.

5. Now edit `client.conf`, enable client mode, and specify the server name or address:

```
client

remote your.vpnserver.com 1194
```

6. Make sure that you have set the correct path for keys copied from the server.

7. Now save the configuration file and start the OpenVPN server:

```
$ service openvpn start
```

8. This should create the `tun0` network interface:

```
$ ifconfig tun0
```

9. Check the new routes created by VPN:

```
$ netstat -rn
```

10. You can test your VPN connection with any What's My IP service. You can also take a DNS leak test with online DNS leak tests.

    For Windows and Mac OS systems, OpenVPN provides respective client tools. You need an OpenVPN profile with the `.ovpn` extension. A template can be found with the OpenVPN client you are using or on the server under OpenVPN examples. The following is the complete path:

```
/usr/share/doc/openvpn/examples/sample-config-
files/client.conf
```

 Note that OpenVPN provides a web-based admin interface to manage VPN clients. This is a commercial offering that provides an easy-to-use admin interface to manage OpenVPN settings and client certificates.

Securing a network with uncomplicated firewall

It is said that the best way to improve server security is to reduce the attack surface. Network communication in any system happens with the help of logical network ports, be it TCP ports or UDP ports. One part of the attack surface is the number of open ports that are waiting for connection to be established. It is always a good idea to block all unrequired ports. Any traffic coming to these ports can be filtered, that is, allowed or blocked with the help of a filtering system.

The Linux kernel provides a built-in packet filtering mechanism called **netfilter**, which is used to filter the traffic coming in or going out of the system. All modern Linux firewall systems use netfilter under the hood. Iptables is a well-known and popular user interface to set up and manage filtering rules for netfilter. It is a complete firewall solution that is highly configurable and highly flexible. However, iptables need effort on the user's part to master the firewall setup. Various frontend tools have been developed to simplify the configuration of iptables. UFW is among the most popular frontend solutions to manage iptables.

Uncomplicated firewall (**UFW**) provides easy-to-use interface for people unfamiliar with firewall concepts. It provides a framework for managing netfilter as well as the command-line interface to manipulate the firewall. With its small command set and plain English parameters, UFW makes it quick and easy to understand and set up firewall rules. At the same time, you can use UFW to configure most of the rules possible with iptables. UFW comes preinstalled with all Ubuntu installations after version 8.04 LTS.

In this recipe, we will secure our Ubuntu server with the help of UFW and also look at some advance configurations possible with UFW.

Getting ready

You will need an access to a root account or an account with root privileges.

How to do it...

Follow these steps to secure network with uncomplicated firewall:

1. UFW comes preinstalled on Ubuntu systems. If it's not, you can install it with the following commands:

   ```
   $ sudo apt-get udpate
   $ sudo apt-get install UFW
   ```

2. Check the status of UFW:

   ```
   $ sudo ufw status
   ```

```
ubuntu@ubuntu:~$ sudo ufw status
Status: inactive
ubuntu@ubuntu:~$ _
```

3. Add a new rule to allow SSH:

   ```
   $ sudo ufw allow ssh
   ```

4. Alternatively, you can use a port number to open a particular port:

   ```
   $ sudo ufw allow 22
   ```

5. Allow only TCP traffic over HTTP (port 80):

   ```
   $ sudo ufw allow http/tcp
   ```

```
ubuntu@ubuntu:~$ sudo ufw allow http/tcp
Rules updated
Rules updated (v6)
ubuntu@ubuntu:~$ _
```

6. Deny incoming FTP traffic:

   ```
   $ sudo ufw deny ftp
   ```

7. Check all added rules before starting the firewall:

   ```
   $ sudo ufw show added
   ```

```
ubuntu@ubuntu:~$ sudo ufw show added
Added user rules (see 'ufw status' for running firewall):
ufw allow 22/tcp
ufw deny 21/tcp
ufw allow 80/tcp
ubuntu@ubuntu:~$ _
```

8. Now enable the firewall:

   ```
   $ sudo ufw enable
   ```

```
ubuntu@ubuntu:~$ sudo ufw enable
Firewall is active and enabled on system startup
ubuntu@ubuntu:~$ _
```

9. Check the `ufw` status, the `verbose` parameter is optional:

   `$ sudo ufw status verbose`

```
ubuntu@ubuntu:~$ sudo ufw status verbose
Status: active
Logging: on (low)
Default: deny (incoming), allow (outgoing), disabled (routed)
New profiles: skip

To                         Action       From
--                         ------       ----
22/tcp                     ALLOW IN     Anywhere
21/tcp                     DENY IN      Anywhere
80/tcp                     ALLOW IN     Anywhere
22/tcp (v6)                ALLOW IN     Anywhere (v6)
21/tcp (v6)                DENY IN      Anywhere (v6)
80/tcp (v6)                ALLOW IN     Anywhere (v6)
```

10. Get a numbered list of added rules:

    `$ sudo ufw status numbered`

```
ubuntu@ubuntu:~$ sudo ufw status numbered
Status: active

     To                    Action       From
     --                    ------       ----
[ 1] 22/tcp                ALLOW IN     Anywhere
[ 2] 21/tcp                DENY IN      Anywhere
[ 3] 80/tcp                ALLOW IN     Anywhere
[ 4] 22/tcp (v6)           ALLOW IN     Anywhere (v6)
[ 5] 21/tcp (v6)           DENY IN      Anywhere (v6)
[ 6] 80/tcp (v6)           ALLOW IN     Anywhere (v6)
```

11. You can also allow all ports in a range by specifying a port range:

    `$ sudo ufw allow 1050:5000/tcp`

12. If you want to open all ports for a particular IP address, use the following command:

```
$ sudo ufw allow from 10.0.2.100
```

13. Alternatively, you can allow an entire subnet, as follows:

```
$ sudo ufw allow from 10.0.2.0/24
```

14. You can also allow or deny a specific port for a given IP address:

```
$ sudo ufw allow from 10.0.2.100 to any port 2222
$ sudo ufw deny from 10.0.2.100 to any port 5223
```

15. To specify a protocol in the preceding rule, use the following command:

```
$ sudo ufw deny from 10.0.2.100 proto tcp to any port 5223
```

16. Deleting rules:

```
$ sudo ufw delete allow ftp
```

17. Delete rules by specifying their numbers:

```
$ sudo ufw status numbered
$ sudo ufw delete 2
```

18. Add a new rule at a specific number:

```
$ sudo ufw insert 1 allow 5222/tcp        # Inserts a rule at
number 1
```

19. If you want to reject outgoing FTP connections, you can use the following command:

```
$ sudo ufw reject out ftp
```

20. UFW also supports application profiles. To view all application profiles, use the following command:

```
$ sudo ufw app list
```

21. Get more information about the app profile using the following command:

```
$ sudo ufw app info OpenSSH
```

22. Allow the application profile as follows:

```
$ sudo ufw allow OpenSSH
```

23. Set ufw logging levels [off|low|medium|high|full] with the help of the following command:

```
$ sudo ufw logging medium
```

24. View firewall reports with the `show` parameter:

    ```
    $ sudo ufw show added     # list of rules added
    $ sudo ufw show raw       # show complete firewall
    ```

25. Reset `ufw` to its default state (all rules will be backed up by UFW):

    ```
    $ sudo ufw reset
    ```

There's more...

UFW also provides various configuration files that can be used:

- ▶ `/etc/default/ufw`: This is the main configuration file.
- ▶ `/etc/ufw/sysctl.conf`: These are the kernel network variables. Variables in this file override variables in `/etc/sysctl.conf`.
- ▶ `/var/lib/ufw/user[6].rules or /lib/ufw/user[6].rules` are the rules added via the `ufw` command.
- ▶ `/etc/ufw/before.init` are the scripts to be run before the UFW initialization.
- ▶ `/etc/ufw/after.init` are the scripts to be run after the UFW initialization.

See also

- ▶ Check logging section of the UFW community page for an explanation of UFW logs at `https://help.ubuntu.com/community/UFW`
- ▶ Check out the UFW manual pages with the following command:

    ```
    $ man ufw
    ```

Securing against brute force attacks

So you have installed minimal setup of Ubuntu, you have setup SSH with public key authentication and disabled password authentication, and you have also allowed only single non-root user to access the server. You also configured a firewall, spending an entire night understanding the rules, and blocked everything except a few required ports. Now does this mean that your server is secured and you are free to take a nice sound sleep? Nope.

Servers are exposed to the public network, and the SSH daemon itself, which is probably the only service open, and can be vulnerable to attacks. If you monitor the application logs and access logs, you can find repeated systematic login attempts that represent brute force attacks.

2ban is a service that can help you monitor logs in real time and modify iptables rules to k suspected IP addresses. It is an intrusion-prevention framework written in Python. It can et to monitor logs for SSH daemon and web servers. In this recipe, we will discuss how to all and configure fail2ban.

Getting ready

You will need access to a root account or an account with similar privileges.

How to do it...

Follow these steps to secure against brute force attacks:

1. Fail2ban is available in the Ubuntu package repository, so we can install it with a single command, as follows:

   ```
   $ sudo apt-get update
   $ sudo apt-get install fail2ban
   ```

2. Create a copy of the `fail2ban` configuration file for local modifications:

   ```
   $ sudo cp /etc/fail2ban/jail.conf /etc/fail2ban/jail.local
   ```

3. Open a new configuration file in your favorite editor:

   ```
   $ sudo nano /etc/fail2ban/jail.local
   ```

4. You may want to modify the settings listed under the `[DEFAULT]` section:

   ```
   # The DEFAULT allows a global definition of the options. They can be overridden
   # in each jail afterwards.

   [DEFAULT]
   ignoreip = 127.0.0.1/8
   bantime  = 600
   findtime = 600
   maxretry = 3
   ```

5. Add your IP address to the ignore IP list.

6. Next, set your e-mail address if you wish to receive e-mail notifications of the ban action:

   ```
   destemail = you@provider.com
   sendername = Fail2Ban
   mta = sendmail
   ```

7. Set the required value for the `action` parameter:

```
action = $(action_mwl)s
```

8. Enable services you want to be monitored by setting `enable=true` for each service. SSH service is enabled by default:

```
[ssh]

enable = true
```

```
[ssh]

enabled  = true
port     = ssh
filter   = sshd
logpath  = /var/log/auth.log
maxretry = 6
```

9. Set other parameters if you want to override the default settings.

10. Fail2ban provides default configuration options for various applications. These configurations are disabled by default. You can enable them depending on your requirement.

11. Restart the `fail2ban` service:

```
$ sudo service fail2ban restart
```

12. Check iptables for the rules created by fail2ban:

```
$ sudo iptables -S
```

```
udaysc: ~ $ sudo iptables -S
-P INPUT ACCEPT
-P FORWARD ACCEPT
-P OUTPUT ACCEPT
-N fail2ban-ssh
-A INPUT -p tcp -m multiport --dports 22 -j fail2ban-ssh
-A fail2ban-ssh -s 61.82.71.252/32 -j REJECT --reject-with icmp-port-unreachable
-A fail2ban-ssh -j RETURN
```

13. Try some failed SSH login attempts, preferably from some other system.

14. Check iptables again. You should find new rules that reject the IP address with failed login attempts:

```
udaysc: ~ $ sudo iptables -S
-P INPUT ACCEPT
-P FORWARD ACCEPT
-P OUTPUT ACCEPT
-N fail2ban-ssh
-A INPUT -p tcp -m multiport --dports 22 -j fail2ban-ssh
-A fail2ban-ssh -s 12.166.225.156/32 -j REJECT --reject-with icmp-port-unreachab
le
-A fail2ban-ssh -j RETURN
```

How it works...

Fail2ban works by monitoring the specified log files as they are modified with new log entries. It uses regular expressions called filters to detect log entries that match specific criteria, such as failed login attempts. Default installation of fail2ban provides various filters that can be found in the `/etc/fail2ban/filter.d` directory. You can always create your own filters and use them to detect log entries that match your criteria.

Once it detects multiple logs matching with the configured filters within the specified timeout, fail2ban adjusts the firewall settings to reject the matching IP address for configured time period.

There's more...

Check out the article about defending against brute force attacks at `http://www.la-samhna.de/library/brutessh.html`.

The preceding articles shows multiple options to defend against SSH brute force attacks. As mentioned in the article, you can use iptables to slow down brute force attacks by blocking IP addresses:

```
$ iptables -A INPUT -p tcp --dport 22 -m state --state NEW -m
recent --set --name SSH -j ACCEPT
$ iptables -A INPUT -p tcp --dport 22 -m recent --update --seconds
60 --hitcount 4 --rttl --name SSH -j LOG --log-prefix "SSH_brute_force "
$ iptables -A INPUT -p tcp --dport 22 -m recent --update --seconds
60 --hitcount 4 --rttl --name SSH -j DROP
```

These commands will create an iptables rule to permit only three SSH login attempts per minute. After three attempts, whether they are successful or not, the attempting IP address will be blocked for another 60 seconds.

Discussing Ubuntu security best practices

In this recipe, we will look at some best practices to secure Ubuntu systems. Linux is considered to be a well secured operating system. It is quite easy to maintain the security and protect our systems from unauthorized access by following a few simple norms or rules.

Getting ready

You will need access to a root or account with `sudo` privileges. These steps are intended for a new server setup. You can apply them selectively for the servers already in productions.

How to do it...

Follow these steps to discuss Ubuntu security best practices:

1. Install updates from the Ubuntu repository. You can install all the available updates or just select security updates, depending on your choice and requirement:

   ```
   $ sudo apt-get update
   $ sudo apt-get upgrade
   ```

2. Change the root password; set a strong and complex root password and note it down somewhere. You are not going to use it every day:

   ```
   $ sudo passwd
   ```

3. Add a new user account and set a strong password for it. You can skip this step if the server has already set up a non-root account, like Ubuntu:

   ```
   $ sudo adduser john
   $ sudo passwd john
   ```

4. Add a new user to the `Sudoers` group:

   ```
   $ sudo adduser john sudo
   ```

5. Enable the public key authentication over SSH and import your public key to new user's `authorized_keys` file.

6. Restrict SSH logins:

   1. Change the default SSH port:

      ```
      port 2222
      ```

   2. Disable root login over SSH:

      ```
      PermitRootLogin no
      ```

3. Disable password authentication:

   PasswordAuthentication no

4. Restrict users and allow IP address:

   AllowUsers john@(your-ip) john@(other-ip)

7. Install fail2ban to protect against brute force attacks and set a new SSH port in the fail2ban configuration:

   ```
   $ sudo apt-get install fail2ban
   ```

8. Optionally, install UFW and allow your desired ports:

   ```
   $ sudo ufw allow from <your-IP> to any port 22 proto tcp
   $ sudo ufw allow 80/tcp
   $ sudo ufw enable
   ```

9. Maintain periodic snapshots (full-disk backups) of your server. Many cloud service providers offer basic snapshot tools.

10. Keep an eye on application and system logs. You may like to set up log-monitoring scripts that will e-mail any unidentified log entry.

How it works...

The preceding steps are basic and general security measures. They may change according to your server setup, package selection, and the services running on your server. I will try to cover some more details about specific scenarios. Also, I have not mentioned application-specific security practices for web servers and database servers. A separate recipe will be included in the respective chapters. Again, these configurations may change with your setup.

The steps listed earlier can be included in a single shell script and executed at first server boot up. Some cloud providers offer an option to add scripts to be executed on the first run of the server. You can also use centralized configuration tools such as Ansible, Chef/Puppet, and some others. Again, these tools come with their own security risks and increase total attack surface. This is a tradeoff between ease of setup and server security. Make sure that you select a well-known tool if you choose this route.

I have also mentioned creating single user account, except root. I am assuming that you are setting up your production server. With production servers, it is always a good idea to restrict access to one or two system administrators. For production servers, I don't believe in setting up multiple user accounts just for accountability or even setting LDAP-like centralized authentication methods to manage user accounts. This is a production environment and not your backyard. Moreover, if you follow the latest trends in immutable infrastructure concepts, then you should not allow even a single user to interfere with your live servers. Again, your mileage may vary.

Another thing that is commonly recommended is to set up automated and unattended security updates. This depends on how trusted your update source is. You live in a world powered by open source tools where things can break. You don't want things to go haywire without even touching the servers. I would recommend setting up unattended updates on your staging or test environment and then periodically installing updates on live servers, manually. Always have a snapshot of the working setup as your plan B.

You may want to skip host-based firewalls such as UFW when you have specialized firewalls protecting your network. As long as the servers are not directly exposed to the Internet, you can skip the local firewalls.

Minimize installed packages and service on single server. Remember the Unix philosophy, *do one thing and do it well,* and follow it. By minimizing the installed packages, you will effectively reduce the attack surface, and maybe save little on resources too. Think of it as a house with a single door verses a house with multiple doors. Also, running single service from one server provides layered security. This way, if a single server is compromised, the rest of your infrastructure remains in a safe state.

Remember that with all other tradeoffs in place, you cannot design a perfectly secured system, there is always a possibility that someone will break in. Direct your efforts to increase the time required for an attacker to break into your servers.

See also

- *First 5 Minutes Troubleshooting A Server* at `http://devo.ps/blog/troubleshooting-5minutes-on-a-yet-unknown-box/`

- Try to break in your own servers at `http://www.backtrack-linux.org/`

- What Can Be Done To Secure Ubuntu Server? at `http://askubuntu.com/questions/146775/what-can-be-done-to-secure-ubuntu-server`

3

Working with Web Servers

In this chapter, we will cover the following recipes:

- ▶ Installing and configuring the Apache web server
- ▶ Serving dynamic contents with PHP
- ▶ Hosting multiple websites with a virtual domain
- ▶ Securing web traffic with HTTPS
- ▶ Installing Nginx with PHP_FPM
- ▶ Setting Nginx as a reverse proxy
- ▶ Load balancing with Nginx
- ▶ Setting HTTPs on Nginx
- ▶ Benchmarking and performance tuning of Apache
- ▶ Securing the web server
- ▶ Troubleshooting the web server

Introduction

A web server is a tool that publishes documents on a network, generally the Internet. HTTP is called a language of the Internet and web servers, apart from browsers, are native speakers of HTTP. Web servers generally listen on one or multiple ports for requests from clients and accept requests in the form of URLs and HTTP headers. On receiving a request, web servers look for the availability of the requested resource and return the contents to the client. The term web server can refer to one or multiple physical servers or a software package, or both of them working together.

Some well known web servers include the Apache web server, Microsoft IIS, and Nginx. Apache web server is the most popular web server package available across platforms such as Windows and Linux. It is an open source project and freely available for commercial use. Nginx, which is again an open source web server project, started to overcome the problems in a high-load environment. Because of its lightweight resource utilization and ability to scale even on minimal hardware, Nginx quickly became a well known name. Nginx offers a free community edition as well as a paid commercial version with added support and extra features. Lastly, Microsoft IIS is a web server specifically designed for Windows servers. Apache still has the major share in the web server market, with Nginx rapidly taking over with some other notable alternatives such as lighttpd and H2O.

Apache is a modularized web server that can be extended by dynamically loading extra modules as and when required. This provides the flexibility to run a bare minimum web server or a fully featured box with modules to support compression, SSL, redirects, language modules, and more. Apache provides multiple connection processing **algorithms** called **multi-processing modules** (**MPM**). It provides an option to create a separate single threaded process for each new request (`mpm_prefork`), a multi-threaded process that can handle multiple concurrent requests (`mpm_worker`), or the latest development of `mpm_event`, which separates the active and idle connections.

Nginx can be considered the next generation of web servers. Its development started to solve the **C10k** problem, that is, handling ten thousand connections at a time. Apache, being a process-driven model, has some limitations when handling multiple concurrent connections. Nginx took advantage of the **event-driven** approach with asynchronous, non-blocking connection handling algorithms. A new connection request is handled by a worker process and placed in an event loop where they are continuously checked for events. The events are processed asynchronously. This approach enables Nginx to run with a much lower memory footprint and lower CPU use. It also eliminates the overload of starting a new process for a new connection. A single worker process started by Nginx can handle thousands of concurrent connections.

It is possible that some terms used throughout this chapter are unknown to you. It is not possible to explain everything in a Cookbook format. A quick Google search for a term will give you more details on them.

Both Apache and Nginx can be configured to process dynamic contents. Apache provides respective language processors such as `mod_php` and `mod_python` to process dynamic contents within the worker process itself. Nginx depends on external processors and uses CGI protocols to communicate with external processors. Apache can also be configured to use an external language processor over CGI, but the choice depends on performance and security considerations.

While both Apache and Nginx provide various similar features, they are not entirely interchangeable. Each one has its own pros and cons. Where Nginx excels at serving static contents, Apache performs much better processing dynamic contents. Many web administrators prefer to use Apache and Nginx together.

 Nginx is commonly used as a frontend caching/reverse proxy handling client requests and serving static contents, while Apache is used as a backend server processing dynamic contents.

Nginx handles a large number of connections and passes limited requests of dynamic contents to backend Apache servers. This configuration also allows users to scale horizontally by adding multiple backend servers and setting Nginx as a load balancer.

In this chapter, we will be working with both Apache and Nginx servers. We will learn how to set up Apache with PHP as a language for dynamic contents. We will look at some important configurations of Apache. Later, we will set up Nginx with an optional PHP processor, PHP_FPM, and configure Nginx to work as a reverse proxy and load balancer. We will also look at performance and security configurations for both the servers.

Installing and configuring the Apache web server

In this recipe, we will simply install the Apache web server from the Ubuntu package repository. We will also look at the basic configuration options and set up our first web page.

Getting ready

You will need access to a root account or an account with `sudo` privileges.

I will be using Apache to refer to the Apache web server. The Apache web server is the most popular project by the Apache Foundation and is generally known as just Apache.

How to do it...

Follow these steps to install and configure the Apache web server:

1. Install Apache2 from the Ubuntu package repository:

    ```
    $ sudo apt-get update
    $ sudo apt-get install apache2
    ```

2. Check if Apache2 has installed successfully. The command `wget` should download the `index.html` file:

```
$ wget 127.0.0.1
```

```
ubuntu@ubuntu:~$ wget 127.0.0.1
--2015-08-12 13:03:37--  http://127.0.0.1/
Connecting to 127.0.0.1:80... connected.
HTTP request sent, awaiting response... 200 OK
Length: 31 [text/html]
Saving to: 'index.html.2'

100%[==================================>] 31          ---.-K/s   in 0s

2015-08-12 13:03:37 (2.59 MB/s) - 'index.html.2' saved [31/31]
```

3. You can also open a browser on a local machine and point it to the server IP address. You should see a default **It works!** page customized for Ubuntu:

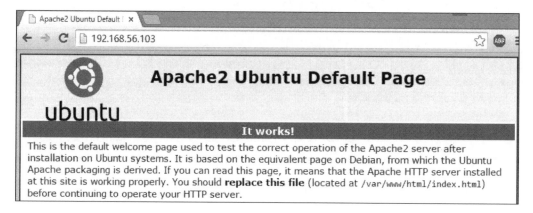

4. Now, let's proceed with creating our first virtual host. First create a directory structure. Change the directory to `/var/www/` and create a new directory for the contents of our site:

```
$ cd /var/www
```

```
$ sudo mkdir example.com
```

5. Change the ownership and group of the directory `example.com`:

```
$ sudo chown ubuntu:www-data example.com
```

6. Set the file permissions to secure web contents:

```
$ sudo chmod 750 example.com
```

7. Create the required directories under the `example.com` directory:

   ```
   $ cd example.com
   $ mkdir public_html
   ```

8. Create a `index.html` file under the `public_html` directory:

   ```
   $ echo '<b>Hello World ...</b>' > public_html/index.html
   ```

9. Next, we need to set up a new virtual host under the Apache configuration.

10. Copy the default **Virtual Host** file under `/etc/apache2/sites-available` and use it as a starting point for our configuration:

    ```
    $ cd /etc/apache2/sites-available
    $ sudo cp 000-default.conf example.com.conf
    ```

11. Edit `example.com.conf` to match it with the following example. Change the parameters as per your requirements:

    ```
    ubuntu@ubuntu:/etc/apache2/sites-available$ cat example.com.conf
    <VirtualHost *:80>
            ServerName example.com
            ServerAlias www.example.com
            ServerAdmin webmaster@example.com
            DocumentRoot /var/www/example.com/public_html

            ErrorLog ${APACHE_LOG_DIR}/error.log
            CustomLog ${APACHE_LOG_DIR}/access.log combined
    </VirtualHost>
    ```

12. Save the changes and exit `example.com.conf`.

13. If you are using the same port as the default `VirtualHost`, do not forget to disable the default one:

    ```
    $ sudo a2dissite 000-default.conf
    ```

14. Finally, enable our new `VirtualHost` with `a2ensite` and reload Apache:

    ```
    $ sudo a2ensite example.com.conf
    $ sudo service apache2 reload
    ```

15. Start your browser and point it to the domain or IP address of your server:

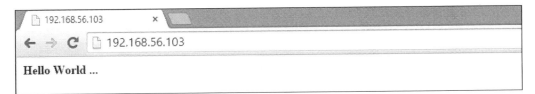

How it works...

The Apache package for Ubuntu is included in the default package repository. We need a single command to install the Apache web server. Installation creates a structure of configuration files under /etc/apache2 and a sample web page under /var/www/html.

As mentioned in the default **It works!** page, Apache2 does not use a single configuration file such as httpd.conf in older versions, but rather separates its configuration across multiple configuration files. These files are named after their respective uses. apache2.conf is now a main configuration file and creates a central configuration by including all other files.

conf-available, mods-available, and sites-available contain configuration snippets and other files for global configurations, modules, and virtual hosts respectively. These configurations are selectively activated under their enabled counterparts with symbolic links for each configuration to be enabled.

envvars contains all environment variables and default values for Apache to work.

ports.conf defines the ports Apache should listen on.

The default web page is created under the /var/www/html directory.

In this recipe, we have created our virtual host for the domain name example.com and hosted it under the directory /var/www/example.com. Next, we have to change the owner and default group of this directory to the user, ubuntu and group, www-data. This grants full access to the user ubuntu and allows read and execute access to the group www-data. If you have observed the contents of the envvars file, you may have noticed that the variable APACHE_RUN_GROUP is set to www-data. This means Apache process will be started as the group www-data. By setting a default group, we have allowed Apache process to read the contents of the example.com directory. We have also enabled write access to the logs directory so that Apache processes can log to this directory.

After creating the virtual host configuration and setting the respective options, all we need to do is enable a new virtual host or site. Apache2 provides the respective commands to enable or disable configurations, modules, and sites. a2ensite will be used to enable the site from options available under sites-available. Basically, this will create a symbolic link under the sites-enabled directory to a specified site configuration. Similarly, a2dissite will disable the site by removing the symbolic link from the sites-enabled directory. Similar commands are available to work with configurations and modules.

There's more...

You may want to get rid of the warning that says Could not reliably determine the server's fully qualified domain name. This warning appears because the Apache process could not find the default FQDN for this server. You can set the default FQDN simply by creating a new configuration file and then enabling this new configuration:

1. Create a new file under the `conf-available` directory:

   ```
   $ sudo vi /etc/apache2/conf-available/fqdn.conf
   ```

2. Add a server name variable to this file:

   ```
   ServerName   localhost
   ```

3. Save the changes and enable this configuration:

   ```
   $ sudo a2enconf fqdn
   ```

4. Reload the Apache server:

   ```
   $ sudo service apache2 reload
   ```

HTTP version 2 support

If you are looking for HTTP2 support, Apache does provide a separate module for that. Apache version 2.4.17 ships with a module, `mod_http2`, that implements the latest HTTP version, HTTP2. It is still an experimental implementation and needs to be enabled manually. This version of Apache (2.4.17) is available with Ubuntu Xenial (16.04) in the default package repository. If you are using Ubuntu 14.04, you can use the external repository as follows:

```
$ sudo add-apt-repository -y ppa:ondrej/apache2
```

Once the required version of Apache is installed, you can enable `mod_http2` as follows:

```
$ sudo a2enmod http2
```

Next, edit the specific virtual host file to enable the HTTP2 protocol for a specific site. Note that you need to configure your site to use an SSL/TLS connection:

```
<VirtualHost *:443>
    Protocols h2 http/1.1
    ...
</VirtualHost>
```

Finally, restart your Apache server:

```
$ sudo service apache2 restart
```

H2O, the new name in web servers, is developed around the HTTP2 protocol. It does support both HTTP 1.1 and a stable implementation of the HTTP2 protocol. You may want to check this out as your local or development server.

See also

You can read more by following the links:

▸ There is a good Q and A about permissions for web directory at `http://serverfault.com/questions/357108/what-permissions-should-my-website-files-folders-have-on-a-linux-webserver`

▸ You can find more details about installing the Apache web server at `https://help.ubuntu.com/lts/serverguide/httpd.html`

▸ Apache official documentation - `http://httpd.apache.org/docs/2.4/`

Serving dynamic contents with PHP

In this recipe, we will learn how to install PHP and set it to work alongside the Apache web server. We will install PHP binaries and then the Apache module `mod_php` to support PHP-based dynamic contents.

Getting ready

You will need access to a root account or an account with `sudo` privileges.

The Apache web server should be installed and working properly.

How to do it...

Follow these steps to serve dynamic contents with PHP:

1. Install PHP7 and the Apache module for PHP support:

```
$ sudo apt-get update
$ sudo apt-get install -y php7.0 libapache2-mod-php7.0
```

2. Check if PHP is properly installed and which version has been installed:

```
$ php -v
```

```
ubuntu@ubuntu:~$ php -v
PHP 7.0.4-7ubuntu2 (cli) ( NTS )
Copyright (c) 1997-2016 The PHP Group
Zend Engine v3.0.0, Copyright (c) 1998-2016 Zend Technologies
    with Zend OPcache v7.0.6-dev, Copyright (c) 1999-2016, by Zend Technologies
```

3. Create `index.php` under the `public_html` directory of our site:

   ```
   $ cd /var/www/example.com/public_html
   $ vi index.php
   ```

4. Add the following contents to `index.php`:

   ```
   <?php echo phpinfo(); ?>
   ```

5. Save and exit the `index.php` file.

6. Open `example.com.conf` from `sites-available`:

   ```
   $ sudo vi /etc/apache2/sites-available/example.com.conf
   ```

7. Add the following line under the `VirtualHost` directive:

   ```
   DirectoryIndex index.php index.html
   ```

```
ubuntu@ubuntu:~$ cat /etc/apache2/sites-available/example.com.conf
<VirtualHost *:80>
        ServerName example.com
        ServerAlias www.example.com
        ServerAdmin webmaster@example.com
        DirectoryIndex index.php index.html
        DocumentRoot /var/www/example.com/public_html
```

8. Save the changes and reload Apache:

   ```
   $ sudo service apache2 reload
   ```

9. Now, access your site with your browser, and you should see a page with information regarding the installed PHP:

```
←  →  C   192.168.56.103
```

PHP Version 7.0.4-7ubuntu2

System	Linux ubuntu 4.4.0-21-generic #37-Ubuntu SMP Mon Apr 18 18:33:37 UTC
Server API	Apache 2.0 Handler
Virtual Directory Support	disabled
Configuration File (php.ini) Path	/etc/php/7.0/apache2
Loaded Configuration File	/etc/php/7.0/apache2/php.ini

How it works...

Here, we have installed PHP binaries on our server along with the Apache module libapache2-mod-php7.0 to support dynamic content coded in PHP. A module, mod_php, runs inside Apache process and processes PHP scripts from within Apache itself. For mod_php to work, Apache needs to run with the mpm_prefork module. PHP setup completes all these settings and restarts the Apache server:

```
Creating config file /etc/php/7.0/apache2/php.ini with new version
Module mpm_event disabled.
Enabling module mpm_prefork.
apache2_switch_mpm Switch to prefork
apache2_invoke: Enable module php7.0
Setting up php7.0 (7.0.4-7ubuntu2) ...
ubuntu@ubuntu:~$
```

After we have installed PHP and mod_php, we simply need to create a PHP script. We have created index.php with little code to display phpinfo. At this stage, if you have both index.html and index.php under the same directory; by default, index.html will take over and be rendered first. You will need to explicitly specify index.php to access the page as http://127.0.0.1/index.php. We have set a directive, DirectoryIndex, under Apache Virtual Host to set index.php as a default index file.

PHP settings

All PHP settings are listed under its own configuration file, php.ini. PHP comes with two sets of configurations, as follows:

/usr/lib/php/7.0/php.ini-development

The /usr/lib/php/7.0/php.ini-productionDevelopment file is customized for a development environment and enables options like display_errors. For production systems, you can use the configuration file, php.ini-production.

The preceding files can be treated as a reference configuration that ships with the PHP installation. A copy of php.ini-production can be found under /etc/php/7.0. Apache and CLI configurations are separated in respective directories. You can directly edit settings under these files or simply use default files by creating a symbolic link to the development or production file as follows:

```
$ cd /etc/php/7.0/apache2
$ sudo mv php.ini php.ini.orig
$ sudo ln -s /usr/lib/php/7.0/php.ini-development php.ini
```

There's more...

Along with PHP, Apache supports various other scripting languages for dynamic content. You can install modules for Perl, Python, Ruby, and other scripting languages.

Add Python support:

```
$ sudo apt-get install libapache2-mod-python
```

Add Perl support:

```
$ sudo apt-get install libapache2-mod-perl2
```

Add Ruby support:

```
$ sudo apt-get install libapache2-mod-passenger
```

Installing the LAMP stack

If you are interested in installing the entire LAMP stack, then Ubuntu provides a single command to do so. Use the following command to install Apache, PHP, and MySQL collectively:

```
$ sudo apt-get install lamp-server^
```

Notice the caret symbol at the end of the command. If you miss this symbol, apt will return an error saying package not found.

> lamp-server is set in the Ubuntu repository as a task to install and configure Apache, PHP, and MySQL collectively. The caret symbol in apt-get command is used to specify the task rather than the package. Alternatively, you can use the tasksel command as $ sudo tasksel install lamp-server. **Tasksel** is a program used to ease the installation of packages that are commonly used together.

Upgrading PHP under Ubuntu 14

As of Ubuntu 14.10, Ubuntu does not provide a package for PHP7 in its repository, but you can use a Debian package repository to upgrade your PHP version. This repository is maintained by Ondřej Surý.

Use the following commands to upgrade to PHP 7:

```
$ sudo apt-get install software-properties-common
$ sudo add-apt-repository ppa:ondrej/php
$ sudo apt-get update
$ sudo apt-get install php7.0
```

Check the PHP version after installation completes:

```
$ php -v
```

Hosting multiple websites with a virtual domain

Setting multiple domains on a single server is a very commonly asked question. In fact, it is very easy to do this with virtual host. In this recipe, we will set up two domains on a single server and set up a sub-domain as well. We will also look at IP-based virtual hosts.

Getting ready

You will need access to a root account or an account with `sudo` privileges.

You will need the Apache server installed and working. This recipe describes configuration for Apache version 2.4

You may need a DNS set up if you want to access configured domains over the Internet.

We will set up two domains, namely `example1.dom` and `example2.com`, and a sub-domain, `dev.example1.com`.

How to do it...

Follow these steps to host multiple websites with a virtual domain:

1. Change the directory to `/var/www` and create a directory structure for the required domains and sub-domain. Also create a blank `index.html` for each domain:

   ```
   $ cd /var/www
   $ sudo mkdir -p example1.com/public_html
   $ sudo touch example1.com/public_html
   $ sudo cp -R example1.com example2.com
   $ sudo cp -R example1.com dev.example1.com
   ```

2. Change the directory ownership and file permissions on the newly created directories:

```
$ sudo chown -R ubuntu:www-data example*
$ sudo chown -R ubuntu:www-data dev.example1.com
$ chmod 750 -R example*
$ chmod 750 -R dev.example1.com
```

 Note the use of the wildcard syntax (chmod 750 -R example*). You can use a similar syntax with various other commands in Linux and save some repeated typing or copy and paste work.

3. Edit the index.html file for each domain with the respective text:

```
ubuntu@ubuntu:/var/www$ cat example1.com/public_html/index.html
<b>Hello from example1.com</b>
ubuntu@ubuntu:/var/www$ cat example2.com/public_html/index.html
<b>Hello from example2.com</b>
ubuntu@ubuntu:/var/www$ cat dev.example1.com/public_html/index.html
<b>Hello from developers at dev.example1.com</b>
```

4. Next, we need to create virtual host configuration for each domain. Change the directory to /etc/apache2/sites-available and copy the default virtual host file 000-default.conf:

```
$ cd /etc/apache2/sites-available
$ sudo cp 000-default.conf example1.com.conf
```

5. Edit the new virtual host file and set ServerName, DocumentRoot, and other variables to match your environment. The final file should look something like this:

```
<VirtualHost *:80>
    ServerName example1.com
    ServerAlias www.example1.com
    DocumentRoot /var/www/example1.com/public_html
    ...
</VirtualHost>
```

6. Now copy this virtual host file to create example2.com.conf and dev.example1.com.conf and modify the respective settings in each of them. You need to update the serverName, serverAlias, and DocumentRoot parameters.

7. Here, we are done with the setup and configuration part. Now enable the virtual hosts and reload the Apache server for the settings to take effect:

```
$ sudo a2ensite example*
$ sudo a2ensite dev.example1.com.conf
$ sudo service apache2 reload
```

8. You can check all enabled virtual hosts with the following command:

```
$ sudo a2query -s
```

9. Next, to test our setup, we need to configure the hosts' setup on the local system. Open and edit the /etc/hosts file and add host entries. If you have Windows as your local system, you can find the hosts file under %systemroot%\System32\drivers\etc:

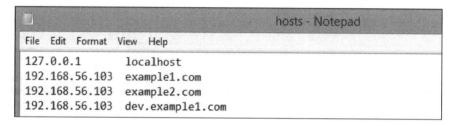

10. Finally, try to access domains by their names. You should see text entered in the respective index.html files for each domain:

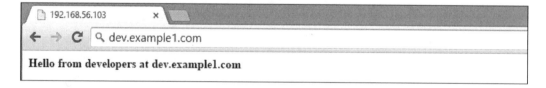

How it works...

Multiple domain hosting works with the concept of **NamedVirtualHost**. We have configured virtual hosts with **ServerName** and **ServerAlias**. When a client sends a request with a domain name, it sends a host name in the request headers. This host name is used by Apache to determine the actual virtual host to serve this request. If none of the available virtual hosts match the requested host header, then the default virtual host or the first virtual host will be used to serve the request.

In this example, we have used hosts file to map test domain names with local IP. With the actual domain name, you need to point DNS servers to the IP address of your web server. Generally, all popular hosting providers host their own DNS servers. You need to add these DNS servers to your domain setting with domain registrar. Then, on your hosting side, you need to set respective **A records** and **CNAME** records. An A record points to an IP address and the CNAME record is an alias for the A record used for pointing a subdomain to an A record. Your hosting provider should give you details on how to configure domains and subdomains.

In previous versions of Apache server, you might need to enable `NameVirtualHost` under the configuration file. Find a line similar to `#NameVirtualHost 172.20.30.40` and uncomment it by removing the # symbol at the start.

You can also set up IP-based virtual hosts. If you have multiple IP addresses available on your server, you can set the virtual host to listen on a particular IP address. Use the following steps to set up an IP-based virtual host:

1. Get a list of the available IP addresses:

    ```
    $ ifconfig | grep "inet addr"
    ubuntu@ubuntu:~$ ifconfig | grep "inet addr"
    inet addr:10.0.2.15  Bcast:10.0.2.255  Mask:255.255.255.0
    inet addr:192.168.56.102  Bcast:192.168.56.255
    Mask:255.255.255.0
    inet addr:127.0.0.1  Mask:255.0.0.0
    ```

2. Edit the virtual host configuration and set it to match the following:

    ```
    Listen 80
    <VirtualHost 192.168.56.102>
            DocumentRoot /var/www/example1.com/public_html
            ServerName example1.com
    </VirtualHost>
    ```

See also

▶ Apache documentation at `https://httpd.apache.org/docs/2.2/vhosts/examples.html`

▶ Refer to the *Installing and configuring the Apache web server* recipe for the installation and configuration of the Apache web server.

Securing web traffic with HTTPS

HTTP is a non-secure protocol commonly used to communicate over the Web. The traffic is transferred in plain text form and can be captured and interpreted by a third-party attacker. **Transport Layer Security** and **Secure Socket Layer** protocols (**TLS/SSL**) can be used to secure the traffic between client and server. These protocols encapsulate normal traffic in an encrypted and secure wrapper. It also validates the identity of the client and server with SSL keys, certificates, and certification authorities.

When HTTP is combined with TLS or SSL, it is abbreviated as HTTPS or HTTP secure. Port 443 is used as a standard port for secured HTTP communication. Nearly all leading web servers provide inbuilt support for enabling HTTPS. Apache has a module called mod_ssl that enables the use of HTTPS.

To set up your servers with SSL/TLS encrypted traffic, you will need an SSL certificate and a key pair that can be used to encrypt traffic. Generally, the certificate and keys are obtained from a trusted signing authority. They charge you some fees to verify your ownership of the web property and allocate the required signed certificates. You can also generate self-signed certificates for internal use. Few certification authorities provide a free SSL certificate. Recently, Mozilla has started a free and automated certificate authority named *Let's Encrypt*. At the time of writing, the service is in public beta and has started allocating certificates. Let's Encrypt offers a client that can be used to obtain certificates and set up automated renewal. You can also find various unofficial clients for Apache and Nginx servers.

In this recipe, we will learn how to create our own self-signed certificate and set up the Apache server to serve contents over a secure channel.

Getting ready

You will need access to a root account or an account with sudo privileges. I assume that you have the Apache server preinstalled. You will also need OpenSSL installed.

Make sure your firewall, if any, allows traffic on port 443. Check *Chapter 2, Networking, Securing network with uncomplicated firewall* recipe for more details on Uncomplicated Firewall.

How to do it...

Follow these steps to secure web traffic with HTTPS:

1. First, we will start by creating a self-signed SSL certificate. Create a directory under /etc/apache2 to hold the certificate and key:

    ```
    $ sudo mkdir /etc/apache2/ssl
    ```

2. Change to the new directory and enter the following command to create a certificate and SSL key:

```
$ cd /etc/apache2/ssl
$ sudo openssl req -x509 -nodes -days 365 \
-newkey rsa:2048 -keyout ssl.key -out ssl.crt
```

3. This will prompt you to enter some information about your company and website. Enter the respective details and press *Enter* for each prompt:

```
Country Name (2 letter code) [AU]:IN
State or Province Name (full name) [Some-State]:MH
Locality Name (eg, city) []:MUM
Organization Name (eg, company) [Internet Widgits Pty Ltd]:example
Organizational Unit Name (eg, section) []:tech
Common Name (e.g. server FQDN or YOUR name) []:example.com
Email Address []:admin@example.com
```

4. After you are done with it, you can check the generated certificate and key:

```
$ ls -l
```

```
ubuntu@ubuntu:/etc/apache2/ssl$ ls -l
total 8
-rw-r--r-- 1 root root 1391 Aug 12 14:55 ssl.crt
-rw-r--r-- 1 root root 1704 Aug 12 14:55 ssl.key
```

5. Next, we need to configure Apache to use SSL. We will enable SSL for the previously created virtual host.

6. Open the Virtual Host configuration file, `example.com.conf`. After removing comments, it should look similar to the following:

```
ubuntu@ubuntu:~$ cat /etc/apache2/sites-available/example.com.conf
<VirtualHost *:80>
        ServerName example.com
        ServerAlias www.example.com
        ServerAdmin webmaster@example.com
        DirectoryIndex index.php index.html
        DocumentRoot /var/www/example.com/public_html

        ErrorLog ${APACHE_LOG_DIR}/error.log
        CustomLog ${APACHE_LOG_DIR}/access.log combined
</VirtualHost>
```

7. Now, copy the entire `<VirtualHost *:80>` ... `</VirtualHost>` tag and paste it at the end of the file.

8. Under the newly copied contents, change the port from `80` to `443`.

9. Add the following lines below the `DocumentRoot` line. This will enable SSL and specify the path to the certificate and key:

    ```
    SSLEngine on

    SSLCertificateFile /etc/apache2/ssl/ssl.crt

    SSLCertificateKeyFile /etc/apache2/ssl/ssl.key
    ```

10. The final file should look something like this:

```
ubuntu@ubuntu:~$ cat /etc/apache2/sites-available/example.com.conf
<VirtualHost *:80>
        ServerName example.com
        ServerAlias www.example.com
        ServerAdmin webmaster@example.com
        DirectoryIndex index.php index.html
        DocumentRoot /var/www/example.com/public_html

        ErrorLog ${APACHE_LOG_DIR}/error.log
        CustomLog ${APACHE_LOG_DIR}/access.log combined
</VirtualHost>

<VirtualHost *:443>
        ServerName example.com
        ServerAlias www.example.com
        ServerAdmin webmaster@example.com
        DirectoryIndex index.php index.html
        DocumentRoot /var/www/example.com/public_html

        SSLEngine on
        SSLCertificateFile /etc/apache2/ssl/ssl.crt
        SSLCertificateKeyFile /etc/apache2/ssl/ssl.key

        ErrorLog ${APACHE_LOG_DIR}/error.log
        CustomLog ${APACHE_LOG_DIR}/access.log combined
</VirtualHost>
```

11. Save the changes, exit `example.com.conf`, and enable the `mod_ssl` module on the Apache server:

    ```
    $ sudo a2enmod ssl
    ```

12. Next, enable the Virtual Host `example.com`. If it's already enabled, it will return a message saying `site example.com already enabled`:

    ```
    $ sudo a2ensite example.com.conf
    ```

13. Reload the Apache server for the changes to take effect:

    ```
    $ sudo service apache2 reload
    ```

14. Now, open your browser on the client system and point it to your domain name or IP address with HTTPS at the start:

    `https://example.com`

15. Your browser may return an error saying **Invalid Certification Authority**. This is fine as we are using a self-signed certificate. Click **Advanced** and then click **Proceed to example.com** to open a specified page:

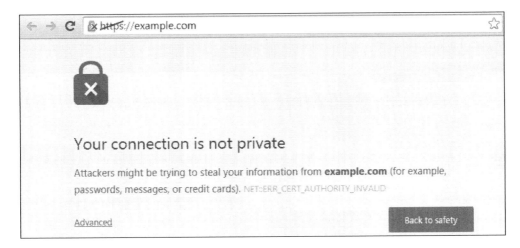

16. Once the page is loaded completely, find the padlock icon in the upper right corner of the browser and click on it. The second section with the green lock icon will display the encryption status. Now your communication with the server is encrypted and secure:

How it works...

We have created a self-signed certificate to secure an HTTP communication. The key will be used to encrypt all communication with clients. Another thing to note is that we have defined a separate Virtual Host entry on port 443. This Virtual Host will be used for all requests that are received over port 443. At the same time, we have allowed non-secured HTTP communication for the same Virtual Host. To disable non-secure communication on port 80, you can simply comment out the original Virtual Host configuration. Alternatively, you can separate both configurations into two files and enable or disable with the a2ensite and a2dissite commands.

Some of the parameters used for generating a key and certificate are as follows:

- ▶ - nodes specifies that we do not want to use a passphrase for a key.
- ▶ - days this specifies the number of days the certificate is valid for. Our certificate is valid for 365 days, that is, a year.
- ▶ - newkey rsa:2048 this option is used to generate a certificate along with a private key. rsa:2048 specifies the 2048 bit long RSA private key.

I have modified the existing Virtual Host entry to demonstrate the minimal configuration required to enable secure HTTP communication. You can always use the default secure Virtual Host configuration available under sites-available/default-ssl.conf. This file provides some additional parameters with respective comments.

The certificate created in this recipe will not be trusted over the Internet but can be used for securing local or internal communication. For production use, it is advisable to get a certificate signed from an external, well known **certification authority**. This will avoid the initial errors in browsers.

There's more...

To get a signed certificate from an external certification authority, you will need a CSR document.

The following are the steps to generate a CSR:

1. Generate a key for the CSR:

   ```
   $ openssl genrsa -des3 -out server.key 2048
   ```

2. You will be asked to enter a passphrase for the key and then verify it. They will be generated with name server.key.

3. Now, remove the passphrase from the key. We don't want to enter a passphrase each time a key is used:

```
$ openssl rsa -in server.key -out server.key.insecure
$ mv server.key server.key.secure
$ mv server.key.insecure server.key
```

4. Next, create the CSR with the following command:

```
$ openssl req -new -key server.key -out server.csr
```

5. A CSR file is created with the name `server.csr`, and now you can submit this CSR for signing purposes.

See also

▸ Refer to the *Installing and configuring the Apache web server* recipe for the installation and configuration of the Apache web server.

▸ Check out the certificates and security in the Ubuntu server guide at `https://help.ubuntu.com/lts/serverguide/certificates-and-security.html`

▸ How to set up client verification at `http://askubuntu.com/questions/511149/how-to-setup-ssl-https-for-your-site-on-ubuntu-linux-two-way-ssl`

▸ Apache documentation on SSL configuration at `http://httpd.apache.org/docs/2.4/ssl/ssl_howto.html`

▸ Free SSL certificate with Mozilla Let's Encrypt at `https://letsencrypt.org/getting-started/`

▸ Easily generate SSL configuration for your web server at Mozilla SSL Configuration Generator at `https://mozilla.github.io/server-side-tls/ssl-config-generator/`

Installing Nginx with PHP_FPM

In this recipe, we will learn how to install and set up Nginx as a web server. We will also install PHP to be able to serve dynamic content. We need to install PHP_FPM (FastCGI Process Manager), as Nginx doesn't support the native execution of PHP scripts. We will install the latest stable version available from the Nginx package repository.

Getting ready

You will need access to a root account or an account with `sudo` privileges.

How to do it...

Follow these steps to install Nginx with PHP_FPM:

1. Update the `apt` package repository and install Nginx. As of writing this Ubuntu 16.04 repository contains latest stable release of Nginx with version 1.10.0:

```
$ sudo apt-get update
$ sudo apt-get install nginx
```

2. Check if Nginx is properly installed and running:

```
$ sudo service nginx status
```

3. Check the installed version of Nginx:

```
$ nginx -v
```

4. You may want to point your browser to the server IP or domain. You should see a default Nginx welcome page:

5. Next, proceed with installing PHP_FPM:

```
$ sudo apt-get install php7.0-fpm
```

6. Configure Nginx to use the PHP processor. Nginx sites are listed at `/etc/nginx/sites-available`. We will modify the default site:

```
$ sudo nano /etc/nginx/sites-available/default
```

7. Find a line stating the priority of the `index` file and add `index.php` as a first option:

```
index index.php index.html index.htm;
```

8. Next, add the following two `location` directives:

```
location / {
    try_files $uri $uri/ /index.php;
}
location ~ \.php$ {
    include fastcgi_params;
    fastcgi_param SCRIPT_FILENAME
    $document_root$fastcgi_script_name;
    fastcgi_param QUERY_STRING    $query_string;
    fastcgi_pass unix:/var/run/php/php7.0-fpm.sock;
}
```

9. Save the changes and exit the file. It should look similar to this:

```
server {
        listen 80 default_server;
        listen [::]:80 default_server;
        root /var/www/html;
        index index.php index.html index.htm;
        server_name _;
        location / {
                try_files $uri $uri/ /index.php;
        }
        location ~ \.php$ {
                include fastcgi_params;
                fastcgi_param SCRIPT_FILENAME
                $document_root$fastcgi_script_name;
                fastcgi_param QUERY_STRING $query_string;
                fastcgi_pass unix:/var/run/php/php7.0-fpm.sock;
        }
}
```

10. Change the PHP settings to disable `PATH_TRANSLATED` support. Find an option, `cgi.fix_pathinfo`, and uncomment it with the value set to 0:

```
$ sudo nano /etc/php/7.0/fpm/php.ini
cgi.fix_pathinfo=0
```

11. Now, restart PHP_FPM and Nginx for the changes to take effect:

```
$ sudo service php7.0-fpm restart
$ sudo service nginx restart
```

12. Create an `index.php` file with some PHP code in it at the path mentioned in the default site configuration:

```
$ sudo nano /var/www/html/index.php
<?php phpinfo(); ?>
```

13. Open your browser and point it to your server. You should see the result of your PHP script:

PHP Version 7.0.4-7ubuntu2.1

System	Linux server-01 4.4.0-22-generic #40-Ubuntu SMP Thu May 12 22:03:46 UT
Server API	FPM/FastCGI
Virtual Directory Support	disabled
Configuration File (php.ini) Path	/etc/php/7.0/fpm
Loaded Configuration File	/etc/php/7.0/fpm/php.ini
Scan this dir for additional .ini files	/etc/php/7.0/fpm/conf.d

How it works...

Here, we have installed the latest stable version of the Nginx server with PHP_FPM to support dynamic content scripted with PHP. The Ubuntu repository for version 16.04 contains the latest stable release of Nginx, So installing Nginx is as easy as a single command. If you are interested in more recent versions Nginx maintains their own package repository for mainline packages. You just need to add repository, the rest of the installation process is similar to a single `apt-get install nginx` command.

 If you are running the Apache server on the same machine, you may want to change the default port Nginx runs on. You can find these settings under site configurations, located at `/etc/nginx/sites-available`. Nginx creates default site configuration with the filename set to `default`. Find the lines that start with `listen` and change the port from its default, `80`, to any port number of your choice.

After installing Nginx, we need to configure it to support dynamic content. Here, we have selected PHP as a dynamic content processor. PHP is a popular scripting language and very commonly used with web servers for dynamic content processing. You can also add support for other modules by installing their respective processors. After installing PHP_FPM, we have configured Nginx to use PHP_FPM and pass all PHP requests to the FPM module on a socket connection.

We have used two location blocks in configuration. The first block search is for static content, such as files and directories, and then if nothing matches, the request is forwarded to `index.php`, which is in turn forwarded to the FastCGI module for processing. This ensures that Nginx serves all static content without executing PHP, and only requests that are not static files and directories are passed to the FPM module.

The following is a brief description of the parameters used under FastCGI configuration:

- The parameter `try_files` configures Nginx to return `404` pages, that is, the *page not found* error, for any requests that do not match website content. This is limited to static files.

- With the parameter `fastcgi_param`, you can forward the script name and query string to the PHP FPM process.

- One more optional parameter is `cgi.fix_pathinfo=0`, under the PHP configuration file `php.ini`. By default, PHP is set to search for the exact script filename and then search for the closest match if the exact name is not found. This may become a security risk by allowing an attacker to execute random scripts with simple guesswork for script names. We have disabled this by setting its value to `0`.

Finally, after we restart PHP_FPM and Nginx, our server is ready to process static as well as dynamic content. All static content will be handled by Nginx itself, and requests for URLs that end with `.php` will be forwarded to PHP_FPM for processing. Nginx may cache the processed result for future use.

There's more...

If you are running Ubuntu 12.10, you may need to install the following dependencies before adding the Nginx repository to the installation sources:

1. Install `python-software-properties` and `software-properties-common`:

   ```
   $ sudo apt-get install python-software-properties
   $ sudo apt-get install software-properties-common
   ```

2. You may want to remove your Apache installation completely. Use the following commands to remove Apache:

   ```
   $ sudo service apache2 stop
   $ sudo apt-get remove --purge apache2 apache2-utils apache2.2-bin apache2-common
   ```

Nginx maintains their own package repositories for stable and mainline releases. These repositories can be used to get the latest updates of Nginx as and when available. Use the stable repository, - `$ sudo add-apt-repository ppa:nginx/stable`.

Use the mainline repository - $ `sudo add-apt-repository ppa:nginx/development`.

See also

▸ Common Nginx pitfalls at `http://wiki.nginx.org/Pitfalls`

▸ Nginx Quick start guide at `http://wiki.nginx.org/QuickStart`

Setting Nginx as a reverse proxy

Apache and Nginx are two popular open source web servers. Both are very powerful, but at the same time have their own disadvantages as well. Apache is not good at handling high load environments with multiple concurrent requests and Nginx does not have inbuilt support for dynamic content processing. Many administrators overcome these problems by using both Apache and Nginx together. Nginx handles all incoming requests and only passes requests for dynamic content to Apache. Additionally, Nginx can provide a catching option which enables the server to respond to a request with results from a similar previous request. This helps to reduce the overall response time and minimize the load sent to Apache.

In this recipe, we will learn how to set up a web server configured with a reverse proxy. We will use Nginx as a reverse proxy, which will serve all static content and pass the requests for dynamic content to Apache.

Getting ready

You will need access to a root account or an account with `sudo` privileges.

I assume that Apache is installed and running with a virtual host, `example.com`.

How to do it...

Follow these steps to set Nginx as a reverse proxy:

1. Install Nginx with the following command:

   ```
   $ sudo apt-get update
   $ sudo apt-get install nginx
   ```

2. Create a new site configuration under `/etc/nginx/sites-available` and add the following content to it:

   ```
   $ sudo nano /etc/nginx/sites-available/reverse_proxy
   server {
       listen 80;
   ```

```
    root /var/www/example.com;

    index index.php index.html index.htm;


    server_name example.com;

    location / {
        try_files $uri $uri/ /index.php;
    }


    location ~ \.php$ {
        proxy_set_header X-Real-IP    $remote_addr;
        proxy_set_header X-Forwarded-For $remote_addr;
        proxy_set_header Host $host;
        proxy_pass http://127.0.0.1:8080;
    }
    location ~* \.(js|css|jpg|jpeg|png|svg|html|htm)$ {
        expires       30d;
    }


    location ~ /\.ht {
        deny all;
    }
}
```

3. Enable this new configuration by creating a symbolic link under `sites-enabled`:

```
$ sudo ln -s /etc/nginx/sites-available/reverse_proxy \
/etc/nginx/sites-enabled/reverse_proxy
```

4. Optionally, disable the default site by removing the symbolic link from `sites-enabled`:

```
$ sudo rm /etc/nginx/sites-enabled/default
```

5. Next, we need to change the Apache settings to listen on port `8080`. This will leave port `80` to be used by Nginx:

```
$ sudo nano /etc/apache2/ports.conf
listen 127.0.0.1:8080
```

6. Also change `NameVirtualHost`, if you are using it:

   `NameVirtualHost 127.0.0.1:8080`

7. Change the virtual hosts settings to listen on port `8080`:

   `$ sudo nano /etc/apache2/sites-available/example.com`

   `<VirtualHost 127.0.0.1:8080>`

   `   ServerName example.com`

   `   ServerAdmin webmaster@example.com`

   `   DocumentRoot /var/www/example.com/public_html`

   `</VirtualHost>`

8. Save the changes and restart Apache for the changes to take effect:

   `$ sudo service apache2 restart`

9. Now, restart Nginx:

   `$ sudo service nginx restart`

10. Check for open ports with the following command:

    `$ sudo netstat -pltn`

```
ubuntu@ubuntu:~$ sudo netstat -pltn | egrep '(apache|nginx)'
tcp        0      0 127.0.0.1:8080          0.0.0.0:*               LISTEN      4753/apache2
tcp        0      0 0.0.0.0:80              0.0.0.0:*               LISTEN      3962/nginx
tcp6       0      0 :::80                   :::*                    LISTEN      3962/nginx
tcp6       0      0 :::443                  :::*                    LISTEN      4753/apache2
ubuntu@ubuntu:~$
```

11. Open your browser and point it to the IP address of your server. It should load the page configured under the Apache virtual host, `example.com`.

How it works...

With the `proxy_pass` parameter, we have simply asked Nginx to pass all requests for PHP scripts to Apache on `127.0.0.1` on port `8080`. Then, we set Apache to listen on the loopback IP and port `8080`, which will receive requests forwarded by Nginx and process them with an internal PHP processor. All non-PHP content will still be served by Nginx from the `/var/www` directory. The `try_files $uri $uri/ /index.php;` option sets Nginx to search for the file with a specified name and then look for the folder; lastly, if both file and folder are not found, send the request to `index.php`, which will then be processed by Apache.

Other options used with proxy pass ensures that Apache and PHP scripts receive the actual hostname and IP of the client and not of the Nginx server. You can use an additional module named `libapache2-mod-rpaf` on Apache. This module provides an option to set a proxy IP address and rename the parameters sent by the proxy server. You can install the module with the following command:

```
$ sudo apt-get install libapache2-mod-rpaf
```

The configuration file for this module is available at `/etc/apache2/mods-available/rpaf.conf`.

You can find various other proxy options and their respective explanations in the Nginx documentation at `http://nginx.org/en/docs/http/ngx_http_proxy_module.html`

Finally, with Nginx set as a frontend, Apache will not have to interact directly with HTTP clients. You may want to disable some of the Apache modules that will not be used in this setup:

```
$ sudo a2dismod deflate cgi negotiation autoindex
```

As always, do not forget to reload Apache after any changes.

There's more...

Nginx can be set to cache the response received from the backend server and thereby minimize repeated requests on backend servers, as well as the response time. Nginx can cache the content in local files and serve new requests from the cache. The cache can be invalidated or even disabled based on the request received. To enable caching, add the following settings to the Nginx site configuration:

```
  proxy_cache_path /data/nginx/cache levels=1:2 keys_zone=backend-
cache:8m max_size=50m;
 proxy_cache_key "$scheme$request_method$host$request_uri$args";
  server {
    ## add other settings heres
   location / {
     proxy_pass 127.0.0.1:8080;
     proxy_cache backend-cache;
     proxy_cache_bypass $http_cache_control;
     add_header X-Proxy-Cache $upstream_cache_status;
     proxy_cache_valid  200 302   10m;
     proxy_cache_valid  404       1m;
   }
 }
```

You may need to create the proxy path directory /data/nginx/cache and set the appropriate file permissions. Set the directory ownership to www-data and restrict permissions to 700. You can use any location for cache data and not necessarily /data/nginx/cache.

This configuration sets the cache validity of 10 minutes, which is quite a lengthy period. This will work if you have static content that rarely changes. Instead, if you are serving dynamic content that is frequently updated, then you can take advantage of microcaching by setting the cache validity to a very small period of a few seconds. Add the following parameters to further improve your caching configuration for microcaching:

  ▶ proxy_cache_lock on: Queues additional requests while the cache is being updated
  ▶ proxy_cache_use_stale updating: Uses stale data while the cache is being updated

HAProxy and Varnish

HAProxy and Varnish are other popular options for the reverse proxy and the caching proxy, respectively. Both of them can offer improved performance when compared with Nginx. HAProxy can also be used as a Layer 4 and Layer 7 load balancer. We covered HAProxy in *Chapter 2, Networking,* in the *Load Balancing with HAProxy* recipe.

See also

  ▶ Nginx admin guide on reverse proxies at https://www.nginx.com/resources/admin-guide/reverse-proxy/
  ▶ Understanding Nginx proxying, load balancing, and caching at https://www.digitalocean.com/community/tutorials/understanding-nginx-http-proxying-load-balancing-buffering-and-caching
  ▶ Nginx proxy module documentation at http://nginx.org/en/docs/http/ngx_http_proxy_module.html

Load balancing with Nginx

When an application becomes popular and the number of requests increases beyond the capacity of a single server, we need to scale horizontally. We can always increase the capacity (vertical scaling) of a server by adding more memory and processing power, but a single server cannot scale beyond a certain limit. While adding separate servers or replicas of the application server, we need a mechanism which directs the traffic between these replicas. The hardware or software tool used for this purpose is known as a load balancer. Load balancers work as transparent mechanisms between the application server and client by distributing the requests between available instances. This is a commonly used technique for optimizing resource utilization and ensuring fault tolerant applications.

Nginx can be configured to work as an efficient Layer 7 as well as Layer 4 load balancer. Layer 7 is application layer of HTTP traffic. With Layer 4 support, Nginx can be used to load balance database servers or even XMPP traffic. With version 1.9.0, Nginx has enabled support for Layer 4 load balancing in their open source offerings.

In this recipe, we will learn how to set up Nginx as a load balancer.

Getting ready

You will need access to a root account or an account with sudo privileges.

You will need a minimum of three servers, as follows:

▶ An Nginx server, which will be set as a load balancer
▶ Two or more application servers with a similar code base set up on all

How to do it...

Follow these steps to set load balancing with Nginx:

1. I assume that you already have Nginx installed. If not, you can refer to the *Installing Nginx with PHP_FPM* recipe of this chapter.

2. Now, create a new configuration file under /etc/nginx/sites-available. Let's call it load_balancer:

   ```
   $ sudo nano /etc/nginx/sites-available/load_balancer
   ```

3. Add the following lines to this load_balancer file. This is the minimum configuration required to get started with load balancing:

```
upstream backend {
    server srv1.example.com;
    server srv2.example.com;
    server 192.168.1.12:8080;
    # other servers if any
}
server {
    listen 80;
    location / {
        proxy_pass http://backend;
    }
}
```

4. Enable this configuration by creating a symlink to `load_balancer` under `sites-enabled`:

```
$ sudo ln -s /etc/nginx/sites-available/load_balancer
/etc/nginx/sites-enabled/load_balancer
```

5. You may want to disable all other sites. Simply remove the respective links under `sites-enabled`.

6. Check the configuration for syntax errors:

```
$ sudo nginx -t
```

```
ubuntu@ubuntu:~$ sudo nginx -t
nginx: the configuration file /etc/nginx/nginx.conf syntax is ok
nginx: configuration file /etc/nginx/nginx.conf test is successful
ubuntu@ubuntu:~$
```

7. Now, reload Nginx for the changes to take effect:

```
$ sudo service nginx reload
```

8. Yes, you are ready to use a load balancer. Open your favorite browser and point it to the IP of your Nginx server. You should see the contents of `example.com` or whatever domain you have used.

How it works...

We have created a very basic configuration for a load balancer. With this configuration, Nginx takes the traffic on port `80` and distributes it between `srv1.example.com` and `srv2.example.com`. With an upstream directive, we have defined a pool of servers that will actually process the requests. The upstream directive must be defined in a HTTP context. Once the upstream directive is defined, it will be available for all site configurations.

 All configuration files defined under `sites-available` are combined in the main configuration file, `/etc/nginx/nginx.conf`, under the HTTP directive. This enables us to set other directives in `site-specific` configurations without specifying the HTTP block.

When defining servers under an `upstream` directive, you can also use the IP address and port of the application server. This is an ideal configuration, especially when both the load balancer and the application servers are on the same private network, and this will help minimize the communication overhead between Nginx and backend servers.

Next, under the `server` block, we have configured Nginx to `proxy_pass` all requests to our `backend` pool.

While setting backend servers, we have not explicitly specified any load balancing algorithm. Nginx provides various load balancing algorithms that define the server that will receive a particular request. By default, Nginx uses a round-robin algorithm and passes requests to each available server in sequential order. Other available options are as follows:

- `least_connection`: This passes the request to the host with the fewest active connections.
- `least_time`: Nginx chooses the host with the lowest latency. This option is available with Nginx plus.
- `ip_hash`: A hash of clients' IP addresses, and is used to determined the host to send the request to. This method guarantees that requests with the same IP address are served by the same host, unless the selected host is down.

Hash uses a user defined key to generate a hash value and then uses the hash to determine the processing host.

There's more...

Nginx provides various other load balancing features, such as weighted load balancing, active and passive health checks, backup servers, and session persistence. With the latest commits to the open source version, it now supports TCP load balancing as well. These settings can be updated at runtime with the help of HTTP APIs. The following are a few examples of different load balancing configurations:

- Set server weights:

```
upstream app-servers {
    server srv1.example.com weight 3;
    server srv2.example.com;
}
```

- Health checkups and backup servers:

```
upstream app-servers {
    server srv1.example.com max_fails 3 fail_timeout 10;
    server srv2.example.com fail_timeout 50;
    192.168.1.12:8080 backup;
}
```

∩ persistence with cookies:

```
ream app-servers {
server srv1.example.com;
server srv2.example.com;
sticky cookie srv_id expires=1h domain=.example.com
ɔath=/;
}
```

Check the Nginx load balancing guide for various other load balancing options and their respective details.

See also

▶ Nginx admin guide for load balancers at `https://www.nginx.com/resources/admin-guide/load-balancer`

Setting HTTPs on Nginx

In this recipe, we will learn how to enable HTTPs communication on the Nginx server.

Getting ready

You will need access to a root account or an account with `sudo` privileges.

How to do it...

Follow these steps to set HTTPs on Nginx:

1. Obtain a certificate and the related keys from a certification authority or create a self-signed certificate. To create a self-signed certificate, refer to the *Securing web traffic with HTTPS* recipe in this chapter.

2. Create a directory to hold all certificate and keys:

    ```
    $ sudo mkdir -p /etc/nginx/ssl/example.com
    ```

3. Move the certificate and keys to the preceding directory. Choose any secure method, such as SCP, SFTP, or any other.

4. Create a virtual host entry or edit it if you already have one:

    ```
    $ sudo nano /etc/nginx/sites-available/example.com
    ```

5. Match your virtual host configuration with the following:

```
server {
  listen 80;
  server_name example.com www.example.com;
  return 301 https://$host$request_uri;
}
server {
  listen 443 ssl;
  server_name example.com www.example.com;

  root /var/www/example.com/public_html;
  index index.php index.html index.htm;

  ssl on;
  ssl_certificate
  /etc/nginx/ssl/example.com/server.crt;
  ssl_certificate_key
  /etc/nginx/ssl/example.com/server.key;
  # if you have received ca-certs.pem from Certification
  Authority
  #ssl_trusted_certificate /etc/nginx/ssl/example.com/ca-
  certs.pem;

  ssl_session_cache shared:SSL:10m;
  ssl_session_timeout 5m;
  keepalive_timeout    70;

  ssl_ciphers "HIGH:!aNULL:!MD5 or HIGH:!aNULL:!MD5:!3DES";
  ssl_prefer_server_ciphers on;
  ssl_protocols  TLSv1.2 TLSv1.1 TLSv1;
  add_header Strict-Transport-Security "max-age=31536000";

  location / {
    try_files $uri $uri/ /index.php;
  }
```

```
        location ~ \.php$ {
          include fastcgi_params;
          fastcgi_pass unix:/var/run/php/php7.0-fpm.sock;
        }
      }
```

6. Enable this configuration by creating a symbolic link to it under `sites-enabled`:

   ```
   $ sudo ln -s /etc/nginx/sites-available/example.com
   /etc/nginx/sites-enabled/example.com
   ```

7. Check the configuration for syntax errors:

   ```
   $ sudo nginx -t
   ```

8. Reload Nginx for the changes to take effect:

   ```
   $ sudo service nginx reload
   ```

9. Open your browser and access the site with domain or IP with HTTPS.

How it works...

When you know some basic configuration parameters, Nginx is quite simple to set up. Here, we have taken a few SSL settings from the default configuration file and added a simple redirection rule to redirect non-HTTPs traffic on port 80 to port 443. The first `server` block takes care of the redirection.

In addition to specifying the server certificate and keys, we have enabled session resumption by setting the cache to be shared across the Nginx process. We also have a timeout value of 5 minutes.

All other settings are common to the Nginx setup. We have allowed the virtual host to match with `example.com`, as well as `www.example.com`. We have set the index to search `index.php`, followed by `index.html` and others. With `location` directives, we have set Nginx to search for files and directories before forwarding the request to a PHP processor. Note that if you create a self-signed certificate, you will notice your browser complaining about invalid certification authority.

See also

▸ Nginx HTTPs guide at `http://nginx.org/en/docs/http/configuring_https_servers.html`

Benchmarking and performance tuning of Apache

In this recipe, we will learn some performance tuning configurations that may help to squeeze out the last bit of performance from the available hardware. Before diving into performance tuning, we need to evaluate our servers and set a benchmark which can be used to measure improvements after any changes. We will be using a well known HTTP benchmarking tool, **Apache Bench** (**ab**). Various other benchmarking tools are available and each one has its own feature set. You can choose the one that best suits your needs.

Getting ready

You will need two systems: one with the web server software installed and another to run Apache Bench. You will need root access or access to an account with similar privileges.

You will also need to modify a few network parameters to handle a large network load. You will also need to set a higher open files limit, in `limits.conf`, on both systems. Check the *Tuning TCP Stack* recipe in *Chapter 2, Networking*.

How to do it...

1. Install the Apache Bench tool. This is available with the package `apache2-utils`:

    ```
    $ sudo apt-get install apache2-utils
    ```

2. If you need to, you can check all the available options of the `ab` tool as follows:

    ```
    $ ab -h
    ```

3. Now we are ready to generate network load. Execute the following command to start `ab`:

    ```
    $ ab -n 10000 -c 200 -t 2 -k "http://192.168.56.103/index.php"
    ```

It will take some time to complete the command depending on the parameters. You should see similar results to the following (partial) output:

```
Total transferred:       16739619 bytes
HTML transferred:        16700040 bytes
Requests per second:     117.96 [#/sec] (mean)
Time per request:        1695.491 [ms] (mean)
Time per request:        8.477 [ms] (mean, across all concurrent requests)
Transfer rate:           8170.87 [Kbytes/sec] received

Connection Times (ms)
              min  mean[+/-sd] median   max
Connect:        0    44  33.6     64     81
Processing:    44   815 363.9    983   1617
Waiting:       44   784 360.2    944   1592
Total:        122   859 340.5   1046   1675
```

Additionally, you may want to benchmark your server for CPU, memory, and IO performance. Check the *Setting performance benchmarks* recipe in *Chapter 13, Performance Monitoring*.

Now that we have a benchmark for server performance with stock installation, we can proceed with performance optimization. The following are some settings that are generally recommended for performance tuning:

- Apache related settings:
  - Remove/disable any unused modules
  - Enable mod_gzip/mod_deflate
  - Turn HostnameLookups off
  - Use IP address in configuration files
  - Use persistence connection by enabling keepalive, then set keepalive timeout
  - Limit the uses of AllowOverride or completely disable it with AllowOverride none
  - Disable ExtendedStatus; this is useful while testing but not in production

- Nginx related settings:
  - Set worker_processes to the count of your CPU cores or simply set it to auto
  - Set the number of worker_connections to test multiple values to find the best match for your servers
  - Set the keepalive_requests and keepalive_timeout values; these reduce the overhead of creating new connections
  - Enable idle connections with upstream servers by setting the keepalive value

❑ Enable log buffering with buffer and flush parameters to `access_log`; this will reduce IO requests while logging

❑ Reduce the log-level - you can set it to warn the user or display an error while in production

❑ Set the `sendfile` directive to use an efficient `sendfile()` call from the operating system

❑ Enable caching and compression

❑ Make sure that you track the performance changes after each set of modifications; this way you will have exact knowledge regarding what worked and what not

❑ You should also tune the TCP stack. The details of the TCP stack settings are covered in *Chapter 2, Networking*.

There's more...

Various other tools are available for benchmarking different features of the web server. The following are some well known tools, as well as a few latest additions:

▶ **Httperf**: A web server benchmarking tool with some advanced options

▶ **Perfkit**: a cloud benchmark tool by Google

▶ **Wrk**: `https://github.com/wg/wrk`

▶ **H2load**: HTTP2 load testing tool at `https://nghttp2.org/documentation/h2load-howto.html`

See also

▶ Apache performance tuning guide at `https://httpd.apache.org/docs/2.4/misc/perf-tuning.html`

▶ Nginx performance tuning guide at `https://www.nginx.com/blog/tuning-nginx/`

Securing the web server

In this recipe, we will learn some steps for securing web server installation.

Getting ready

You will need access to a root account or an account with `sudo` privileges.

You may need to have a web server stack installed and running.

How to do it...

Follow these steps to secure the web server:

1. Disable any unwanted modules. You can check all enabled modules with the following command:

   ```
   $ a2query -m
   ```

2. Disable modules with the following command:

   ```
   $ sudo a2dismod status
   ```

3. Hide the web server's identity. For Apache, edit `/etc/apache2/conf-available/security.conf` and set the following values:

   ```
   ServerSignature Off
   ServerTokens Prod
   ```

4. You may want to check other options under `security.conf`.

5. Next, disable the Apache server status page:

   ```
   $ sudo a2dismod status
   ```

6. For Nginx, edit `/etc/nginx/nginx.conf` and uncomment the following line:

   ```
   # server_tokens off;
   ```

7. In production environments, minimize the detail shown on error pages. You can enable the PHP Suhosin module and strict mode.

8. Disable directory listing. On Apache, add the following line to the virtual host configuration:

   ```
   <Directory /var/www/example.com>
     Options -Indexes
   </Directory>
   ```

9. You can also disable directory listing globally by setting `Options -Indexes` in `/etc/apache2/apache2.conf`.

10. Restrict access to the following directories:

```
<Directory /var/www/ >
   Order deny,allow    # order of Deny and Allow
   Deny from all    # Deny web root for all
</Directory>
```

11. Disable directory level settings and the use of `.htaccess`. This also helps improve performance:

```
<Directory />
   AllowOverride None    # disable use of .htaccess
</Directory>
```

12. Disable the following symbolic links:

```
<Directory />
   Options -FollowSymLinks
</Directory>
```

13. You can also install `mod_security` and `mod_evasive` for added security. `mod_security` acts as a firewall by monitoring traffic in real time, whereas `mod_evasive` provides protection against Denial of Service attacks by monitoring request data and requester IP.

14. For Apache, you can install `mod_security` as a plugin module as follows:

```
$ sudo apt-get install libapache2-modsecurity
$ sudo a2enmod mod-security
```

15. On Nginx, you need to first compile `mod_security` and then compile Nginx with `mod_security` enabled.

16. Turn of server side includes and CGI scripts:

```
<Directory />
   Options -ExecCGI -Includes
</Directory>
```

17. Limit request body, headers, request fields, and max concurrent connections; this will help against DOS attacks.

18. Set the following variables on Apache:

    `TimeOut`

    `KeepAliveTimeout`

    `RequestReadTimeout`

    `LimitRequestBody`

    `LimitRequestFields`

    `LimitRequestFieldSize`

    `LimitRequestLine`

    `MaxRequestWorkers`

19. For Nginx, configure the following variables to control buffer overflow attacks:

    `client_body_buffer_size`

    `client_header_buffer_size`

    `client_max_body_size`

    `large_client_header_buffers`

20. Enable logging and periodically monitor logs for any new or unrecognized events:

```
<VirtualHost *:80>
  ErrorLog /var/log/httpd/example.com/error_log
  CustomLog /var/log/httpd/example.com/access_log combined
</VirtualHost>
```

21. Set up HTTPs and set it to use modern ciphers. You can also disable the use of SSL and enforce TLS.

How it works...

In this recipe, I have listed the various options available to make your web server more secure. It is not necessary to set all these settings. Disabling some of these settings, especially `FollowSymlinks` and `AllowOverride`, may not suit your requirements or your environment. You can always choose the settings that apply to your setup.

Various settings listed here are available in their respective configuration files, mostly under `/etc/apache2` for the Apache web server and `/etc/nginx` for the Nginx server.

Also, do not forget to reload or restart your server after setting these options.

You should also set your Ubuntu environment to be more secure. You can find more details on securing Ubuntu in *Chapter 2, Networking*.

See also

▶ Installing mod_evasive at https://www.linode.com/docs/websites/apache-tips-and-tricks/modevasive-on-apache

▶ Apache security tips at http://httpd.apache.org/docs/2.4/misc/security_tips.html

▶ Setting up mod_security at https://www.digitalocean.com/community/tutorials/how-to-set-up-mod_security-with-apache-on-debian-ubuntu

Troubleshooting the web server

In this recipe, we will cover some common issues with Apache and Nginx and list the basic steps for overcoming those issues. The steps mentioned here are general troubleshooting methods; you may need to change them based on your setup and environment.

Getting ready

You may need root level access to your web server system.

How to do it...

Web server problems can be grouped in a few broad categories, such as a server not working, a particular domain or virtual host is not accessible, problems with a specific module configuration, and access denied errors. The following section lists each of these problems and their possible solutions.

Web server not accessible

1. The first step is to check your local Internet connection. Try to access the server from another system from another network.

2. Check if the DNS settings point to your web server.

3. If your network is working properly, then try to ping to the server IP address.

4. On the web server, check the firewall or any other tool that may block communication.

5. Open a `telnet` connection to web server on port `80`, or whatever port you have used for web server. If you see output similar to following screenshot, then your web server is working:

```
ubuntu@ubuntu:~$ telnet 192.168.56.103 80
Trying 192.168.56.103...
Connected to 192.168.56.103.
Escape character is '^]'.
```

6. Make sure that the web server port is not being used by some other process:

`$ sudo netstat -plutn`

```
Active Internet connections (only servers)
Proto Recv-Q Send-Q Local Address           Foreign Address         State       PID/Program name
tcp        0      0 127.0.0.1:8080          0.0.0.0:*               LISTEN      1069/apache2
tcp        0      0 0.0.0.0:80              0.0.0.0:*               LISTEN      994/nginx
tcp        0      0 0.0.0.0:22              0.0.0.0:*               LISTEN      948/sshd
tcp6       0      0 :::22                   :::*                    LISTEN      948/sshd
```

7. If required, reload or restart the web server process:

`$ sudo service apache2 reload/restart`

8. Check the Apache/Nginx logs listed under the `/var/log/` directory and view the entire file in a scrollable format:

`$ less /var/log/apache2/error.log`

9. See the continuous stream of logs as they are added to the log file:

`$ tail -f /var/log/nginx/error.log`

10. You may want to run Apache with extended log levels. Find the variable `LogLevel` in `/etc/apache2/apache2.conf` and set its value to `debug`:

`$ sudo nano /etc/apache2/apache2.conf`

`LogLevel debug`

11. Run Apache in debug single process mode:

`$ sudo apache2ctl -X  # debug mode single worker`

Virtual host not accessible

1. Make sure you have enabled virtual host configuration:

`ubuntu@ubuntu:~$ a2query -s`

`example.com (enabled by site administrator)`

2. Check the virtual host configuration for any syntax errors:

```
ubuntu@ubuntu:~$ sudo apache2ctl -t
Syntax OK
```

3. On Nginx, use the following command:

```
ubuntu@ubuntu:~$ sudo nginx -t
nginx: the configuration file /etc/nginx/nginx.conf syntax
is ok
nginx: configuration file /etc/nginx/nginx.conf test is
successful
```

4. Check the virtual host's details and other Apache configurations:

```
$ sudo apache2ctl -S
```

```
ubuntu@ubuntu:~$ sudo apache2ctl -S
VirtualHost configuration:
127.0.0.1:8080          example.com (/etc/apache2/sites-enabled/example.com.conf:1)
ServerRoot: "/etc/apache2"
Main DocumentRoot: "/var/www"
Main ErrorLog: "/var/log/apache2/error.log"
Mutex default: dir="/var/lock/apache2" mechanism=fcntl
Mutex mpm-accept: using_defaults
Mutex watchdog-callback: using_defaults
Mutex ssl-stapling: using_defaults
Mutex ssl-cache: using_defaults
PidFile: "/var/run/apache2/apache2.pid"
Define: DUMP_VHOSTS
Define: DUMP_RUN_CFG
User: name="www-data" id=33
Group: name="www-data" id=33
```

5. Make sure your virtual host IP and port configuration matches the one defined with NamedVirtualHost.

6. Check DocumentRoot - does it point to proper files?

   ❏ On Apache:

   ```
   <VirtualHost *:80>
           DocumentRoot /var/www/html
   <VirtualHost>
   ```

   ❏ On Nginx:

   ```
   server {
           root /usr/share/nginx/html;
   }
   ```

7. Crosscheck your `ServerName` and `ServerAlias` variables - do they match your domain name?

    ❑ On Apache, these settings should look similar to this:

```
<VirtualHost *:80>
    ServerName example.com
    ServerAlias www.example.com
</virtualHost>
```

    ❑ On Nginx, the `ServerName` is defined as this:

```
server {
    server_name example.com www.example.com;
}
```

Access denied or forbidden errors

Check directory permissions for the virtual host root directory. Are they accessible to the web server? Check the web server user and group (commonly `www-data`) have ready permissions. If required, you can set permissions with `chown` and `chmod` commands.

```
ubuntu@ubuntu:~$ ls -l /var/www/
drwxr-x--- 3 ubuntu www-data 4096 Aug  4 23:00 example.com
drwxr-xr-x 2 ubuntu www-data 4096 Aug  2 23:04 public_html
```

Secondly, make sure that you have properly set directory permissions in the virtual host configuration. Are they restricting file access?

Use the following commands to set directory permissions in the virtual host configuration:

```
<Directory /var/www/>
    AllowOverride None
    Order Deny,Allow
    Deny from all
</Directory>
```

Apache downloads .php files

Make sure that the `mod_php` module is installed and enabled:

```
ubuntu@ubuntu:~$ ls -l /etc/apache2/mods-available | grep php
-rw-r--r-- 1 root root  897 Jul  2 21:26 php7.0.conf
-rw-r--r-- 1 root root   59 Jul  2 21:26 php7.0.load

ubuntu@ubuntu:~$ a2query -m | grep php
php7.0 (enabled by maintainer script)
```

4
Working with Mail Servers

In this chapter, we will cover the following recipes:

- ▶ Sending e-mails with Postfix
- ▶ Enabling IMAP and POP3 with Dovecot
- ▶ Adding e-mail accounts
- ▶ Mail filtering with spam-assassin
- ▶ Troubleshooting the mail server
- ▶ Installing the Zimbra mail server

Introduction

In this chapter, we will learn how to set up an e-mail server. We will be using Postfix MTA to send e-mails and Dovecot to enable receiving e-mails. We will also install the Zimbra e-mail server, which is all-in-one one package to set up sending and receiving e-mails and web access. By the end of this chapter, you will be able to send e-mails with your own e-mail server.

Sending e-mails with Postfix

In this recipe, we will set up Postfix **Mail Transfer Agent** (**MTA**). This will be a very basic setup which will enable us to send and receive e-mails from our server. Postfix is an open source MTA which routes e-mails to their destination. It is a default MTA for Ubuntu and is available in Ubuntu's main package repository.

Getting ready

You will need access to a root account or an account with `sudo` privileges.

A domain name (FQDN) is required while configuring Postfix. You can configure your local server for testing, but make sure that you set the proper host entries and hostname.

How to do it...

Follow these steps to send e-mails with Postfix:

1. Install Postfix and `mailutils` with the following commands:

    ```
    $ sudo apt-get update
    $ sudo apt-get install postfix mailutils -y
    ```

2. The installation process will prompt you to enter some basic configuration details. When asked for **General type of mail configuration:**, select **Internet Site** and then click on **<Ok>**:

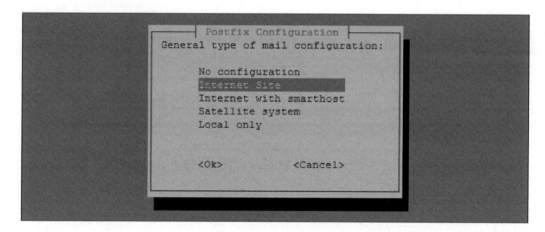

3. On the next screen, enter your domain name, for example, `mail.example.com`, and answer the other questions. You can leave them with default values:

4. After installation completes, we need to modify the Postfix configuration under `/etc/postfix/main.cf`:

   ```
   $ sudo nano /etc/postfix/main.cf
   ```

5. Set `myhostname` to point to your domain name:

   ```
   myhostname = mail.example.com
   ```

6. Ensure `mynetworks` is set to the local network. This will secure your server from spammers:

   ```
   mynetworks = 127.0.0.0/8 [::ffff:127.0.0.0]/104 [::1]/128
   ```

7. Also check `mydestination`. It should contain your domain name:

   ```
   mydestination = example.com, ubuntu, localhost.localdomain,
   localhost
   ```

```
myhostname = mail.example.com
alias_maps = hash:/etc/aliases
alias_database = hash:/etc/aliases
myorigin = /etc/mailname
mydestination = mail.example.com, ubuntu, localhost.localdomain, localhost
relayhost =
mynetworks = 127.0.0.0/8 [::ffff:127.0.0.0]/104 [::1]/128
```

8. Change the mail storage format to `Maildir` from the default `mbox`. Search and uncomment the following line:

   ```
   home_mailbox = Maildir/
   ```

9. Optionally, you can change the TLS keys used by Postfix. Find the `TLS parameters` section and point the variables to your key path:

```
# TLS parameters
smtpd_tls_cert_file=/etc/ssl/certs/ssl-cert-snakeoil.pem
smtpd_tls_key_file=/etc/ssl/private/ssl-cert-snakeoil.key
smtpd_use_tls=yes
```

10. Save the configuration file and exit.

11. Now, reload Postfix for the changes to take effect:

    ```
    $ sudo service postfix reload
    ```

    Test if everything is working as expected. Open a telnet connection to the mail server:

    ```
    $ telnet localhost 25
    ```

You should see an output similar to the following screenshot:

```
ubuntu@ubuntu:~$ telnet localhost 25
Trying ::1...
Connected to localhost.
Escape character is '^]'.
220 mail.example.com ESMTP Postfix (Ubuntu)
```

12. Now, send your first e-mail from this server. Type `sendmail user@domain` and press *Enter*. Then, type your message, and when done with that press *Ctrl + D* to send an e-mail.

13. To read your e-mails, log in with the user you send e-mails to. Start the mail program with the command `mail`. This should show you a list of e-mails received by this user account. The output should look similar to following screenshot:

```
root@ubuntu:~# mail
"/var/mail/root": 1 message 1 new
>N   1 ubuntu                Tue Sep  1 15:34  10/375
?
```

14. To read any e-mail, type in the mail number and press *Enter*. Type `q` followed by *Enter* to quit the mail reader.

How it works...

Postfix installation is quite a simple task; you need to be sure that you have configured the proper settings and then you are up and running in minutes. The Postfix installation process itself prompts for basic settings.

 If you miss providing configuration during installation, you can always recall the same dialogue box with the `reconfigure` command as follows:

$ `sudo dpkg-reconfigure postfix`

Other parameters include `mynetworks` and `mydestination`. With `mynetwork`, we have restricted the uses of the mail server to the local network. Only users on the local network can use this server to send and receive e-mails. The parameter `mydestination` specifies the domain names that Postfix is going to serve. For all other domains that are not listed under `mydestination`, Postfix will simply act as a forwarder.

We have configured Postfix to use the `Maildir` format for storing e-mails. This is a new storage format and provides various improvements over the default format, `mbox`. Also, `Maildir` is used by various IMAP and POP servers. With `Maildir`, each new message is stored in a separate file. This avoids file locking when working with messages and provides protection against mailbox corruption.

Now if you send an e-mail to a local domain, it will be delivered to the inbox of the respective user, which can be read with `mail` command. If you send e-mails to an external mail server, such as Gmail, chances are your mail gets delivered to spam. You need to include a number of different parameters in your e-mail headers and then make sure that your server IP is not blacklisted. It would be a good idea to use an external mail server such as Mail Chimp or Gmail for sending e-mails.

See also

▶ An article by Jeff Atwood on sending e-mails through code. This may help you get your e-mails out of spam: `http://blog.codinghorror.com/so-youd-like-to-send-some-email-through-code/`

▶ Mailbox formats: `http://wiki.dovecot.org/MailboxFormat`

▶ The difference between port 465 and 587: `http://stackoverflow.com/questions/15796530/what-is-the-difference-between-ports-465-and-587`

Enabling IMAP and POP3 with Dovecot

In this recipe, we will learn how to install and set up Dovecot to enable accessing e-mails over IMAP and POP3 protocols. This will enable mail clients such as thunderbird to download e-mails on a user's local system.

Getting ready

You will need access to a root account or an account with `sudo` privileges

Make sure that you have set up Postfix and are able to send and receive e-mails on your server.

You may need an e-mail client to connect to and test the Dovecot setup.

How to do it...

Follow these steps to enable IMAP and POP3 with Dovecot:

1. First, install the Dovecot binaries from the Ubuntu main repository:

   ```
   $ sudo apt-get update
   $ sudo apt-get install dovecot-imapd dovecot-pop3d
   ```

2. You will be prompted for a hostname to be used for certificate generation. Type in a full hostname, for example `mail.example.com`. You can skip this step if you already have certificates.

3. Next, proceed with configuring Dovecot. Open the file `/etc/dovecot/dovecot.conf`:

   ```
   $ sudo nano /etc/dovecot/dovecot.conf
   ```

4. Find the `Enable installed protocols` section and add a new line to set the protocols that you want Dovecot to support:

   ```
   protocols = pop3 pop3s imap imaps
   ```

5. Open `/etc/dovecot/conf.d/10-mail.conf` and set the mailbox to be used. Dovecot supports `mbox` as well as `Maildir`. Make sure you set the correct path of your `mail` directory:

   ```
   mail_location = mbox:~/mail:INBOX=/var/spool/mail/%u
   ```

6. Open `/etc/dovecot/conf.d/10-ssl.conf` and uncomment or change the following lines to enable SSL authentication. Here, I have used certificates created by Postfix. You can use your own certificates or use the one generated by Dovecot:

   ```
   ssl = yes
   ssl_cert = < /etc/ssl/certs/ssl-cert-snakeoil.pem
   ssl_key =</etc/ssl/private/ssl-cert-snakeoil.key
   ```

7. Restart the Dovecot daemon:

   ```
   $ sudo service dovecot restart
   ```

8. Test Dovecot by creating a telnet connection. You should see an output similar to the following:

   ```
   $ telnet localhost pop3
   ```

```
ubuntu@ubuntu:~$ telnet localhost pop3
Trying ::1...
Connected to localhost.
Escape character is '^]'.
+OK Dovecot (Ubuntu) ready.
```

How it works...

Dovecot is one of the most popular **Mail Delivery Agents** (**MDA**) with support for IMAP and POP3 protocols. It works with both major mailbox formats, namely `mbox` and `Maildir`. The installation process is simple, and a minimal configuration can get you started with your own IMAP or POP3 service.

Dovecot developers have tried to simplify the configuration by separating it across various small files for each section. All these configuration files are located under `/etc/dovecot/conf.d`. If you prefer to use a single configuration file, you can replace the default file with the entire working configuration. To get all enabled configurations, use the `doveconf -n` command:

```
# mv /etc/dovecot/dovecot.conf /etc/dovecot/dovecot.conf.old
# doveconf -n > /etc/dovecot/dovecot.conf
```

In this recipe, we have configured Dovecot to support POP3, POP3 secure, IMAP, and IMAP secure. You can choose a single protocol or any combination of them. After setting protocol support, we have set the mailbox type to `mbox`. If you are using `Maildir` as your mailbox format, instead replace the mailbox setting with following line:

```
mail_location = maildir:~/Maildir
```

Now, when a user wants to check his e-mails, they need to authenticate with the Dovecot server. At this stage, only users with a user account on the server will be able to access their e-mails with Dovecot. To support users without creating a user account, we will need to set up Virtual Users, which is covered in the next recipes.

If you plan to skip SSL setup, you may need to enable plain text authentication under the configuration file, `/etc/dovecot/conf.d/10-auth.conf`. Find and uncomment the following line and set it to `no`:

```
disable_plaintext_auth = yes
```

The default setting is to allow plain text authentication over SSL connections only. That means the clients that do not support SSL will not be allowed to log in.

See also

▸ Dovecot wiki Quick-configuration at `http://wiki2.dovecot.org/QuickConfiguration`

Adding e-mail accounts

In this recipe, we will learn how to add e-mail accounts to Postfix. The easiest way to add a new e-mail account to Postfix is to add a new user account on your server. Postfix will check for user accounts and deliver e-mails to respective users. We will create a virtual user setup so that we do not need to create user accounts for each e-mail user.

Getting ready

You will need access to a root account or an account with `sudo` privileges.

I assume that you have completed your basic Postfix setup and that it is working properly.

How to do it...

Follow these steps to add e-mail account:

1. Create a new user account:

    ```
    $ useradd -s /usr/bin/nologin -m vmail
    ```

2. Get the UID and GID for this account:

    ```
    $ grep vmail /etc/passwd
    vmail:x:1001:1001::/home/vmail:/usr/bin/nologin
    ```

    ```
    ubuntu@ubuntu:~$ grep vmail /etc/passwd
    vmail:x:1001:1001::/home/vmail:/usr/bin/nologin
    ubuntu@ubuntu:~$
    ```

3. Create a base directory layout for domains and users:

    ```
    $ sudo mkdir -p /home/vmail/example.org/bob
    $ sudo mkdir -p /home/vmail/example.net/alice
    ```

4. Allow only the user vmail to access these files:

    ```
    $ sudo chown -R vmail:vmail /home/vmail
    $ chmod -R 700 /home/vmail
    ```

5. Next, configure Postfix. Edit /etc/postfix/main.cf and add the following lines:

    ```
    virtual_mailbox_base = /home/vmail
    virtual_mailbox_domains = /etc/postfix/virtual_domains
    virtual_mailbox_maps = hash:/etc/postfix/virtual_maps
    virtual_alias_maps = hash:/etc/postfix/virtual_alias
    virtual_uid_maps = static:1001  # user ID for user vmail
    virtual_gid_maps = static:1001  # group ID for user vmail
    ```

6. Create the file `virtual_domains` under `/etc/postfix`:

   ```
   $ sudo nano /etc/postfix/virtual_domains
   ```

   ```
   example.org
   example.net
   ```

7. Create the `virtual_maps` file:

   ```
   $ sudo nano /etc/postfix/virtual_maps
   bob@example.org   example.org/bob/
   alice@example.org   example.org/alice/
   @example.org   example.org/catchall/    # catch all address
   ```

8. Create the `virtual_alias` file and optionally set a `redirect`:

   ```
   $ sudo nano /etc/postfix/virtual_alias
   # redirect emails for tim to bob

   tim@example.org   bob@example.org
   ```

9. Now generate database of virtual maps and aliases by hashing respective files:

   ```
   $ sudo postmap /etc/postfix/virtual_maps
   $ sudo postmap /etc/postfix/virtual_alias
   ```

10. Reload Postfix and send an e-mail to the newly created address:

    ```
    $ sudo postfix reload
    $ sendmail bob@example.org
    ```

How it works...

Here, we have created a virtual mailbox setup to enable our Postfix server to serve multiple domains as well as add e-mail users without creating user accounts on the server. All e-mails received by virtual users will be stored under the home directory of the vmail user (`virtual_mailbox_base` in Postfix configuration). When you need to add a new e-mail account, simply add the e-mail address with its respective domain to the `virtual_maps` file. In case you need to support a new domain, you can easily add it to the `virtual_domains` file.

The third file we used is `virtual_alias`. You can set e-mail forwarding in this file. It is handy when you need to create a new alias for an e-mail address or forward e-mails to one or multiple accounts. We have set a `catchall` entry in the `virtual_alias` file; this setting will redirect all e-mails received on nonexistent accounts to `catchall@example.org`, which can be checked by the domain administrator.

There's more...

Using files for virtual users and domains is good for getting started with setup. But once you need to add more and more user accounts and domains it is a good idea to move the users and domains to a database server. This can be easily done by changing the lookup table type. Postfix supports a variety of lookup table types, which include LDAP, MySQL, PGSQL, memcache, SQLite, and many others.

To use MySQL as a backend database, complete the following steps:

1. Create respective tables for `virtual_domain`, `virtual_maps`, and `virtual_alias`.

2. Change the Postfix configuration to use MySQL as a lookup table:

   ```
   virtual_mailbox_domains = mysql:/etc/postfix/mysql-virtual-domains
   virtual_mailbox_maps = mysql:/etc/postfix/mysql-virtual-maps
   virtual_alias_maps = mysql:/etc/postfix/mysql-virtual-alias
   ```

3. Add the respective details to each file using the following commands:

   $ sudo nano /etc/postfix/mysql-virtual-domains

   ```
   user = mysql_user
   password = mysql_password
   hosts = 127.0.0.1
   dbname = mysql_db_name
   query = SELECT 1 FROM virtual_domains WHERE name='%s'
   ```

   $ sudo nano /etc/postfix/mysql-virtual-maps

   ```
   . . .
   query = SELECT 1 FROM virtual_users WHERE email='%s'
   ```

   $ sudo nano /etc/postfix/mysql-virtual-alias

   ```
   . . .
   query = SELECT destination FROM virtual_aliases WHERE
   source='%s'
   ```

4. You can test your mapping with the following command. This should output 1 as a result:

   $ postmap -q bob@example.org mysql:/etc/postfix/mysql-virtual-maps

5. Finally, restart the Postfix daemon.

Web console for virtual mailbox administration

The **Vimbadmin** package provides a web console for virtual mailbox administration. It is a PHP-based open source package. You can get source code and installation instructions at `https://github.com/opensolutions/ViMbAdmin`.

See also

▶ Postfix guide at `http://www.postfix.org/VIRTUAL_README.html`

▶ Postfix lookup table types at `http://www.postfix.org/DATABASE_README.html#types`

Mail filtering with spam-assassin

In this recipe, we will learn how to install and set up a well-known e-mail filtering program, spam-assassin.

Getting ready

You will need access to a root account or an account with `sudo` privileges.

You need to have Postfix installed and working.

How to do it...

Follow these steps to filter mail with spam-assassin:

1. Install spam-assassin with the following command:

```
$ sudo apt-get update
$ sudo apt-get install spamassassin spamc
```

2. Create a user account and group for spam-assassin:

```
$ sudo groupadd spamd
$ sudo useradd -g spamd -s /usr/bin/nologin \
-d /var/log/spamassassin -m spamd
```

3. Change the default settings for the spam daemon. Open `/etc/default/spamassassin` and update the following lines:

```
ENABLED=1
SAHOME="/var/log/spamassassin/"
OPTIONS="--create-prefs --max-children 5 --username spamd -
-helper-home-dir ${SAHOME} -s ${SAHOME}spamd.log"
PIDFILE="${SAHOME}spamd.pid"
CRON=1
```

4. Optionally, configure spam rules by changing values in `/etc/spamassassin/local.cf`:

```
trusted_networks 10.0.2.  # set your trusted network
required_score 3.0    # 3 + will be marked as spam
```

5. Next, we need to change the Postfix settings to pass e-mails through spam-assassin. Open `/etc/postfix/master.cf` and find the following line:

```
smtp        inet  n      -      -      -      -
smtpd
```

6. Add the content filtering option:

```
-o content_filter=spamassassin
```

```
#
# service type  private unpriv  chroot  wakeup  maxproc command + args
#                (yes)   (yes)   (yes)   (never) (100)
#
smtp       inet  n        -       -       -              smtpd
-o content_filter=spamassassin
```

7. Define the content filter block by adding the following lines to the end of the file:

```
spamassassin unix -      n       n       -       -
pipe
        user=spamd argv=/usr/bin/spamc -f -e
        /usr/sbin/sendmail -oi -f ${sender} ${recipient}
```

```
spamassassin unix -      n       n       -       -       pipe
        user=spamd argv=/usr/bin/spamc -f -e
        /usr/sbin/sendmail -oi -f ${sender} ${recipient}
```

8. Finally, restart spam-assassin and Postfix:

```
$ sudo service spamassassin start
$ sudo service postfix reload
```

9. You can check spam-assassin and mail logs to verify that spam-assassin is working properly:

```
$ less /var/log/spamassassin/spamd.log
$ less /var/log/mail.log
```

How it works...

Spam filtering works with the help of a piping mechanism provided by Postfix. We have created a new Unix pipe which will be used to filter e-mails. Postfix will pass all e-mails through this pipe, which will be then scanned through spam-assassin to determine the spam score. If given e-mail scores below the configured threshold, then it passes the filter without any modification; otherwise, spam-assassin adds a spam header to the e-mail.

Spam-assassin works with a Bayesian classifier to classify e-mails as spam or not spam. Basically, it checks the content of the e-mail and determines the score based on content.

There's more...

You can train spam-assassin's Bayesian classifier to get more accurate spam detections.

The following command will train spam-assassin with spam contents (--spam):

```
$ sudo sa-learn --spam -u spamd --dir ~/Maildir/.Junk/* -D
```

To train with non-spam content, use the following command (--ham):

```
$ sudo sa-learn --ham -u spamd --dir ~/Maildir/.INBOX/* -D
```

If you are using the mbox format, replace --dir ~/Maildir/.Junk/* with the option --mbox.

See also

- ▶ Sa-learn - train SpamAssassin's Bayesian classifier at https://spamassassin. apache.org/full/3.2.x/doc/sa-learn.html and https://wiki.apache. org/spamassassin/BayesInSpamAssassin
- ▶ Learn about Bayesian classification at https://en.wikipedia.org/wiki/ Naive_Bayes_classifier

Troubleshooting the mail server

Sometimes you may face problems such as e-mails not being sent, delayed delivery or mail bouncing, issues while fetching e-mails, and login failures. In this recipe, we will learn how to identify the exact problem behind these issues. We will learn how to use debugging tools and read the logs of Postfix and Dovecot.

Getting ready

You will need access to a root account or an account with `sudo` privileges.

It is assumed that you have already installed Postfix and Dovecot servers.

How to do it...

Follow these steps to troubleshoot the mail server:

1. Start with checking the status of Postfix and Dovecot. If you get output that says `stop/waiting` or `not running` then the respective service is not running:

    ```
    $ sudo service postfix status
    $ sudo service dovecot status
    ```

    ```
    ubuntu@ubuntu:~$ sudo service postfix status
     * postfix is running
    ubuntu@ubuntu:~$ sudo service dovecot status
    dovecot start/running, process 5260
    ```

2. Try to restart the respective services. Restarting may give you error messages. Also check for startup logs under `/var/log/mail.log`:

    ```
    $ sudo service postfix restart
    $ less /var/log/mail.log
    ```

3. You can use a `tail` command to monitor the stream of logs while the service is running. You can easily filter the output of `tail` by piping it to a `grep` command:

    ```
    $ tail -f /var/log/mail.log
    ```

    Use `grep` to only view selected logs:

    ```
    $ tail -f /var/log/mail.log | grep "dovecot"
    ```

    ```
    ubuntu@ubuntu:~$ tail -f /var/log/mail.log | grep dovecot
    Sep  1 16:17:45 ubuntu dovecot: anvil: Warning: Killed with signal 15 (by pid=1 uid=
    0 code=kill)
    Sep  1 16:17:45 ubuntu dovecot: log: Warning: Killed with signal 15 (by pid=1 uid=0
    code=kill)
    Sep  1 16:17:45 ubuntu dovecot: master: Dovecot v2.2.9 starting up (core dumps disab
    led)
    Sep  1 16:18:14 ubuntu dovecot: pop3-login: Aborted login (no auth attempts in 9 sec
    s): user=<>, rip=::1, lip=::1, secured, session=<RUB/Sa0eIAAAAAAAAAAAAAAAAAAAAAAAB>
    ```

4. Use `grep -v` to filter/remove selected logs:

```
$ tail -f /var/log/mail.log | grep -v "dovecot"
```

```
ubuntu@ubuntu:~$ tail -f /var/log/mail.log | grep -v dovecot
Sep  1 16:50:15 ubuntu postfix/smtp[5426]: 5DA06380726: to=<root@example.com>, relay
=none, delay=4733, delays=4713/0.01/20/0, dsn=4.4.3, status=deferred (Host or domain
 name not found. Name service error for name=example.com type=MX: Host not found, tr
y again)
```

5. You can check other log files such as `/var/log/mail.err` and `/var/log/upstart/dovecot.log`.

   You may want to enable verbose logging to get detailed debugging information. To enable debug mode on Dovecot, edit `10-logging.conf` and enable `auth_verbose` and `mail_debug` variables:

```
$ sudo nano /etc/dovecot/conf.d/10-logging.conf
```

```
auth_verbose = yes
mail_debug = yes
```

   Restart Dovecot:

```
$ sudo service dovecot restart
```

6. To enable verbose logging on Postfix, edit `master.cf` file and add the `-v` argument:

```
$ sudo nano /etc/postfix/master.cf
```

```
smtp      inet  n        -        -        -        -           smtpd
-v
```

   Restart Postfix.

7. Turn off chroot operations:

```
$ sudo nano /etc/postfix/master.cf
```

```
smtp      inet  n        -        n        -        -           smtpd
```

8. Check user account with Dovecot:

```
$ doveadm username useremail@example.com
```

9. If you have set virtual users, check if they are working properly:

```
$ postmap -q bob@example.org mysql:/etc/postfix/mysql-virtual-maps
```

10. Check respective ports used by Postfix and Dovecot. Postfix uses ports `25`, `465`, `587` and Dovecot uses port `993` and `995`:

```
$ telnet localhost 993
```

11. Check `netstat` to make sure services are listening:

    ```
    $ sudo netstat -plutn
    ```

```
ubuntu@ubuntu:~$ sudo netstat -plutn
Active Internet connections (only servers)
Proto Recv-Q Send-Q Local Address          Foreign Address        State       PID/Program name
tcp        0      0 0.0.0.0:143            0.0.0.0:*              LISTEN      5260/dovecot
tcp        0      0 0.0.0.0:22             0.0.0.0:*              LISTEN      776/sshd
tcp        0      0 0.0.0.0:25             0.0.0.0:*              LISTEN      5687/master
tcp        0      0 0.0.0.0:993            0.0.0.0:*              LISTEN      5260/dovecot
tcp        0      0 0.0.0.0:995            0.0.0.0:*              LISTEN      5260/dovecot
tcp        0      0 0.0.0.0:110            0.0.0.0:*              LISTEN      5260/dovecot
tcp6       0      0 :::143                 :::*                  LISTEN      5260/dovecot
```

12. Check for DNS resolution and MX records:

    ```
    $ host -t mx example.com
    ```

13. Check if spam filters and antivirus scanners are working properly.

See also

▸ Postfix debugging - `http://www.postfix.org/DEBUG_README.html`

▸ Postfix book (troubleshooting) at `http://www.postfix-book.com/debugging.html`

▸ Dovecot troubleshooting at `http://wiki2.dovecot.org/WhyDoesItNotWork`

Installing the Zimbra mail server

Until now, we have installed Postfix, Dovecot, spam-assassin, and other tools separately. In this recipe, we will learn how to install the Zimbra collaboration server, which covers all tools in a single package. The Zimbra server contains Postfix, MySQL, OpenLDAP, ClamAV, and Spam-Assassin, Calendar, and various other features. Zimbra provides a paid option as well as an open source version. We will be installing an open source version of the Zimbra server in single server mode.

Getting ready

As always, you will need access to a root account or an account with `sudo` privileges.

For Zimbra to work properly, you will need the following minimum configuration for your server:

▸ At least 1.5 GHz of CPU 2 GHz recommended

▸ Minimum 8 GB of memory

▸ Minimum 10 GB of storage 20 GB recommended

You will need to set proper DNS and MX records for your domain.

You will also need various ports, as follows:

- Postfix/LMTP 25, 7025
- HTTP 80, 443
- POP3 110, 995
- IMAP 143, 993
- LDAP 389

How to do it...

Follow these steps to install Zimbra collaboration server:

1. Install the dependency packages before starting with the Zimbra installation:

   ```
   $ sudo apt-get update
   $ sudo apt-get install libperl5.18 libaio1 unzip pax sysstat
   sqlite3 libgmp10
   ```

2. Download and extract the Zimbra open source package using the following command:

   ```
   $ wget https://files.zimbra.com/downloads/8.6.0_GA/zcs-
   8.6.0_GA_1153.UBUNTU14_64.20141215151116.tgz
   $ tar -zxvf zcs-8.6.0_GA_1153.UBUNTU14_64.20141215151116.tgz
   $ cd zcs-8.6.0_GA_1153.UBUNTU14_64.20141215151116
   ```

3. Make sure you have set the proper hostname and hosts entries in respective files:

   ```
   $ cat /etc/hosts
   127.0.0.1 localhost
   119.9.107.28    mail.server.local    mail
   $ cat /etc/hostname
   mail.server.local
   ```

4. Start the Zimbra installation by executing the installer:

   ```
   $ sudo ./install.sh
   ```

5. The installation process will ask you to agree with License Agreement. Type y and press *Enter* to continue:

```
License Terms for the Zimbra Collaboration Suite:
  http://www.zimbra.com/license/zimbra-public-eula-2-5.html



Do you agree with the terms of the software license agreement? [N] y
```

6. On acceptance of agreement, Zimbra will check for dependencies and then ask for the component selection. I have chosen to skip a few components. Type y when asked for confirmation:

```
Select the packages to install

Install zimbra-ldap [Y] y

Install zimbra-logger [Y] y
```

7. Type y when asked for package selection confirmation.

8. The installation process will take some time. As installation completes, the Zimbra configuration menu will be displayed. Here, you need to set an admin account password:

```
 4) zimbra-mta:                           Enabled
 5) zimbra-snmp:                          Enabled
 6) zimbra-store:                         Enabled
      +Create Admin User:                 yes
      +Admin user to create:              admin@mail.server01.local
******* +Admin Password                   UNSET
      +Anti-virus quarantine user:        virus-quarantine.3rmlo2nfq@mail.server01.local
      +Enable automated spam training:    yes
```

9. On the main menu, select 6 to choose `zimbra-store` and then type 4 for the admin password. The new prompt will ask for the admin account password:

```
Select, or 'r' for previous menu [r] 4

Password for admin@mail.server01.local (min 6 characters): [Vfs7tvEVf] password
```

10. Then, type `r` to come back to the main menu and then type `a` to apply settings, and again press *Enter* to save settings:

```
*** CONFIGURATION COMPLETE - press 'a' to apply
Select from menu, or press 'a' to apply config {? - help} a
Save configuration data to a file? [Yes]
Save config in file: [/opt/zimbra/config.8466]
Saving config in /opt/zimbra/config.8466...done.
The system will be modified - continue? [No] y
```

11. Finally, apply all configurations when asked. Zimbra will ask you to send installation notification to Zimbra. Choose `Yes` by typing `y` to notify Zimbra:

```
Notify Zimbra of your installation? [Yes] y
Notifying Zimbra of installation via http://www.zimbra.com/cgi-bin/notify.cgi?VER=8.6.0_
GA_1153_UBUNTU14_64&MAIL=admin@mail.server01.local

Notification complete
```

12. Now you can access your Zimbra server with the domain name of your server or IP address. Your browser may prompt for a non-trusted server certificate, as shown in the following screenshot:

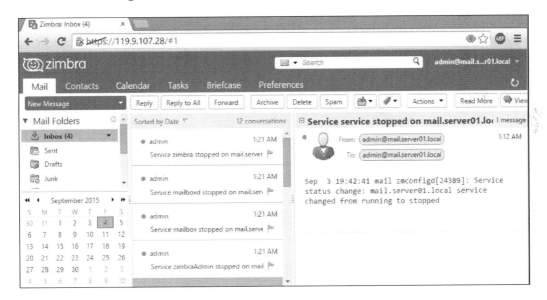

13. You can access the **Inbox** panel on port `7071, https://yourserver.tld:7071`.

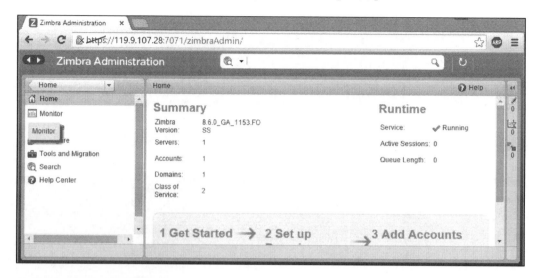

How it works...

Zimbra combines various commonly used packages in a single package and provides a web interface to work with them. It reduces the efforts required in installing and configuring all tools separately. For any additional features, you can always switch to the Zimbra collaboration server, Network Edition.

There's more...

If you are planning to use Zimbra on your local network, you will need a DNS server set up. Alternatively, you can use the tool `dnsmasq`. It is a small package that sets up a quick DNS environment on your local network.

See also

▸ Zimbra open source features at `https://www.zimbra.com/open-source/features`

5
Handling Databases

In this chapter, we will cover the following recipes:

- ▸ Installing relational databases with MySQL
- ▸ Storing and retrieving data with MySQL
- ▸ Importing and exporting bulk data
- ▸ Adding users and assigning access rights
- ▸ Installing web access for MySQL
- ▸ Setting backups
- ▸ Optimizing MySQL performance – queries
- ▸ Optimizing MySQL performance – configuration
- ▸ Creating MySQL replicas for scaling and high availability
- ▸ Troubleshooting MySQL
- ▸ Installing MongoDB
- ▸ Storing and retrieving data with MongoDB

Introduction

In this chapter, we will learn how to set up database servers. A database is the backbone of any application, enabling an application to efficiently store and retrieve crucial data to and from persistent storage. We will learn how to install and set up relational databases with MySQL and NoSQL databases with MongoDB.

MySQL is a popular open source database server used by various large scale applications. It is a mature database system that can be scaled to support large volumes of data. MySQL is a relational database and stores data in the form of rows and columns organized in tables. It provides various storage engines, such as MyISAM, InnoDB, and in-memory storage. MariaDB is a fork of a MySQL project and can be used as a drop-in replacement for MySQL. It was started by the developers of MySQL after Oracle took over Sun Microsystems, the owner of the MySQL project. MariaDB is guaranteed to be open source and offers faster security releases and advanced features. It provides additional storage engines, including XtraDB by Percona and Cassandra for the NoSQL backend. PostgreSQL is another well-known name in relational database systems.

NoSQL, on the other hand, is a non-relational database system. It is designed for distributed large-scale data storage requirements. For some types of data, it is not efficient to store it in the tabular form offered by relational database systems, for example, data in the form of a document. NoSQL databases are used for these types of data. Some emerging NoSQL categories are document storage, key value store, BigTable, and the graph database.

In this chapter, we will start by installing MySQL, followed by storing and manipulating data in MySQL. We will also cover user management and access control. After an introduction to relational databases, we will cover some advanced topics on scaling and high availability. We will learn how to set up the web administration tool, PHPMyAdmin, but the focus will be on working with MySQL through command line access. In later recipes, we will also cover the document storage server, MongoDB.

Installing relational databases with MySQL

In this recipe, we will learn how to install and configure the MySQL database on an Ubuntu server.

Getting ready

You will need access to a root account or an account with `sudo` privileges.

Make sure that the MySQL default port `3306` is available and not blocked by any firewall.

How to do it...

Follow these steps to install the relational database MySQL:

1. To install the MySQL server, use the following command:

```
$ sudo apt-get update
$ sudo apt-get install mysql-server-5.7
```

The installation process will download the necessary packages and then prompt you to enter a password for the MySQL root account. Choose a strong password:

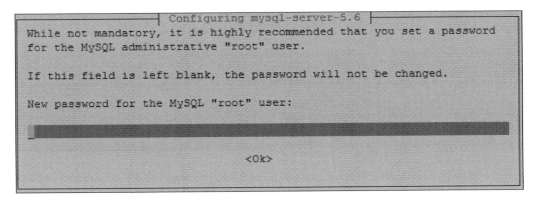

2. Once the installation process is complete, you can check the server status with the following command. It should return an output similar to the following:

    ```
    $ sudo service mysql status
    mysql.service - MySQL Community Server
       Loaded: loaded (/lib/systemd/system/mysql.service
       Active: active (running) since Tue 2016-05-10 05:
    ```

3. Next, create a copy of the original configuration file:

    ```
    $ cd /etc/mysql/mysql.conf.d
    $ sudo cp mysqld.cnf mysqld.cnf.bkp
    ```

4. Set MySQL to listen for a connection from network hosts. Open the configuration file /etc/mysql/mysql.conf.d/mysqld.cnf and change bind-address under the [mysqld] section to your server's IP address:

    ```
    $ sudo nano /etc/mysql/mysql.conf.d/mysqld.cnf
    bind-address = 10.0.2.6
    ```

    ```
    # Instead of skip-networking the default is now to listen only on
    # localhost which is more compatible and is not less secure.
    bind-address            = 10.0.2.6
    #
    ```

> For MySQL 5.5 and 5.6, the configuration file can be found at /etc/mysql/my.cnf

5. Optionally, you can change the default port used by the MySQL server. Find the [mysqld] section in the configuration file and change the value of the port variable as follows:

```
port = 30356
```

Make sure that the selected port is available and open under firewall.

6. Save the changes to the configuration file and restart the MySQL server:

```
$ sudo service mysql restart
```

7. Now open a connection to the server using the MySQL client. Enter the password when prompted:

```
$ mysql -u root -p
```

8. To get a list of available commands, type \h:

```
mysql> \h
```

```
List of all MySQL commands:
Note that all text commands must be first on line and end with ';'
?         (\?) Synonym for `help'.
clear     (\c) Clear the current input statement.
connect   (\r) Reconnect to the server. Optional arguments are db and host.
delimiter (\d) Set statement delimiter.
edit      (\e) Edit command with $EDITOR.
ego       (\G) Send command to mysql server, display result vertically.
```

How it works...

MySQL is a default database server available in Ubuntu. If you are installing the Ubuntu server, you can choose MySQL to be installed by default as part of the LAMP stack. In this recipe, we have installed the latest production release of MySQL (5.7) from the Ubuntu package repository. Ubuntu 16.04 contains MySQL 5.7, whereas Ubuntu 14.04 defaults to MySQL version 5.5.

If you prefer to use an older version on Ubuntu 16, then use following command:

```
$ sudo add-apt-repository `deb http://archive.ubuntu.com/ubuntu
trusty universe'
```

```
$ sudo apt-get update
```

```
$ sudo apt-get install mysql-server-5.6
```

After installation, configure the MySQL server to listen for connections from external hosts. Make sure that you open your database installation to trusted networks such as your private network. Making it available on the Internet will open your database to attackers.

There's more...

Securing MySQL installation

MySQL provides a simple script to configure basic settings related to security. Execute this script before using your server in production:

```
$ mysql_secure_installation
```

This command will start a basic security check, starting with changing the `root` password. If you have not set a strong password for the root account, you can do it now. Other settings include disabling remote access to the root account and removing anonymous users and unused databases.

MySQL is popularly used with PHP. You can easily install PHP drivers for MySQL with the following command:

```
$ sudo apt-get install php7.0-mysql
```

See also

> ▸ The Ubuntu server guide mysql page at
>   `https://help.ubuntu.com/14.04/serverguide/mysql.html`

Storing and retrieving data with MySQL

In this recipe, we will learn how to create databases and tables and store data in those tables. We will learn the basic **Structured Query Language** (**SQL**) required for working with MySQL. We will focus on using the command-line MySQL client for this tutorial, but you can use the same queries with any client software or code.

Getting ready

Ensure that the MySQL server is installed and running. You will need administrative access to the MySQL server. Alternatively, you can use the root account of MySQL.

How to do it...

Follow these steps to store and retrieve data with MySQL:

1. First, we will need to connect to the MySQL server. Replace `admin` with a user account on the MySQL server. You can use root as well but it's not recommended:

   ```
   $ mysql -u admin -h localhost -p
   ```

2. When prompted, enter the password for the `admin` account. If the password is correct, you will see the following MySQL prompt:

```
ubuntu@ubuntu:~$ mysql -u admin -h localhost -p
Enter password:
Welcome to the MySQL monitor.  Commands end with ; or \g.
Your MySQL connection id is 7
Server version: 5.7.12-0ubuntu1 (Ubuntu)
```

3. Create a database with the following query. Note the semi-colon at the end of query:

   mysql > create database myblog;

4. Check all databases with a `show` databases query. It should list `myblog`:

   mysql > show databases;

```
mysql> show databases;
+--------------------+
| Database           |
+--------------------+
| information_schema |
| myblog             |
| mysql              |
| performance_schema |
| replication_test   |
+--------------------+
5 rows in set (0.03 sec)
```

5. Select a database to work with, in this case `myblog`:

   mysql > use myblog;

   Database changed

6. Now, after the database has changed, we need to create a table to store our data. Use the following query to create a table:

```
CREATE TABLE `articles` (
    `id` int(11) NOT NULL AUTO_INCREMENT,
    `title` varchar(255) NOT NULL,
    `content` text NOT NULL,
    `created_at` timestamp NOT NULL DEFAULT
CURRENT_TIMESTAMP,
    PRIMARY KEY (`id`)
) ENGINE=InnoDB AUTO_INCREMENT=1;
```

7. Again, you can check tables with the `show tables` query:

   mysql > show tables;

```
mysql> show tables;
+-------------------+
| Tables_in_myblog |
+-------------------+
| articles          |
+-------------------+
1 row in set (0.00 sec)
```

8. Now, let's insert some data in our table. Use the following query to create a new record:

```
mysql > INSERT INTO `articles` (`id`, `title`, `content`,
`created_at`)
VALUES (NULL, 'My first blog post', 'contents of article',
CURRENT_TIMESTAMP);
```

```
mysql> INSERT INTO `articles` (`id`, `title`, `content`, `created_at`)
    -> VALUES (NULL, 'My first blog post', 'contents of article', CURRENT_TIMEST
AMP);
Query OK, 1 row affected (0.04 sec)
```

9. Retrieve data from the table. The following query will select all records from the articles table:

```
mysql > Select * from articles;
```

```
mysql> select * from articles;
+----+----------------------+---------------------+---------------------+
| id | title                | content             | created_at          |
+----+----------------------+---------------------+---------------------+
|  1 | New title            | contents of article | 2015-09-15 16:42:26 |
|  2 | My second  blog post | contents of blog 2  | 2015-09-15 16:44:15 |
+----+----------------------+---------------------+---------------------+
2 rows in set (0.00 sec)
```

10. Retrieve the selected records from the table:

```
mysql > Select * from articles where id = 1;
```

11. Update the selected record:

```
mysql > update articles set title="New title" where id=1;
```

```
mysql> update articles set title = "New title" where id = 1;
Query OK, 1 row affected (0.01 sec)
Rows matched: 1  Changed: 1  Warnings: 0
```

12. Delete the record from the `articles` table using the following command:

```
mysql > delete from articles where id = 2;
```

How it works...

We have created a relational database to store blog data with one table. Actual blog databases will need additional tables for comments, authors, and various entities. The queries used to create databases and tables are known as **Data Definition Language** (**DDL**), and queries that are used to select, insert, and update the actual data are known as **Data Manipulation Language** (**DML**).

MySQL offers various data types to be used for columns such as `tinyint`, `int`, `long`, `double`, `varchar`, `text`, `blob`, and so on. Each data type has its specific use and a proper selection may help to improve the performance of your database.

Importing and exporting bulk data

In this recipe, we will learn how to import and export bulk data with MySQL. Many times it happens that we receive data in CSV or XML format and we need to add this data to the database server for further processing. You can always use tools such as MySQL workbench and phpMyAdmin, but MySQL provides command-line tools for the bulk processing of data that are more efficient and flexible.

How to do it...

Follow these steps to import and export bulk data:

1. To export a database from the MySQL server, use the following command:

   ```
   $ mysqldump -u admin -p mytestdb > db_backup.sql
   ```

2. To export specific tables from a database, use the following command:

   ```
   $ mysqldump -u admin -p mytestdb table1 table2 >
   table_backup.sql
   ```

3. To compress exported data, use `gzip`:

   ```
   $ mysqldump -u admin -p mytestdb | gzip > db_backup.sql.gz
   ```

4. To export selective data to the CSV format, use the following query. Note that this will create `articles.csv` on the same server as MySQL and not your local server:

   ```
   SELECT id, title, contents FROM articles
   INTO OUTFILE '/tmp/articles.csv'
   FIELDS TERMINATED BY ',' ENCLOSED BY '"'
   LINES TERMINATED BY '\n';
   ```

5. To fetch data on your local system, you can use the MySQL client as follows:

   ❑ Write your query in a file:

   ```
   $ nano query.sql
   select * from articles;
   ```

   ❑ Now pass this query to the `mysql` client and collect the output in CSV:

   ```
   $ mysql -h 192.168.2.100 -u admin -p myblog < query.sql >
   output.csv
   ```

   The resulting file will contain tab separated values.

6. To import an SQL file to a MySQL database, we need to first create a database:

   ```
   $ mysqladmin -u admin -p create mytestdb2
   ```

7. Once the database is created, import data with the following command:

   ```
   $ mysql -u admin -p mytestdb2 < db_backup.sql
   ```

8. To import a CSV file in a MySQL table, you can use the `Load Data` query. The following is the sample CSV file:

```
ubuntu@ubuntu:~$ cat /tmp/articles.csv
"1","New title","contents of article"."2015-09-15 16:42:26"
"2","My second blog post","contents of blog 2"."2015-09-15 16:44:15"
ubuntu@ubuntu:~$
```

Now use the following query from the MySQL console to import data from CSV:

```
LOAD DATA INFILE 'c:/tmp/articles.csv'
INTO TABLE articles
FIELDS TERMINATED BY ','  ENCLOSED BY '"'
LINES TERMINATED BY \n IGNORE 1 ROWS;
```

See also

▶ MySQL select-into syntax at
   https://dev.mysql.com/doc/refman/5.6/en/select-into.html

▶ MySQL load data infile syntax at
   https://dev.mysql.com/doc/refman/5.6/en/load-data.html

▶ Importing from and exporting to XML files at
   https://dev.mysql.com/doc/refman/5.6/en/load-xml.html

Adding users and assigning access rights

In this recipe, we will learn how to add new users to the MySQL database server. MySQL provides very flexible and granular user management options. We can create users with full access to an entire database or limit a user to simply read the data from a single database. Again, we will be using queries to create users and grant them access rights. You are free to use any tool of your choice.

Getting ready

You will need a MySQL user account with administrative privileges. You can use the MySQL root account.

How to do it...

Follow these steps to add users to MySQL database server and assign access rights:

1. Open the MySQL shell with the following command. Enter the password for the admin account when prompted:

   ```
   $ mysql -u root -p
   ```

2. From the MySQL shell, use the following command to add a new user to MySQL:

   ```
   mysql> create user 'dbuser'@'localhost' identified by
   'password';
   ```

3. You can check the user account with the following command:

   ```
   mysql> select user, host, password from mysql.user where
   user = 'dbuser';
   ```

```
mysql> select user, host, password from mysql.user where user = 'blog_admin';
+-------------+-----------+---------------------------------------------+
| user        | host      | password                                    |
+-------------+-----------+---------------------------------------------+
| blog_admin  | localhost | *59C70DA2F3E3A5BDF46B68F5C8B8F25762BCCEF0   |
+-------------+-----------+---------------------------------------------+
1 row in set (0.00 sec)
```

4. Next, add some privileges to this user account:

   ```
   mysql> grant all privileges on *.* to 'dbuser'@'localhost'
   with grant option;
   ```

5. Verify the privileges for the account as follows:

   ```
   mysql> show grants for 'dbuser'@'localhost'
   ```

```
mysql> show grants for 'blog_admin'@'localhost';
+-------------------------------------------------------------------------+
| Grants for blog_admin@localhost                                         |
+-------------------------------------------------------------------------+
| GRANT ALL PRIVILEGES ON *.* TO 'blog_admin'@'localhost' IDENTIFIED BY PASSWORD
 '*59C70DA2F3E3A5BDF46B68F5C8B8F25762BCCEF0' WITH GRANT OPTION |
+-------------------------------------------------------------------------+
1 row in set (0.00 sec)
```

6. Finally, exit the MySQL shell and try to log in with the new user account. You should log in successfully:

```
mysql> exit
$ mysql -u dbuser -p
```

How it works...

MySQL uses the same database structure to store user account information. It contains a hidden database named MySQL that contains all MySQL settings along with user accounts. The statements create user and grant work as a wrapper around common insert statements and make it easy to add new users to the system.

In the preceding example, we created a new user with the name dbuser. This user is allowed to log in only from localhost and requires a password to log in to the MySQL server. You can skip the identified by 'password' part to create a user without a password, but of course, it's not recommended.

To allow a user to log in from any system, you need to set the host part to a %, as follows:

```
mysql> create user 'dbuser'@'%' identified by 'password';
```

You can also limit access from a specific host by specifying its FQDN or IP address:

```
mysql> create user 'dbuser'@'host1.example.com' identified by 'password';
```

Or

```
mysql> create user 'dbuser'@'10.0.2.51' identified by 'password';
```

Note that if you have an anonymous user account on MySQL, then a user created with username'@'% will not be able to log in through localhost. You will need to add a separate entry with username'@'localhost.

Next, we give some privileges to this user account using a `grant` statement. The preceding example gives all privileges on all databases to the user account `dbuser`. To limit the database, change the database part to `dbname.*`:

```
mysql> grant all privileges on dbname.* to 'dbuser'@'localhost' with
grant option;
```

To limit privileges to certain tasks, mention specific privileges in a `grant` statement:

```
mysql> grant select, insert, update, delete, create
    -> on dbname.* to 'dbuser'@'localhost';
```

The preceding statement will `grant select`, `insert`, `update`, `delete`, and `create` privileges on any table under the `dbname` database.

There's more...

Similar to preceding add user example, other user management tasks can be performed with SQL queries as follows:

Removing user accounts

You can easily remove a user account with the `drop` statement, as follows:

```
mysql> drop user 'dbuser'@'localhost';
```

Setting resource limits

MySQL allows setting limits on individual accounts:

```
mysql> grant all on dbname.* to 'dbuser'@'localhost'
    ->      with max_queries_per_hour 20
    ->          max_updates_per_hour 10
    ->          max_connections_per_hour 5
    ->          max_user_connections 2;
```

See also

▶ MySQL user account management at `https://dev.mysql.com/doc/refman/5.6/en/user-account-management.html`

Installing web access for MySQL

In this recipe, we will set up a well-known web-based MySQL administrative tool—phpMyAdmin.

Getting ready

You will need access to a root account or an account with `sudo` privileges.

You will need a web server set up to serve PHP contents.

How to do it...

Follow these steps to install web access for MySQL:

1. Enable the `mcrypt` extension for PHP:

   ```
   $ sudo php5enmod mcrypt
   ```

2. Install `phpmyadmin` with the following commands:

   ```
   $ sudo apt-get update
   $ sudo apt-get install phpmyadmin
   ```

3. The installation process will download the necessary packages and then prompt you to configure `phpmyadmin`:

```
┤ Configuring phpmyadmin ├

The phpmyadmin package must have a database installed and configured
before it can be used.  This can be optionally handled with
dbconfig-common.

If you are an advanced database administrator and know that you want to
perform this configuration manually, or if your database has already
been installed and configured, you should refuse this option.  Details
on what needs to be done should most likely be provided in
/usr/share/doc/phpmyadmin.

Otherwise, you should probably choose this option.

Configure database for phpmyadmin with dbconfig-common?

              <Yes>                          <No>
```

4. Choose `<yes>` to proceed with the configuration process.

5. Enter the MySQL admin account password on the next screen:

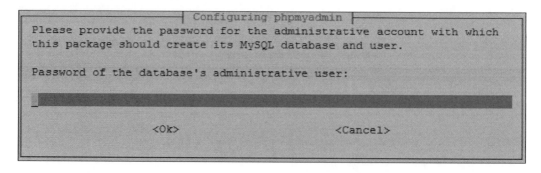

6. Another screen will pop up; this time, you will be asked for the new password for the `phpmyadmin` user. Enter the new password and then confirm it on the next screen:

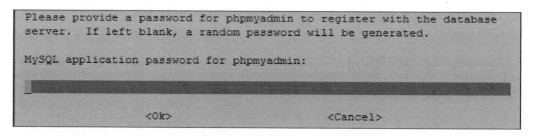

7. Next, `phpmyadmin` will ask for web server selection:

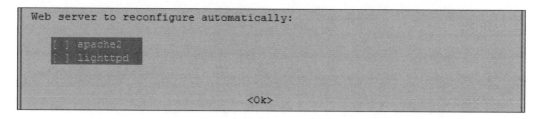

8. Once the installation completes, you can access phpMyAdmin at `http://server-ip/phpmyadmin`. Use your admin login credentials on the login screen. The `phpmyadmin` screen will look something like this:

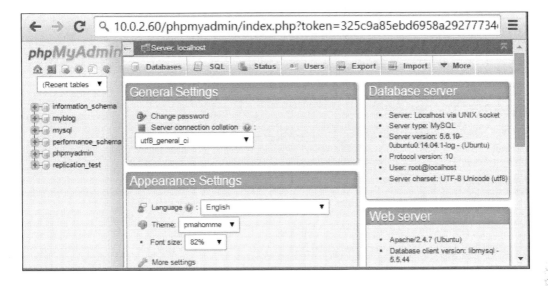

How it works...

PHPMyAdmin is a web-based administrative console for MySQL. It is developed in PHP and works with a web server such as Apache to serve web access. With PHPMyAdmin, you can do database tasks such as create databases and tables; select, insert, update data; modify table definitions; and a lot more. It provides a query console which can be used to type in custom queries and execute them from same screen.

With the addition of the Ubuntu software repository, it has become easy to install PHPMyAdmin with a single command. Once it is installed, a new user is created on the MySQL server. It also supports connecting to multiple servers. You can find all configuration files located in the `/etc/phpmyadmin` directory.

There's more...

If you want to install the latest version of phpMyAdmin, you can download it from their official website, `https://www.phpmyadmin.net/downloads/`. You can extract downloaded contents to your `web` directory and set MySQL credentials in the `config.inc.php` file.

See also

- Read more about phpMyAdmin in the Ubuntu server guide at `https://help.ubuntu.com/lts/serverguide/phpmyadmin.html`

- Install and secure phpMyAdmin at `https://www.digitalocean.com/community/tutorials/how-to-install-and-secure-phpmyadmin-on-ubuntu-14-04`

Setting backups

In this recipe, we will learn how to back up the MySQL database.

Getting ready

You will need administrative access to the MySQL database.

How to do it...

Follow these steps to set up the backups:

1. Backing up the MySQL database is the same as exporting data from the server. Use the `mysqldump` tool to back up the MySQL database as follows:

   ```
   $ mysqldump -h localhost -u admin -p mydb > mydb_backup.sql
   ```

2. You will be prompted for the admin account password. After providing the password, the backup process will take time depending on the size of the database.

3. To back up all databases, add the `--all-databases` flag to the preceding command:

   ```
   $ mysqldump --all-databases -u admin -p alldb_backup.sql
   ```

4. Next, we can restore the backup created with the `mysqldump` tool with the following command:

   ```
   $ mysqladmin -u admin -p create mydb
   ```
   ```
   $ mysql -h localhost -u admin -p mydb < mydb_backup.sql
   ```

5. To restore all databases, skip the database creation part:

   ```
   $ mysql -h localhost -u admin -p < alldb_backup.sql
   ```

How it works...

MySQL provides a very general tool, `mysqldump`, to export all data from the database server. This tool can be used with any type of database engine, be it MyISAM or InnoDB or any other. To perform an online backup of InnoDB tables, `mysqldump` provides the `--single-transaction` option. With this option set, InnoDB tables will not be locked and will be available to other applications while backup is in progress.

Oracle provides the MySQL Enterprise backup tool for MySQL Enterprise edition users. This tool includes features such as incremental and compressed backups. Alternatively, Percona provides an open source utility known as **Xtrabackup**. It provides incremental and compressed backups and many more features.

Some other backup methods include copying MySQL table files and the `mysqlhotcopy` script for InnoDB tables. For these methods to work, you may need to pause or stop the MySQL server before backup.

You can also enable replication to mirror all data to the other server. It is a mechanism to maintain multiple copies of data by automatically copying data from one system to another. In this case, the primary server is called **Master** and the secondary server is called **Slave**. This type of configuration is known as Master-Slave replication. Generally, applications communicate with the Master server for all read and write requests. The Slave is used as a backup if the Master goes down. Many times, the Master-Slave configuration is used to load balance database queries by routing all read requests to the Slave server and write requests to the Master server. Replication can also be configured in Master-Master mode, where both servers receive read-write requests from clients.

See also

▶   MySQL backup methods at `http://dev.mysql.com/doc/refman/5.6/en/backup-methods.html`

▶   Percona XtraBackup at `https://www.percona.com/doc/percona-xtrabackup/2.2/index.html`

▶   MySQL binary log at `http://dev.mysql.com/doc/refman/5.6/en/binary-log.html`

Optimizing MySQL performance – queries

MySQL performance optimizations can be divided into two parts. One is query optimization and the other is MySQL server configuration. To get optimum results, you have to work on both of these parts. Without proper configuration, queries will not provide consistent performance; on the other hand, without proper queries and a database structure, queries may take much longer to produce results.

In this recipe, we will learn how to evaluate query performance, set indexes, and identify the optimum database structure for our data.

Getting ready

You will need access to an admin account on the MySQL server.

You will need a large dataset to test queries. Various tools are available to generate test data. I will be using test data available at `https://github.com/datacharmer/test_db`.

How to do it...

Follow these steps to optimize MySQL performance:

1. The first and most basic thing is to identify key columns and add indexes to them:

    ```
    mysql> alter table salaries add index (salary);
    ```

2. Enable the slow query log to identify long-running queries. Enter the following commands from the MySQL console:

    ```
    mysql> set global log_slow_queries = 1;

    mysql> set global slow_query_log_file =
    '/var/log/mysql/slow.log';
    ```

3. Once you identify the slow and repeated query, execute that query on the database and record query timings. The following is a sample query:

    ```
    mysql> select count(*) from salaries where salary between
    30000 and 65000 and from_date > '1986-01-01';
    ```

    ```
    mysql> select count(*) from salaries where salary between 30000 and 65000 and fr
    om_date > '1986-01-01';
    +----------+
    | count(*) |
    +----------+
    |  1646072 |
    +----------+
    1 row in set (3.67 sec)
    ```

4. Next, use `explain` to view the query execution plan:

    ```
    mysql> explain select count(*) from salaries where salary
    between 30000 and 65000 and from_date > '1986-01-01';
    ```

    ```
    mysql> explain select count(*) from salaries where salary between 30000 and 6500
    0 and from_date > '1986-01-01';
    +----+-------------+----------+------+---------------+------+---------+------+--------+-------------+
    | id | select_type | table    | type | possible_keys | key  | key_len | ref  | rows   | Extra       |
    +----+-------------+----------+------+---------------+------+---------+------+--------+-------------+
    |  1 | SIMPLE      | salaries | ALL  | NULL          | NULL | NULL    | NULL | 756234 | Using where |
    +----+-------------+----------+------+---------------+------+---------+------+--------+-------------+
    1 row in set (0.04 sec)
    ```

5. Add required indexes, if any, and recheck the query execution plan. Your new index should be listed under `possible_keys` and key columns of `explain` output:

```
mysql> alter table `salaries` add index ( `from_date` ) ;
```

6. If you found that MySQL is not using a proper index or using another index than expected then you can explicitly specify the index to be used or ignored:

```
mysql> select * from salaries use index (salaries) where
salary between 30000 and 65000 and from_date > '1986-01-
01';
```

```
mysql> select * from salaries where salary between 30000
and 65000 and from_date > '1986-01-01' ignore index
(from_date);
```

Now execute the query again and check query timings for any improvements.

7. Analyze your data and modify the table structure. The following query will show the minimum and maximum length of data in each column. Add a small amount of buffer space to the reported maximum length and reduce additional space allocation if any:

```
mysql> select * from `employees` procedure analyse();
```

The following is the partial output for the `analyse()` procedure:

```
| employees.employees.emp_no      | 10001      | 499999      |              5 |
     6 |              0 |    0 | 253321.7634      | 300552.3312 | MEDIUM
INT(6) UNSIGNED NOT NULL |
| employees.employees.birth_date | 1952-02-01 | 1965-02-01 |             10 |
    10 |              0 |    0 | 10.0000      | NULL      | DATE N
OT NULL                         |
| employees.employees.first_name | Aamer      | Zvonko      |              3 |
    14 |              0 |    0 | 6.2157      | NULL      | VARCHA
R(14) NOT NULL                   |
```

8. Check the database engines you are using. The two major engines available in MySQL are MyISAM and InnoDB:

```
mysql> show create table employees;
```

How it works...

MySQL uses SQL to accept commands for data processing. The query contains the operation, such as `select`, `insert`, and `update`; the target that is a table name; and conditions to match the data. The following is an example query:

```
select * from employee where id = 1001;
```

In the preceding query, `select *` is the operation asking MySQL to select all data for a row. The target is the `employee` table, and `id = 1001` is a condition part.

Once a query is received, MySQL generates query execution plan for it. This step contains various steps such as parsing, preprocessing, and optimization. In parsing and pre-processing, the query is checked for any syntactical errors and the proper order of SQL grammar. The given query can be executed in multiple ways. Query optimizer selects the best possible path for query execution. Finally, the query is executed and the execution plan is stored in the query cache for later use.

The query execution plan can be retrieved from MySQL with the help of the `explain` query and explain extended. Explain executes the query until the generation of the query execution plan and then returns the execution plan as a result. The execution plan contains table names used in this query, key fields used to search data, the number of rows needed to be scanned, and temporary tables and file sorting used, if any. The query execution plan shows possible keys that can be used for query execution and then shows the actual key column used. **Key** is a column with an index on it, which can be a primary index, unique index, or non-unique index. You can check the MySQL documentation for more details on query execution plans and `explain` output.

If a specific column in a table is being used repeatedly, you should consider adding a proper index to that column. **Indexes** group similar data together, which reduces the look up time and total number of rows to be scanned. Also keep in mind that indexes use large amounts of memory, so be selective while adding indexes.

Secondly, if you have a proper index set on a required column and the query optimization plan does not recognize or use the index, you can force MySQL to use a specific index with the `USE INDEX index_name` statement. To ignore a specific index, use the statement `IGNORE INDEX index_name`.

You may get a small improvement with table maintenance commands. **Optimize table** is useful when a large part of the table is modified or deleted. It reorganizes table index data on physical storage and improves I/O performance. **Flush table** is used to reload the internal cache. **Check table** and **Analyze table** check for table errors and data distribution respectively. The improvements with these commands may not be significant for smaller tables. Reducing the extra space allocated to each column is also a good idea for reducing total physical storage used. Reduced storage will optimize I/O performance as well as cache utilization.

You should also check the storage engines used by specific tables. The two major storage engines used in MySQL are MyISAM and InnoDB. InnnoDB provides full transactional support and uses row-level locking, whereas MyISAM does not have transaction support and uses table-level locking. MyISAM is a good choice for faster reads where you have a large amount of data with limited writes on the table. MySQL does support the addition of external storage engines in the form of plugins. One popular open source storage engine is **XtraDB** by Percona systems.

There's more...

If your tables are really large, you should consider partitioning them. Partitioning tables distributes related data across multiple files on disk. Partitioning on frequently used keys can give you a quick boost. MySQL supports various different types of partitioning such as hash partitions, range partitions, list partitions, key partitions, and also sub-partitions.

You can specify hash partitioning with table creation as follows:

```
create table employees (
    id int not null,
    fname varchar(30),
    lname varchar(30),
    store_id int
) partition by hash(store_id) partitions 4;
```

Alternatively, you can also partition an existing table with the following query:

```
mysql> alter table employees partition by hash(store_id) partitions
4;
```

Sharding MySQL

You can also shard your database. Sharding is a form of horizontal partitioning where you store part of the table data across multiple instances of a table. The table instance can exist on the same server under separate databases or across different servers. Each table instance contains parts of the total data, thus improving queries that need to access limited data. Sharding enables you to scale a database horizontally across multiple servers.

The best implementation strategy for sharding is to try to avoid it for as long as possible. Sharding requires additional maintenance efforts on the operations side and the use of proxy software to hide sharding from an application, or to make your application itself sharding aware. Sharding also adds limitations on queries that require access to the entire table. You will need to create cross-server joins or process data in the application layer.

See also

▸ The MySQL optimization guide at `https://dev.mysql.com/doc/refman/5.6/en/optimization.html`

▸ MySQL query execution plan information at `https://dev.mysql.com/doc/refman/5.6/en/execution-plan-information.html`

▸ InnoDB storage engine at `https://dev.mysql.com/doc/refman/5.6/en/innodb-storage-engine.html`

▸ Other storage engines available in MySQL at `https://dev.mysql.com/doc/refman/5.6/en/storage-engines.html`

▸ Table maintenance statements at `http://dev.mysql.com/doc/refman/5.6/en/table-maintenance-sql.html`

▸ MySQL test database at `https://github.com/datacharmer/test_db`

Optimizing MySQL performance – configuration

MySQL has hundreds of settings that can be configured. Version 5.7 ships with many improvements in default configuration values and requires far fewer changes. In this recipe, we will look at some of the most important parameters for tuning MySQL performance.

Getting ready

You will need access to a root account or an account with `sudo` privileges.

You will need access to a root account on the MySQL server.

How to do it...

Follow these steps to improve MySQL configuration:

1. First, create a backup of the original configuration file:

   ```
   $ cd /etc/mysql/mysql.conf.d
   $ sudo cp mysqld.cnf mysqld.cnf.bkp
   ```

2. Now open `my.cnf` for changes:

   ```
   $ sudo nano /etc/mysql/mysql.conf.d/mysqld.cnf
   ```

3. Adjust the following settings for your InnoDB tables:

   ```
   innodb_buffer_pool_size = 512M  # around 70% of total ram
   innodb_log_file_size  = 64M
   innodb_file_per_table = 1
   innodb_log_buffer_size = 4M
   ```

4. If you are using MyISAM tables, set the key buffer size:

   ```
   key_buffer_size = 64M
   ```

5. Enable the slow query log:

   ```
   slow_query_log = 1
   slow_query_log_file = /var/lib/mysql/mysql-slow.log
   long_query_time = 2
   ```

6. Disable the query cache:

   ```
   query_cache_size = 0
   ```

7. Set the maximum connections as per your requirements:

   ```
   max_connections = 300
   ```

8. Increase the temporary table size:

   ```
   tmp_table_size = 32M
   ```

9. Increase `max_allowed_packet` to increase the maximum packet size:

   ```
   max_allowed_packet = 32M
   ```

10. Enable binary logging for easy recovery and replication:

    ```
    log_bin = /var/log/mysql/mysql-bin.log
    ```

11. Additionally, you can use `mysqltuner.pl`, which gives general recommendations about the MySQL best practices:

    ```
    $ wget http://mysqltuner.pl/ -O mysqltuner.pl
    $ perl mysqltuner.pl
    ```

How it works...

The preceding example shows some important settings for MySQL performance tuning. Ensure that you change one setting at a time and assess its results. There is no silver bullet that works for all, and similarly, some of these settings may or may not work for you. Secondly, most settings can be changed at runtime with a `SET` statement. You can test settings in runtime and easily reverse them if they do not work as expected. Once you are sure that settings work as expected, you can move them to the configuration file.

The following are details on the preceding settings:

- `innodb_buffer_pool_size`: the size of the cache where InnoDB data and indexes are cached. The larger the buffer pool, the more data can be cached in it. You can set this to around 70% of available physical memory as MySQL uses extra memory beyond this buffer. It is assumed that MySQL is the only service running on server.
- `log_file_size`: the size of the redo logs. These logs are helpful in faster writes and crash recovery.
- `innodb_file_per_table`: This determines whether to use shared table space or separate files for each table. MySQL 5.7 defaults this setting to ON.
- `key_buffer_size`: determines the key buffer for MyISAM tables.
- `slow_query_log` and `long_query_time` enable slow query logging and set slow query time respectively. Slow query logging can be useful for identifying repeated slow queries.
- `Query_cache_size` caches the result of a query. It is identified as a bottleneck for concurrent queries and MySQL 5.6 disables it by default.

- ▶ `max_connections` sets the number of maximum concurrent connections allowed. Set this value as per your application's requirements. Higher values may result in higher memory consumption and an unresponsive server. Use connection pooling in the application if possible.

- ▶ `max_allowed_packet` sets the size of the packet size that MySQL can send at a time. Increase this value if your server runs queries with large result sets. `mysqld` set it to `16M` and `mysqldump` set it to `24M`. You can also set this as a command-line parameter.

- ▶ `log_bin` enables binary logging, which can be used for replication and also for crash recovery. Make sure that you set proper rotation values to avoid large dump files.

There's more...

MySQL performance tuning primer script: This script takes information from show status and show variables statements. It gives recommendations for various settings such as slow query log, max connections, query cache, key buffers, and many others. This shell script is available at `http://day32.com/MySQL`.

You can download and use this script as follows:

```
$ wget http://day32.com/MySQL/tuning-primer.sh
$ sh tuning-primer.sh
```

Percona configuration wizard

Percona systems provide a developer-friendly, web-based configuration wizard to create a configuration file for your MySQL server. The wizard is available at `http://tools.percona.com`

MySQL table compression

Depending on the type of data, you can opt for compressed tables. Compression is useful for tables with long textual contents and read-intensive workloads. Data and indexes are stored in a compressed format, resulting in reduced I/O and a smaller database size, though it needs more CPU cycles to compress and uncompress data. To enable compression, you need an InnoDB storage engine with `innodb_file_per_table` enabled and the file format set to Barracuda. Check MySQL documents for more details on InnoDB compression at `https://dev.mysql.com/doc/innodb/1.1/en/innodb-compression.html`.

See also

- ▶ MySQL tuner script at `https://github.com/major/MySQLTuner-perl`
- ▶ MySQL docs at `https://dev.mysql.com/doc/refman/5.7/en/optimization.html`

▶ InnoDB table compression at `https://dev.mysql.com/doc/refman/5.7/en/innodb-table-compression.html`

Creating MySQL replicas for scaling and high availability

When your application is small, you can use a single MySQL server for all your database needs. As your application becomes popular and you get more and more requests, the database starts becoming a bottleneck for application performance. With thousands of queries per second, the database write queue gets longer and read latency increases. To solve this problem, you can use multiple replicas of the same database and separate read and write queries between them.

In this recipe, we will learn how to set up replication with the MySQL server.

Getting ready

You will need two MySQL servers and access to administrative accounts on both.

Make sure that port `3306` is open and available on both servers.

How to do it...

Follow these steps to create MySQL replicas:

1. Create the replication user on the Master server:

```
$ mysql -u root -p
mysql> grant replication slave on *.* TO
'slave_user'@'10.0.2.62' identified by 'password';
mysql> flush privileges;
mysql> quit
```

2. Edit the MySQL configuration on the Master server:

```
$ sudo nano /etc/mysql/my.cnf
[mysqld]
bind-address = 10.0.2.61     # your master server ip
server-id = 1
log-bin = mysql-bin
binlog-ignore-db = "mysql"
```

3. Restart MySQL on the Master server:

```
$ sudo service mysql restart
```

4. Export MySQL databases on the Master server. Open the MySQL connection and lock the database to prevent any updates:

```
$ mysql -u root -p
mysql> flush tables with read lock;
```

5. Read the Master status on the Master server and take a note of it. This will be used shortly to configure the Slave server:

```
mysql> show master status;
```

```
mysql> show master status;
+-------------------+----------+--------------+------------------+--------------
| File              | Position | Binlog_Do_DB | Binlog_Ignore_DB | Executed_Gt
+-------------------+----------+--------------+------------------+--------------
| mysql-bin.000010  |   2214   |              | mysql            |
+-------------------+----------+--------------+------------------+--------------
1 row in set (0.00 sec)
```

6. Open a separate terminal window and export the required databases. Add the names of all the databases you want to export:

```
$ mysqldump -u root -p --databases testdb >
master_dump.sql
```

7. Now, unlock the tables after the database dump has completed:

```
mysql> UNLOCK TABLES;
mysql> quit;
```

8. Transfer the backup to the Slave server with any secure method:

```
$ scp master_backup.sql
ubuntu@10.0.2.62:/home/ubuntu/master_backup.sql
```

9. Next, edit the configuration file on the Slave server:

```
$ sudo nano /etc/mysql/my.cnf
[mysqld]
bind-address = 10.0.2.62
server-id = 2
relay_log=relay-log
```

10. Import the dump from the Master server. You may need to manually create a database before importing dumps:

```
$ mysqladmin -u admin -p create testdb
$ mysql -u root -p < master_dump.sql
```

11. Restart the MySQL server:

```
$ sudo service mysql restart
```

12. Now set the Master configuration on the Slave. Use the values we received from show master status command in step 5:

```
$ mysql -u root -p
mysql > change master to
master_host='10.0.2.61', master_user='slave_user',
master_password='password', master_log_file='mysql-
bin.000010',
master_log_pos=2214;
```

13. Start the Slave:

```
mysql> start slave;
```

14. Check the Slave's status. You should see the message Waiting for master to send event under Slave_IO_state:

```
mysql> show slave status\G
```

```
mysql> show slave status\G
*************************** 1. row ***************************
               Slave_IO_State: Waiting for master to send event
                  Master_Host: 10.0.2.6
                  Master_User: slave_user
                  Master_Port: 3306
                Connect_Retry: 60
              Master_Log_File: mysql-bin.000010
          Read_Master_Log_Pos: 2214
```

Now you can test replication. Create a new database with a table and a few sample records on the Master server. You should see the database replicated on the Slave immediately.

How it works...

MySQL replication works with the help of binary logs generated on the Master server. MySQL logs any changes to the database to local binary logs with a lightweight buffered and sequential write process. These logs will then be read by the slave. When the slave connects to the Master, the Master creates a new thread for this replication connection and updates the slave with events in a binary log, notifying the slave about newly written events in binary logs.

On the slave side, two threads are started to handle replication. One is the IO thread, which connects to the Master and copies updates in binary logs to a local log file, relay_log. The other thread, which is known as the SQL thread, reads events stored on relay_log and applies them locally.

In the preceding recipe, we have configured Master-Slave replication. MySQL also supports Master-Master replication. In the case of Master-Slave configuration, the Master works as an active server, handling all writes to database. You can configure slaves to answer read queries, but most of the time, the slave server works as a passive backup server. If the Master fails, you manually need to promote the slave to take over as Master. This process may require downtime.

To overcome problems with Master - Slave replication, MySQL can be configured in **Master-Master** relation, where all servers act as a Master as well as a slave. Applications can read as well as write to all participating servers, and in case any Master goes down, other servers can still handle all application writes without any downtime. The problem with Master-Master configuration is that it's quite difficult to set up and deploy. Additionally, maintaining data consistency across all servers is a challenge. This type of configuration is lazy and asynchronous and violates ACID properties.

In the preceding example, we configured the `server-id` variable in the `my.cnf` file. This needs to be unique on both servers. MySQL version 5.6 adds another UUID for the server, which is located at `data_dir/auto.cnf`. If you happen to copy `data_dir` from Master to host or are using a copy of a Master virtual machine as your starting point for a slave, you may get an error on the slave that reads something like **master and slave have equal mysql server UUIDs**. In this case, simply remove `auto.cnf` from the slave and restart the MySQL server.

There's more...

You can set MySQL load balancing and configure your database for high availability with the help of a simple load balancer in front of MySQL. HAProxy is a well known load balancer that supports TCP load balancing and can be configured in a few steps, as follows:

1. Set your MySQL servers to Master - Master replication mode.
2. Log in to `mysql` and create one user for `haproxy` health checks and another for remote administration:

    ```
    mysql> create user 'haproxy_admin'@'haproxy_ip';
    
    mysql> grant all privileges on *.* to 'haproxy_admin'@'haproxy_ip'
    identified by 'password' with
    grant option;
    
    mysql> flush privileges;
    ```

3. Next, install the MySQL client on the HAProxy server and try to log into the `mysql` server with the `haproxy_admin` account.

4. Install HAProxy and configure it to connect to `mysql` on the TCP port:

```
listen mysql-cluster
    bind haproxy_ip:3306
    mode tcp
    option mysql-check user haproxy_check
    balance roundrobin
    server mysql-1 mysql_srv_1_ip:3306 check
    server mysql-2 mysql_srv_2_ip:3306 check
```

5. Finally, start the `haproxy` service and try to connect to the `mysql` server with the `haproxy_admin` account:

```
$ mysql -h haproxy_ip -u hapoxy_admin -p
```

See also

▸ MySQL replication configuration at `http://dev.mysql.com/doc/refman/5.6/en/replication.html`

▸ How MySQL replication works at `https://www.percona.com/blog/2013/01/09/how-does-mysql-replication-really-work/`

▸ MySQL replication formats at `http://dev.mysql.com/doc/refman/5.5/en/replication-formats.html`

Troubleshooting MySQL

In this recipe, we will look at some common problems with MySQL and learn how to solve them.

Getting ready

You will need access to a root account or an account with `sudo` privileges.

You will need administrative privileges on the MySQL server.

How to do it...

Follow these steps to troubleshoot MySQL:

1. First, check if the MySQL server is running and listening for connections on the configured port:

   ```
   $ sudo service mysql status
   $ sudo netstat -pltn
   ```

2. Check MySQL logs for any error messages at `/var/log/mysql.log` and `mysql.err`.

3. You can try to start the server in interactive mode with the `verbose` flag set:

   ```
   $ which mysqld
   /usr/sbin/mysqld
   $ sudo /usr/sbin/mysqld --user=mysql --verbose
   ```

4. If you are accessing MySQL from a remote system, make sure that the server is set to `listen` on a public port. Check for `bind-address` in `my.cnf`:

   ```
   bind-address   = 10.0.247.168
   ```

5. For any access denied errors, check if you have a user account in place and if it is allowed to log in from a specific IP address:

   ```
   mysql> select user, host, password from mysql.user where user = 'username';
   ```

6. Check the user has access to specified resources:

   ```
   mysql > grant all privileges on databasename.* to 'username'@'%';
   ```

7. Check your firewall is not blocking connections to MySQL.

8. If you get an error saying `mysql server has gone away`, then increase `wait_timeout` in the configuration file. Alternatively, you can re-initiate a connection on the client side after a specific timeout.

9. Use a `repair table` statement to recover the crashed MyISAM table:

   ```
   $ mysql -u root -p
   mysql> repair table databasename.tablename;
   ```

10. Alternatively, you can use the `mysqlcheck` command to repair tables:

    ```
    $ mysqlcheck -u root -p --auto-repair \
    --check --optimize databasename
    ```

See also

▶   InnoDB troubleshooting at `https://dev.mysql.com/doc/refman/5.7/en/innodb-troubleshooting.html`

Installing MongoDB

Until now, we have worked with the relational database server, MySQL. In this recipe, we will learn how to install and configure MongoDB, which is a not only SQL (NoSQL) document storage server.

Getting ready

You will need access to a root account or an account with `sudo` privileges.

How to do it...

To get the latest version of MongoDB, we need to add the MongoDB source to Ubuntu installation sources:

1. First, import the MongoDB GPG public key:

    ```
    $ sudo apt-key adv \
    --keyserver hkp://keyserver.ubuntu.com:80 \
    --recv 7F0CEB10
    ```

2. Create a `list` file and add an install source to it:

    ```
    $ echo "deb http://repo.mongodb.org/apt/ubuntu
    "$(lsb_release
    -sc)"/mongodb-org/3.0 multiverse" | sudo tee
    /etc/apt/sources.list.d/mongodb-org-3.0.list
    ```

3. Update the `apt` repository sources and install the MongoDB server:

    ```
    $ sudo apt-get update
    $ sudo apt-get install -y mongodb-org
    ```

4. After installation completes, check the status of the MongoDB server:

    ```
    $ sudo service mongod status
    ```

5. Now you can start using the MongoDB server. To access the Mongo shell, use the following command:

    ```
    $ mongo
    ```

How it works...

We have installed the MongoDB server from the MongoDB official repository. The Ubuntu package repository includes the MongoDB package in it, but it is not up to date with the latest release of MongoDB. With GPG keys, Ubuntu ensures the authenticity of the packages being installed. After importing the GPG key, we have created a `list` file that contains the installation source of the MongoDB server.

After installation, the MongoDB service should start automatically. You can check logs at `/var/log/mongodb/mongod.log`.

See also

▶ MongoDB installation guide at `http://docs.mongodb.org/manual/tutorial/install-mongodb-on-ubuntu/`

Storing and retrieving data with MongoDB

In this recipe, we will look at basic CRUD operations with MongoDB. We will learn how to create databases, store, retrieve, and update stored data. This is a recipe to get started with MongoDB.

Getting ready

Make sure that you have installed and configured MongoDB. You can also use the MongoDB installation on a remote server.

How to do it...

Follow these steps to store and retrieve data with MongoDB:

1. Open a shell to interact with the Mongo server:

    ```
    $ mongo
    ```

2. To open a shell on a remote server, use the command given. Replace `server_ip` and `port` with the respective values:

    ```
    $ mongo server_ip:port/db
    ```

3. To create and start using a new database, type `use dbname`. Since schemas in MongoDB are dynamic, you do not need to create a database before using it:

    ```
    > use testdb
    ```

4. You can type `help` in Mongo shell to get a list of available commands and help regarding a specific command:

    > `help`: Let's insert our first document:

    > **db.users.insert({'name':'ubuntu','uid':1001})**

    ```
    > db.users.insert({'name':'ubuntu','uid':1001})
    WriteResult({ "nInserted" : 1 })
    >
    ```

5. To view the created database and collection, use the following commands:

    > **show dbs**

    ```
    > show dbs
    local     0.078GB
    test      0.078GB
    testdb    0.078GB
    >
    ```

    > **show collections**

    ```
    > show collections
    system.indexes
    users
    >
    ```

6. You can also insert multiple values for a key, for example, which groups a user belongs to:

    > **db.users.insert({'name':'root','uid':1010, 'gid':[1010, 1000, 1111]})**

7. Check whether a document is successfully inserted:

    > **db.users.find()**

    ```
    > db.users.find()
    { "_id" : ObjectId("55f7d9b28b756ea94f93a10d"), "name" : "root", "uid" : 1010, "
    gid" : [ 1010, 1000, 1111 ] }
    { "_id" : ObjectId("560ce2a7cf3368a229826104"), "name" : "root", "uid" : 1010, "
    gid" : [ 1010, 1000, 1111 ] }
    >
    ```

8. To get a single record, use `findOne()`:

    > **db.users.findOne({uid:1010})**

9. To update an existing record, use the `update` command as follows:

   ```
   > db.users.update({name:'ubuntu'}, {$set:{uid:2222}})
   ```

10. To remove a record, use the `remove` command. This will remove all records with a name equal to `ubuntu`:

    ```
    > db.users.remove({'name':'ubuntu'})
    ```

11. To drop an entire collection, use the `drop()` command:

    ```
    > db.users.drop()
    ```

12. To drop a database, use the `dropDatabase()` command:

    ```
    > db.users.dropDatabase()
    ```

How it works...

The preceding examples show very basic CRUD operations with the MongoDB shell interface. MongoDB shell is also a JavaScript shell. You can execute all JS commands in a MongoDB shell. You can also modify the shell with the configuration file, `~/.mongorc.js`. Similar to shell, MongoDB provides language-specific drivers, for example, MongoDB PHP drivers to access MongoDB from PHP.

MongoDB works on the concept of collections and documents. A collection is similar to a table in MySQL and a document is a set of key value stores where a key is similar to a column in a MySQL table. MongoDB does not require any schema definitions and accepts any pair of keys and values in a document. Schemas are dynamically created. In addition, you do not need to explicitly create the collection. Simply type a collection name in a command and it will be created if it does not already exist. In the preceding example, `users` is a collection we used to store all data. To explicitly create a collection, use the following command:

```
> use testdb
```

```
> db.createCollection('users')
```

You may be missing the `where` clause in MySQL queries. We have already used that with the `findOne()` command:

```
> db.users.findOne({uid:1010})
```

You can use `$lt` for less than, `$lte` for less than or equal to, `$gt` for greater than, `$gte` for greater than or equal to, and `$ne` for not equal:

```
> db.users.findOne({uid:{$gt:1000}})
```

In the preceding example, we have used the `where` clause with the equality condition `uid=1010`. You can add one more condition as follows:

```
> db.users.findOne({uid:1010, name:'root'})
```

To use the `or` condition, you need to modify the command as follows:

```
> db.users.find ({$or:[{name:'ubuntu'}, {name:'root'}]})
```

You can also extract a single key (column) from the entire document. The `find` command accepts a second optional parameter where you can specify a select criteria. You can use values `1` or `0`. Use `1` to extract a specific key and `0` otherwise:

```
> db.users.findOne({uid:1010}, {name:1})
```

```
> db.users.findOne({uid:1010}, {name:1})
{ "_id" : ObjectId("55f7d9b28b756ea94f93a10d"), "name" : "root" }
>
```

```
> db.users.findOne({uid:1010}, {name:0})
```

```
> db.users.findOne({uid:1010}, {name:0})
{
        "_id" : ObjectId("55f7d9b28b756ea94f93a10d"),
        "uid" : 1010,
        "gid" : [
                1010,
                1000,
                1111
        ]
}
>
```

There's more...

You can install a web interface to manage the MongoDB installation. There are various open source web interfaces listed on Mongo documentation at `http://docs.mongodb.org/ecosystem/tools/administration-interfaces/`.

When you start a mongo shell for the first time, you may see a warning message regarding `transperent_hugepage` and defrag. To remove those warnings, add the following lines to `/etc/init/mongod.conf`, below the `$DAEMONUSER /var/run/mongodb.pid` line:

```
if test -f /sys/kernel/mm/transparent_hugepage/enabled; then
  echo never > /sys/kernel/mm/transparent_hugepage/enabled
fi
if test -f /sys/kernel/mm/transparent_hugepage/defrag; then
  echo never > /sys/kernel/mm/transparent_hugepage/defrag
fi
```

Find more details on this Stack Overflow post at `http://stackoverflow.com/questions/28911634/how-to-avoid-transparent-hugepage-defrag-warning-from-mongodb`

See also

- ▸ Mongo CRUD tutorial at `https://docs.mongodb.org/manual/applications/crud/`
- ▸ MongoDB query documents at `https://docs.mongodb.org/manual/tutorial/query-documents/`

Network Storage

In this chapter, we will cover the following recipes:

- ▸ Installing the Samba server
- ▸ Adding users to the Samba server
- ▸ Installing the secure FTP server
- ▸ Synchronizing files with Rsync
- ▸ Performance tuning the Samba server
- ▸ Troubleshooting the Samba server
- ▸ Installing the Network File System

Introduction

Often we need to store a lot of data and local systems don't have enough space. Sometimes, we need to quickly share this data across multiple systems and users. Also, when you have a big network, chances are you have Linux systems as well as Windows or Mac. Centralized networked storage can help to solve these storage and sharing problems. Linux provides various options, such as Samba and NFS, to host a centralized storage server and share data across multiple computers.

In this chapter, we will learn how to set up a centralized storage system. We will set up the Samba server and NFS server. We will learn how to enable synchronization with Rsync and set Windows clients to access storage servers.

Installing the Samba server

In this recipe, we will learn how to install Samba as our network storage server. Samba is a collection of open source applications that implement **Server Message Block** (**SMB**) and **Common Internet File System** (**CIFS**) protocols on Unix systems. This allows Samba to be accessible across different types of network system. Samba provides various other functionalities, such as a domain controller for the networks of Windows systems. In this recipe, we will focus on using Samba as a storage server.

Getting ready

You will need access to a root account or an account with `sudo` privileges

If your server is using any firewall system, make sure to open the necessary network ports. Samba runs on TCP 139 and 445 and UDP ports 137 and 138. Check *Chapter 2, Networking*, for more details on firewall configuration.

How to do it...

Follow these steps to install the Samba server:

1. Install the Samba server with the following command:

```
$ sudo apt-get update
$ sudo apt-get install samba -y
```

2. After installation is complete, you can check the Samba version with the following command:

```
$ smbd --version
```

3. Next, we need to configure Samba to enable sharing on the network. First, create a backup of the original configuration file:

```
$ sudo cp /etc/samba/smb.conf /etc/samba/smb.conf.orignl
```

4. Next, open `smb.conf` and replace its contents with the following:

```
[global]
workgroup = WORKGROUP
server string = Samba Server
netbios name = ubuntu
security = user
map to guest = bad user
```

```
dns proxy = no
[Public]
path = /var/samba/shares/public
browsable =yes
writable = yes
guest ok = yes
read only = no
create mask = 644
```

5. Next, we need to create a shared directory:

   ```
   $ sudo mkdir -p /var/samba/shares/public
   ```

6. Change the directory permissions to make it world writable:

   ```
   $ sudo chmod 777 /var/samba/shares/public
   ```

7. Restart the Samba service for the changes to take effect:

   ```
   $ sudo service smbd restart
   ```

Now you can access this Samba share on the Windows client. Open Windows Explorer and in the address bar, type in \\ubuntu or \\your-server-ip. You should see the shared directory, Public, as follows:

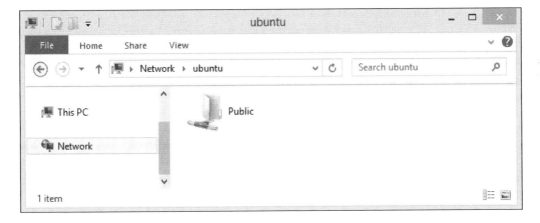

How it works...

Samba is quite an old technology, especially in the age of Cloud storage such as Dropbox and Amazon S3. However, when it comes to private networking, Samba offers a hassle-free setup and is always available for free. All you need is a small server with some free storage space. The release of Samba 4 has added **Active Directory** (**AD**) support. Now it's possible to set up Windows AD on Linux servers. Support for AD comes with a wide range of other features, including DNS for name resolution, centralized storage, and authentication with LDAP and Kerberos.

As you can see in the preceding example, setting up Samba is quick and easy, and you can easily get started with network storage within minutes. We can install the Samba server with a single command, as Samba packages are available in the Ubuntu default package repository. After installation, we have created a new quick and dirty configuration file which defines a few parameters, such as the server name (netbios name) and a share definition. We have created a publicly-shared directory where everyone can read and write the contents.

Once you are done with installation and initial testing, make sure that you remove public sharing and enable authenticated access to your Samba shares. You don't want the server to fill up with data from unknown people. In the next recipes, we will take a closer look at user management and access control for Samba shares.

There's more...

To secure your Samba installation and limit access to your local network or subnet, you can use the following configuration parameters:

```
[globals]
hosts deny = ALL
hosts allow = xxx.xxx.xxx.xxx/yy 127.
interfaces = eth0 lo
bind interfaces only = Yes
```

This configuration limits Samba to listen only on listed interfaces. In this case, its eth0, the Ethernet network, and lo, localhost. Connection requests from all other hosts are denied.

Tools for personal file sharing

If you need a simple file sharing tool for your personal use and do not want to set up and configure Samba, then you can try using a tool named OwnCloud. It is very similar to Dropbox and is open source. It gives you web access to all your files and documents. Plus, you get desktop and mobile client apps to sync all files to a remote server.

Another good tool is BitTorrent Sync. Again, this is a file synchronization tool, but this time it is peer-to-peer file synchronization. If you really care about the privacy and security of data, then this tool is made for you. All files are synchronized between two or more systems (say, your desktop and laptop) without the use of any centralized server.

See also

▸ Ubuntu server guide for Samba at `https://help.ubuntu.com/lts/serverguide/samba-fileserver.html`

Adding users to the Samba server

In the previous recipe, we installed the Samba server and created a public share accessible to everyone. In this recipe, we will learn how to add authentication to the Samba server and password protect shared directories.

Getting ready

You will need access to a root account or an account with `sudo` privileges.

Make sure that the Samba server is installed and running.

How to do it...

Follow these steps to add users to the Samba server:

1. Create a new user account. You can use any existing account or add a new Samba only account with the following command. Change `smbuser` to your desired username:

   ```
   $ sudo useradd -d /home/smbuser -s /sbin/nologin smbuser
   ```

2. Now, we need to allocate a Samba password to this new user. First, enter your `sudo` password, followed by the new password for your Samba account, and then verify the password:

   ```
   $ sudo smbpasswd -a smbuser
   ```

```
ubuntu@ubuntu:/var/samba/shares/public$ sudo smbpasswd -a smbuser
[sudo] password for ubuntu:
New SMB password:
Retype new SMB password:
ubuntu@ubuntu:/var/samba/shares/public$
```

3. Create a shared directory for this user and change its ownership:

```
$ sudo chown smbuser:smbuser /var/samba/share/smbuser
```

4. Next, edit the Samba configuration to add the preceding share:

```
[Private]
path = /var/samba/shares/smbuser
browsable = yes
writable = yes
valid users = smbuser
```

5. Save the changes to the configuration file and reload the Samba server:

```
$ sudo service smbd reload
```

6. Now, check in Windows Explorer. You should see the new shared directory. On trying to open that directory, you will be asked for a Samba username and password:

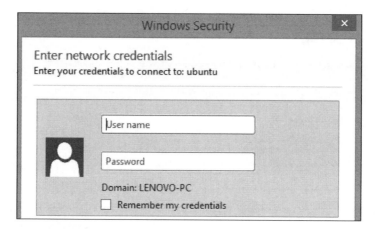

How it works...

Samba allows various different types of configuration for shared resources. In the previous recipe, we learned how to set up a public share, and in this recipe we have created a private share for a single user. We have created a new user with the `nologin` permission. This will allow `smbuser` to access only the Samba shared directory and nothing else. You can also use existing user accounts on the Ubuntu server.

After adding a user, we set a password to be used with the Samba server. Samba maintains a database of passwords separately from Ubuntu passwords. You can enable or disable Samba users with the following commands:

- Enable a Samba user:

  ```
  $ sudo smbpasswd -e username
  ```

- Disable a Samba user:

  ```
  $ sudo smbpasswd -d username
  ```

- Remove a Samba user:

  ```
  $ sudo smbpasswd -x username
  ```

To enable multiple users to access a shared resource, you can specify the list of users under the valid users line, as follows:

```
valid users = userone, usertwo, userthree
```

Similarly, you can limit write permissions to a set of users, as follows:

```
write list = userone, usertwo
```

Samba also supports the sharing of users, `home` directories. This will enable users to create shares for all existing Ubuntu users with a single block of configuration. Add the following lines to the Samba configuration to enable the sharing of `home` directories:

```
[homes]
browseable = No
valid users = %S
```

After this configuration, user's home directories will be available at `//server-name/user-name`. You will be required to provide a username and password to access these shares. Home directories are by default shared as read only. To enable write permissions, add the following line to the preceding block:

```
writable = yes
```

Note that on Windows, you will not be able to access multiple `home` directories from a single Windows system. Windows does not allow multiple user authentications to a single host.

Alternatively, to share a directory with a group of users, you can use group sharing. Use the following line to share a directory with a group of users:

```
path=/var/samba/shares/group-share
valid users = @groupname
```

Then, set group ownership on the directory, `group-share`:

```
$ sudo chgrp groupname /var/samba/shares/group-share
```

There are some other directives such as `create mask`, `directory mask`, `force user`, and `force group`. These directives can be used to determine the permissions and ownership of the newly created files under Samba share.

After any changes to the Samba configuration file, use `testparm` to check the configuration for any syntax errors:

```
$ testparm
```

It should show the Loaded services file OK message, as listed in following screenshot:

```
ubuntu@ubuntu:~$ testparm
Load smb config files from /etc/samba/smb.conf
rlimit_max: increasing rlimit_max (1024) to minimum Windows limit (16384)
Processing section "[Private]"
Loaded services file OK.
Server role: ROLE_STANDALONE
Press enter to see a dump of your service definitions

[global]
        server string = Samba Server %v
```

There's more...

With the release of version 4, Samba can be set as a domain controller. Check the official documentation for more details at the following link:

`https://wiki.samba.org/index.php/Setup_a_Samba_Active_Directory_Domain_Controller`

You can also configure the Samba server to authenticate against the LDAP server. LDAP installation and configuration is covered in *Chapter 14, Centralized Auth Service*. For more details on Samba and LDAP integration, check out the Ubuntu server guide at `https://help.ubuntu.com/lts/serverguide/samba-ldap.html`.

See also

► Linux home server Samba guide at `http://www.brennan.id.au/18-Samba.html#useraccounts`

Installing the secure FTP server

In this recipe, we will learn how to install the **File Transfer Protocol** (**FTP**) server and configure it to use SSL encryption.

Getting ready

You will need access to a root account or an account with `sudo` privileges.

How to do it...

Follow these steps to install the secure FTP server:

1. Install `vsftpd` with the following command:

   ```
   $ sudo apt-get update
   $ sudo apt-get install vsftpd
   ```

2. After installation, we can configure `vsftpd` by editing `/etc/vsftpd.conf`.

3. First create the SSL certificate for the FTP server:

   ```
   sudo openssl req -x509 -nodes -days 365 -newkey rsa:2048 -keyout /etc/ssl/private/vsftpd.pem -out /etc/ssl/private/vsftpd.pem
   ```

4. Next, configure Vsftpd. Add or edit the following lines in `vsftpd.conf`:

   ```
   anonymous_enable=no
   local_enable=yes
   write_enable=yes
   chroot_local_user=yes
   Add the SSL certificate created in the previous step:
   rsa_cert_file=/etc/ssl/private/vsftpd.pem
   rsa_private_key_file=/etc/ssl/private/vsftpd.pem
   ssl_enable=yes
   ssl_ciphers=high
   force_local_data_ssl=yes
   force_local_logins_ssl=yes
   ```

5. Save and exit the configuration file.

6. Restart the Vsftpd server:

```
$ sudo service vsftpd restart
```

7. Now you can use any FTP client that supports the SFTP protocol to connect to your FTP server. The following is the configuration screen for SFTP client FileZilla:

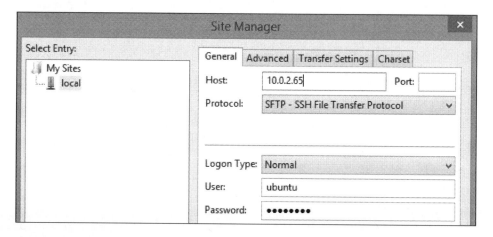

How it works...

FTP is an insecure protocol and you should avoid using it, especially in a production environment. Limit use of FTP to downloads only and use more secure methods, such as SCP, to upload and transfer files on servers. If you have to use FTP, make sure that you have disabled anonymous access and enable SFTP to secure your data and login credentials.

In this recipe, we have installed Vsftpd, which is a default FTP package in the Ubuntu repository. Vsftpd stands for very secure FTP daemon, and it is designed to protect against possible FTP vulnerabilities. It supports both FTP and SFTP protocols.

As Vsftpd is available in the Ubuntu package repository, installation is very simple, using only a single command. After Vsftpd installed, we created an SSL certificate to be used with an FTP server. With this configuration, we will be using the SFTP protocol, which is more secure than FTP. You can find more details about SSL certificates in *Chapter 3, Working with Web Servers*.

Under the Vsftpd configuration, we have modified some settings to disable anonymous logins, allowed local users to use FTP, enabled write access, and used chroot for local users. Next, we have set a path for previously generated SSL certificates and enabled the use of SSL. Additionally, you can force the use of TLS over SSL by adding the following lines to the configuration file:

```
ssl_tlsv1=yes
ssl_sslv2=no
ssl_sslv3=no
```

There's more...

This recipe covers FTP as a simple and easy-to-use tool for network storage. FTP is inherently insecure and you must avoid its use in a production environment. Server deployments can easily be automated with simple Git hooks or the sophisticated integration of continuous deployment tools such as Chef, Puppet, or Ansible.

See also

▶ Ubuntu server FTP guide at `https://help.ubuntu.com/lts/serverguide/ftp-server.html`

Synchronizing files with Rsync

In this recipe, we will learn how to use the Rsync utility to synchronize files between two directories or between two servers.

How to do it...

Follow these steps to synchronize files with Rsync:

1. Set up key-based authentication between source and destination servers. We can use password authentication as well, which is described later in this recipe.

2. Create a sample directory structure on the source server. You can use existing files as well:

   ```
   ubuntu@src$ mkdir sampledir
   ubuntu@src$ touch sampledir/file{1..10}
   ```

3. Now, use the following command to synchronize the entire directory from the
    source server to your local system. Note the / after `sampledir`. This will copy
    contents of `sampledir` in the `backup`. Without /, the entire `sampledir` will be
    copied to the `backup`:

    ubuntu@dest$ rsync -azP -e ssh
    ubuntu@10.0.2.8:/home/ubuntu/sampledir/ backup

    As this is the first time, all files from `sampledir` on the remote server will be
    downloaded in a `backup` directory on your local system. The output of the
    command should look like the following screenshot:

    ```
    ubuntu@dest:~$ rsync -azP -e ssh ubuntu@10.0.2.8:/home/ubuntu/sampledir/ backup
    receiving incremental file list
    ./
    file1
                  0 100%    0.00kB/s    0:00:00 (xfr#1, to-chk=22/24)
    file10
                  0 100%    0.00kB/s    0:00:00 (xfr#2, to-chk=21/24)
    file11
    ```

4. You can check the downloaded files with the `ls` command:

    $ ls -l backup

5. Add one new file on the remote server under `sampledir`:

    ubuntu@src$ touch sampledir/file22

6. Now re-execute the `rsync` command on the destination server. This time, `rsync` will
    only download a new file and any other update files. The output should look similar to
    the following screenshot:

    ubuntu@dest$ rsync -azP -e ssh
    ubuntu@10.0.2.8:/home/ubuntu/sampledir backup

    ```
    ubuntu@dest:~$ rsync -azP -e ssh ubuntu@10.0.2.8:/home/ubuntu/sampledir/ backup
    receiving incremental file list
    ./
    file22
                  0 100%    0.00kB/s    0:00:00 (xfr#1, to-chk=7/25)
    ubuntu@dest:~$
    ```

7. To synchronize two local directories, you can simply specify the source and
    destination path with `rsync`, as follows:

    $ rsync /var/log/mysql ~/mysql_log_backup

How it works...

Rsync is a well known command line file synchronization utility. With Rsync, you can synchronize files between two local directories, as well as files between two servers. This tool is commonly used as a simple backup utility to copy or move files around systems. The advantage of using Rsync is that file synchronization happens incrementally, that is, only new and modified files will be downloaded. This saves bandwidth as well as time. You can quickly schedule a daily backup with a cron and Rsync. Open a cron jobs file with `ctontab-e` and add the following line to enable daily backups:

```
$ crontab -e     # open crontab file
@daily rsync -aze ssh ubuntu@10.0.2.50:/home/ubuntu/sampledir
/var/backup
```

In the preceding example, we have used a pull operation, where we are downloading files from the remote server. Rsync can be used to upload files as well. Use the following command to push files to the remote server:

```
$ rsync -azP -e ssh backup
ubuntu@10.0.2.50:/home/ubuntu/sampledir
```

Rsync provides tons of command line options. Some options that are used in the preceding example are –a, a combination of various other flags and stands for achieve. This option enables recursive synchronization and preserves modification time, symbolic links, users, and group permissions. Option -z is used to enable compression while transferring files, while option -P enables progress reports and the resumption of interrupted downloads by saving partial files.

We have used one more option, -e, which specifies which remote shell to be used while downloading files. In the preceding command, we are using SSH with public key authentication. If you have not set public key authentication between two servers, you will be asked to enter a password for your account on the remote server. You can skip the -e flag and rsync will use a non-encrypted connection to transfer data and login credentials.

Note that the SSH connection is established on the default SSH port, port 22. If your remote SSH server runs on a port other than 22, then you can use a slightly modified version of the preceding command as follows:

```
rsync -azP -e "ssh -p port_number" source destination
```

Anther common option is --exclude, which specifies the pattern for file names to be excluded. If you need to specify multiple exclusion patterns, then you can specify all such patterns in a text file and include that file in command with the options --exclude-from=filename. Similarly, if you need to include some specific files only, you can specify the inclusion pattern with options --include=pattern or --include-from=filename.

Exclude a single file or files matching with a single pattern:

```
$ rsync -azP --exclude 'dir*' source/ destination/
```

Exclude a list of patterns or file names:

```
$ rsync -azP --exclude-from 'exclude-list.txt' source/
destination/
```

By default, Rsync does not delete destination files, even if they are deleted from the source location. You can override this behavior with a `--delete` flag. You can create a backup of these files before deleting them. Use the `--backup` and `--backup-dir` options to enable backups. To delete files from the source directory, you can use the `--remove-source-files` flag. Another handy option is `--dry-run`, which simulates a transfer with the given flags and displays the output, but does not modify any files. You should use `--dry-run` before using any deletion flags.

Use this to remove source files with `--dry-run`:

```
$ rsync --dry-run --remove-source-files -azP source/
destination/
```

There's more...

Rsync is a great tool to quickly synchronize the files between source and destination, but it does not provide bidirectional synchronization. It means the changes are synchronized from source to destination and not vice versa. If you need bi-directional synchronization, you can use another utility, Unison. You can install Unison on Debian systems with the following command:

```
$ sudo apt-get -y install unison
```

Once installed, Unison is very similar to Rsync and can be executed as follows:

```
$ unison /home/ubuntu/documents
ssh://10.0.2.56//home/ubuntu/documents
```

You can get more information about Unison in the manual pages with the following command:

```
$ man unison
```

If you wish to have your own Dropbox-like mirroring tool which continuously monitors for local file changes and quickly replicates them to network storage, then you can use Lsyncd. Lsyncd is a live synchronization or mirroring tool, which monitors the local directory tree for any events (with inotify and `fsevents`), and then after few seconds spawns a synchronization process to mirror all changes to a remote location. By default, Lsyncd uses Rsync for synchronization.

As always, Lsyncd is available in the Ubuntu package repository and can be installed with a single command, as follows:

```
$ sudo apt-get install lsyncd
```

To get more information about Lsyncd, check the manual pages with the following command:

```
$ man lsyncd
```

See also

▶ Ubuntu Rsync community page at `https://help.ubuntu.com/community/rsync`

Performance tuning the Samba server

In this recipe, we will look at Samba configuration parameters in order to get optimum performance out of your Samba installation.

Getting ready

You will need root access or an account with `sudo` privileges.

It is assumed that you have installed the Samba server and it is properly working.

How to do it...

1. Open the Samba configuration file located at `/etc/samba/smb.conf`:

    ```
    $ sudo vi /etc/samba/smb.conf
    ```

2. Add or edit the following options under the `global` section of the configuration file:

    ```
    [global]
    log level = 1
    socket options = TCP_NODELAY IPTOS_LOWDELAY SO_RCVBUF=131072 SO_SNDBUF=131072 SO_KEEPALIVE
    read raw = Yes
    write raw = Yes
    strict locking = No
    oplocks = yes
    max xmit = 65535
    dead time = 15
    ```

```
getwd cache = yes
aio read size = 16384
aio write size = 16384
use sendfile = true
```

3. Save the configuration file and restart the Samba service:

```
$ sudo service smbd restart
```

How it works...

The Samba server provides various configuration parameters. It uses TCP sockets to connect with clients and for data transfer. You should compare Samba's performance with similar TCP services such as FTP.

The preceding example lists some commonly used configuration options for Samba. Some of these options may work for you and some of them may not. The latest Samba version ships with default values for these options that work fairly well for common network conditions. As always, test these options one at a time or in a group, and benchmark each modification to get optimum performance.

The explanation for the preceding is as follows:

- ▸ log level: The default log level is set to 0. Samba produces a lot of debugging information and writing all this to disk is a slow operation. Increasing the log level results in increased logs and poor performance. Unless you are debugging the server, it is good to have the log level set to the lowest value.

- ▸ socket options: These are the TCP/IP stack level options.

- ▸ read raw and write raw: These options enable Samba to use large read and writes to a network up to 64 KB in a single request. Some older clients may have issues with raw reads and writes. Check your setup before using these options.

- ▸ dead time and so_keepalive: These options set periodic checks for dead connections and close such connections and free unused memory.

- ▸ oplocks: This allows clients to cache files locally and results in overall performance improvement. The default setting disables oplocks.

- ▸ aio read size and aio write size: This **Asynchronous IO (AIO)** allows Samba to read and write asynchronously when a file's size is bigger than the specified size values.

You can find various other options and respective explanations in the Samba manual pages. Use the following command to open the manual pages on your server:

```
$ man smbd
```

Troubleshooting the Samba server

In this recipe, we will look at the various tools available for troubleshooting Samba shares.

How to do it...

Samba troubleshooting can be separated in to three parts: network connectivity, Samba process issues, and Samba configuration issues. We will go through each of them step by step. As a first step for troubleshooting, let's start with network testing.

Checking network connectivity

Follow these steps to check network connectivity:

1. Send ping requests to the Samba server to check network connectivity:

    ```
    $ ping samba-server-ip
    ```

2. Check name resolution. Ping the Samba server by its name. Windows uses `netbios` for name resolution:

    ```
    $ ping samba-server-name
    ```

3. Check the Samba configuration for network restrictions. Temporarily open Samba to all hosts.

4. Use `tcpdump` to check Samba network communication. Start `tcpdump` as follows and let it run for some time while accessing the Samba server from clients. All packets will be logged in a file named `tcpdump` in the current directory:

    ```
    $ sudo tcpdump -p -s 0 -w tcpdumps port 445 or port 139
    ```

    ```
    ubuntu@ubuntu:~$ sudo tcpdump -p -s 0 -w tcpdumps port 445 or port 139
    [sudo] password for ubuntu:
    tcpdump: listening on eth0, link-type EN10MB (Ethernet), capture size 65535 byte
    s
    ```

5. If you know the client IP address, you can filter `tcpdumps` with the following command:

    ```
    $ sudo tcpdump -s 0 -w tcpdumps host client_IP
    ```

6. Connect to the Samba process with `telnet`:

   `$ echo "hello" | telnet localhost 139`

```
ubuntu@ubuntu:~$ echo "hello" | telnet localhost 139
Trying ::1...
Connected to localhost.
Escape character is '^]'.
Connection closed by foreign host.
```

7. Check whether your Samba server uses a firewall. If so, check the allowed ports on your firewall. If the firewall is on, make sure you have allowed the Samba ports as follows:

```
ubuntu@ubuntu:~$ sudo ufw show added
Added user rules (see 'ufw status' for running firewall):
ufw allow 139
ufw allow 445
ubuntu@ubuntu:~$
```

8. Try connecting to FTP or a similar TCP service on the Samba server. This may identify the problems with the TCP stack.

9. Use `nmblookup` to test `netbios name` resolution for Windows systems.

Checking the Samba service

Follow these steps to check Samba service:

1. Check whether the Samba service has started properly:

   `$ sudo service samba status`

2. Use `netstat` to check the Samba daemon is listening on the network:

   `$ sudo netstat -plutn`

```
ubuntu@ubuntu:~$ sudo netstat -plutn | grep smbd
tcp       0      0 0.0.0.0:445          0.0.0.0:*          LISTEN
704/smbd
tcp       0      0 0.0.0.0:139          0.0.0.0:*          LISTEN
704/smbd
tcp6      0      0 :::445               :::*              LISTEN
704/smbd
tcp6      0      0 :::139               :::*              LISTEN
704/smbd
```

3. Use `ps` to check the Samba processes. Look for the process name, `smbd`, in the output of the following command:

   ```
   $ ps aux
   ```

4. Use `strace` to view the Samba process logs. This will list all filesystem activities by `smbd` process:

   ```
   $ strace smbd
   ```

Checking Samba logs

Follow these steps to check Samba logs:

1. Check Samba log files for any warning or errors.

2. Increase the log level to get more debugging information:

   ```
   [global]
   log level = 3
   ```

3. Enable logging for a specific client with client-specific configuration. First, set the following options under `smb.conf` to enable client-specific configuration:

   ```
   [global]
       log level = 0
       log file = /var/log/samba/log.%m
       include = /etc/samba/smb.conf.%m
   ```

4. Now create a new configuration file for a specific client:

   ```
   $ sudo vi /etc/samba/smb.conf.client1
   [global]
   log level = 3
   ```

5. Similarly, you can create separate logs for each Samba user:

   ```
   [global]
       log level = 0
       log file = /var/log/samba/log.%u
       include = /etc/samba/smb.conf.%u
   ```

Checking Samba configuration

Follow these steps to check Samba configuration:

1. Check the registered users and accounts in the Samba server user database with the `pdbedit` command:

    ```
    $ sudo pdbedit -L
    ```

    ```
    ubuntu@ubuntu:~$ sudo pdbedit -L
    smbuser:1001:
    ubuntu:1000:ubuntu
    ubuntu@ubuntu:~$
    ```

2. Check the shares with the `smbtree` command:

    ```
    ubuntu@ubuntu:~$ smbtree
    Enter ubuntu's password:
    WORKGROUP
            \\UBUNTU                          Samba Server 4.1.6-Ubuntu
                    \\UBUNTU\Private
                    \\UBUNTU\IPC$                        IPC Service (Samba Server 4.1.6-
    Ubuntu)
    ubuntu@ubuntu:~$
    ```

3. Use the `testparm` command to find any errors in the Samba configuration:

    ```
    $ testparm
    ```

4. Check for allowed users and group names. Make sure that group names start with the @ symbol.

5. Back up your configuration files and then use minimal configuration to test Samba:

    ```
    [global]
        workgroup = WORKGROUP
        security = user
        browsable = yes
    [temp]
        path = /tmp
        public = yes
    ```

Publicly writable directories are not good for server security.
Remove the preceding configuration as soon as testing is finished.

6. Test your configuration with `smbcclient`. It should list all Samba shares:

```
$ smbclient -L localhost -U%
```

```
ubuntu@ubuntu:~$ smbclient -L localhost -U%
Domain=[WORKGROUP] OS=[Unix] Server=[Samba 4.1.6-Ubuntu]

        Sharename       Type        Comment
        ---------       ----        -------
        IPC$            IPC         IPC Service (Samba Server 4.1.6-Ubuntu)
        Private         Disk
Domain=[WORKGROUP] OS=[Unix] Server=[Samba 4.1.6-Ubuntu]
```

See also

▶ Samba docs troubleshooting at `https://www.samba.org/samba/docs/using_samba/ch12.html`

Installing the Network File System

Network File System (**NFS**) is a distributed filesystem protocol that allows clients to access remote files and directories as if they are available on the local system. This allows client systems to leverage large centrally shared storage. Users can access the same data from any system across the network. A typical setup for NFS includes a server that runs the NFS daemon, nfsd, and lists (export) files and directories to be shared. A client system can mount these exported directories as their local file system.

In this recipe, we will learn how to install the NFS server and client systems.

Getting ready

You will need two Ubuntu systems: one as a central NFS server and another as a client. For this recipe, we will refer to the NFS server with the name `Host` and the NFS client with the name `Client`. The following is an example IP address configuration for the `Host` and `Client` systems:

```
Host - 10.0.2.60
Client - 10.0.2.61
```

You will need access to a root account on both servers, or at least an account with `sudo` privileges.

How to do it...

Follow these steps to install NFS:

1. First, we need to install the NFS server:

    ```
    $ sudo apt-get update
    $ sudo apt-get install nfs-kernel-server
    ```

2. Create the directories to be shared:

    ```
    $ sudo mkdir /var/nfs
    ```

3. Add this directory to NFS exports under /etc/exports:

    ```
    $ sudo nano /etc/exports
    ```

4. Add the following line to /etc/exports:

    ```
    /var/nfs       *(rw,sync,no_subtree_check)
    ```

5. Save and close the exports file.

6. Now, restart the NFS service:

    ```
    $ sudo service nfs-kernel-server restart
    ```

7. Next, we need to configure the client system to access NFS shares.

8. Create a mount point for NFS shares.

9. Install the nfs-common package on the client side:

    ```
    $ sudo apt-get install nfs-common
    $ sudo mkdir -p /var/nfsshare
    ```

10. Mount the NFS shared directory on the newly-created mount point:

    ```
    $ sudo mount 10.0.2.60:/var/nfs /var/nfsshare
    ```

11. Confirm the mounted share with the following command:

    ```
    $ mount -t nfs
    ```

12. Now, change the directory to /var/nfsshare, and you are ready to use NFS.

How it works...

In the preceding example, we have installed the NFS server and then created a directory that will share with clients over the network. The configuration file `/etc/exports` contains all NFS shared directories. The syntax to add new exports is as follows:

```
directory_to_share    client_IP_or_name(option1, option2,
option..n)
```

The options used in exports are as follows:

- `rw`: This enables read/write access. You can enable read-only access with the `ro` option.

- `sync`: This forces the NFS server to write changes to disk before replying to requests. sync is the default option; you can enable async operations by explicitly stating async. Async operations may get a little performance boost but at the cost of data integrity.

- `no_subtree_check`: This disables subtree checking, which provides more stable and reliable NFS shares.

You can check the `exports` documentation for more export options. Use the `man` command to open the `exports` manual pages, as follows:

```
$ man exports
```

In the preceding example, we have used the `mount` command to mount the NFS share. Once the client system has restarted, this mount will be removed. To remount the NFS share on each reboot, you can add the following line to `/etc/fstab` file:

```
10.0.2.60:/var/nfs   /var/nfsshare   nfs4   _netdev,auto  0  0
```

To mount all shares exported by the NFS server, you can use the following command:

```
$ sudo mount 10.0.2.60:/ /var/nfsshare
```

There's more...

NFS 4.1 adds support for pNFS, which enables clients to access the storage device directly and in parallel. This architecture eliminates scalability and performance issues with NFS deployments.

See also

- NFS exports options at `http://manpages.ubuntu.com/manpages/trusty/man5/exports.5.html`
- Parallel NFS at `http://www.pnfs.com/`
- NFS documentation in manual pages, by using the following command:

```
$ man nfs
```

7

Cloud Computing

In this chapter, we will cover the following recipes:

- ▶ Creating virtual machine with KVM
- ▶ Managing virtual machines with virsh
- ▶ Setting up your own cloud with OpenStack
- ▶ Adding a cloud image to OpenStack
- ▶ Launching a virtual instance with OpenStack
- ▶ Installing Juju a service orchestration framework
- ▶ Managing services with Juju

Introduction

Cloud computing has become the most important terminology in the computing sphere. It has reduced the effort and cost required to set up and operate the overall computing infrastructure. It has helped various businesses quickly start their business operations without wasting time planning their IT infrastructure, and has enabled really small teams to scale their businesses with on-demand computing power.

The term **cloud** is commonly used to refer to a large network of servers connected to the Internet. These servers offer a wide range of services and are available for the general public on a pay-per-use basis. Most cloud resources are available in the form of **Software as a Service (SaaS)**, **Platform as a Service (PaaS)**, or **Infrastructure as a Service (IaaS)**. A SaaS is a software system hosted in the cloud. These systems are generally maintained by large organizations; a well-known example that we commonly use is Gmail and the Google Docs service. The end user can access these application through their browsers. He or she can just sign up for the service, pay the required fees, if any, and start using it without any local setup. All data is stored in the cloud and is accessible from any location.

PaaS provide a base platform to develop and run applications in the cloud. The service provider does the hard work of building and maintaining the infrastructure and provides easy-to-use APIs that enable developers to quickly develop and deploy an application. Heroku and the Google App Engine are well-known examples of PaaS services.

Similarly, IaaS provides access to computing infrastructure. This is the base layer of cloud computing and provides physical or virtual access to computing, storage, and network services. The service builds and maintains actual infrastructure, including hardware assembly, virtualization, backups, and scaling. Examples include Amazon AWS and the Google Compute Engine. Heroku is a platform service built on top of the AWS infrastructure.

These cloud services are built on top of virtualization. Virtualization is a software system that enables us to break a large physical server into multiple small virtual servers that can be used independently. One can run multiple isolated operating systems and applications on a single large hardware server. Cloud computing is a set of tools that allows the general public to utilize these virtual resources at a small cost.

Ubuntu offers a wide range of virtualization and cloud computing tools. It supports hypervisors, such as KVM, XEN, and QEMU; a free and open source cloud computing platform, OpenStack; the service orchestration tool Juju and machine provisioning tool MAAS. In this chapter, we will take a brief look at virtualization with KVM. We will install and set up our own cloud with OpenStack and deploy our applications with Juju.

Creating virtual machine with KVM

Ubuntu server gives you various options for your virtualization needs. You can choose from KVM, XEN, QEMU, VirtualBox, and various other proprietary and open source tools. KVM, or Kernel virtual machine, is the default hypervisor on Ubuntu. In this recipe, we will set up a virtual machine with the help of KVM. Ubuntu, being a popular cloud distribution provides prebuilt cloud images that can be used to start virtual machines in the cloud. We will use one of these prebuilt images to build our own local virtual machine.

Getting ready

As always, you will need access to the root account or an account with sudo privileges.

How to do it...

Follows these steps to install KVM and launch a virtual machine using cloud image:

1. To get started, install the required packages:

    ```
    $ sudo apt-get install kvm cloud-utils \
    genisoimage bridge-utils
    ```

Before using KVM, you need to check whether your CPU supports hardware virtualization, which is required by KVM. Check CPU support with the following command:

`$ kvm-ok`

You should see output like this:

`INFO: /dev/kvm exists`

KVM acceleration can be used.

2. Next, download the cloud images from the Ubuntu servers. I have selected the Ubuntu 14.04 Trusty image:

```
$ wget http://cloud-
images.ubuntu.com/releases/trusty/release/ubuntu-14.04-server-
cloudimg-amd64-disk1.img -O trusty.img.dist
```

This image is in a compressed format and needs to be converted into an uncompressed format. This is not strictly necessary but should save on-demand decompression when an image is used. Use the following command to convert the image:

```
$ qemu-img convert -O qcow2 trusty.img.dist trusty.img.orig
```

3. Create a copy-on-write image to protect your original image from modifications:

```
$ qemu-img create -f qcow2 -b trusty.img.orig trusty.img
```

4. Now that our image is ready, we need a `cloud-config` disk to initialize this image and set the necessary user details. Create a new file called `user-data` and add the following data to it:

```
$ sudo vi user-data
#cloud-config
password: password
chpasswd: { expire: False }
ssh_pwauth: True
```

This file will set a password for the default user, `ubuntu`, and enable password authentication in the SSH configuration.

5. Create a disk with this configuration written on it:

```
$ cloud-localds my-seed.img user-data
```

6. Next, create a network bridge to be used by virtual machines. Edit `/etc/network/interfaces` as follows:

```
auto eth0
iface eth0 inet manual

auto br0
iface br0 inet dhcp
    bridge_ports eth0
```

> On Ubuntu 16.04, you will need to edit files under the `/etc/network/interfaces.d` directory. Edit the file for `eth0` or your default network interface, and create a new file for `br0`. All files are merged under `/etc/network/interfaces`.

7. Restart the networking service for the changes to take effect. If you are on an SSH connection, your session will get disconnected:

```
$ sudo service networking restart
```

8. Now that we have all the required data, let's start our image with KVM, as follows:

```
$ sudo kvm -netdev bridge,id=net0,br=br0 \
-net user -m 256 -nographic \
-hda trusty.img -hdb my-seed.img
```

This should start a virtual machine and route all input and output to your console. The first boot with `cloud-init` should take a while. Once the boot process completes, you will get a login prompt. Log in with the username `ubuntu` and the password specified in user-data.

9. Once you get access to the shell, set a new password for the user `ubuntu`:

```
$ sudo passwd ubuntu
```

After that, uninstall the cloud-init tool to stop it running on the next boot:

```
$ sudo apt-get remove cloud-init
```

Your virtual machine is now ready to use. The next time you start the machine, you can skip the second disk with the cloud-init details and route the system console to VNC, as follows:

```
$ sudo kvm -netdev bridge,id=net0,br=br0 \
-hda trusty.img \
-m 256 -vnc 0.0.0.0:1 -daemonize
```

How it works...

Ubuntu provides various options to create and manage virtual machines. The previous recipe covers basic virtualization with KVM and prebuilt Ubuntu Cloud images. KVM is very similar to desktop virtualization tools such as VirtualBox and VMware. It comes as a part of the Qemu emulator and uses hardware acceleration features from the host CPU to boost the performance of virtual machines. Without hardware support, the machines need to run inside the Qemu emulator.

After installing KVM, we have used Ubuntu cloud image as our pre-installed boot disk. Cloud images are prebuilt operating system images that do not contain any user data or system configuration. These images need to be initialized before being used. Recent Ubuntu releases contain a program called cloud-init, which is used to initialize the image at first boot. The cloud-init program looks for the metadata service on the network and queries user-data once the service is found. In our case, we have used a secondary disk to pass user data and initialize the cloud image.

We downloaded the prebuilt image from the Ubuntu image server and converted it to uncompressed format. Then, we created a new snapshot with the backing image set to the original prebuilt image. This should protect our original image from any modifications so that it can be used to create more copies. Whenever you need to restore a machine to its original state, just delete the newly created snapshot images and recreate it. Note that you will need to use the cloud-init process again during such restores.

This recipe uses prebuilt images, but you can also install the entire operating system on virtual machines. You will need to download the required installation medium and attach a blank hard disk to the VM. For installation, make sure you set the VNC connection to follow the installation steps.

There's more...

Ubuntu also provides the `virt-manager` graphical interface to create and manage KVM virtual machines from a GUI. You can install it as follows:

```
$ sudo apt-get install virt-manager
```

Alternatively, you can also install Oracle VirtualBox on Ubuntu. Download the `.deb` file for your Ubuntu version and install it with `dpkg -i`, or install it from the package manager as follows:

1. Add the Oracle repository to your installation sources. Make sure to substitute `xenial` with the correct Ubuntu version:

   ```
   $ sudo vi /etc/apt/sources.list

   deb http://download.virtualbox.org/virtualbox/debian xenial
   contrib
   ```

2. Add the Oracle public keys:

```
wget -q
https://www.virtualbox.org/download/oracle_vbox_2016.asc -O- |
sudo apt-key add -
```

3. Install VirtualBox:

```
$ sudo apt-get update && sudo apt-get install virtualbox-5.0
```

See also

▸ VirtualBox downloads: `https://www.virtualbox.org/wiki/Linux_Downloads`

▸ Ubuntu Cloud images on a local hypervisor: `https://help.ubuntu.com/community/UEC/Images#line-105`

▸ The Ubuntu community page for KVM: `https://help.ubuntu.com/community/KVM`

Managing virtual machines with virsh

In the previous recipe, we saw how to start and manage virtual machines with KVM. This recipe covers the use of Virsh and virt-install to create and manage virtual machines. The `libvirt` Linux library exposes various APIs to manage hypervisors and virtual machines. Virsh is a command-line tool that provides an interface to libvirt APIs.

To create a new machine, Virsh needs the machine definition in XML format. virt-install is a Python script to easily create a new virtual machine without manipulating bits of XML. It provides an easy-to-use interface to define a machine, create an XML definition for it and then load it in Virsh to start it.

In this recipe, we will create a new virtual machine with virt-install and see how it can be managed with various Virsh commands.

Getting ready

You will need access to the root account or an account with `sudo` privileges.

▸ Install the required packages, as follows:

```
$ sudo apt-get update
```

```
$ sudo apt-get install -y qemu-kvm libvirt-bin virtinst
```

▸ Install packages to create the cloud init disk:

```
$ sudo apt-get install genisoimage
```

▸ Add your user to the `libvirtd` group and update group membership for the current session:

```
$ sudo adduser ubuntu libvirtd
$ newgrp libvirtd
```

How to do it...

We need to create a new virtual machine. This can be done either with an XML definition of the machine or with a tool called virt-install. We will again use the prebuilt Ubuntu Cloud images and initialize them with a secondary disk:

1. First, download the Ubuntu Cloud image and prepare it for use:

```
$ mkdir ubuntuvm && cd ubuntuvm
$ wget -O trusty.img.dist \
http://cloud-images.ubuntu.com/releases/trusty/release/ubuntu-
14.04-server-cloudimg-amd64-disk1.img
$ qemu-img convert -O qcow2 trusty.img.dist trusty.img.orig
$ qemu-img create -f qcow2 -b trusty.img.orig trusty.img
```

2. Create the initialization disk to initialize your cloud image:

```
$ sudo vi user-data
#cloud-config
password: password
chpasswd: { expire: False }
ssh_pwauth: True
$ sudo vi meta-data
instance-id: ubuntu01;
local-hostname: ubuntu
$ genisoimage -output cidata.iso -volid cidata -joliet \
-rock user-data meta-data
```

3. Now that we have all the necessary data, let's create a new machine, as follows:

```
$ virt-install --import --name ubuntu01 \
--ram 256 --vcpus 1 --disk trusty.img \
--disk cidata.iso,device=cdrom \
--network bridge=virbr0 \
--graphics vnc,listen=0.0.0.0 --noautoconsole -v
```

This should create a virtual machine and start it. A display should be opened on the local VNC port 5900. You can access the VNC through other systems available on the local network with a GUI.

 You can set up local port forwarding and access VNC from your local system as follows:

```
$ ssh kvm_hostname_or_ip -L 5900:127.0.0.1:5900
$ vncviewer localhost:5900
```

4. Once the cloud-init process completes, you can log in with the default user, ubuntu, and the password set in user-data.

5. Now that the machine is created and running, we can use the virsh command to manage this machine. You may need to connect virsh and qemu before using them:

```
$ virsh connect qemu:///system
```

6. Get a list of running machines with virsh list. The --all parameter will show all available machines, whether they are running or stopped:

```
$ virsh list --all # or virsh --connect qemu:///system list
```

7. You can open a console to a running machine with virsh as follows. This should give you a login prompt inside the virtual machine:

```
$ virsh console ubuntu01
```

To close the console, use the *Ctrl +]* key combination.

8. Once you are done with the machine, you can shut it down with virsh shutdown. This will call a shutdown process inside the virtual machine:

```
$ virsh shutdown ubuntu01
```

You can also stop the machine without a proper shutdown, as follows:

```
$ virsh destroy ubuntu01
```

9. To completely remove the machine, use virsh undefine. With this command, the machine will be deleted and cannot be used again:

```
$ virsh destroy ubuntu01
```

How it works...

Both the `virt-install` and `virsh` commands collectively give you an easy-to-use virtualization environment. Additionally, the system does not need to support hardware virtualization. When it's available, the virtual machines will use KVM and hardware acceleration, and when KVM is not supported, Qemu will be used to emulate virtual hardware.

With `virt-install`, we have easily created a KVM virtual machine. This command abstracts the XML definition required by libvirt. With a list of various parameters, we can easily define all the components with their respective configurations. You can get a full list of `virt-install` parameters with the `--help` flag.

> The `virtinst` package, which installs `virt-install`, also contains some more commands, such as `virt-clone`, `virt-admin`, and `virt-xml`. Use tab completion in your bash shell to get a list of all `virt-*` commands.

Once the machine is defined and running, it can be managed with `virsh` subcommands. Virsh provides tons of subcommands to manage virtual machines, or domains as they are called by libvirt. You can start or stop machines, pause and resume them, or stop them entirely. You can even modify the machine configuration to add or remove devices as needed, or create a clone of an existing machine. To get a list of all machine (domain) management commands, use `virsh help domain`.

Once you have your first virtual machine, it becomes easier to create new machines using the XML definition from it. You can dump the XML definition with `virsh dumpxml machine`, edit it as required, and then create a new machine using XML configuration with `virsh create configuration.xml`.

There are a lot more options available for the `virsh` and `virt-install` commands; check their respective manual pages for more details.

There's more...

In the previous example, we used cloud images to quickly start a virtual machine. You do not need to use cloud machines, and you can install the operating system on your own using the respective installation media.

Download the installation media and then use following command to start the installation. Make sure you change the `-c` parameter to the downloaded ISO file, along with the location:

```
$ sudo virt-install -n ubuntu -r 1024 \
--disk path=/var/lib/libvirt/images/ubuntu01.img,bus=virtio,size=4 \
-c ubuntu-16.04-server-i386.iso \
--network network=default,model=virtio
--graphics vnc,listen=0.0.0.0 --noautoconsole -v
```

The command will wait for the installation to complete. You can access the GUI installation using the VNC client.

Forward your local port to access VNC on a KVM host. Make sure you replace 5900 with the respective port from virsh vncdisplay node0:

```
$ ssh kvm_hostname_or_ip -L 5900:127.0.0.1:5900
```

Now you can connect to VNC at `localhost:5900`.

Easy cloud images with uvtool

Ubuntu provides another super easy tool named uvtool. This tool focuses on the creation of virtual machines out of Ubuntu Cloud images. It synchronizes cloud images from Ubuntu servers to your local machine. Later, these images can be used to launch virtual machines in minutes. You can install and use uvtool with the following commands:

```
$ sudo apt-get install uvtool
```

Download the Xenial image from the cloud images:

```
$ uvt-simplestreams-libvirt sync release=xenial arch=amd64
```

Start a virtual machine:

```
$ uvt-kvm create virtsys01
```

Finally, get the IP of a running system:

```
$ uvt-kvm ip virtsys01
```

Check out the manual page with the `man uvtool` command and visit the official uvtool page at `https://help.ubuntu.com/lts/serverguide/cloud-images-uvtool.html` for more details.

See also

- Check out the manual pages for virt-install using $ `man virt-install`
- Check out the manual pages for virsh using $ `man virsh`
- The official Libvirt site: `http://libvirt.org/`
- The Libvirt documentation on Ubuntu Server guide: `https://help.ubuntu.com/lts/serverguide/libvirt.html`

Setting up your own cloud with OpenStack

We have already seen how to create virtual machines with KVM and Qemu, and how to manage them with tools such as virsh and virt-manager. This approach works when you need to work with a handful of machines and manage few hosts. To operate on a larger scale, you need a tool to manage host machines, VM configurations, images, network, and storage, and monitor the entire environment. OpenStack is an open source initiative to create and manage a large pool of virtual machines (or containers). It is a collection of various tools to deploy IaaS clouds. The official site defines OpenStack as an operating system to control a large pool of compute, network, and storage resources, all managed through a dashboard.

OpenStack was primarily developed and open-sourced by Rackspace, a leading cloud service provider. With its thirteenth release, Mitaka, OpenStack provides tons of tools to manage various components of your infrastructure. A few important components of OpenStack are as follows:

- **Nova**: Compute controller
- **Neutron**: OpenStack networking
- **Keystone**: Identity service
- **Glance**: OpenStack image service
- **Horizon**: OpenStack dashboard
- **Cinder**: Block storage service
- **Swift**: Object store
- **Heat**: Orchestration program

OpenStack in itself is quite a big deployment. You need to decide the required components, plan their deployment, and install and configure them to work in sync. The installation itself can be a good topic for a separate book. However, the OpenStack community has developed a set of scripts known as DevStack to support development with faster deployments. In this recipe, we will use the DevStack script to quickly install OpenStack and get an overview of its workings. The official OpenStack documentation provides detailed documents for the Ubuntu based installation and configuration of various components. If you are planning a serious production environment, you should read it thoroughly.

Getting ready

You will need a non-root account with `sudo` privileges. The default account named `ubuntu` should work.

The system should have at least two CPU cores with at least 4 GB of RAM and 60 GB of disk space. A static IP address is preferred. If possible, use the minimal installation of Ubuntu.

 If you are performing a fresh installation of Ubuntu Server, press *F4* on the first screen to get installation options, and choose **Install Minimal System**. If you are installing inside a virtual machine, choose **Install Minimal Virtual Machine**. You may need to go to the installation menu with the *Esc* key before using *F4*.

DevStack scripts are available on GitHub. Clone the repository or download and extract it to your installation server. Use the following command to clone:

```
$ git clone https://git.openstack.org/openstack-dev/devstack \
-b stable/mitaka --depth 1
$ cd devstack
```

You can choose to get the latest release by selecting the master branch. Just skip the `-b stable/mitaka` option from the previous command.

How to do it...

Once you obtain the DevStack source, it's as easy as executing an installation script. Before that, we will create a minimal configuration file for passwords and basic network configuration:

1. Copy the sample configuration to the root of the `devstack` directory:

    ```
    $ cp samples/local.conf
    ```

2. Edit `local.conf` and update passwords:

    ```
    ADMIN_PASSWORD=password
    DATABASE_PASSWORD=password
    RABBIT_PASSWORD=password
    SERVICE_PASSWORD=$ADMIN_PASSWORD
    ```

3. Add basic network configuration as follows. Update IP address range as per your local network configuration and set `FLAT_INTERFACE` to your primary Ethernet interface:

    ```
    FLOATING_RANGE=192.168.1.224/27
    ```

```
FIXED_RANGE=10.11.12.0/24
FIXED_NETWORK_SIZE=256
FLAT_INTERFACE=eth0
```

Save the changes to the configuration file.

4. Now, start the installation with the following command. As the Mitaka stable branch has not been tested with Ubuntu Xenial (16.04), we need to use the FORCE variable. If you are using the master branch of DevStack or an older version of Ubuntu, you can start the installation with the `./stack.sh` command:

    ```
    $ FORCE=yes ./stack.sh
    ```

    The installation should take some time to complete, mostly depending on your network speed. Once the installation completes, the script should output the dashboard URL, keystone API endpoint, and the admin password:

```
This is your host IP address: 192.168.1.10
This is your host IPv6 address: ::1
Horizon is now available at http://192.168.1.10/dashboard
Keystone is serving at http://192.168.1.10:5000/
The default users are: admin and demo
The password: password
ubuntu@ubuntu:~/devstack$
```

5. Now, access the OpenStack dashboard and log in with the given username and password. The admin account will give you an admin interface. The login screen looks like this:

6. Once you log in, your admin interface should look something like this:

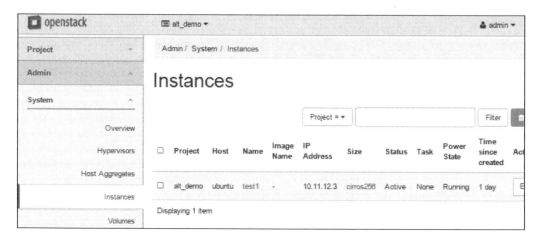

Now, from this screen, you can deploy new virtual instances, set up different cloud images, and configure instance flavors.

How it works...

We used DevStack, an unattended installation script, to install and configure basic OpenStack deployment. This will install OpenStack with the bare minimum components for deploying virtual machines with OpenStack. By default, DevStack installs the identity service, Nova network, compute service, and image service. The installation process creates two user accounts, namely `admin` and `dummy`. The `admin` account gives you administrative access to the OpenStack installation and the `dummy` account gives you the end user interface. The DevStack installation also adds a Cirros image to the image store. This is a basic lightweight Linux distribution and a good candidate to test OpenStack installation.

The default installation creates a basic flat network. You can also configure DevStack to enable Neutron support, by setting the required options in the configuration. Check out the DevStack documentation for more details.

There's more...

Ubuntu provides its own easy-to-use OpenStack installer. It provides options to install OpenStack, along with LXD support and OpenStack Autopilot, an enterprise offering by Canonical. You can choose to install on your local machine (all-in-one installation) or choose a **Metal as a Service** (**MAAS**) setup for a multinode deployment. The single-machine setup will install OpenStack on multiple LXC containers, deployed and managed through Juju. You will need at least 12 GB of main memory and an 8-CPU server. Use the following commands to get started with the Ubuntu OpenStack installer:

```
$ sudo apt-get update
$ sudo apt-get install conjure-up
$ conjure-up openstack
```

While DevStack installs a development-focused minimal installation of OpenStack, various other scripts support the automation of the OpenStack installation process. A notable project is OpenStack Ansible. This is an official OpenStack project and provides production-grade deployments. A quick GitHub search should give you a lot more options.

See also

- ▶ A step-by-step detailed guide to installing various OpenStack components on Ubuntu server: `http://docs.openstack.org/mitaka/install-guide-ubuntu/`
- ▶ DevStack Neutron configuration: `http://docs.openstack.org/developer/devstack/guides/neutron.html`
- ▶ OpenStack Ansible: `https://github.com/openstack/openstack-ansible`
- ▶ A list of OpenStack resources: `https://github.com/ramitsurana/awesome-openstack`
- ▶ Ubuntu MaaS: `http://www.ubuntu.com/cloud/maas`
- ▶ Ubuntu Juju: `http://www.ubuntu.com/cloud/juju`
- ▶ Read more about LXD and LXC in *Chapter 8, Working with Containers*

Adding a cloud image to OpenStack

In the previous recipe, we installed and configured OpenStack. Now, to start using the service, we need to upload virtual machine images. The OpenStack installation uploads a test image named Cirros. This is a small Linux distribution designed to be used as a test image in the cloud. We will upload prebuilt cloud images available from Ubuntu.

Getting ready

Make sure you have installed the OpenStack environment and you can access the OpenStack dashboard with valid credentials. It is not necessary to have an admin account to create and upload images.

Select the cloud image of your choice and get its download URL. Here, we will use the Trusty Ubuntu Server image. The selected image format is QCOW2, though OpenStack support various other image formats. The following is the URL for the selected image:

```
https://cloud-images.ubuntu.com/trusty/current/trusty-server-
cloudimg-amd64-disk1.img
```

How to do it...

The OpenStack dashboard provides a separate section for image management. You can see the images that are already available and add or remove your own images. Follow these steps to create your own image:

1. Log in to your OpenStack dashboard. On successful login, you should get an **Overview** page for your account.

2. Now, from the left-hand side **Project** menu, under the **Compute** submenu, click on **Images**:

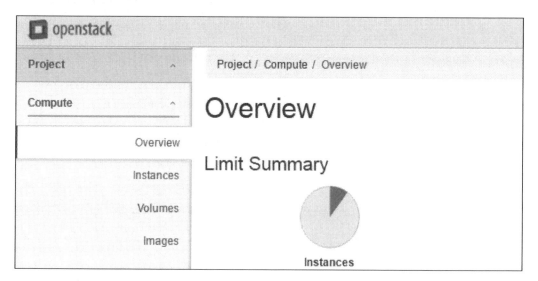

This should show you a list of all publicly available images—something like this:

3. Click on the **Create Image** button to add a new image. This should open a popup box with various details. Here, you can choose to add an image URL or enter an image path if you have downloaded the image to your local machine.

4. Fill in the name and other required details. Under **Image Source**, select the image location, and in the next box, **Image Location**, enter the URL for the Ubuntu Cloud image.

5. Under **Format**, select the image format of your selected image. In this case, it's **QCOW2**.

6. Enter amd64 under **Architecture**. Make sure you match this with your selected image.

7. Enter the minimum disk and RAM size. As we have selected an Ubuntu image, the minimum disk size should be 5 GB and minimum RAM 256 MB. These values will affect the selection of instance flavors while creating a new instance.

8. Finally, click on the **Create Image** button to save the details and add the image to OpenStack. This will download the image from the source URL and save it in the image repository. The resulting image will be listed under the **Project** tab, as follows:

Now, the image is ready can be used to launch new cloud instances.

How it works...

OpenStack is a cloud virtualization platform and needs operating system images to launch virtual machines in the cloud. The Glance OpenStack imaging service provides the image-management service. It supports various types of image, including Qemu format, raw disk files, ISO images, and images from other virtualization platforms, as well as Docker images. Like every other thing in OpenStack, image management works with the help of APIs provided by Glance.

OpenStack, being a cloud platform, is expected to have ready-to-use images that can be used to quickly start a virtual instance. It is possible to upload the operating system installation disk and install the OS to a virtual instance, but that would be a waste of resources. Instead, it is preferable to have prebuilt cloud images. Various popular operating systems provide their respective cloud images, which can be imported to cloud systems. In the previous example, we used the Ubuntu Cloud image for the Ubuntu Trusty release.

We imported the image by specifying its source URI. Local image files can also be uploaded by selecting the image file as an image source. You can also build your own images and upload them to the image store to be used in the cloud. Along with the image source, we need to provide a few more parameters, which include the type of the image being uploaded and the minimum resource requirements of that image. Once the image has been uploaded, it can be used to launch a new instance in the cloud. Also, the image can be marked as public so that it is accessible to all OpenStack users. You will need specific rights for your OpenStack account to create public images.

There's more...

OpenStack images can also be managed from the command line with the client called `glance`. To access the respective APIs from the command line, you need to authenticate with the Glance server. Use the following steps to use `glance` from the command line:

1. First, add authentication parameters to the environment:

```
export OS_USERNAME=demo
export OS_PASSWORD=password
export OS_AUTH_URL=http://10.196.69.158/identity
export OS_TENANT_ID=8fe52bb13ca44981aa15d9b62e9133f4
```

> DevStack makes things even easier by providing a script, openrc. It's located under the `root` directory of DevStack and can be used as follows:
>
> `$ source openrc demo    # source openrc username`
>
> You are then ready, without multiple export commands.

2. Now, use the following command to obtain the image list for the specified user:

   `$ glance image-list`

```
ubuntu@ubuntu:~$ glance image-list
+--------------------------------------+----------------------------------+
| ID                                   | Name                             |
+--------------------------------------+----------------------------------+
| 6948c538-7f52-4439-8e81-e26cdefc8b08 | cirros-0.3.4-x86_64-uec          |
| ad7a5ef1-f500-4e5d-a44e-22710c066938 | cirros-0.3.4-x86_64-uec-kernel   |
| c1b1b13e-1d4c-49c4-8dd6-0e25c3c12ba1 | cirros-0.3.4-x86_64-uec-ramdisk  |
| abf59bb4-68e6-4b89-8b77-8fdaeff7163e | Ubuntu Trusty                    |
| ffddf013-5f6c-4c47-b4fe-e087957680fd | Ubuntu Xenial                    |
+--------------------------------------+----------------------------------+
```

You can get a list of available command-line options with `glance help`.

See also

▶ Read more about OpenStack image management: `http://docs.openstack.org/image-guide/`

▶ Command-line image management: `http://docs.openstack.org/user-guide/common/cli_manage_images.html`

▶ Dashboard image management: `http://docs.openstack.org/user-guide/dashboard_manage_images.html`

▶ Glance documentation: `http://docs.openstack.org/developer/glance/`

Launching a virtual instance with OpenStack

Now that we have OpenStack installed and have set our desired operating system image, we are ready to launch our first instance in a self-hosted cloud.

Getting ready

You will need credentials to access the OpenStack dashboard.

Uploading your own image is not necessary; you can use the default Cirros image to launch the test instance.

Log in to the OpenStack dashboard and set the SSH key pair in the **Access & Security** tab available under the **Projects** menu. Here, you can generate a new key pair or import your existing public key.

 If you generate a new key pair, a file with the .pem extension will be downloaded to your local system. To use this key with PuTTy, you need to use PuTTYgen and extract the public and private keys.

How to do it...

OpenStack instances are the same virtual machines that we launch from the command line or desktop tools. OpenStack give you a web interface to launch your virtual machines from. Follow these steps to create and start a new instance:

1. Select the **Instance** option under the **Projects** menu and then click on the **Launch Instance** button on the right-hand side. This should open a modal box with various options, which will look something like this:

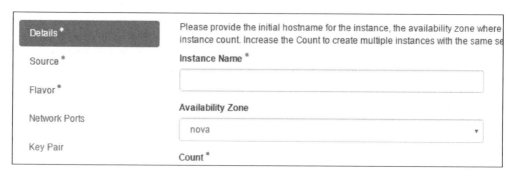

2. Now, start filling in the necessary details. All fields that are marked with ***** are required fields. Let's start by naming our instance. Enter the name in the **Instance Name** field.

3. Set the value of **Count** to the number of instances you want to launch. We will leave it at the default value of **1**.

4. Next, click on the **Source** tab. Here, we need to configure the source image for our instance. Set **Select Boot Source** to **Image** and select **No** for **Create New Volume**. Then, from the **Available Images** section, search the desired image and click on the button with the **+** sign to select the image. The list should contain our recently uploaded image. The final screen should look something like this:

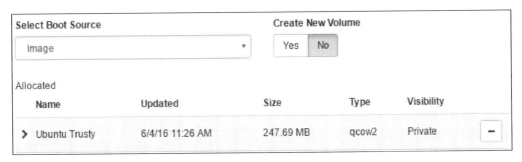

5. Next, on the **Flavor** tab, we need to select the desired resources for our instance. Select the desired flavor by clicking on the **+** button. Make sure that the selected row does not contain any warning signs.

6. Now, from the **Key Pair** tab, select the SSH key pair that we just created. This is required to log in to your instance.

7. Finally, click on the **Launch Instance** button from the bottom of the modal box. A new instance should be created and listed under the instances list. It will take some time to start; wait for the **Status** column to show **Active**:

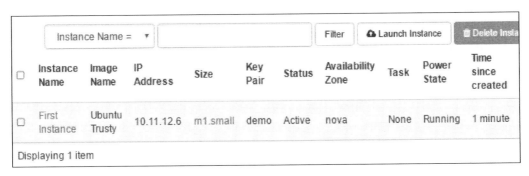

8. You are now ready to access your virtual instance. Log in to your host console and try to ping the IP address of your instance. Then, open an SSH session with the following command:

    ```
    $ ssh -i your_key ubuntu@instance_ip
    ```

    This should give you a shell inside your new cloud instance. Try to ping an external server, such as an OpenDNS server, from within an instance to ensure connectivity.

    To make this instance available on your local network, you will need to assign a floating IP address to it. Click on the drop-down arrow from the **Actions** column and select **Associate Floating IP**. This should add one more IP address to your instance and make it available on your local network.

How it works...

OpenStack instances are the same as the virtual machines that we build and operate with common virtualization tools such as VirtualBox and Qemu. OpenStack provides a central console for deploying and managing thousands of such machines on multiple hosts. Under the hood, OpenStack uses the same virtualization tools as the others. The preferred hypervisor is KVM, and if hardware acceleration is not available, Qemu emulation is used. OpenStack supports various other hypervisors, including VMware, XEN, Hyper-V, and Docker. In addition, a lightervisor, LXD, is on its way to a stable release. Other than virtualization, OpenStack adds various other improvements, such as image management, block storage, object storage, and various network configurations.

In the previous example, we set various parameters before launching a new instance; these include the instance name, resource constraints, operating system image, and login credentials. All these parameters will be passed to the underlying hypervisor to create and start the new virtual machine. A few other options that we have not used are volumes and networks. As we have installed a very basic OpenStack instance, new developments in network configurations are not available for use. You can update your DevStack configuration and install the OpenStack networking component Neutron.

Volumes, on the other hand, are available and can be used to obtain disk images of the desired size and format. You can also attach multiple volumes to a single machine, providing extended storage capacity. Volumes can be created separately and do not depend on the instance. You can reuse an existing volume with a new instance, and all data stored on it will be available to the new instance.

Here, we have used a cloud image to start a new instance. You can also choose a previously stored instance snapshot, create a new volume, or use a volume snapshot. The volume can be a permanent volume, which has its life cycle separate from the instance, or an ephemeral volume, which gets deleted along with the instance. Volumes can also be attached at instance runtime or even removed from an instance, provided they are not a boot source.

Other options include configuration and metadata. The configuration tab provides an option to add initialization scripts that are executed at first boot. This is very similar to cloud-init data. The following is a short example of a cloud-init script:

```
#cloud-config
package_update: true
package_upgrade: true
password: password
chpasswd: { expire: False }
ssh_pwauth: True
ssh_authorized_keys:
  - your-ssh-public-key-contents
```

This script will set a password for the default user (ubuntu in the case of Ubuntu images), enable password logins, add an SSH key to authorize keys, and update and upgrade packages.

The metadata section adds arbitrary data to instances in the form of key-value pairs. This data can be used to identify an instance from a group and automate certain tasks.

Once an instance has been started, you have various management options from the **Actions** menu available on the instance list. From this menu, you can create instance snapshots; start, stop, or pause instances; edit security groups; get the VNC console; and so on.

There's more...

Similar to the `glance` command-line client, a compute client is available as well and is named after the compute component. The `nova` command can be used to create and manage cloud instances from the command line. You can get detailed parameters and options with the `nova help` command or, to get help with a specific subcommand, `nova help <subcommand>`.

See also

- ▸ The cloud-init official documentation: `https://cloudinit.readthedocs.io/en/latest/`
- ▸ More on cloud-init: `https://help.ubuntu.com/community/CloudInit`
- ▸ OpenStack instance guide: `http://docs.openstack.org/user-guide/dashboard_launch_instances.html`
- ▸ Command-line cheat sheet: `http://docs.openstack.org/user-guide/cli_cheat_sheet.html#compute-nova`

Installing Juju a service orchestration framework

Up to now in this chapter, we have learned about virtualization and OpenStack for deploying and managing virtual servers. Now, it's time to look at a service-modeling tool, Juju. Juju is a service-modeling tool for Ubuntu. Connect it to any cloud service, model your application, and press deploy—done. Juju takes care of lower-level configuration, deployments, and scaling, and even monitors your services.

Juju is an open source tool that offers a GUI and command-line interface for modeling your service. Applications are generally deployed as collections of multiple services. For example, to deploy WordPress, you need a web server, a database system, and perhaps a load balancer. Service modeling refers to the relations between these services. Services are defined with the help of **charms**, which are collections of configurations and deployment instructions, such as dependencies and resource requirements. The Juju store provides more than 300 predefined and ready-to-use charms.

Once you model your application with the required charms and their relationships, these models can be stored as a bundle. A bundle represents a set of charms, their configurations, and their relationships with each other. The entire bundle can be deployed to a cloud or local system with a single command. Also, similar to charms, bundles can be shared and are available on the Juju store.

This recipe covers the installation of Juju on Ubuntu Server. With the release of Xenial, the latest Ubuntu release, Canonical has also updated the Juju platform to version 2.0.

Getting ready

You need access to the root account or an account with `sudo` privileges.

Make sure you have the SSH keys generated with your user account. You can generate a new key pair with the following command:

```
$ ssh-keygen -t rsa -b 2048
```

How to do it...

Juju 2.0 is available in the Ubuntu Xenial repository, so installation is quite easy. Follow these steps to install Juju, along with LXD for local deployments:

1. Install Juju, along with the LXD and ZFSUtils packages. On Ubuntu 16, LXD should already be installed:

    ```
    $ sudo apt-get update
    $ sudo apt-get install juju-2.0 lxd zfsutils-linux
    ```

2. The LXD installation creates a new group, `lxd`, and adds the current user to it. Update your group membership with `newgrp` so that you don't need to log out and log back in:

```
$ newgrp lxd
```

3. Now, we need to initialize LXD before using it with Juju. We will create a new ZFS pool for LXD and configure a local `lxd` bridge for container networking with NAT enabled:

```
$ sudo lxd init
Name of the storage backend to use (dir or zfs): zfs
Create a new ZFS pool (yes/no)? yes
Name of the new ZFS pool: lxdpool
Would you like to use an existing block device (yes/no)? no
Size in GB of the new loop device (1GB minimum): 20
Would you like LXD to be available over the network (yes/no)? no
Do you want to configure the LXD bridge (yes/no)? yes
```

LXD has been successfully configured.

4. Now that LXD has been configured, we can bootstrap Juju and create a controller node. The following command will bootstrap Juju with LXD for local deployments:

```
$ juju bootstrap juju-controller lxd
```

This command should take some time to finish as it needs to fetch the container image and the install Juju tools inside the container.

5. Once the bootstrap process completes, you can check the list of controllers, as follows:

```
$ juju list-controllers
CONTROLLER              MODEL     USER          SERVER
local.juju-controller*  default   admin@local
10.155.16.114:17070
```

6. You can also check the LXD container created by Juju using the `lxc list` command:

```
$ lxc list
```

7. From Juju 2.0 onwards, every controller will install the Juju GUI by default. This is a web application to manage the controller and its models. The following command will give you the URL of the Juju GUI:

```
$ juju gui
...
https://10.201.217.65:17070/gui/2331544b-1e16-49ba-8ac7-
2f13ea147497/
...
```

8. You may need to use port forwarding to access the web console. Use the following command to quickly set up iptables forwarding:

```
$ sudo iptables -t nat -A PREROUTING -p tcp --dport 17070 -j
DNAT \
--to-destination 10.201.217.65:17070
```

9. You will also need a username and password to log in to the GUI. To get these details, use the following command:

```
$ juju show-controller --show-passwords juju-controller
...
accounts:
    admin@local:
      user: admin@local
      password: 8fcb8aca6e22728c6ac59b7cba322f39
```

When you log in to the web console, it should look something like this:

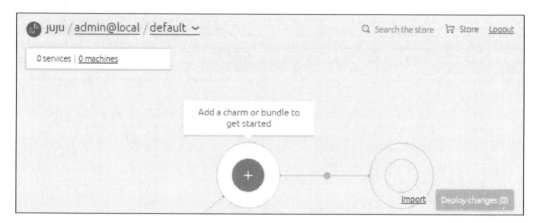

Now, you are ready to use Juju and deploy your applications either with a command line or from the web console.

How it works...

Here, we installed and configured the Juju framework with LXD as a local deployment backend. Juju is a service-modeling framework that makes it easy to compose and deploy an entire application with just a few commands. Now, we have installed and bootstrapped Juju. The bootstrap process creates a controller node on a selected cloud; in our case, it is LXD. The command provides various optional arguments to configure controller machines, as well as pass the credentials to the bootstrap process. Check out the bootstrap help menu with the `juju bootstrap --help` command.

We have used LXD as a local provider, which does not need any special credentials to connect and create new nodes. When using pubic cloud providers or your own cloud, you will need to provide your username and password or access keys. This can be done with the help of the `add-credentials <cloud>` command. All added credentials are stored in a plaintext file: `~/.local/share/juju/credentials.yaml`. You can view a list of available cloud credentials with the `juju list-credentials` command.

The controller node is a special machine created by Juju to host and manage data and models related to an environment. The container node hosts two models, namely admin and default, and the admin model runs the Juju API server and database system. Juju can use multiple cloud systems simultaneously, and each cloud can have its own controller node.

From version 2.0 onwards, every controller node installs the Juju GUI application by default. The Juju GUI is a web application that provides an easy-to-use visual interface to create and manage various Juju entities. With its simple interface, you can easily create new models, import charms, and set up relations between them. The GUI is still available as a separate charm and can be deployed separately to any machine in a Juju environment. The command-line tools are more than enough to operate Juju, and it is possible to skip the installation of the GUI component using the `--no-gui` option with the `bootstrap` command.

There's more...

In the previous example, we used LXD as a local deployment backend for Juju. With LXD, Juju can quickly create new containers to deploy applications. Along with LXD, Juju supports various other cloud providers. You can get a full list of supported cloud providers with the `list-clouds` option:

```
$ juju list-clouds
```

Juju also provides the option to fetch updates to a supported cloud list. With the `update-clouds` subcommand, you can update your local cloud with the latest developments from Juju.

Along with public clouds, Juju also supports OpenStack deployments and MaaS-based infrastructures. You can also create your own cloud configuration and add it to Juju with the `juju add-cloud` command. Like with LXD, you can use virtual machines or even physical machines for Juju-based deployments. As far as you can access the machine with SSH, you can use it with Juju. Check out the cloud-configuration manual for more details: `https://jujucharms.com/docs/devel/clouds-manual`

See also

▸ Read more about Juju concepts at `https://jujucharms.com/docs/devel/juju-concepts`

▸ Get to know Juju-supported clouds or how to add your own at `https://jujucharms.com/docs/devel/clouds`

▸ The Juju GUI: `https://jujucharms.com/docs/devel/controllers-gui`

▸ Juju controllers: `https://jujucharms.com/docs/devel/controllers`

▸ Refer to *Chapter 8, Working with Containers* for more details about LXD containers

▸ Learn how to connect Juju to a remote LXD server: `https://insights.ubuntu.com/2015/11/16/juju-and-remote-lxd-host/`

Managing services with Juju

In the previous recipe, we learned how to install the Juju service orchestration framework. Now, we will look at how to use Juju to deploy and manage a service.

Getting ready

Make sure you have installed and bootstrapped Juju.

How to do it...

We will deploy a sample WordPress installation with a load balancer. The MySQL service will be used as the database for WordPress. Both services are available in the Juju Charm store.

Follow these steps to manage services with Juju:

1. Let's start by deploying the WordPress service with `juju deploy`. This should give you the following output:

```
$ juju deploy wordpress
Added charm "cs:trusty/wordpress-4" to the model.
Deploying charm "cs:trusty/wordpress-4" with the charm series
"trusty".
```

2. Now, deploy a MySQL service to store WordPress contents:

```
$ juju deploy mysql
Added charm "cs:trusty/mysql-38" to the model.
Deploying charm "cs:trusty/mysql-38" with the charm series
"trusty".
```

3. Now, you can use `juju status` to confirm your deployed services. It should show you the deployed services, their relations, and respective machine statuses, as follows:

```
$ juju status
```

```
ubuntu@ubuntu:~$ juju status
[Services]
NAME         STATUS        EXPOSED  CHARM
mysql        maintenance   false    cs:trusty/mysql-38
wordpress    unknown       false    cs:trusty/wordpress-4

[Relations]
SERVICE1     SERVICE2    RELATION      TYPE
mysql        mysql       cluster       peer
wordpress    wordpress   loadbalancer  peer
```

4. Now that both services have been deployed, we need to connect them together so that `wordpress` can use the database service. Juju calls this a relation, and it can be created as follows:

```
$ juju add-relation mysql wordpress
```

5. Finally, we need to expose our `wordpress` service so that it can be accessed outside our local network. By default, all charms start as unexposed and are accessible only on a local network:

```
$ juju expose wordpress
```

You can get the IP address or DNS name of the `wordpress` instance with the `juju status` command from the `Machines` section. Note that in a local LXD environment, you may need a forwarded port to access WordPress.

How it works...

In this example, we deployed two separate services using Juju. Juju will create two separate machines for each of them and deploy the service as per the instructions in the respective charms. These two services need to be connected with each other so that `wordpress` knows the existence of the MySQL database. Juju calls these connections relations. Each charm contains a set of hooks that are triggered on given events. When we create a relation between WordPress and MySQL, both services are informed about it with the `database-relation-changed` hook. At this point, both services can exchange the necessary details, such as MySQL ports and login credentials. The WordPress charm will set up a MySQL connection and initialize a database.

Once both services are ready, we can expose them to be accessed on a public network. Here, we do not need MySQL to be accessible by WordPress users, so we have only exposed the `wordpress` service. WordPress can access MySQL internally, with the help of a relation.

You can use the Juju GUI to visualize your model and add or remove charms and their relations. At this point, if you open a GUI, you should see your charms plotted on the graph and connected with each other through a small line, indicating a relation. The GUI also provides an option to set constraints on a charm and configure charm settings, if any.

Note that both charms internally contain scaling options. WordPress is installed behind an Nginx reverse proxy and can be scaled with extra units as and when required. You can add new units to the service with a single command, as follows:

```
$ juju add-unit mysql -n 1
```

There's more...

When you no longer need these services, the entire model can be destroyed with the `juju destroy-model <modelname>` command. You can also selectively destroy particular services with the `remove-service` command and remove relations with `remove-relations`. Check out the Juju manual page for tons of commands that are not listed in the Juju help menu.

See also

- How to create your own charm: `https://jujucharms.com/docs/stable/authors-charm-writing`
- More about hooks: `https://jujucharms.com/docs/stable/authors-hook-environment`

8
Working with Containers

In this chapter, we will cover the following recipes:

- ▶ Installing LXD, the Linux container daemon
- ▶ Deploying your first container with LXD
- ▶ Managing LXD containers
- ▶ Managing LXD containers – advanced options
- ▶ Setting resource limits on LXD containers
- ▶ Networking with LXD
- ▶ Installing Docker
- ▶ Starting and managing Docker containers
- ▶ Creating images with a Dockerfile
- ▶ Understanding Docker volumes
- ▶ Deploying WordPress using a Docker network
- ▶ Monitoring Docker containers
- ▶ Securing Docker containers

Introduction

Containers are quite an old technology and existed in the form of chroot and FreeBSD Jails. Most of us have already used containers in some form or other. The rise of Docker gave containers the required adoption and popularity. Ubuntu has also released a new tool named LXD with Ubuntu 15.04.

A container is a lightweight virtual environment that contains a process or set of processes. You might already have used containers with chroot. Just as with containers, we create an isolated virtual environment to group and isolate a set of processes. The processes running inside the container are isolated from the base operating system environment, as well as other containers running on the same host. Such processes cannot access or modify anything outside the container. A recent development in the Linux kernel to support namespaces and cgroups has enabled containers to provide better isolation and resource-management capabilities.

One of the reasons for the widespread adoption of containers is the difference between containers and hypervisor-based virtualization, and the inefficiencies associated with virtual machines. A VM requires its own kernel, whereas containers share the kernel with the host, resulting in a fast and lightweight isolated environment. Sharing the kernel removes much of the overhead of VMs and improves resource utilization, as processes communicate with a single shared kernel. You can think of containers as OS-level virtualization.

With containers, the entire application can be started within milliseconds, compared to virtual minutes. Additionally, the image size becomes much smaller, resulting in easier and faster cloud deployments. The shared operating system results in smaller footprints, and saved resources can be used to run additional containers on the same host. It is normal to run hundreds of containers on your laptop.

However, containerization also has its own shortcomings. First, you cannot run cross-platform containers. That is, containers must use the same kernel as the host. You cannot run Windows containers on a Linux host, and vice versa. Second, the isolation and security is not as strong as hypervisor-based virtualization. Containers are largely divided into two categories: OS containers and application containers. As the name suggests, application containers are designed to host a single service or application. Docker is an application container. You can still run multiple processes in Docker, but it is designed to host a single process.

OS containers, on the other hand, can be compared to virtual machines. They provide user space isolation. You can install and run multiple applications and run multiple processes inside OS containers. LXC on Linux and Jails on BSD are examples of OS containers.

In this chapter, we will take a look at LXC, an OS container, and Docker, an application container. In the first part of the chapter, we will learn how to install LXC and deploy a containerized virtual machine. In subsequent recipes, we will work with Docker and related technologies. We will learn to create and deploy a container with Docker.

Installing LXD, the Linux container daemon

LXC is a system built on the modern Linux kernel and enables the creation and management of virtual Linux systems or containers. As discussed earlier, LXC is not a full virtualization system and shares the kernel with the host operating system, providing lightweight containerization. LXC uses Linux namespaces to separate and isolate the processes running inside containers. This provides much better security than simple chroot-based filesystem isolation. These containers are portable and can easily be moved to another system with a similar processor architecture.

Ubuntu 15.04 unveiled a new tool named LXD, which is a wrapper around LXC. The official page calls it a container hypervisor and a new user experience for LXC. Ubuntu 16.04 comes preinstalled with its latest stable release, LXD 2.0. With LXD, you no longer need to work directly with lower-level LXC tools.

LXD adds some important features to LXC containers. First, it runs unprivileged containers by default, resulting in improved security and better isolation for containers. Second, LXD can manage multiple LXC hosts and can be used as an orchestration tool. It also supports the live migration of containers across hosts.

LXD provides a central daemon named LXD and a command-line client named `lxc`. Containers can be managed with the command-line client or the REST APIs provided by the LXD daemon. It also provides an OpenStack plugin, nova-compute-lxd, to deploy containers on the OpenStack cloud.

In this recipe, we will learn to install and configure the LXD daemon. This will set up a base for the next few recipes in this chapter.

Getting ready

You will need access to the root account or an account with `sudo` privileges.

Make sure that you have enough free space available on disk.

How to do it...

Ubuntu 16.04 ships with the latest release of LXD preinstalled. We just need to initialize the LXD daemon to set the basic settings.

1. First, update the `apt` cache and try to install LXD. This should install updates to the LXD package, if any:

   ```
   $ sudo apt-get update
   $ sudo apt-get install lxd
   ```

If you are using Ubuntu 14.04, you can install LXD using the following command:

```
$ sudo apt-get -t trusty-backports install lxd
```

2. Along with LXD, we will need one more package named ZFS—the most important addition to Ubuntu 16.04. We will be using ZFS as a storage backend for LXD:

```
$ sudo apt-get install zfsutils-linux
```

3. Once LXD has been installed, we need to configure the daemon before we start using it. Use `lxd init` to start the initialization process. This will ask some questions about the LXD configuration:

```
$ sudo lxd init
Name of the storage backend to use (dir or zfs): zfs
Create a new ZFS pool (yes/no)? yes
Name of the new ZFS pool: lxdpool
Would you like to use an existing block device (yes/no)? no
Size in GB of the new loop device (1GB minimum): 10
Would you like LXD to be available over the network (yes/no)?
no
Do you want to configure the LXD bridge (yes/no)? yes
Warning: Stopping lxd.service, but it can still be activated
by: lxd.socket
LXD has been successfully configured.
```

Now, we have our LXD setup configured and ready to use. In the next recipe, we will start our first container with LXD.

How it works...

Ubuntu 16.04 comes preinstalled with LXD and makes it even easier to start with system containers or operating system virtualization. In addition to LXD, Ubuntu now ships with inbuilt support for ZFS (OpenZFS), a filesystem with support for various features that improve the containerization experience. With ZFS, you get faster clones and snapshots with copy-on-write, data compression, disk quotas, and automated filesystem repairs.

LXD is a wrapper around lower-level LXC or Linux containers. It provides the REST API for communicating and managing LXC components. LXD runs as a central daemon and adds some important features, such as dynamic resource restrictions and live migrations between multiple hosts. Containers started with LXD are unprivileged containers by default, resulting in improved security and isolation.

This recipe covers the installation and initial configuration of the LXD daemon. As mentioned previously, LXD comes preinstalled with Ubuntu 16. The installation commands should fetch updates to LXD, if any. We have also installed `zfsutils-linux`, a user space package to interact with ZFS. After the installation, we initialized the LXD daemon to set basic configuration parameters, such as the default storage backend and network bridge for our containers.

We selected ZFS as the default storage backend and created a new ZFS pool called `lxdpool`, backed by a simple loopback device. In a production environment, you should opt for a physical device or separate partition. If you have already created a ZFS pool, you can directly name it by choosing `no` for `Create new ZFS pool`. To use a separate storage device or partition, choose `yes` when asked for block storage.

> Use the following commands to get ZFS on Ubuntu 14.04:
> ```
> $ sudo apt-add-repository ppa:zfs-native/stable
> $ sudo apt-get update && sudo apt-get install ubuntu-zfs
> ```

ZFS is the recommended storage backend, but LXD also works with various other options, such as **Logical Volume Manager** (**LVM**) and **btrfs** (pronounced "butter F S"), that offer nearly the same features as ZFS or a simple directory-based storage system.

Next, you can choose to make LXD available on the network. This is necessary if you are planning a multi-host setup and support for migration. The initialization also offers to configure the `lxdbr0` bridge interface, which will be used by all containers. By default, this bridge is configured with IPv6 only. Containers created with the default configuration will have their `veth0` virtual Ethernet adapter attached to `lxdbr0` through a NAT network. This is the gateway for containers to communicate with the outside world. LXD also installs a local DHCP server and the `dnsmasq` package. DHCP is used to assign IP addresses to containers, and `dnsmasq` acts as a local name-resolution service.

If you misplace the network bridge configuration or need to update it, you can use the following command to get to the network configuration screen:

```
$ sudo dpkg-reconfigure -p medium lxd
```

There's more...

The LXD 2.0 version, which ships with Ubuntu 16, is an LTS version. If you want to get your hands on the latest release, then you can install stable versions from the following repository:

```
$ sudo add-apt-repository ppa:ubuntu-lxc/lxd-stable
```

For development releases, change the PPA to `ppa:ubuntu-lxc/lxd-git-master`.

For more information, visit the LXC download page at `https://linuxcontainers.org/lxc/downloads/`.

If you still want to install LXC, you can. Use the following command:

```
$ sudo apt-get install lxc
```

This will install the required user space package and all the commands necessary to work directly with LXC. Note that all LXC commands are prefixed with `lxc-`, for example, `lxc-create` and `lxc-info`. To get a list of all commands, type `lxc-` in your terminal and press *Tab* twice.

See also

- ▶ For more information, check the LXD page of the Ubuntu Server guide: `https://help.ubuntu.com/lts/serverguide/lxd.html`
- ▶ The LXC blog post series is at `https://www.stgraber.org/2013/12/20/lxc-1-0-blog-post-series/`
- ▶ The LXD 2.0 blog post series is at `https://www.stgraber.org/2016/03/11/lxd-2-0-blog-post-series-012/`
- ▶ Ubuntu 16.04 switched to Systemd, which provides its own container framework, systemd-nspawn; read more about systemd containers on its Ubuntu man page at `http://manpages.ubuntu.com/manpages/xenial/man1/systemd-nspawn.1.html`
- ▶ See how to get started with systemd containers at `https://community.flockport.com/topic/32/systemd-nspawn-containers`

Deploying your first container with LXD

In this recipe, we will create our first container with LXD.

Getting ready

You will need access to the root account or an account with `sudo` privileges.

How to do it...

LXD works on the concept of remote servers and images served by those remote servers. Starting a new container with LXD is as simple as downloading a container image and starting a container out of it, all with a single command. Follow these steps:

1. To start your first container, use the `lxc launch` command, as follows:

   ```
   $ lxc launch ubuntu:14.04/amd64 c1
   ```

   LXC will download the required image (`14.04/amd64`) and start the container. You should see the progress like this:

   ```
   ubuntu@ubuntu:~$ lxc launch ubuntu:14.04/amd64 c1
   Creating c1
   Retrieving image: 100%
   Starting c1
   ubuntu@ubuntu:~$
   ```

2. As you can see in the screenshot, `lxc launch` downloads the required image, creates a new container, and then starts it as well. You can see your new container in a list of containers with the `lxc list` command, as follows:

   ```
   $ lxc list
   ```

   ```
   ubuntu@ubuntu:~$ lxc list
   +------+---------+----------------------+------+------------+-----------+
   | NAME | STATE   |         IPV4         | IPV6 |    TYPE    | SNAPSHOTS |
   +------+---------+----------------------+------+------------+-----------+
   | c1   | RUNNING | 10.201.233.13 (eth0) |      | PERSISTENT | 0         |
   +------+---------+----------------------+------+------------+-----------+
   ubuntu@ubuntu:~$
   ```

3. Optionally, you can get more details about the containers with the `lxc info` command:

   ```
   $ lxc info c1
   ```

4. Now that your container is running, you can start working with it. With the `lxc` `exec` command, you can execute commands inside a container. Use the following command to obtain the details of Ubuntu running inside a container:

```
$ lxc exec c1 -- lsb_release -a
```

```
ubuntu@ubuntu:~$ lxc exec c1 -- lsb_release -a
No LSB modules are available.
Distributor ID: Ubuntu
Description:    Ubuntu 14.04.4 LTS
Release:        14.04
Codename:       trusty
```

5. You can also open a bash shell inside a container, as follows:

```
$ lxc exec c1 -- bash
```

How it works...

Creating images is a time-consuming task. With LXD, the team has solved this problem by downloading the prebuilt images from trusted remote servers. Unlike LXC, where images are built locally, LXD downloads them from the remote servers and keep a local cache of these images for later use. The default installation contains three remote servers:

- **Ubuntu**: This contains all Ubuntu releases
- **Ubuntu-daily**: This contains all Ubuntu daily builds
- **images**: This contains all other Linux distributions

You can get a list of available remote servers with this command:

```
$ lxc remote list
```

Similarly, to get a list of available images on a specific remote server, use the following command:

```
$ lxc image list ubuntu:
```

In the previous example, we used 64-bit Ubuntu 14.04 from one of the preconfigured remote servers (`ubuntu:`). When we start a specific container, LXD checks the local cache for the availability of the respective image; if it's not available locally, the required images gets fetched from the remote server and cached locally for later use. These images are kept in sync with remote updates. They also expire if not used for a specific time period, and expired images are automatically removed by LXD. By default, the expiration period is set to 10 days.

You can find a list of various configuration parameters for LXC and LXD documented on GitHub at `https://github.com/lxc/lxd/blob/` `master/doc/configuration.md`.

The `lxc launch` command creates a new container and then starts it as well. If you want to just create a container without starting it, you can do that with the `lxc init` command, as follows:

```
$ lxc init ubuntu:xenial c2
```

All containers (or their `rootfs`) are stored under the `/var/lib/lxd/containers` directory, and images are stored under the `/var/lib/lxd/images` directory.

 All LXD containers are non-privileged containers by default. You do not need any special privileges to create and manage containers. On the other hand, LXD does support privileged containers as well.

While starting a container, you can specify the set of configuration parameters using the `--config` flag. LXD also supports configuration profiles. Profiles are a set of configuration parameters that can be applied to a group of containers. Additionally, a container can have multiple profiles. LXD ships with two preconfigured profiles: `default` and `docker`.

To get a list of profiles, use the `lxc profile list` command, and to get the contents of a profile, use the `lxc profile show <profile_name>` command.

Sometimes, you may need to start a container to experiment with something—execute a few random commands and then undo all the changes. LXD allows us to create such throwaway or ephemeral containers with the `-e` flag. By default, all LXD containers are permanent containers. You can start an ephemeral container using the `--ephemeral` or `-e` flag. When stopped, an ephemeral container will be deleted automatically.

With LXD, you can start and manage containers on remote servers as well. For this, the LXD daemon needs to be exposed to the network. This can be done at the time of initializing LXD or with the following commands:

```
$ lxc config set core.https_address "[::]"
$ lxc config set core.trust_password some-password
```

Next, make sure that you can access the remote server and add it as a remote for LXD with the `lxc remote add` command:

```
$ lxc remote add remote01 192.168.0.11  #  lxc remote add name server_ip
```

Now, you can launch containers on the remote server, as follows:

```
$ lxc launch ubuntu:xenial remote01:c1
```

There's more...

Unlike LXC, LXD container images do not support password-based SSH logins. The container still has the SSH daemon running, but login is restricted to a public key. You need to add a key to the container before you can log in with SSH. LXD supports file management with the `lxc file` command; use it as follows to set your public key inside an Ubuntu container:

```
$ lxc file push ~/.ssh/id_rsa.pub \
c1/home/ubuntu/.ssh/authorized_keys \
--mode=0600 --uid=1000
```

Once the public key is set, you can use SSH to connect to the container, as follows:

```
$ ssh ubuntu@container_IP
```

Alternatively, you can directly open a root session inside a container and get a bash shell with `lxc exec`, as follows:

```
$ lxc exec c1 -- bash
```

See also

- ▸ The LXD getting started guide: `https://linuxcontainers.org/lxd/getting-started-cli/`
- ▸ The Ubuntu Server guide for LXC: `https://help.ubuntu.com/lts/serverguide/lxd.html`
- ▸ Container images are created using tools such as debootstrap, which you can read more about at `https://wiki.debian.org/Debootstrap`
- ▸ Creating LXC templates from scratch: `http://wiki.pcprobleemloos.nl/using_lxc_linux_containers_on_debian_squeeze/creating_a_lxc_virtual_machine_template`

Managing LXD containers

We have installed LXD and deployed our first container with it. In this recipe, we will learn various LXD commands that manage the container lifecycle.

Getting ready...

Make sure that you have followed the previous recipes and created your first container.

How to do it...

Follow these steps to manage LXD containers:

1. Before we start with container management, we will need a running container. If you have been following the previous recipes, you should already have a brand new container running on your system. If your container is not already running, you can start it with the `lxc start` command:

    ```
    $ lxc start c1
    ```

2. To check the current state of a container, use `lxc list`, as follows:

    ```
    $ lxc list c1
    ```

    This command should list only containers that have c1 in their name.

3. You can also set the container to start automatically. Set the `boot.autostart` configuration option to `true` and your container will start automatically on system boot. Additionally, you can specify a delay before autostart and a priority in the autostart list:

    ```
    $ lxc config set c1 boot.autostart true
    ```

4. Once your container is running, you can open a bash session inside a container using the `lxc exec` command:

    ```
    $ lxc exec c1 -- bash
    root@c1:~# hostname
    c1
    ```

    This should give you a root shell inside a container. Note that to use bash, your container image should have a bash shell installed in it. With alpine containers, you need to use `sh` as the shell as alpine does not contain the bash shell.

5. LXD provides the option to pause a container when it's not being actively used. A paused container will still hold memory and other resources assigned to it, but not receive any CPU cycles:

```
$ lxc pause c1
```

```
ubuntu@ubuntu:~$ lxc list c1
+------+--------+----------------------+------+------------+-----------+
| NAME | STATE  |         IPV4         | IPV6 |    TYPE    | SNAPSHOTS |
+------+--------+----------------------+------+------------+-----------+
| c1   | FROZEN | 10.201.233.13 (eth0) |      | PERSISTENT | 0         |
+------+--------+----------------------+------+------------+-----------+
```

6. Containers that are paused can be started again with `lxc start`.

7. You can also restart a container with the `lxc restart` command, with the option to perform a stateful or stateless restart:

```
$ lxc restart --stateless c1
```

8. Once you are done working with the container, you can stop it with the `lxc stop` command. This will release all resources attached to that container:

```
$ lxc stop c1
```

At this point, if your container is an ephemeral container, it will be deleted automatically.

9. If the container is no longer required, you can explicitly delete it with the `lxc delete` command:

```
$ lxc delete c1
```

There's more...

For those who do not like to work with command line tools, you can use a web-based management console known as LXD GUI. This package is still in beta but can be used on your local LXD deployments. It is available on GitHub at `https://github.com/dobin/lxd-webgui`.

See also

▸ Get more details about LXD at `https://www.stgraber.org/2016/03/19/lxd-2-0-your-first-lxd-container-312/`

▸ LXC web panel: `https://lxc-webpanel.github.io/install.html`

Managing LXD containers – advanced options

In this recipe, we will learn about some advanced options provided by LXD.

How to do it...

Follow these steps to deal with LXD containers:

1. Sometimes, you may need to clone a container and have it running as a separate system. LXD provides a `copy` command to create such clones:

   ```
   $ lxc copy c1 c2    # lxc copy source destination
   ```

   You can also create a temporary copy with the `--ephemeral` flag and it will be deleted after one use.

2. Similarly, you can create a container, configure it as per you requirements, have it stored as an image, and use it to create more containers. The `lxc publish` command allows you to export existing containers as a new image. The resulting image will contain all modifications from the original container:

   ```
   $ lxc publish c1 --alias nginx    # after installing nginx
   ```

   The container to be published should be in the stopped state. Alternatively, you can use the `--force` flag to publish a running container, which will internally stop the container before exporting.

3. You can also move the entire container from one system to another. The `move` command helps you with moving containers across hosts. If you move a container on the same host, the original container will be renamed. Note that the container to be renamed must not be running:

   ```
   $ lxc move c1 c2 # container c1 will be renamed to c2
   ```

4. Finally, we have the snapshot and restore functionality. You can create snapshots of the container or, in simple terms, take a backup of its current state. The snapshot can be a stateful snapshot that stores the container's memory state. Use the following command to create a snapshot of your container:

   ```
   $ lxc snapshot c1 snap1    # lxc snapshot container cnapshot
   ```

5. The `lxc list` command will show you the number of snapshots for a given container. To get the details of every snapshot, check the container information with the `lxc info` command:

   ```
   $ lxc info c1
   ...
   ```

```
Snapshots:
    c1/shap1 (taken at 2016/05/22 10:34 UTC) (stateless)
```

 You can skip the snapshot name and LXD will name it for you. But, as of writing this, there's no option to add a description with snapshots. You can use the filename to describe the purpose of each snapshot.

6. Once you have the snapshots created, you can restore it to go back to a point or create new containers out of your snapshots and have both states maintained. To restore your snapshot, use `lxc restore`, as follows:

```
$ lxc restore c1 snap1    # lxc restore container snapshot
```

7. To create a new container out of your snapshot, use `lxc copy`, as follows:

```
$ lxc copy c1/snap1 c4  # lxc copy container/snapshot
new_container
```

8. When you no longer need a snapshot, delete it with `lxc delete`, as follows:

```
$ lxc delete c1/snap1      # lxc delete container/snapshot
```

How it works...

Most of these commands work with the `rootfs` or `root` filesystem of `containers`. The `rootfs` is stored under the `/var/lib/lxd/containers` directory. Copying creates a copy of the `rootfs` while deleting removes the `rootfs` for a given container. These commands benefit with the use of the ZFS file system. Features such as copy-on-write speed up the copy and snapshot operations while reducing the total disk space use.

Setting resource limits on LXD containers

In this recipe, we will learn to set resource limits on containers. LXD uses the cgroups feature in the Linux kernel to manage resource allocation and limits. Limits can be applied to a single container through configuration or set in a profile, applying limits to a group of containers at once. Limits can be dynamically updated even when the container is running.

How to do it...

We will create a new profile and configure various resource limits in it. Once the profile is ready, we can use it with any number of containers. Follow these steps:

1. Create a new profile with the following command:

```
$ lxc profile create cookbook
Profile cookbook created
```

2. Next, edit the profile with `lxc profile edit`. This will open a text editor with a default profile structure in YML format:

```
$ lxc profile edit cookbook
```

Add the following details to the profile. Feel free to select any parameters and change their values as required:

```
name: cookbook
config:
  boot.autostart: "true"
  limits.cpu: "1"
  limits.cpu.priority: "10"
  limits.disk.priority: "10"
  limits.memory: 128MB
  limits.processes: "100"
description: A profile for Ubuntu Cookbook Containers
devices:
  eth0:
    nictype: bridged
    parent: lxdbr0
    type: nic
```

Save your changes to the profile and exit the text editor.

3. Optionally, you can check the created profile, as follows:

```
$ lxc profile show cookbook
```

```
ubuntu@ubuntu:~$ lxc profile show cookbook
name: cookbook
config:
  boot.autostart: "true"
  limits.cpu: "1"
  limits.cpu.priority: "10"
  limits.disk.priority: "10"
```

4. Now, our profile is ready and can be used with a container to set limits. Create a new container using our profile:

```
$ lxc launch ubuntu:xenial c4 -p cookbook
```

5. This should create and start a new container with the cookbook profile applied to it. You can check the profile in use with the lxc info command:

```
$ lxc info c4
```

```
ubuntu@ubuntu:~$ lxc info c4
Name: c4
Architecture: x86_64
Created: 2016/05/22 17:44 UTC
Status: Running
Type: persistent
Profiles: cookbook
Pid: 13300
```

6. Check the memory limits applied to container c4:

```
$ lxc exec c4 -- free -m
```

7. Profiles can be updated even when they are in use. All containers using that profile will be updated with the respective changes, or return a failure message. Update your profile as follows:

```
$ lxc profile set cookbook limits.memory 256MB
```

How it works...

LXD provides multiple options to set resource limits on containers. You can apply limits using profiles or configure containers separately with the lxc config command. The advantage of creating profiles is that you can have various parameters defined in one central place, and all those parameters can be applied to multiple containers at once. A container can have multiple profiles applied and also have configuration parameters explicitly set. The overlapping parameters will take a value from the last applied profile. Also the parameters that are set explicitly using lxc config will override any values set by profiles.

The LXD installation ships with two preconfigured profiles. One is **default**, which is applied to all containers that do not receive any other profile. This contains a network device for a container. The other profile, named **docker**, configures the required kernel modules to run Docker inside the container. You can view the parameters of any profile with the lxc profile show profile_name command.

In the previous example, we used the `edit` option to edit the profile and set multiple parameters at once. You can also set each parameter separately or update the profile with the `set` option:

```
$ lxc profile set cookbook limits.memory 256MB
```

Similarly, use the `get` option to read any single parameter from a profile:

```
$ lxc profile get cookbook limits.memory
```

Profiles can also be applied to a running container with `lxc profile apply`. The following command will apply two profiles, `default` and `cookbook`, to an existing container, `c6`:

```
$ lxc profile apply c6 default,cookbook
```

 We could have skipped the network configuration in the `cookbook` profile and had our containers use the default profile along with `cookbook` to combine both configurations.

Updating the profiles will update the configuration for all container using that profile. To modify a single container, you can use `lxc config set` or pass the parameters directly to a new container using the `-c` flag:

```
$ lxc launch ubuntu:xenial c7 -c limits.memory=64MB
```

Similar to `lxc profile`, you can use the edit option with `lxc config` to modify multiple parameters at once. The same command can also be used to configure or read server parameters. When used without any container name, the command applies to the LXD daemon.

There's more...

The `lxc profile` and `lxc config` commands can also be used to attach local devices to containers. Both commands provide the option to work with various devices, which include network, disk IO, and so on. The simplest example will be to pass a local directory to a container, as follows:

```
$ lxc config device add c1 share disk \
source=/home/ubuntu path=home/ubuntu/shared
```

▸ Read more about setting resource limits at `https://www.stgraber. org/2016/03/26/lxd-2-0-resource-control-412`

▸ For more details about LXC configuration, check the help menu for the `lxc profile` and `lxc config` commands, as follows:

```
$ lxc config --help
```

Networking with LXD

In this recipe, we will look at LXD network setup. By default, LXD creates an internal bridge network. Containers are set to access the Internet through **Network Address Translation (NAT)** but are not accessible from the Internet. We will learn to open a service on a container to the Internet, share a physical network with a host, and set a static IP address to a container.

Getting ready

As always, you will need access to the root account or an account with `sudo` privileges.

Make sure that you have created at least one container.

How to do it...

By default, LXD sets up a NAT network for containers. This is a private network attached to the `lxdbr0` port on the host system. With this setup, containers get access to the Internet, but the containers themselves or the services running in the containers are not accessible from an outside network. To open a container to an external network, you can either set up port forwarding or use a bridge to attach the container directly to the host's network:

1. To set up port forwarding, use the `iptables` command, as follows:

   ```
   $ sudo iptables -t nat -A PREROUTING -p tcp -i eth0 \
   --dport 80 -j DNAT --to 10.106.147.244:80
   ```

   This will forward any traffic on the host TCP port `80` to the containers' TCP port `80` with the IP `10.106.147.244`. Make sure that you change the port and IP address as required.

2. You can also set a bridge that connects all containers directly to your local network. The bridge will use an Ethernet port to connect to the local network. To set a bridge network with the host, we first need to create a bridge on the host and then configure the container to use that bridge adapter.

   To set up a bridge on the host, open the `/etc/network/interfaces` file and add the following lines:

   auto br0

   iface br0 inet dhcp

       bridge_ports eth0

   Make sure that you replace `eth0` with the name of the interface connected to the external network.

3. Enable IP forwarding under `sysctl`. Find the following line in `/etc/sysctl.conf` and uncomment it:

   net.ipv4.ip_forward=1

4. Start a new bridge interface with the `ifup` command:

   $ sudo ifup br0

> Note that if you are connected to a server over SSH, your connection will break. Make sure to have a snapshot of the working state before changing your network configuration.

5. If required, you can restart the networking service, as follows:

   $ sudo service networking restart

6. Next, we need to update the LXD configuration to use our new bridge interface. Execute a reconfiguration of the LXD daemon and choose <No> when asked to create a new bridge:

   $ sudo dpkg-reconfigure -p medium lxd

Would you like to setup a network bridge for LXD containers now?

           <Yes>

7. Then on the next page, choose `<Yes>` to use an existing bridge:

```
Do you want to use an existing bridge?

            <Yes>                           <No>
```

8. Enter the name of the newly created bridge interface:

```
A valid network interface name (e.g. lxdbr0).

Bridge interface name:

br0_

                    <Ok>
```

This should configure LXD to use our own bridge network and skip the internal bridge. You can check the new configuration under the default profile:

```
$ lxc profile show default
```

```
description: Default LXD profile
devices:
  eth0:
    name: eth0
    nictype: bridged
    parent: br0
    type: nic
```

9. Now, start a new container. It should receive the IP address from the router on your local network. Make sure that your local network has DHCP configured:

```
ubuntu@ubuntu:~$ lxc list
+------+---------+-----------------------+------+------------+-----------+
| NAME |  STATE  |          IPV4         | IPV6 |    TYPE    | SNAPSHOTS |
+------+---------+-----------------------+------+------------+-----------+
|  c5  | RUNNING | 192.168.0.104 (eth0)  |      | PERSISTENT |     0     |
+------+---------+-----------------------+------+------------+-----------+
```

How it works...

By default, LXD sets up a private network for all containers. A separate bridge, `lxdbr0`, is set up and configured in the default profile. This network is shared (NAT) with the host system, and containers can access the Internet through this network. In the previous example, we used IPtables port forwarding to make the container port 80 available on the external network. This way, containers will still use the same private network, and a single application will be exposed to the external network through the host system. All incoming traffic on host port 80 will be directed to the container's port 80.

You can also set up your own bridge connected to the physical network. With this bridge, all your containers can connect to and be directly accessible over your local network. Your local DHCP will be used to assign IP addresses to containers. Once you create a bridge, you need to configure it with LXD containers either through profiles or separately with container configuration. In the previous example, we reconfigured the LXD network to set a new bridge.

> If you are using virtual machines for hosting containers and want to set up a bridge, then make sure that you have enabled promiscuous mode on the network adapter of the virtual machine. This can be enabled from the network settings of your hypervisor. Also, a bridge setup may not work if your physical machine is using a wireless network.

LXD supports more advanced network configuration by attaching the host `eth` interface directly to a container. The following settings in the container configuration will set the network type to a physical network and use the host's `eth0` directly inside a container. The `eth0` interface will be unavailable for the host system till the container is live:

```
$ lxc config device add c1 eth0 nic nictype=physical parent=eth0
```

There's more...

LXD creates a default bridge with the name `lxdbr0`. The configuration file for this bridge is located at `/etc/default/lxd-bridge`. This file contains various configuration parameters, such as the address range for the bridge, default domain, and bridge name. An interesting parameter is the additional configuration path for dnsmasq configurations.

The LXD bridge internally uses dnsmasq for DHCP allocation. The additional configuration file can be used to set up various dnsmasq settings, such as address reservation and name resolution for containers.

Edit `/etc/default/lxd-bridge` to point to the dnsmasq configuration file:

```
# Path to an extra dnsmasq configuration file
LXD_CONFILE="/etc/default/dnsmasq.conf"
```

Then, create a new configuration file called `/etc/default/dnsmasq.conf` with the following contents:

```
dhcp-host=c5,10.71.225.100
server=/lxd/10.71.225.1
#interface=lxdbr0
```

This will reserve the IP `10.71.225.100` for the container called `c5`, and you can also ping containers with that name, as follows:

```
$ ping lxd.c5
```

See also

- Read more about bridge configuration at `https://wiki.debian.org/LXC/SimpleBridge`
- Find out more about LXD bridge at the following links:
    - `https://insights.ubuntu.com/2016/04/07/lxd-networking-lxdbr0-explained/`
    - `http://askubuntu.com/questions/754323/lxd-2-0-local-networking`
    - `https://insights.ubuntu.com/2015/11/10/converting-eth0-to-br0-and-getting-all-your-lxc-or-lxd-onto-your-lan/`
- Read more about dnsmasq at `https://wiki.debian.org/HowTo/dnsmasq`
- Sample dnsmasq configuration file: `http://oss.segetech.com/intra/srv/dnsmasq.conf`
- Check the dnsmasq manual pages with the `man dnsmasq` command

Installing Docker

In last few recipes, we learned about LXD, an operating system container service. Now, we will look at a hot new technology called Docker. Docker is an application container designed to package and run a single service. It enables developers to enclose an app with all dependencies in an isolated container environment. Docker helps developers create a reproducible environment with a simple configuration file called a Dockerfile. It also provides portability by sharing the Dockerfile, and developers can be sure that their setup will work the same on any system with the Docker runtime.

Docker is very similar to LXC. Its development started as a wrapper around the LXC API to help DevOps take advantage of containerization. It added some restrictions to allow only a single process to be running in a container, unlike a whole operating system in LXC. In subsequent versions, Docker changed its focus from LXC and started working on a new standard library for application containers, known as **libcontainer**.

It still uses the same base technologies, such as Linux namespaces and control groups, and shares the same kernel with the host operating system. Similarly, Docker makes use of operating system images to run containers. Docker images are a collection of multiple layers, with each layer adding something new to the base layer. This something new can include a service, such as a web server, application code, or even a new set of configurations. Each layer is independent of the layers above it and can be reused to create a new image.

Being an application container, Docker encourages the use of a microservice-based distributed architecture. Think of deploying a simple **WordPress** blog. With Docker, you will need to create at least two different containers, one for the MySQL server and the other for the WordPress code with PHP and the web server. You can separate PHP and web servers in their own containers. While this looks like extra effort, it makes your application much more flexible. It enables you to scale each component separately and improves application availability by separating failure points.

While both LXC and Docker use containerization technologies, their use cases are different. LXC enables you to run an entire lightweight virtual machine in a container, eliminating the inefficiencies of virtualization. Docker enables you to quickly create and share a self-dependent package with your application, which can be deployed on any system running Docker.

In this recipe, we will cover the installation of Docker on Ubuntu Server. The recipes after that will focus on various features provided by Docker.

Getting ready

You will need access to the root account or an account with `sudo` privileges.

How to do it...

Recently, Docker released version 1.11 of the Docker engine. We will follow the installation steps provided on the Docker site to install the latest available version:

1. First, add a new gpg key:

```
$ sudo apt-key adv --keyserver hkp://p80.pool.sks-
keyservers.net:80 --recv-keys
58118E89F3A912897C070ADBF76221572C52609D
```

2. Next, add a new repository to the local installation sources. This repository is maintained by Docker and contains Docker packages for 1.7.1 and higher versions:

```
$ echo "deb https://apt.dockerproject.org/repo ubuntu-xenial
main" | \
sudo tee /etc/apt/sources.list.d/docker.list
```

> If you are using an Ubuntu version other than 16.04 (Xenial), then make sure that you replace the repository path with the respective codename. For example, on Ubuntu 14.04 (Trusty), use the following repository:
>
> ```
> deb https://apt.dockerproject.org/repo ubuntu-
> trusty main
> ```

3. Next, update the `apt` package list and install Docker with the following commands:

```
$ sudo apt-get update
$ sudo apt-get install docker-engine
```

4. Once the installation completes, you can check the status of the Docker service, as follows:

```
$ sudo service docket status
```

5. Check the installed Docker version with `docker version`:

```
$ sudo docker version
Client:
 Version:      1.11.1
 API version:  1.23
 . . .
Server:
 Version:      1.11.1
 API version:  1.23
 . . .
```

6. Download a test container to test the installation. This container will simply print a welcome message and then exit:

```
$ sudo docker run hello-world
```

```
ubuntu@cookbook:~$ sudo docker run hello-world

Hello from Docker.
This message shows that your installation appears to be working correctly.

To generate this message, Docker took the following steps:
 1. The Docker client contacted the Docker daemon.
 2. The Docker daemon pulled the "hello-world" image from the Docker Hub.
```

7. At this point, you need to use `sudo` with every Docker command. To enable a non-sudo user to use Docker, or to simply avoid the repeated use of `sudo`, add the respective usernames to the `docker` group:

```
$ sudo gpasswd -a ubuntu docker
```

 The `docker` group has privileges equivalent to the root account. Check the official Docker installation documentation for more details.

Now, update group membership, and you can use Docker without the `sudo` command:

```
$ newgrp docker
```

How it works...

This recipe installs Docker from the official Docker repository. This way, we can be sure to get the latest version. The Ubuntu 16.04 repository also contains the package for Docker with version 1.10. If you prefer to install from the Ubuntu repository, it's an even easier task with a single command, as follows:

```
$ sudo apt-get install docker.io
```

As of writing this, Docker 1.11 is the latest stable release and the first release to have been built on Open Container Initiative standards. This version is built on **runc** and **containerd**.

There's more...

Docker provides a quick installation script, which can be used to install Docker with a single command. This scripts reads the basic details of your operating system, such as the distribution and version, and then executes all the required steps to install Docker. You can use the bootstrap script as follows:

```
$ sudo curl -sSL https://get.docker.com | sudo sh
```

Note that with this command, the script will be executed with `sudo` privileges. Make sure you cross-check the script's contents before executing it. You can download the script without executing it, as follows:

```
$ curl -sSL https://get.docker.com -o docker_install.sh
```

See also

- The Docker installation guide: `http://docs.docker.com/installation/ubuntulinux/`
- Operating system containers versus application containers: `https://blog.risingstack.com/operating-system-containers-vs-application-containers/`
- What Docker adds to lxc-tools: `http://stackoverflow.com/questions/17989306/what-does-docker-add-to-lxc-tools-the-userspace-lxc-tools`
- A curated list of Docker resources: `https://github.com/veggiemonk/awesome-docker`

Starting and managing Docker containers

So, we have installed the latest Docker binary. In this recipe, we will start a new container with Docker. We will see some basic Docker commands to start and manage Docker containers.

Getting ready

Make sure that you have installed Docker and set your user as a member of the Docker group.

You may need `sudo` privileges for some commands.

How to do it...

Let's create a new Docker container and start it. With Docker, you can quickly start a container with the `docker run` command:

1. Start a new Docker container with the following command:

   ```
   $ docker run -it --name dc1 ubuntu /bin/bash
   Unable to find image 'ubuntu:trusty' locally
   trusty: Pulling from library/ubuntu
   6599cadaf950: Pull complete
   23eda618d451: Pull complete
   ...
   Status: Downloaded newer image for ubuntu:trusty
   root@bd8c99397e52:/#
   ```

   Once a container has been started, it will drop you in a new shell running inside it. From here, you can execute limited Ubuntu or general Linux commands, which will be executed inside the container.

2. When you are done with the container, you can exit from the shell by typing `exit` or pressing *Ctrl + D*. This will terminate your shell and stop the container as well.

3. Use the `docker ps` command to list all the containers and check the status of your last container:

   ```
   $ docker ps -a
   ```

By default, `docker ps` lists all running containers. As our container is no longer running, we need to use the `-a` flag to list all available containers.

4. To start the container again, you can use the `docker start` command. You can use the container name or ID to specify the container to be started:

```
$ docker start -ia dc1
```

```
ubuntu@cookbook:~$ docker start -ia dc1
root@708fea034cbe:/#
root@708fea034cbe:/# exit
exit
ubuntu@cookbook:~$
```

The `-i` flag will start the container in interactive mode and the `-a` flag will attach to a terminal inside the container. To start a container in detached mode, use the `start` command without any flags. This will start the container in the background and return to the host shell:

```
$ docker start dc1
```

5. You can open a terminal inside a detached container with `docker attach`:

```
$ docker attach dc1
```

6. Now, to detach a terminal and keep the container running, you need the key combinations *Ctrl + P* and *Ctrl + Q*. Alternatively, you can type `exit` or press *Ctrl + C* to exit the terminal and stop the container.

7. To get all the details of a container, use the `docker inspect` command with the name or ID of the container:

```
$ docker inspect dc1 | less
```

This command will list all the details of the container, including container status, network status and address, and container configuration files.

 Use `grep` to filter container information. For example, to get the IP address from the `docker inspect` output, use this:
```
$ docker inspect dc1 | grep-iipaddr
```

8. To execute a command inside a container, use `docker exec`. For example, the following command gets the environment variables from the `dc1` container:

```
$ docker exec dc1 env
```

This one gets the IP address of a container:

```
$ docker exec dc1 ifconfig
```

```
ubuntu@cookbook:~$ docker exec dc1 ifconfig
eth0    Link encap:Ethernet  HWaddr 02:42:ac:11:00:02
        inet addr:172.17.0.2  Bcast:0.0.0.0  Mask:255.255.0.0
        inet6 addr: fe80::42:acff:fe11:2/64 Scope:Link
        UP BROADCAST RUNNING MULTICAST  MTU:1500  Metric:1
        RX packets:8 errors:0 dropped:0 overruns:0 frame:0
```

9. To get the processes running inside a container, use the `docker top` command:

```
$ docker top dc1
```

```
ubuntu@cookbook:~$ docker top dc1
UID              PID           PPID          C
STIME            TTY           TIME          CMD
root             6495          866           0
05:23            pts/12        00:00:00      /bin/bash
```

10. Finally, to stop the container, use `docker stop`, which will gracefully stop the container after stopping processes running inside it:

```
$ docker stop dc1
```

11. When you no longer need the container, you can use `docker rm` to remove/delete it:

```
$ docker rm dc1
```

Want to remove all stopped containers with a single command? Use this:
```
$ docker rm $(dockerps -aq)
```

How it works...

We started our first Docker container with the `docker run` command. With this command, we instructed the Docker daemon to start a new container with an image called Ubuntu, start an interactive session (`-i`), and allocate a terminal (`-t`). We also elected to name our container with the `--name` flag and execute the `/bin/bash` command inside a container once it started.

The Docker daemon will search for Ubuntu images in the local cache or download the image from Docker Hub if the specified image is not available in the local cache. Docker Hub is a central Docker image repository. It will take some time to download and extract all the layers of the images. Docker maintains container images in the form of multiple layers. These layers can be shared across multiple container images. For example, if you have Ubuntu running on a server and you need to download the Apache container based on Ubuntu, Docker will only download the additional layer for Apache as it already has Ubuntu in the local cache, which can be reused.

Docker provides various other commands to manage containers and images. We have already used a few of them in the previous example. You can get the full list of all available commands from the command prompt itself, by typing `docker` followed by the *Enter* key. All commands are listed with their basic descriptions. To get more details on any specific subcommand, use its `help` menu, as follows:

```
$ docker rmi --help
```

There's more...

Docker images can be used to quickly create `runc` containers, as follows:

```
$ sudo apt-get install runc
$ mkdir -p runc/rootfs && cd runc
$ docker run --name alpine alpine sh
$ docker export alpine > alpine.tar
$ tar -xf alpine.tar -C rootfs
$ runc spec
$ sudo runc start alpine
```

See also

▸ Docker run documentation: `http://docs.docker.com/engine/reference/commandline/run/`

▸ Check manual entries for any Docker command: `$ man docker create`

Creating images with a Dockerfile

This recipe explores image creation with Dockerfiles. Docker images can be created in multiple ways, which includes using Dockerfiles, using `docker commit` to save the container state as a new image, or using `docker import`, which imports chroot directory structure as a Docker image.

In this recipe, we will focus on **Dockerfiles** and related details. Dockerfiles help in automating identical and repeatable image creation. They contain multiple commands in the form of instructions to build a new image. These instructions are then passed to the Docker daemon through the `docker build` command. The Docker daemon independently executes these commands one by one. The resulting images are committed as and when necessary, and it is possible that multiple intermediate images are created. The build process will reuse existing images from the image cache to speed up build process.

Getting ready

Make sure that your Docker daemon is installed and working properly.

How to do it...

1. First, create a new empty directory and enter it. This directory will hold our Dockerfile:

    ```
    $ mkdir myimage
    ```

    ```
    $ cd myimage
    ```

2. Create a new file called `Dockerfile`:

    ```
    $ touch Dockerfile
    ```

3. Now, add the following lines to the newly created file. These lines are the instructions to create an image with the Apache web server. We will look at more details later in this recipe:

    ```
    FROM ubuntu:trusty

    MAINTAINER ubuntu server cookbook


    # Install base packages
    RUN apt-get update && apt-get -yq install apache2 && \
    apt-get clean && \
    rm -rf /var/lib/apt/lists/*


    RUN echo "ServerName localhost" >>
    /etc/apache2/apache2.conf


    ENV APACHE_RUN_USER www-data
    ENV APACHE_RUN_GROUP www-data
    ENV APACHE_LOG_DIR /var/log/apache2
    ```

```
ENV APACHE_PID_FILE /var/run/apache2.pid

ENV APACHE_LOCK_DIR /var/www/html


VOLUME ["/var/www/html"]

EXPOSE 80

CMD ["/usr/sbin/apache2", "-D", "FOREGROUND"]
```

4. Save the changes and start the `docker build` process with the following command:

   `$ docker build.`

```
ubuntu@cookbook:~/ubuntu_nginx$ docker build .
Sending build context to Docker daemon 3.072 kB
Step 1 : FROM ubuntu:trusty
 ---> 1d073211c498
Step 2 : MAINTAINER ubuntu server cookboox
 ---> Running in 24b4e9d4db7b
 ---> b5449baf8533
Removing intermediate container 24b4e9d4db7b
Step 3 : RUN apt-get update && apt-get -yq install apache2 && apt-get clean && r
m -rf /var/lib/apt/lists/*
 ---> Running in c92dac5c8d28
```

This will build a new image with Apache server installed on it. The build process will take a little longer to complete and output the final image ID:

```
Step 12 : CMD /usr/sbin/apache2 -D FOREGROUND
 ---> Running in d75bff891353
 ---> e9cfe1181171
Removing intermediate container d75bff891353
Successfully built e9cfe1181171
```

5. Once the image is ready, you can start a new container with it:

   `$ docker run -p 80:80 -d image_id`

   Replace `image_id` with the image ID from the result of the build process.

6. Now, you can list the running containers with the `docker ps` command. Notice the `ports` column of the output:

`$ docker ps`

```
ubuntu@cookbook:~$ docker run -p 80:80 -d e9cfe1181171
255c06f2478db50e33a501535c19880d825153fd6134f507514d6dfd525d1d75
ubuntu@cookbook:~$ docker ps
CONTAINER ID        IMAGE                    COMMAND                CREATED
    STATUS              PORTS                   NAMES
255c06f2478d        e9cfe1181171           "/usr/sbin/apache2 -D"  6 seconds ago
    Up 4 seconds        0.0.0.0:80->80/tcp     sad_keller
ubuntu@cookbook:~$
```

Apache server's default page should be accessible at your host domain name or IP address.

How it works...

A Dockerfile is a document that contains several commands to create a new image. Each command in a Dockerfile creates a new container, executes that command on the new container, and then commits the changes to create a new image. This image is then used as a base for executing the next command. Once the final command is executed, Docker returns the ID of the final image as an output of the `docker build` command.

This recipe demonstrates the use of a Dockerfile to create images with the Apache web server. The Dockerfile uses a few available instructions. As a convention, the instructions file is generally called **Dockerfile**. Alternatively, you can use the `-f` flag to pass the instruction file to the Docker daemon. A Dockerfile uses the following format for instructions:

`# comment`

`INSTRUCTION argument`

All instructions are executed one by one in a given order. A Dockerfile must start with the FROM instruction, which specifies the base image to be used. We have started our Dockerfile with **Ubuntu:trusty** as the base image. The next line specifies the maintainer or the author of the Dockerfile, with the MAINTAINER instruction.

Followed by the author definition, we have used the RUN instruction to install Apache on our base image. The RUN instruction will execute a given command on the top read-write layer and then commit the results. The committed image will be used as a starting point for the next instruction. If you've noticed the RUN instruction and the arguments passed to it, you can see that we have passed multiple commands in a chained format. This will execute all commands on a single image and avoid any cache-related problems. The apt-get clean and rm commands are used to remove any unused files and minimize the resulting image size.

After the RUN command, we have set some environment variables with the ENV instruction. When we start a new container from this image, all environment variables are exported to the container environment and will be accessible to processes running inside the container. In this case, the process that will use such a variable is the Apache server.

Next, we have used the VOLUME instruction with the path set to /var/www/html. This instruction creates a directory on the host system, generally under Docker root, and mounts it inside the container on the specified path. Docker uses volumes to decouple containers from the data they create. So even if the container using this volume is removed, the data will persist on the host system. You can specify volumes in a Dockerfile or in the command line while running the container, as follows:

```
$ docker run -v /var/www/html image_id
```

You can use docker inspect to get the host path of the volumes attached to container.

Finally, we have used the EXPOSE instruction, which will expose the specified container port to the host. In this case, it's port 80, where the Apache server will be listening for web requests. To use an exposed port on the host system, we need to use either the -p flag to explicitly specify the port mapping or the -P flag, which will dynamically map the container port to the available host port. We have used the -p flag with the argument 80:80, which will map the container port 80 to the host port 80 and make Apache accessible through the host.

The last instruction, CMD, sets the command to be executed when running the image. We are using the executable format of the CMD instruction, which specifies the executable to be run with its command-line arguments. In this case, our executable is the Apache binary with -D FOREGROUND as an argument. By default, the Apache parent process will start, create a child process, and then exit. If the Apache process exits, our container will be turned off as it no longer has a running process. With the -D FOREGROUND argument, we instruct Apache to run in the foreground and keep the parent process active. We can have only one CMD instruction in a Dockerfile.

The instruction set includes some more instructions, such as ADD, COPY, and ENTRYPOINT. I cannot cover them all because it would run into far too many pages. You can always refer to the official Docker site to get more details. Check out the reference URLs in the *See also* section.

There's more...

Once the image has been created, you can share it on Docker Hub, a central repository of public and private Docker images. You need an account on Docker Hub, which can be created for free. Once you get your Docker Hub credentials, you can use `docker login` to connect your Docker daemon with Docker Hub and then use `docker push` to push local images to the Docker Hub repository. You can use the respective `help` commands or manual pages to get more details about `docker login` and `docker push`.

Alternatively, you can also set up your own local image repository. Check out the Docker documents for deploying your own registry at `https://docs.docker.com/registry/deploying/`.

 GitLab, an open source Git hosting server, now supports container repositories. This feature has been added in GitLab version 8.8. Refer to *Chapter 11*, *Git Hosting*, for more details and installation instructions for GitLab.

We need a base image or any other image as a starting point for the Dockerfile. But how do we create our own base image?

Base images can be created with tools such as **debootstrap** and **supermin**. We need to create a distribution-specific directory structure and put all the necessary files inside it. Later, we can create a tarball of this directory structure and import the tarball as a Docker image using the `docker import` command.

See also

- Dockerfile reference: `https://docs.docker.com/reference/builder/`
- Dockerfile best practices: `https://docs.docker.com/articles/dockerfile_best-practices`
- More Dockerfile best practices: `http://crosbymichael.com/dockerfile-best-practices.html`
- Create a base image: `http://docs.docker.com/engine/articles/baseimages/`

Understanding Docker volumes

One of the most common questions seen on Docker forums is how to separate data from containers. This is because any data created inside containers is lost when the container gets deleted. Using `docker commit` to store data inside Docker images is not a good idea. To solve this problem, Docker provides an option called data volumes. Data volumes are special shared directories that can be used by one or more Docker containers. These volumes persist even when the container is deleted. These directories are created on the host file system, usually under the `/var/lib/docker/` directory.

In this recipe, we will learn to use Docker volumes, share host directories with Docker containers, and learn basic backup and restore tricks that can be used with containers.

Getting ready

Make sure that you have the Docker daemon installed and running. We will need two or more containers.

You may need `sudo` privileges to access the `/var/lib/docker` directory.

How to do it...

Follow these steps to understand Docker volumes:

1. To add a data volume to a container, use the `-v` flag with the `docker run` command, like so:

   ```
   $ docker run -dP -v /var/lib/mysql --name mysql\
   -e MYSQL_ROOT_PASSWORD= passwdmysql:latest
   ```

   This will create a new MySQL container with a volume created at `/var/lib/mysql` inside the container. If the directory already exists on the volume path, the volume will overlay the directory contents.

2. Once the container has been started, you can get the host-specific path of the volume with the `docker inspect` command. Look for the `Mounts` section in the output of `docker inspect`:

   ```
   $ docker inspect mysql
   ```

```
"Mounts": [
    {
        "Name": "99999cdfbab177220de964b63c6f6a3a283b68067765d9199fb7bd09350
1d548",
        "Source": "/var/lib/docker/volumes/99999cdfbab177220de964b63c6f6a3a2
83b68067765d9199fb7bd093501d548/_data",
        "Destination": "/var/lib/mysql",
        "Driver": "local",
        "Mode": "",
        "RW": true
    }
```

3. To mount a specific directory from the host system as a data volume, use the following syntax:

```
$ mkdir ~/mkdir
$ docker run -dP -v ~/mysql:/var/lib/mysql \
--name mysql mysql:latest
```

   This will create a new directory named mysql at the home path and mount it as a volume inside a container at /var/lib/mysql.

4. To share a volume between multiple containers, you can use named volume containers.

   First, create a container with a volume attached to it. The following command will create a container with its name set to mysql:

```
$ docker run -dP -v /var/lib/mysql --name mysql\
-e MYSQL_ROOT_PASSWORD= passwd mysql:latest
```

5. Now, create a new container using the volume exposed by the mysql container and list all the files available in the container:

```
$ docker run --rm --volumes-from mysql ubuntu ls -l
/var/lib/mysql
```

```
ubuntu@cookbook:~$ docker run --rm --volumes-from mysql ubuntu ls -l /var/lib/my
sql
total 188444
-rw-r------ 1 999 999         56 Nov 10 06:10 auto.cnf
-rw-r------ 1 999 999       1319 Nov 10 06:10 ib_buffer_pool
-rw-r------ 1 999 999 50331648 Nov 10 06:10 ib_logfile0
-rw-r------ 1 999 999 50331648 Nov 10 06:10 ib_logfile1
-rw-r------ 1 999 999 79691776 Nov 10 06:10 ibdata1
```

6. To back up data from the `mysql` container, use the following command:

```
$ docker run --rm--volumes-from mysql -v ~/backup:/backup \
$ tar cvf /backup/mysql.tar /var/lib/mysql
```

7. Docker volumes are not deleted when containers are removed. To delete volumes along with a container, you need to use the `-v` flag with the `docker rm` command:

```
$ dockerrm -v mysql
```

How it works...

Docker volumes are designed to provide persistent storage, separate from the containers' life cycles. Even if the container gets deleted, the volume still persists unless it's explicitly specified to delete the volume with the container. Volumes can be attached while creating a container using the `docker create` or `docker run` commands. Both commands support the `-v` flag, which accepts volume arguments. You can add multiple volumes by repeatedly using the volume flag. Volumes can also be created in a Dockerfile using the VOLUME instruction.

When the `-v` flag is followed by a simple directory path, Docker creates a new directory inside a container as a data volume. This data volume will be mapped to a directory on the host filesystem under the `/var/lib/docker` directory. Docker volumes are read-write enabled by default, but you can mark a volume to be read-only using the following syntax:

```
$ docker run -dP -v /var/lib/mysql:ro --name mysql mysql:latest
```

Once a container has been created, you can get the details of all the volumes used by it, as well as its host-specific path, with the `docker inspect` command. The Mounts section from the output of `docker inspect` lists all volumes with their respective names and paths on the host system and path inside a container.

Rather than using a random location as a data volume, you can also specify a particular directory on the host to be used as a data volume. Add a host directory along with the volume argument, and Docker will map the volume to that directory:

```
$ docker run -dP -v ~/mysql:/var/lib/mysql \
--name mysql mysql:latest
```

In this case, `/var/lib/mysql` from the container will be mapped to the `mysql` directory located at the user's home address.

Need to share a single file from a host system with a container? Sure, Docker supports that too. Use `docker run -v` and specify the file source on the host and destination inside the container. Check out following example command:

```
$ docker run --rmd -v ~/.bash_history:/.bash_history ubuntu
```

The other option is to create a named data volume container or data-only container. You can create a named container with attached volumes and then use those volumes inside other containers using the `docker run --volumes-from` command. The data volumes container need not be running to access volumes attached to it. These volumes can be shared by multiple containers, plus you can create temporary, throwaway application containers by separating persistent data storage. Even if you delete a temporary container using a named volume, your data is still safe with a volume container.

From Docker version 1.9 onwards, a separate command, `docker volume`, is available to manage volumes. With this update, you can create and manage volumes separately from containers. Docker volumes support various backend drivers, including AUFS, OverlayFS, BtrFS, and ZFS. A simple command to create a new volume will be as follows:

```
$ docker volume create --name=myvolume
$ docker run -v myvolume:/opt alpine sh
```

See also

- The Docker volumes guide: `http://docs.docker.com/engine/userguide/dockervolumes/`
- Clean up orphaned volumes with this script: `https://github.com/chadoe/docker-cleanup-volumes`

Deploying WordPress using a Docker network

In this recipe, we will learn to use a Docker network to set up a WordPress server. We will create two containers, one for MySQL and the other for WordPress. Additionally, we will set up a private network for both MySQL and WordPress.

How to do it...

Let's start by creating a separate network for WordPress and the MySQL containers:

1. A new network can be created with the following command:

   ```
   $ docker network create wpnet
   ```

2. Check whether the network has been created successfully with `docker network ls`:

```
$ docker network ls
```

```
ubuntu@cookbook:~$ docker network create wpnet
d2405dfb37f4d450e09b0f62ca097fd85da9017016184a8ee038c5e27e5b30cd
ubuntu@cookbook:~$ docker network ls
NETWORK ID          NAME                DRIVER
d3c35f350f8e        bridge              bridge
fd9b429d3539        none                null
b9e3d814828e        host                host
d2405dfb37f4        wpnet               bridge
```

3. You can get details of the new network with the `docker network inspect` command:

```
$ docker network inspect wpnet
```

```
ubuntu@cookbook:~$ docker network inspect wpnet
[
    {
        "Name": "wpnet",
        "Id": "d2405dfb37f4d450e09b0f62ca097fd85da9017016184a8ee038c5e27e5b30cd"

        "Scope": "local",
        "Driver": "bridge",
        "IPAM": {
            "Driver": "default",
            "Config": [
                {}
            ]
        },
        "Containers": {},
        "Options": {}
```

4. Next, start a new MySQL container and set it to use wpnet:

```
$ docker run --name mysql -d \
-e MYSQL_ROOT_PASSWORD=password \
--net wpnet mysql
```

5. Now, create a container for WordPress. Make sure the WORDPRESS_DB_HOST argument matches the name given to the MySQL container:

```
$ docker run --name wordpress -d -p 80:80 \
--net wpnet\
-e WORDPRESS_DB_HOST=mysql\
-e WORDPRESS_DB_PASSWORD=password wordpress
```

6. Inspect wpnet again. This time, it should list two containers:

```
    "Containers": {
        "278abce759709f28a45dac29fc79ca13104a7be5bdb45c3bfff326a3ae6a6262":
{
            "EndpointID": "84ce992c28743857d3ca478bcaead36262f58f5d81433a9dd
46e06ef63913910",
            "MacAddress": "02:42:ac:12:00:02",
            "IPv4Address": "172.18.0.2/16",
            "IPv6Address": ""
        },
        "d0318648190de753188f9d8aa42c5f58e0333f2b503ddb6c9e260ac98e37be2e":
{
            "EndpointID": "dc3aa8f8b0c01ef9c7080fc875dd7a2e4d1a5e3d459249d64
ed5fd117b8faa1a",
            "MacAddress": "02:42:ac:12:00:03",
            "IPv4Address": "172.18.0.3/16",
            "IPv6Address": ""
        }
    },
```

Now, you can access the WordPress installation at your host domain name or IP address.

How it works...

Docker introduced the **container networking model** (**CNM**) with Docker version 1.9. CNM enables users to create small, private networks for a group of containers. Now, you can set up a new software-assisted network with a simple `docker network create` command. The Docker network supports bridge and overlay drivers for networks out of the box. You can use plugins to add other network drivers. The bridge network is a default driver used by a Docker network. It provides a network similar to the default Docker network, whereas an overlay network enables multihost networking for Docker clusters.

This recipe covers the use of a bridge network for wordpress containers. We have created a simple, isolated bridge network using the `docker network` command. Once the network has been created, you can set containers to use this network with the `--net` flag to `docker run` command. If your containers are already running, you can add a new network interface to them with the `docker network connect` command, as follows:

```
$ # docker network connect network_name container_name
$ docker network connect wpnet mysql
```

Similarly, you can use `docker network disconnect` to disconnect or remove a container from a specific network. Additionally, this network provides an inbuilt discovery feature. With discovery enabled, we can communicate with other containers using their names. We used this feature while connecting the MySQL container to the wordpress container. For the `WORDPRESS_DB_HOST` parameter, we used the container name rather than the IP address or FQDN.

If you've noticed, we have not mentioned any port mapping for the `mysql` container. With this new wpnet network, we need not create any port mapping on the MySQL container. The default MySQL port is exposed by the `mysql` container and the service is accessible only to containers running on the wpnet network. The only port available to the outside world is port `80` from the wordpress container. We can easily hide the WordPress service behind a load balancer and use multiple wordpress containers with just the load balancer exposed to the outside world.

There's more...

Docker also supports links to create secure communication links between two or more containers. You can set up a WordPress site using linked containers as follows:

1. First, create a `mysql` container:

   ```
   $ docker run --name mysql -d \
   -e MYSQL_ROOT_PASSWORD=password mysql
   ```

2. Now, create a `wordpress` container and link it with the `mysql` container:

   ```
   $ docker run --name wordpress -d -p 80:80 --link mysql:mysql
   ```

   And you are done. All arguments for `wordpress`, such as DB_HOST and ROOT_PASSWORD, will be taken from the linked `mysql` container.

The other option to set up WordPress is to set up both WordPress and MySQL in a single container. This needs process management tools such as **supervisord** to run two or more processes in a single container. Docker allows only one process per container by default.

See also

You can find the respective Dockerfiles for MySQL and WordPress containers at the following addresses:

- ▸ Docker Hub WordPress: `https://hub.docker.com/_/wordpress/`
- ▸ Docker Hub MySQL: `https://hub.docker.com/_/mysql/`
- ▸ Docker networking: `https://blog.docker.com/2015/11/docker-multi-host-networking-ga/`
- ▸ Networking for containers using libnetwork: `https://github.com/docker/libnetwork`

Monitoring Docker containers

In this recipe, we will learn to monitor Docker containers.

How to do it...

Docker provides inbuilt monitoring with the `docker stats` command, which can be used to get a live stream of the resource utilization of Docker containers.

1. To monitor multiple containers at once using their respective IDs or names, use this command:

```
$ docker stats mysql f9617f4b716c
```

```
CONTAINER          CPU %              MEM USAGE / LIMIT      MEM %
  NET I/O          BLOCK I/O
mysql              0.03%              438.5 MB / 4.145 GB    10.58%
  2.656 kB / 1.301 kB    32.49 MB / 290.1 MB
wordpress          0.00%              84.7 MB / 4.145 GB     2.04%
  1.301 kB / 1.36 kB     54.92 MB / 49.15 kB
```

If you need to monitor all running containers, use the following command:

```
$ docker stats $(dockerps -q)
```

2. With `docker logs`, you can fetch logs of your application running inside a container. This can be used similarly to the `tail -f` command:

   ```
   $ docker logs -f ubuntu
   ```

3. Docker also records state change events from containers. These events include start, stop, create, kill, and so on. You can get real-time events with `docker events`:

   ```
   $ docker events
   ```

   To get past events, use the `--since` flag with `docker events`:

   ```
   $ docker events --since '2015-11-01'
   ```

4. You can also check the changes in the container filesystem with the `docker diff` command. This will list newly added (A), changed (C), or deleted (D) files.

   ```
   $ docker diff ubuntu
   ```

5. Another useful command is `docker top`, which helps look inside a container. This commands displays the processes running inside a container:

   ```
   $ docker top ubuntu
   ```

How it works...

Docker provides various inbuilt commands to monitor containers and the processes running inside them. It uses native system constructs such as namespaces and cgroups. Most of these statistics are collected from the native system. Logs are directly collected from running processes.

Need something more, possibly a tool with graphical output? There are various such tools available. One well-known tool is **cAdvisor** by Google. You can run the tool itself as a Docker container, as follows:

```
docker run -d -p 8080:8080 --name cadvisor \
   --volume=/:/rootfs:ro \
   --volume=/var/run:/var/run:rw \
   --volume=/sys:/sys:ro \
   --volume=/var/lib/docker/:/var/lib/docker:ro \
google/cadvisor:latest
```

Once the container has been started, you can access the UI at your server domain or IP on port `8080` or any other port that you use. cAdvisor is able to monitor both LXC and Docker containers. In addition, it can report host system resources.

There's more...

Various external tools are available that provide monitoring and troubleshooting services. **Sysdig** is a similar command-line tool that can be used to monitor Linux systems and containers. Read some examples of using sysdig at `https://github.com/draios/sysdig/wiki/Sysdig%20Examples`.

Also, check out Sysdig Falco, an open source behavioral monitor with container support.

See also

- ▶ Docker runtime metrics at `http://docs.docker.com/engine/articles/runmetrics/`
- ▶ cAdvisor at GitHub: `https://github.com/google/cadvisor`

Securing Docker containers

In this recipe, we will learn Docker configurations that may result in slightly improved security for your containers. Docker uses some advanced features in the latest Linux kernel, which include kernel namespaces to provide process isolation, control groups to control resource allocation, and kernel capabilities and user namespaces to run unprivileged containers. As stated on the Docker documentation page, Docker containers are, by default, quite secure.

This recipe covers some basic steps to improve Docker security and reduce the attack surface on the Ubuntu host as well as the Docker daemon.

How to do it...

The first and most common thing is to use the latest versions of your software. Make sure that you are using the latest Ubuntu version with all security updates applied and that your Docker version is the latest stable version:

1. Upgrade your Ubuntu host with the following commands:

   ```
   $ sudo apt-get update
   $ sudo apt-get upgrade
   ```

2. If you used a Docker-maintained repository when installing Docker, you need not care about Docker updates, as the previous commands will update your Docker installation as well.

3. Set a proper firewall on your host system. Ubuntu comes preinstalled with UFW; you simply need to add the necessary rules and enable the firewall. Refer to *Chapter 2, Networking* for more details on UFW configuration.

   On Ubuntu systems, Docker ships with the **AppArmor** profile. This profile is installed and enforced with a Docker installation. Make sure you have AppArmor installed and working properly. AppArmor will provide better security against unknown vulnerabilities:

   ```
   $ sudo apparmor_status
   ```

4. Next, we will move on to configure the Docker daemon. You can get a list of all available options with the `docker daemon --help` command:

   ```
   $ docker daemon --help
   ```

5. You can configure these settings in the Docker configuration file at `/etc/default/docker`, or start the Docker daemon with all required settings from the command line.

6. Edit the Docker configuration and add the following settings to the `DOCKER_OPTS` section:

   ```
   $ sudo nano /etc/default/docker
   ```

7. Turn off inter-container communication:

   ```
   --icc=false
   ```

8. Set default ulimit restrictions:

   ```
   --default-ulimitnproc=512:1024 --default-ulimitnofile=50:100
   ```

9. Set the default storage driver to overlayfs:

   ```
   ---storage-driver=overlay
   ```

10. Once you have configured all these settings, restart the Docker daemon:

    ```
    $ sudo service docker restart
    ```

11. Now, you can use the security bench script provided by Docker. This script checks for common security best practices and gives you a list of all the things that need to be improved.

12. Clone the script from the Docker GitHub repository:

    ```
    $ git clone https://github.com/docker/docker-bench-security.git
    ```

13. Execute the script:

```
$ cd docker-bench-security
$ sh docker-bench-security.sh
```

```
[INFO] 1 - Host Configuration
[WARN] 1.1  - Create a separate partition for containers
[PASS] 1.2  - Use an updated Linux Kernel
[PASS] 1.5  - Remove all non-essential services from the host - Network
[PASS] 1.6  - Keep Docker up to date
[INFO] 1.7  - Only allow trusted users to control Docker daemon
```

Try to fix the issues reported by this script.

14. Now, we will look at Docker container configurations.

The most important part of a Docker container is its image. Make sure that you download or pull the images from a trusted repository. You can get most of the images from the official Docker repository, Docker Hub.

15. Alternatively, you can build the images on your own server. Dockerfiles for the most popular images are quite easily available and you can easily build images after verifying their contents and making any changes if required.

When building your own images, make sure you don't add the root user:

```
RUN group add -r user && user add -r -g user user
USER user
```

16. When creating a new container, make sure that you configure CPU and memory limits as per the containers requirements. You can also pass container-specific ulimit settings when creating containers:

```
$ docker run --cpu-shares1024 --memory 512 --cpuset-cpus 1
```

17. Whenever possible, set your containers to read-only:

```
$ docker run --read-only
```

18. Use read-only volumes:

```
$ docker run -v /shared/path:/container/path:ro ubuntu
```

19. Try not to publish application ports. Use a private Docker network or Docker links when possible. For example, when setting up WordPress in the previous recipe, we used a Docker network and connected WordPress and MySQL without exposing MySQL ports.

20. You can also publish ports to a specific container with its IP address. This may create problems when using multiple containers, but is good for a base setup:

```
$ docker run -p 127.0.0.1:3306:3306 mysql
```

See also

▸ Most of these recommendations are taken from the Docker security cheat sheet at `https://github.com/konstruktoid/Docker/blob/master/Security/CheatSheet.md`

▸ The Docker bench security script: `https://github.com/docker/docker-bench-security`

▸ The Docker security documentation: `http://docs.docker.com/engine/articles/security/`

9
Streaming with Ampache

In this chapter, we will cover the following recipes:

- ▶ Installing the Ampache server
- ▶ Uploading contents and creating catalogs
- ▶ Setting on-the-fly transcoding
- ▶ Enabling API access for remote streaming
- ▶ Streaming music with Ampache

Introduction

This chapter covers the installation and configuration of the open source audio and video streaming service, Ampache. It is a web-based streaming application that allows you to upload your own audio/video contents and access them across multiple Internet-enabled devices. You can easily set up your home media server using Ampache and your old personal computer running Ubuntu. We will focus on installing Ampache on the Ubuntu server, but you can install Ampache on any Linux distribution of your choice.

Installing the Ampache server

This recipe covers the installation of the Ampache server. It is a simple PHP-based web application. Once installed and set up, you can use a web interface to play your audio/video files or use any of the various popular streaming clients to stream content over the intranet or even the Internet.

Getting ready

We will be using Ubuntu Server 16.04, but you can choose to have any version of Ubuntu.

Additionally, we will need the Samba server. It will be used as shared network storage.

As always, access to a root account or an account with sudo privileges will be required.

How to do it...

Ampache is a web application developed in PHP. We will start the installation with the LAMP stack. This recipe covers installation with the Apache web server, but you can choose any other web server:

1. Install the LAMP stack if it's not already installed:

    ```
    $ sudo apt-get update
    $ sudo apt-get install apache2 mysql-server-5.5 php7 \
    php7-mysql php7-curl libapache2-mod-php7
    ```

     For more details on Apache and PHP installation, check
    Chapter 3, Working with Web Server.

2. Next, download the latest Ampache server source code. Ampache is a PHP application:

    ```
    $ wget https://github.com/ampache/ampache/archive/3.8.0.tar.gz
    Extract achieve contents under a web root directory
    $ tar -xf 3.8.0.tar.gz -C /var/www
    $ mv /var/www/ampache-3.8.0 /var/www/ampache
    ```

3. We also need to create some configuration files. You can use the default configuration that ships with the Ampache setup and rename the existing files:

    ```
    $ cd /var/www/ampache
    $ mv rest/.htaccess.dist rest/.htaccess
    $ mv play/.htaccess.dist play/.htaccess
    $ mv channel/.htaccess.dist channel/.htaccess
    ```

4. The Ampache web setup will save the configuration under the `config` directory. It will need write access to that directory:

   ```
   $ chmod 777 -R config
   ```

5. Next, we need to configure the Apache web server, enable `mod_rewrite`, and set a virtual host pointing to the Ampache directory.

6. Enable `mod_rewrite` with the following command:

   ```
   $ sudo a2enmod rewrite
   ```

7. Create a new virtual host configuration:

   ```
   $ cd /etc/apache2/sites-available/
   $ sudo vi ampache.conf
   ```

8. Add the following lines to `ampache.conf`:

   ```
   <VirtualHost *:80>
       DocumentRoot /var/www/ampache
         <Directory /var/www/ampache/>
       DirectoryIndex index.php
       AllowOverride All
       Order allow,deny
       Allow from all
       </Directory>
       ErrorLog ${APACHE_LOG_DIR}/error.log
       LogLevel warn
       CustomLog ${APACHE_LOG_DIR}/access.log combined
   </VirtualHost>
   ```

9. Now, disable any default configuration that is using port `80`, or alternatively you can use a port other than `80` for Ampache installation.

10. Reload the Apache server for the changes to take effect:

    ```
    $ sudo service apache2 reload
    ```

Here, we have installed and configured the base setup. Now, we can move on to configuration through a web-based installer. You can access the web installer at the domain name or IP address of your server. The installer should greet you with a big Ampache logo and a language selection box; something similar to the following:

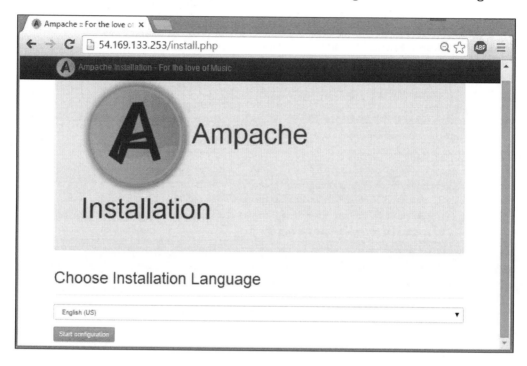

11. Select the language of your choice and click the **Start configuration** button.
12. On the next page, Ampache will check all the requirements and show you a list of settings that need to be fixed. These are mostly the configuration changes and file permissions.

13. Most of these requirements should already be marked with a green **OK** button. You need to fix things that are marked in red. The requirements screen will look as follows:

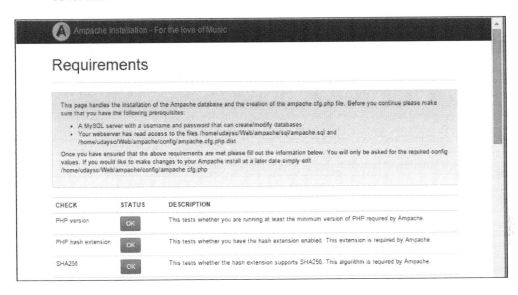

14. Click the **Continue** button when you are done reviewing all the requirements.

15. On the next page, you need to configure the MySQL settings. Fill in the necessary details and select **Create Database User** to create a new Ampache user under the MySQL server:

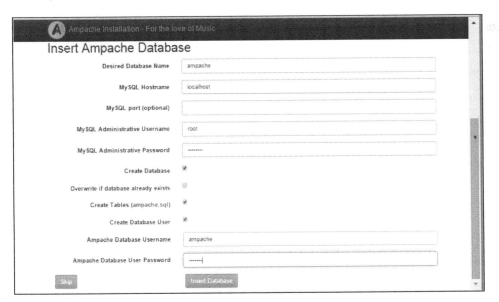

16. Click **Insert Database** to configure database settings.

17. The next screen will confirm the database settings and write the configuration changes to a file under the `config` directory. You can choose to change the installation type and enable transcoding configuration from this screen. Once done, click the **Continue** button to write the configuration file. If you see any errors, scroll to the bottom of the page and click the **write** button to write config changes.

18. Finally, the web setup will ask for admin account credentials for the Ampache server. The **Create Admin Account** form will be shown with **Username** and **Password** fields, as follows. Set the admin account username and password and click the **Create Account** button:

19. Once the account is created, the Ampache installation script will redirect you to the web player screen. If it shows a login screen, use the admin account credentials created in the last step to log in. The landing page of the web player will be rendered as follows:

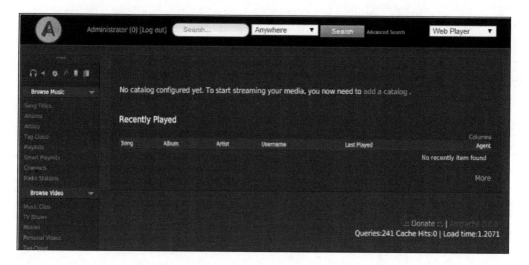

You have completed the Ampache setup process. Now you need to upload content and enjoy your own streaming server. We will learn to create a catalog and upload content in the next recipe.

How it works...

Ampache is a web application written in PHP. We have downloaded the latest Ampache code and set it to work with our web server using Virtual Host configuration. Ampache provides sample `htaccess` files that set required redirection rules. We have enabled respective rules by renaming the sample files. If you are using a web server other than Apache, make sure you check the Ampache documentation for your web server. It supports Nginx and lighttpd as web servers.

Ampache has made it easy to cross-check all requirements and configure your database connection using the web installer. The installer checks for the required PHP settings and extensions and returns a simple page with things that need to fixed. Next, we can configure database settings and push schema directly from the web installer.

Once everything is configured, the web installer returns the login page, from where you can access the Ampache server.

There's more...

The Ampache community have created a Docker image for the Ampache server. If you have a Docker system set up, you can quickly get started with Ampache with its Docker image.

You can get the Dockerfile at `https://github.com/ampache/ampache-docker`.

Ampache is also available in the Ubuntu package repository and can be installed with the following single command:

```
$ sudo apt-get install ampache mysql-server-5.5
```

The currently available version of Ampache is 3.6. If you don't care about the latest and greatest updates, you can use the Ubuntu repository for quick and easy installation.

See also

- Ampache installation guide: `https://github.com/ampache/ampache/wiki/Installation`

Uploading contents and creating catalogs

So, we have installed the Ampache streaming server. Now, we will learn how to upload our audio/video content and create our first catalog.

Getting ready

You will need audio and video files to be uploaded on your server and enough space to save all this content. I will be using podcasts from Ubuntu podcasts in the MP3 format.

Upload all content to your Ampache server and note the directory path. I will be using the `podcasts` directory under `home` for my user.

Open the Ampache server homepage and log in with admin credentials.

How to do it...

Ampache provides the admin page, where you can perform all administrative tasks, such as catalogue management, user management, and other configurations. We will create a new catalogue from the admin panel and then point it to already uploaded content:

1. From your Ampache homepage, click on the admin icon in the upper-left corner of the screen. This should list all administrative tools:

2. Now, click on the **Add a Catalog** link. This should load the **Add a Catalog** page:

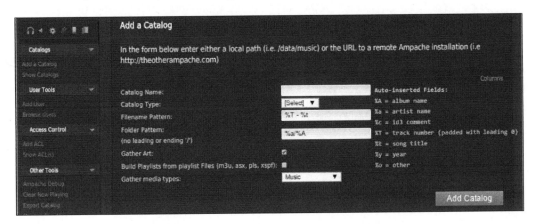

3. Enter the catalog name. Use a name that describes your content. I will use `Ubuntu podcasts`.

4. Set the **Catalog Type** to `local`, as we will be loading content from your local filesystem.

5. Enter the path for your MP3 (or video) files, `/home/ubuntu/podcasts` in my case.

6. Click on the **Add Catalog** button. This will create a new catalog and import all content to it. The process will check for meta tags and try to collect more information about the content. It will take some time to process all the files and add details to the Ampache database:

7. Finally, click **Continue** to complete catalog creation and go to the catalog list:

8. Once catalog creation is complete, you can go to the homepage by clicking the home icon (first) in the upper-left of the screen and then clicking on the song title link. This should list all the files available under your catalog directory:

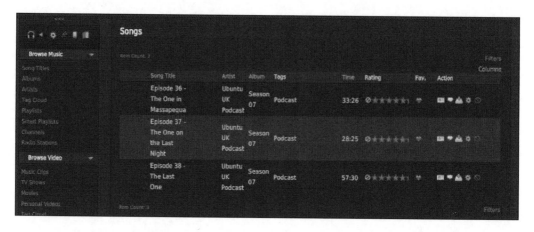

9. From this song list, you can play songs/podcasts, add or remove ratings, add them to playlists, and more:

How it works...

Catalog creation simply reads the content from the upload directory and adds the respective details to the MySQL database. The process tries to gather more details about content using information collected from meta tags and track titles or file names. This information is then used to group the content by artist and album. Note that Ampache is not tagging software where you upload random content and receive a well-organized media library. For Ampache to work well, you need to have properly tagged and well-organized content.

Setting on-the-fly transcoding

Transcoding means converting media from one format to another. Suppose your music files are in a format different to MP3 and your media player only understands MP3 format. In that case, you need to convert your music files to MP3. This conversion task is done by transcoder programs. There are various transcoding programs available, such as `ffmpeg` and `avconv`. These programs need codec before they can convert media from source format to destination format. We need to separately install and configure these components.

Ampache supports on-the-fly transcoding of media files. That is, your music that is not in an MP3 format can be converted into the MP3 format just before it is delivered to your music player, and your high definition video content can be optimized for mobile consumption to reduce bandwidth use.

In this recipe, we will learn how to install and configure transcoding programs with Ampache.

Getting ready

Make sure you have working a setup of the Ampache server.

You will need access to a root account or an account with root privileges.

How to do it...

Ampache depends on external libraries for transcoding to work. We will first install the dependencies and then configure Ampache to work with them:

1. First, add the `ffmpeg` PPA to the Ubuntu installation sources:

   ```
   $ sudo apt-add-repository ppa:mc3man/trusty-media
   $ sudo apt-get update
   ```

2. Now, install `ffmpeg` and other required codecs:

   ```
   $ sudo apt-get install flac mp3splt lame faad ffmpeg vorbis-tools
   ```

3. Next, we need to configure Ampache and enable transcoding. Open the configuration file located at `/var/www/ampache/config/ampache.cfg.php`, find the following lines in the file, and uncomment them:

   ```
   max_bit_rate = 576
   min_bit_rate = 48
   transcode_flac = required
   transcode_mp3 = allowed
   encode_target = mp3
   transcode_cmd = "ffmpeg"
   ```

   Here, we have set `ffmpeg` for the encoding/decoding of media files. You can choose any encoder of your choice. Change the value of `transcode_cmd` respectively.

4. Next, enable debug mode to get details of the transcoding. Find the debug section in the configuration file and set it as follows:

   ```
   debug = true
   Enable log file path which is, by default, set to null
   log_path = "/var/log/ampache"
   ```

5. Save the changes to the configuration file and reload the Apache web server:

```
$ sudo service apache2 reload
```

Now your transcoding setup should be working. You should be able to upload media in a different format and play it as MP3 or other respective formats.

It often happens that we have content in a format that is not supported by the device we are using for playback. Maybe the device does not have the required codec or the hardware is not capable of playing a high bit rate. We may even need to convert content to a lower bit rate and reduce the bandwidth used to stream. The transcoding feature of Ampache helps us to cover these scenarios.

With transcoding, you can convert the content to the desired device-supported format before actually starting the streaming. This is called on-the-fly transcoding. The contents are encoded in a new format as and when needed. Once the conversion is completed, the new format can be cached for repeat use. In the above example, we set Ampache to convert FLAC files to MP3 using the ffmpeg tool. Now whenever we request a file that is originally available in the FLAC format, Ampache will convert it to MP3 before streaming it to our device.

Ampache uses external, well-established media conversion tools for transcoding. Any tool that works with the Ubuntu command line can be configured to work with Ampache. Refer to the Ampache configuration file to get more details and configuration examples.

Enabling API access for remote streaming

A streaming client needs to get the details of the media available on the streaming server. The client needs to authenticate with server access the catalog and list of songs and even request offline access to store media locally. With Ampache, we can use its REST and XML APIs. Through these APIs, clients can communicate with Ampache. You can even write your own client tool using any of the supported APIs.

This recipe covers the setup process for streaming content to remote devices. As of writing this, Ampache allows all users to use all available APIs. We will learn how to modify this setting and configure it to limit access based on user accounts.

Getting ready

Open Ampache in your browser and log in with admin credentials.

How to do it...

We will create a separate user account for remote streaming. From the Ampache homepage, click on the admin icon in the top-left corner and then click on the **Add User** link from the **User Tools** section. An add user menu will be shown that looks like this:

1. Fill in the **Username, E-mail,** and **Password** fields for the new user account and set **User Access** to User.

2. Click the **Add User** button to create this user and then click **Continue**.

3. We will use this new user account to log in from the remote client.

4. Next, we need to configure access rights and allow this user to use APIs to stream music.

5. Click on the admin icon and then click on the **Add ACL** link under the **Access Control** section.

6. Set the name for this access control list.

7. Set level to **Read/Write**.

8. Set the user to the user account created in the previous step.

9. Set **ACL type** to `Stream Access`.

10. Set the start and end IP addresses to `0.0.0.0` and `255.255.255.255` respectively.

11. Click **Create ACL** to save the settings.

12. Click on the **Add ACL** link again and repeat the preceding settings, except, for **ACL Type** that choose `API/RPC`.

13. Now you can use Ampache streaming from your mobile client. When asked for your username and password, use our new user account, and for the streaming server URL, use your Ampache FQDN followed by `/ampache`, for example:

    `http://myampachehost.com/ampache`

14. If your client needs an API key, you can generate one from the **User Tools** section.

15. Click on the **Browse Users** link and then select the user account in question. Click the edit icon to update user details and then click on the generate API key icon.

16. Finally, click the **Update User** button to save your changes.

How it works...

By default, the Ampache server creates an Access Control List that allows all access to all users. It is a good idea to create a separate user and grant only the required permissions. Here, we have created a new user account with access to the REST API and to stream content. This will allow better control over users and content, as well as allow us to set various user-specific default settings, such as default bitrate and encoding formats.

Streaming music with Ampache

We have set up the Ampache server and configured it for streaming. In this recipe, we will learn how to set up an Android client to play content from our Ampache server.

Getting ready

You will need an Android or iOS phone or tablet. We will focus on the configuration of an Android client, but the same configuration should work with an iOS device, and even desktop clients such as VLC.

How to do it...

Follow these steps to stream music with Ampache:

1. First, install Just Player on your Android device. It is an Ampache client and uses XML APIs to stream content from Ampache. It is available from the Play Store.

2. Once installed, open the settings of Just Player and search for Ampache under cloud player.

3. We need to add our Ampache server details here. Enter the server URL as the domain name or IP address of your Ampache server and append `/ampache` at the end, for example:

    ```
    http://myampacheserver.com/ampache
    ```

4. Next, enter the username and password in their respective fields. You can use the user account created in the last recipe.

5. Click **Check** to confirm the settings and then save.

Now you should be able to access your Ampache songs on your Android device or phone.

10
Communication Server with XMPP

In this chapter, we will cover the following recipes:

- ▶ Installing Ejabberd
- ▶ Creating users and connecting with the XMPP client
- ▶ Configuring the Ejabberd installation
- ▶ Creating web client with Strophe.js
- ▶ Enabling group chat
- ▶ Chat server with Node.js

Introduction

Extensible Messaging and Presence Protocol (**XMPP**) is a communication protocol that provides near-real-time message passing between two or more entities. XMPP is based on XML and transfers data in predefined formats that are known to server as well as client systems. Being an XML-based protocol, you can easily extend XMPP to suit your requirements. It also provides various standard extensions to extend the base functionality of the XMPP server.

In this chapter, we will learn how to set up our own XMPP server. The main focus will be on implementing a simple chat application. In later recipes, we will also look at a Node.js and socket-based alternative to implementing the messaging server.

We will be working with a popular XMPP server **Ejabberd**. It is a well-known XMPP implementation supported by ProcessOne. Ejabberd is based on Erlang, a functional programming language specifically designed for soft real-time communication.

Installing Ejabberd

In this recipe, we will learn how to install the Ejabberd XMPP server. We will be using an integrated installation package that is available from the Ejabberd download site. You can also install Ejabberd from the Ubuntu package repository, but that will give you an older, and probably outdated, version.

Getting ready

You will need an Ubuntu server with root access or an account with `sudo` privileges.

How to do it...

The following are the steps to install Ejabberd:

1. Download the Ejabberd installer with the following command. We will be downloading the 64-bit package for Debian-based systems.

2. Make sure you get the updated link to download the latest available version:

   ```
   $ wget https://www.process-one.net/downloads/downloads-
   action.php?file=/ejabberd/15.11/ejabberd_15.11-0_amd64.deb -O
   ejabberd.deb
   ```

3. Once the download completes, you will have an installer package with the `.deb` extension. Use the `dpkg` command to install Ejabberd from this package:

   ```
   $ sudo dpkg -i ejabberd.deb
   ```

4. When installation completes, check the location of the Ejabberd executable:

   ```
   $ whereis ejabberd
   ```

```
ubuntu@ubuntu:~$ whereis ejabberd
ejabberd: /opt/ejabberd-15.11/bin/ejabberd.init /opt/ejabberd-15.11/bin/ejabberd
.service
ubuntu@ubuntu:~$
```

5. Now you can start the Ejabberd server, as follows:

   ```
   $ sudo /opt/ejabberd-15.11/bin/ejabberdctl start
   ```

6. The `start` command does not create any output. You can check the server status with the `ejabberdctl status` command:

```
$ sudo /opt/ejabberd-15.11/bin/ejabberdctl status
```

```
ubuntu@ubuntu:/opt/ejabberd-15.11$ sudo bin/ejabberdctl start
ubuntu@ubuntu:/opt/ejabberd-15.11$ sudo bin/ejabberdctl status
The node ejabberd@localhost is started with status: started
ejabberd 15.11 is running in that node
ubuntu@ubuntu:/opt/ejabberd-15.11$
```

7. Now your XMPP server is ready to use. Ejabberd includes a web-based admin panel. Once the server has started, you can access it at `http://server_ip:5280/admin`. It should ask you to log in, as shown in the following screenshot:

8. The admin panel is protected with a username and password. Ejabberd installation creates a default administrative user account with the username and password both set to `admin`.

 In older versions of Ejabberd, you needed to create an admin account before logging in. The Ejabberd configuration file grants all admin rights to the username admin. The following command will help you to create a new admin account:

```
$ sudo ejabberdctl register_user admin ubuntu password
```

9. To log in, you need a JID (XMPP ID) as a username, which is a username and hostname combination. The hostname of my server is `ubuntu` and the admin JID is `admin@ubuntu`. Once you have entered the correct username and password, an admin console will be rendered as follows:

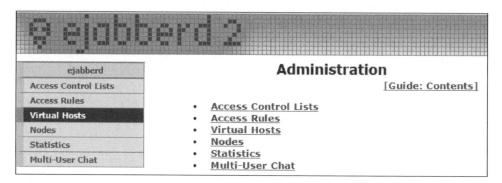

How it works...

Ejabberd binaries are available as a Debian package. It includes a minimum Erlang runtime and all other dependencies. You can download the latest package from the Ejabberd download page.

The installer unpacks all the contents at the `/opt/ejabberd-version` directory. You can get an exact location of the installation with the `whereis` command. All executable files are generally located under the `bin` directory. We will mostly be working with `ejabberdctl`, which is a command line administrative tool. It provides various options to manage and monitor Ejabberd installation. You can see the full list of supported options by entering `ejabberdctl` without any options.

The following screenshot shows the partial output of executing `ejabberdctl` without any options:

```
ubuntu@ubuntu:/opt/ejabberd-15.11$ sudo bin/ejabberdctl
Usage: ejabberdctl [--node nodename] [--auth user host password] command [option
s]

Available commands in this ejabberd node:

    add_rosteritem localuser localserver user server nick group subs
         Add an item to a user's roster (supports ODBC)

    backup file
         Store the database to backup file
```

If the server is not running, you will only see options to start the server or launch a debug console.

If you have noticed, I am using `sudo` with each `ejabberdctl` command. You can avoid the use of the `sudo` command by switching to the `ejabberd` user, which is created at the time of Ejabberd installation. The installer creates a system user account, `ejabberd`, and sets its `home` directory to the Ejabberd installation directory, `/opt/ejabberd-version`. You will still need to use `sudo` to switch user accounts as the `ejabberd` user has no password set. Use the following command to log in as the `ejabberd` user:

```
$ sudo su ejabberd
```

In addition to creating the system user to run the Ejabberd process, the installer also creates an `ejabberd` admin account. The username and password for the administrator account is set to admin/admin. Make sure that you change this password before using your server in production. The installation process also creates a default XMPP host. The hostname is set to match your server hostname. It can be modified from the configuration file.

Once the server has started, you can access the handy web administrative console to manage most of the Ejabberd settings. You can add new users, create access control lists and set access rules, check the participating servers (`node`), and all hosted XMPP domains (`host`). Additionally, you can enable or disable Ejabberd modules separately for each domain. That means if you are using the same server to host `xmpp1.example1.com` and `xmpp2.example2.com`, you can enable a multi-user chat for `xmpp1.example1.com` and disable the same module for `xmpp2.example2.com`.

See also

▸ Ejabberd download page at `https://www.process-one.net/en/ejabberd/downloads/`

Creating users and connecting with the XMPP client

We have installed the XMPP server, Ejabberd. In this recipe, we will learn how to add new user accounts to the Ejabberd server. We will also learn how to configure the XMPP client and connect to our server.

Getting ready

Make sure that you have installed the Ejabberd server and it is running properly.

Additionally, you will need XMPP client software. You can choose from multiple free and open source clients such as pidgin, PSI, Adium, Gajim, and many more. I will be using PSI as it provides various low-level administrative features.

How to do it...

Ejabberd supports multiple methods for registering a new user account. These include adding a new user from the command line, creating a new user from the admin panel, and allowing clients to register with the server using in-band registration. Here, we will create a new user from a command line admin tool. Later in this recipe, I will briefly explain another two methods.

Follow these steps to create a user account and connect it with a XMPP client:

1. Use the following command to register a new user using the `ejabberdctl` command:

   ```
   $ # ejabberdctl register username host password
   $ sudo ejabberdctl register user1 ubuntu password
   ```

   ```
   ejabberd-15.11$ sudo bin/ejabberdctl register user1 ubuntu password
   [sudo] password for ubuntu:
   User user1@ubuntu successfully registered
   ejabberd-15.11$
   ```

2. You can get a list of registered users with the `registered_users` option to `ejabberdctl`:

   ```
   $ # ejabberdctl  registered_users host
   $ sudo ejabberdctl registered_users ubuntu
   ```

   ```
   ejabberd-15.11$ sudo bin/ejabberdctl registered_users ubuntu
   admin
   user1
   ejabberd-15.11$
   ```

3. Now you can create a connection to the server with the XMPP client and your new account. Download and install the XMPP client tool, PSI.

4. Open PSI, click the **General** tab, and then select **Account Setup**. This will open the **XMPP Accounts** window, which looks something like this:

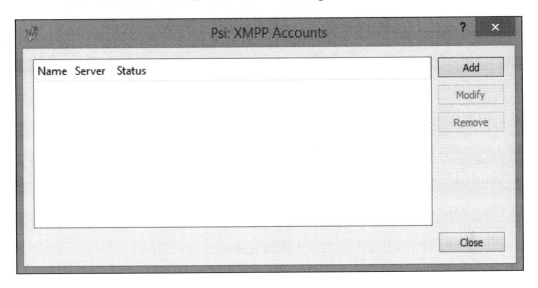

5. Click the **Add** button in the **XMPP Accounts** window. This will open another window named **Add Accounts**:

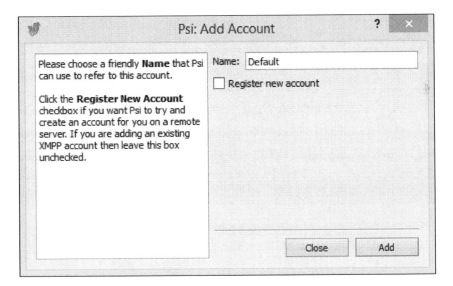

6. Now, in the **Add Account** window, enter the name for this connection, or you can choose to keep the name as **Default**. Click the **Add** button to open one more window.

7. In the newly opened window, enter the account details that we created with the `ejabberdctl` command:

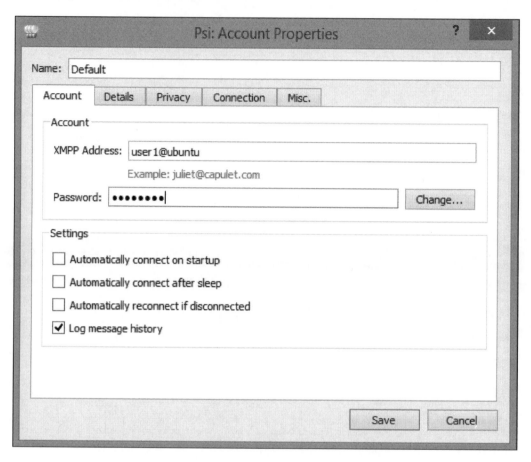

8. On the **Account** tab, enter the full XMPP address (JID) and password for your account.

 If your server IP address is mapped with a domain name and your JID refers to the same domain, you can click **Save** and the account setup is completed for you. If not, you need to provide a server IP or FQDN in the **Connection** tab.

9. Click on the **Connection** tab, then click to check the **Manually Specify Server Host/Port:** checkbox, and then enter the server IP or FQDN and change the port to match your configuration:

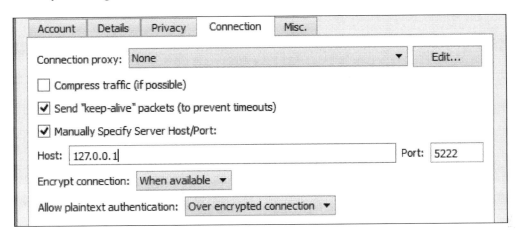

10. Next, click the **Save** button to complete the account setup and then click **Close** to close the account setup window. Your account will be listed in the main window of **Psi**, as follows:

11. Now you are ready to connect to your XMPP server. Select the listed account and change the drop-down box at the bottom to **Online**. This will start the connection process and set the user status as Online.

12. The PSI client will show a prompt regarding self-signed certificates if you are using the default certificate provided by Ejabberd. Click **Trust this certificate** to proceed.

It will take a few seconds to complete the connection process. Once connected, your PSI status will change to **Online**:

13. Now click **General** menu to add XMPP contacts or to join a group chat or to send a message to existing contact. To change your Instant Messaging account status, click on the **Status** menu and select your desired option.

How it works...

The preceding example demonstrates the account creation and client setup process for connecting with the XMPP server. We have used an administrative command to create an XMPP account and then configured client software to use the existing account.

You can also create a new account from the Ejabberd web console. The web console lists all the configured hostnames under the Virtual Hosts section, and each host lists options for user and access management, and other administration tools. Both these options need the server administrator to create an account.

Additionally, XMPP supports an extension that enables a user to self-register with the server. This is called in-band registration (xep-0077), where a user can send his registration request with his desired username, password, and other details, such as email, and the server creates a new user account. This is useful with public XMPP servers where administrators cannot handle all registration requests. The Ejabberd server supports in-band registration with the mod_register plugin, which is enabled by default. From the client side, you can use any XMPP client that supports in-band registration. If you have noticed, PSI also supports in-band registration and provides an option to register a new account in the **Add Account** process:

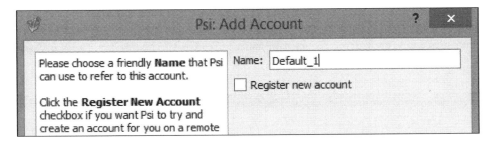

There's more...

When it is an XMPP administration task, PSI is a handy tool. It provides a debug console where you can monitor all XML data transfers between the client and server, as well as send arbitrary XML stanzas to the server. You can access the XML console from right-clicking the menu of your PSI account. Once opened, check **Enable** checkbox to enable traffic monitoring. The **XML Console** looks similar to the following screenshot:

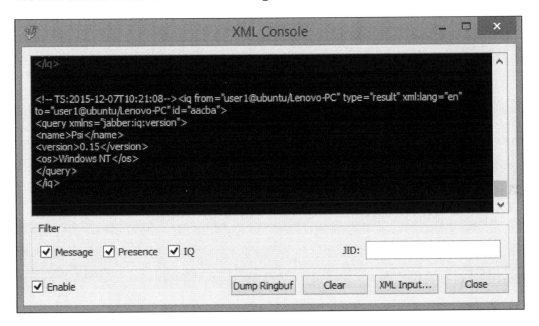

XML Console also allows the filtering of traffic based on packet type. Button **Dump Ringbuf** can be used to dump any traffic before opening the **XML Console**.

Another option is service discovery from the right-click menu. You need to log in as an administrator to see all the options under service discovery. From here, you can monitor user accounts and various services that are available on the server. The **Service Discovery** window looks something like this:

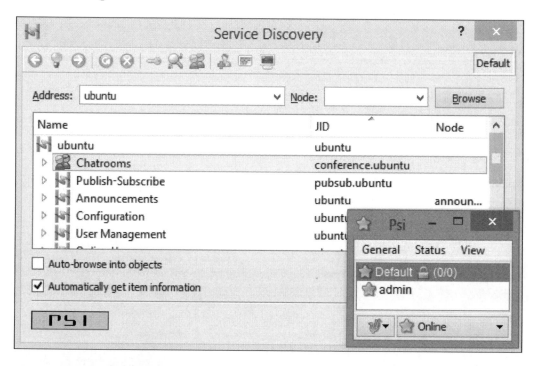

▶   A list of XMPP client tools at `https://xmpp.org/xmpp-software/clients/`

Configuring the Ejabberd installation

Ejabberd comes with various default settings that make it easy to get started. We can install Ejabberd and start using it as soon as installation completes. This works when we are testing our setup, but when we need a production server, we need to make a number of changes to the default installation. Ejabberd provides a central configuration file through which we can easily configure our XMPP installation.

This recipe covers the basic configuration of the Ejabberd server.

Getting ready

Make sure that you have installed the Ejabberd server.

You will need access to a root account or an account with `sudo` privileges.

How to do it...

Ejabberd configuration files are located under the `conf` directory in the Ejabberd installation. On the Ubuntu server, it should be `/opt/ejabberd-version/conf`.

Follow these steps to configure the Ejabberd installation:

1. Open the `ejabberd.yml` file. It contains configuration settings in the YML format.

2. Let us start by setting the domain for our XMPP service. This is located under the `SERVED HOSTNAMES` section in the configuration file. The default setting uses the server hostname as a host for the XMPP service.

3. Add a fully qualified domain name under the `hosts` section. You can choose to keep the default host entry or remove it:

```
###.    ========================
###'    SERVED HOSTNAMES

hosts:
  - "ubuntu"
  - "xmpp.example.com"
```

4. Next, you may want to change the default ports for XMPP connections. Search for the `LISTENING PORTS` section in `ejabberd.yml` and change the respective ports. I will use the default port configuration. The following is the configuration snippet listing `port 5222`:

```
###.    ========================
###'    LISTENING PORTS
listen:
  -
    port: 5222
    module: ejabberd_c2s
    certfile: "/opt/ejabberd-15.11/conf/server.pem"
    starttls: true
```

5. The LISTENING PORTS section contains different port configurations, each serving a separate service. Three of them are enabled by default and serve a client to server connection (5222), server to server connection (5269), and HTTP module for admin console and http_bind service (5280).

6. The same section contains the parameter named certfile, which specifies the SSL certificate file to be used while creating client connections. The default settings point to a certificate created by the Ejabberd installation process. You can change it to your own signed certificate.

7. Also note the shaper and access settings. These settings specify the connection throttling and access control settings used for the client to server connections respectively.

8. At the end of the LISTENING PORTS section, there is a configuration for BOSH (port 5280) connections, as well as the web admin panel. This section also enables web socket connections with the ejabberd_http_ws module.

9. Under the AUTHENTICATION section, you can configure the authentication mechanism to be used. By default, Ejabberd uses internal authentication but it can be set to use external scripts, system-level authentication, external databases, or even a centralized LDAP service. The following is the list of all supported options:

```
###.   ====================
###'   AUTHENTICATION

auth_method: internal
##  auth_method: external
##  auth_method: odbc
##  auth_method: pam
##  auth_method: ldap
```

10. Default internal authentication works well enough and we will proceed with it. If you are planning to use a different authentication mechanism, make sure that you comment out internal authentication.

11. You can also enable anonymous login support, where clients can open an XMPP connection without a username and password. Simply uncomment the respective settings from Anonymous login support:

```
##
## Anonymous login support:
##   auth_method: anonymous
##   anonymous_protocol: sasl_anon | login_anon | both
##   allow_multiple_connections: true | false
```

12. Next, under the DATABASE SETUP section, you can set Ejabberd to use an external database system. Ejabberd supports all leading relational database systems, including SQLite. The following is the list of all supported database systems:

```
###.
###'   DATABASE SETUP
## MySQL server:
## PostgreSQL server:
## SQLite:
## ODBC compatible or MSSQL server:
```

13. The default database settings use an inbuilt database server known as **Mnesia**. It provides in-memory and disk-based storage and can be easily replicated across Ejaberd nodes. Mnesia works well even for very busy XMPP operations.

14. To define an admin user, search for the ACCESS CONTROL LISTS section and add your desired username and hostname under the admin users list:

```
###.
###'   ACCESS CONTROL LISTS
acl:
  admin:
    user:
      - "admin": "ubuntu"
```

This same section includes a list of blocked users.

You can also define your own access control lists, which can be used to restrict permissions to specific hostnames or users. The Access Rules section define the rules applicable to listed ACLs.

15. Finally, under the `modules` section, you can configure the modules to be used by Ejabberd. Modules are plugins to extend the functionality of the Ejabberd server. Comment out the modules that you are not planning to use. You can also enable or disable any module in runtime from the web admin panel. The following is the partial list of modules:

```
## Modules enabled in all ejabberd virtual hosts.
modules:
  mod_adhoc: {}
  mod_admin_extra: {}
  mod_announce: # recommends mod_adhoc
    access: announce
  mod_blocking: {} # requires mod_privacy
  mod_caps: {}
  mod_carboncopy: {}
```

Each module is named after respective XEPs (XMPP extensions). You can get details of the functionality of any module by looking for the related XEP. Also check the Ejabberd documentation to find out the dependencies between modules.

16. Once you are done with all the configuration, you can restart the Ejabberd server with `ejabberdctl restart` or reload configuration changes with the `ejabberdctl reload_config` command:

```
$ sudo bin/ejabberdctl reload_config
```

How it works...

Most of the core settings of Ejabberd are controlled through the configuration file, `ejabberd.yml`. Alternatively, you can change settings with the `ejabberdctl` command, but those settings will not persist after restart. If you need the settings to be permanent, change them in the configuration file. You can always reload the configuration file changes without restarting the server.

While editing the configuration file, make sure that you follow the indentation and spacing as shown in examples. Ejabberd configuration follows the YML format and any change in spacing will leave that setting undefined. The good news is that the latest version of Ejabberd will prompt you about any mistakes in configuration.

There's another file named `ejabberdctl.cfg` that contains Erlang runtime settings. You may need to update those parameters while performance tuning the Ejabberd server.

There's more...

The Ejabberd server is highly extensible and customizable thanks to its modular architecture. Most Ejabberd features are implemented as external modules. Modules are pluggable components that can be used to extend core functionality. These modules can be enabled or disabled as per requirements and do not affect the core functionality. Ejabberd modules are written in either Erlang or Elixir.

Ejabberd modules work with the hook mechanism implemented in the Ejabberd core. Hooks are nothing but simple events such as message received, user logged in, and connection time out. You can get a full list of supported hooks in the Ejabberd documentation, although it may not be a complete list. Each hook gets its own handler chain, with each handler assigned with a priority number. When you enable a module, it registers a given handler with a respective hook and a position or priority in the handler chain. When a hook is triggered by an event, it executes each handler in a chain, one after another. Additionally, a handler function may request to stop processing hooks and not to execute any further handlers.

The Ejabberd administrative command `ejabberdctl` provides an option to search for and install external modules. Ejabberd takes care of downloading the module, compiling, and installing it. You can even write your own module and add it to the local repository for installation. Check Ejabberd's developer documents for more details on module development.

See also

- List of XMPP extensions at `http://xmpp.org/xmpp-protocols/xmpp-extensions/`
- Ejabberd document at `link - https://www.process-one.net/docs/ejabberd/guide_en.html`
- Ejabberd developer documentation at `http://docs.ejabberd.im/developer/modules/`
- Ejabberd hooks at `http://docs.ejabberd.im/developer/hooks/`

Creating web client with Strophe.js

In this recipe, we will learn how to use web technologies to create a web-based XMPP client. I will demonstrate the use of the popular JavaScript library **StropheJS** to create a basic web client and connect to the XMPP server.

Strophe is a collection of libraries that can be used to communicate with the XMPP server. It contains **libstrophe**, which is a C-based implementation of XMPP client functionalities, and Strophe.js, which is a JavaScript implementation. Strophe provides core XMPP client functionality and can be extended with custom modules. The community has contributed various extensions to support additional XMPP functions.

With a limit on page count, I will focus on a simple demo of Strophe.js where we download the code and modify an example to connect with our XMPP server.

Getting ready

You will need the XMPP server installed and running. You can also use public XMPP servers, but make sure that you register with them and obtain your username (JID) and password.

You will need at least two user accounts to communicate with each other.

As we are using a web-based connection, it needs a **Bidirectional-streams Over Synchronous HTTP (BOSH)** extension enabled on the XMPP server. Ejabberd supports this functionality with `mod_http_bind` and it should be enabled by default.

Download and extract the latest source achieve from the Strophe.js site: `http://strophe.im/strophejs/`.

Optionally, you will need a web server set up to access a web client.

How to do it...

I assume the source code is located in the StropheJS directory. We will use one of the examples shipped with the StropheJS source:

1. Change the directory to `examples` under the extracted StropheJS code. This directory contains multiple examples, demonstrating different features of StropheJS. We will use `echobot.js` and `echobot.html` as our starting point.

2. Open `echobot.js` and change the `BOSH_SERVICE` URL on the first line, as follows:

   ```
   var BOSH_SERVICE = 'http://hostname:5280/http-bind';
   ```

3. Replace the hostname with your XMPP domain or XMPP server IP address. For example, if your XMPP server is available at `xmpp.mysrv.com`, then the `BOSH_SERVICE` URL will be as follows:

   ```
   var BOSH_SERVICE = 'http://xmpp.mysrv.com:5280/http-bind';
   ```

4. Optionally, you can enable debug logging to watch actual data exchanged between client and server. Find the `$(document).ready()` section and uncomment the following lines:

```
// uncomment the following lines to spy on the wire
traffic.
connection.rawInput = function (data) { log('RECV: ' +
data); };
connection.rawOutput = function (data) { log('SEND: ' +
data); };
```

5. Save the changes to `echobot.js` and open `echobot.html` in your browser. You should see a page with two text fields, one for **JID** and another for **Password**:

6. Enter your JID (XMPP username) and respective password and click **connect**.

7. Now, Strophe.js will try to open an XMPP connection and log in with the given details. If the connection is successful, you should see the following screen:

8. The last line includes your JID, with a unique identifier for the current session appended at the end. This form of JID is also called **full JID**.

9. Open a separate client connection with, say, PSI, log in with some other user, and send a message on your given JID. This should print your message on the web page and the same message will be echoed back to the sender. Your web page should look similar to the following screenshot:

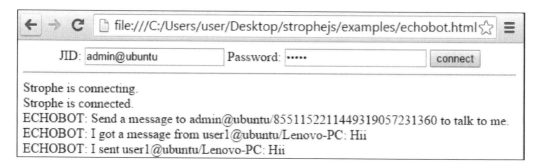

When you are done playing around, click **disconnect** to properly close the XMPP connection.

How it works...

Strophe.js is a JavaScript-based XMPP client library that makes it easy to write your own web-based XMPP clients. Strophe handles all actual communication parts, such as the encoding and decoding of XML stanzas, the connection procedure, and so on. You can use simple APIs provided by Strophe to create your client. Strophe.js uses jQuery to work with the HTML DOM, so if you are familiar with jQuery you will feel at home when working with Strophe.

If you browse through the code in echobot.js, you will see two main event handlers: onConnect and onMessage. These event handlers are attached to specific events and are executed when that event occurs. The onConnect handler is attached to a connection object to capture any change in connection state, and onMessage is attached as a handler for message events. It will be triggered when our client receives any message from the server.

If you are interested in the syntax for the addHandler function, it is as follows:

```
addHandler: function (handler,ns,name,type,id,from,options)
```

The `handler` parameter is the actual function to manipulate an incoming message object; `ns` is the XMPP namespace and can be used to receive packets only from a certain namespace. It defaults to jabber:client, the name parameter, which is the name of an element to act upon—in our case, it is `message`. You can use `iq` or `presence` to receive respective data types. Other parameters add more filtering options, where you can specify a specific ID for the message, type of the message packet (chat or normal or group, defaults to chat) and other options.

The handler function `onMessage` gets triggered whenever a `connection` object receives a new message from the server. Then, it parses the received data and extracts all required information. As it is an echo bot, it simply reads the message and echoes it back to the sender. The new message packet is generated with the following lines:

```
var reply = $msg({to: from, from: to, type: 'chat'})
    .cnode(Strophe.copyElement(body));
```

The message is passed to a `connection` object with the following lines, which in turn sends it to the server:

```
connection.send(reply.tree());
```

The last section initiates the Strophe client on page load (`ready`). When we click on the **connect** button, a `click` handler in this section gets triggered and opens a new connection with the XMPP server. The same button is changed to disconnect so that we can send a proper disconnect request to the server.

There's more...

Strophe.js supports WebSocket-based XMPP connections, and the latest version of Ejabberd has also added support for WebSockets. WebSockets provides noticeable performance improvements and reduces connection time over BOSH connections. In the preceding example, we have used the BOSH protocol, which can be replaced with WebSocket simply by changing the `BOSH_SERVICE` URL as follows:

```
var BOSH_SERVICE = 'ws:// hostname:5280/websocket';
```

If you need a secure WebSocket connection, use the `wss` protocol instead of:

```
wsvar BOSH_SERVICE = 'wss:// hostname:5280/websocket';
```

You should check other examples, mainly `prebind` and `restore`. Both demonstrate connection features that can help in reducing connection delay.

See also

▶ StropheJS official page at `http://strophe.im/strophejs/`

▶ StropheJS GitHub repo at `https://github.com/strophe/strophejs`

▶ StropheJS API documentation at `http://strophe.im/strophejs/doc/1.1.3/files/strophe-js.html`

▶ StropheJS plugins at `https://github.com/metajack/strophejs-plugins`

Enabling group chat

In this recipe, we will learn how to set up and use the group chat feature of XMPP. Group chat is also called **Multi User Chat** (**MUC**). Ejabberd supports MUC with the help of an extension and is enabled by default.

Getting ready

You will need the Ejabberd server set up and running. Make sure you have enabled MUC with the `mod_muc` and `mod_muc_admin` modules.

You will need two users for the group chat. One of them needs to have admin rights to set up MUC and create rooms.

Check your XMPP client for the support of MUC or conference protocol. I will be using PSI as a client for this recipe.

How to do it...

For multi-user chat, we need two or more users logged in on the server at the same time, plus a chat room. Let's first set up our chat client with user accounts and create a chat room.

Follow these steps to enable group chat:

1. Open PSI and set up two different accounts. Log in to the XMPP server and set the **Status** to **Online**. Your PSI window should look something like this:

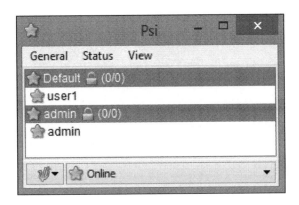

2. You can access the MUC statistics on the Ejabberd web panel to check available rooms.

3. Now we will create our first chat room. In PSI, click the **General** menu, select **Service Discovery**, and then select your **admin** account:

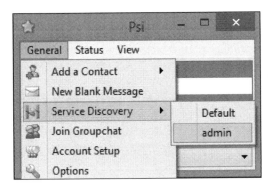

4. This will open a **Service Discovery** window with a list of all administrative services on your Ejabberd XMPP server:

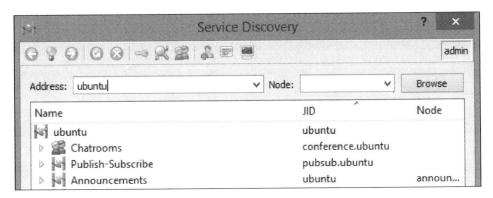

5. Look for the **Chatrooms** node under the **Name** column and double-click it to browse its options. A new window will pop up, which should look something like this:

6. Now type the name of the chat room you want to create under the **Room information** section. Set your nickname as it should be displayed to other participants and click the **Join** button.

7. This will open a new window for your chat room. You will notice the chat room name on the title bar of the window. As the user admin created this room, he is assigned as a moderator:

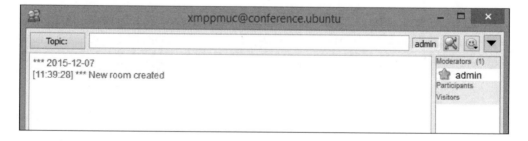

8. For now, the admin is the only participant in this room. Repeat the same steps with other user accounts to get them to join this room. Make sure that you use the same room name again. Once a new user joins the room, the admin user will get notified. Both users can see each other in the participants section:

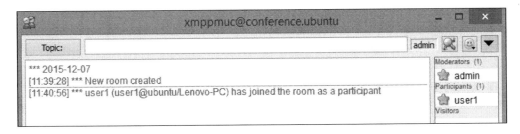

 You can always share your room name with other users to let them in.

How it works...

A group chat works in a similar way to a one on one chat. In a one-on-one chat, we send a message to the JID of a specific user, while in a multi-user chat we send a message to the JID of a chat room. As the message is received on room ID, XMPP takes care of forwarding it to all participants in that room.

There's more...

By default, XMPP chat rooms are not persistent and will be deleted when all participants leave that room. PSI uses the default configuration to quickly create a new chat room. Once the chat room is created, you can configure it in the same chat room window. Click on the options button, the downward triangle in the upper-right corner of the chat room window, and then select **Configure room**:

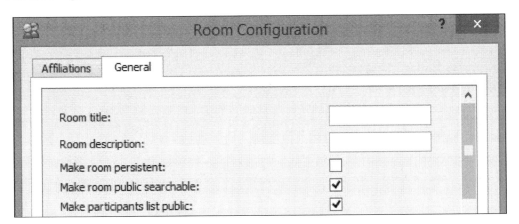

On the first tab, you can set members, administrators, and ban user accounts. On the **General** tab, you can set other room configurations. You can mark a room as persistent and make it private password-protected. This tab contains a number of other options; check them at your leisure.

You may have noticed we have used an admin account to create a chat room. You can allow non-admin users to act as an MUC admin. Open the Ejabberd configuration and search for `muc_admin` configuration. Add your desired username below the admin entry and set it to **allow**.

See also

▸ Candy - JavaScript-based multi-user chat client at `https://candy-chat.github.io/candy/`

▸ Strophe.js MUC plugin at `https://github.com/metajack/strophejs-plugins/tree/master/muc`

Chat server with Node.js

Up to now, this chapter has covered XMPP and its usages. It is a good, mature protocol with multiple servers developed around it. Sometimes, however, you may need to set up a quick application that uses a simple message transfer, or develop a small chat application for your team. For such projects, XMPP servers may turn out to be overkill. You may not use all the features of XMPP and waste resources, even for a basic setup. Plus, developing an XMPP application is a time consuming process.

In this case, you can quickly start using Node.js-based socket communication. Node.js has gained popularity in the developer community. It is a framework developed in a commonly known language, JavaScript. In this recipe, we will learn how to develop a message passing application using Node.js sockets. We will use Socket.io, a popular Node.js library, to work with sockets and a demo app provided by Socket.io.

Getting ready

You will need access to a root account or an account with `sudo` privileges.

How to do it...

We are going to set up a Node.js-based application, so we need to install Node.js on our Ubuntu server.

Follow these steps to install Node.js:

1. Install Node.js with the following command:

    ```
    $ sudo apt-get update
    $ sudo apt-get install nodejs
    ```

2. Optionally, check your Node.js version:

    ```
    $ node -v
    ```

3. Next, download the sample application from the Socket.io GitHub repo:

    ```
    $ wget https://github.com/rauchg/chat-example/archive/master.zip
    ```

4. Unzip the downloaded contents. This will create a new directory named `chat-sample-master`:

    ```
    $ unzip master.zip
    ```

5. Change the path to the newly created directory:

    ```
    $ cd chat-sample-master
    ```

6. Next, we will need to install the dependencies for this sample application. Use the following Node.js command to install all dependencies.

    ```
    $ npm install
    ```

7. This will fetch all dependencies and install them in the `node_modules` directory under `chat-sample-master`. Once the `install` command completes, you can start your application with the following command:

    ```
    $ node index.js
    ubuntu: ~/chat-example-master $ node index.js listening on *:3000
    ```

8. This will start an inbuilt HTTP server and set it to listen on default port `3000`. Now you can access the app at `http://server-ip:3000`. The screen will look similar to the following image:

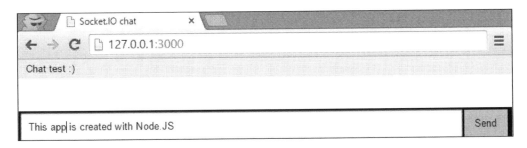

9. Open another instance in a separate browser window and start sending your messages.

How it works...

We have set up a very simple application that listens on a given Node.js socket. To send a message, we have used the `socket.emit()` function, which writes the data from text box to socket:

```
$('form').submit(function(){
        socket.emit('chat message', $('#m').val());
        ...
});
```

When this message is received on the server side, the server writes it to all connected sockets, resulting in a group chat scenario:

```
io.on('connection', function(socket){
    socket.on('chat message', function(msg){
        io.emit('chat message', msg);
    });
});
```

Similarly, to receive a message, we keep listening on the socket, and when an event chat message happens, we write the received data to an HTML page as a message:

```
socket.on('chat message', function(msg){
        $('#messages').append($('<li>').text(msg));
});
```

This is very basic application and can be extended easily to implement one-on-one chat. All we need is a unique ID for all clients and a little modification to the interface to separate messages. Right now, the message is sent as it is; you can collect the message and create a JSON object to contain sender and receiver IDs, plus any additional information.

The advantage of using NodeJS is quick and easy development. JavaScript is a commonly used language and you can easily get support from the large community. You can always develop the application as per your requirements. The disadvantage is regarding scaling; you will need to code the clustering mechanism on your own, whereas for XMPP, clustering is implemented by nearly all leading servers.

There's more...

The Node.js setup available with the Ubuntu repository is not the latest one. You can download the latest version from the node official download page.

Download NodeJS binaries for Linux. Choose your desired version by visiting the NodeJS download page. As of writing this, the latest stable version is 5.1:

```
$ wget https://nodejs.org/download/release/v5.1.0/node-v5.1.0-linux-x64.tar.xz
```

Extract binaries and move it to `/use/local` so that it is accessible globally:

```
$ tar Jxv --strip=1 -C /usr/local/
```

Check the node version with the following command:

```
$ node -v
```

See also

▸   Node.js download page: `https://nodejs.org/en/download`

▸   Node: how to install: `https://github.com/nodejs/help/issues/41`

▸   Sample chat application on GitHub: `https://github.com/rauchg/chat-example`

11

Git Hosting

In this chapter, we will cover the following recipes:

- ▸ Installing Git
- ▸ Creating a local repository with Git CLI
- ▸ Storing file revisions with Git commit
- ▸ Synchronizing the repository with a remote server
- ▸ Receiving updates with Git pull
- ▸ Creating repository clones
- ▸ Installing GitLab, your own Git hosting
- ▸ Adding users to the GitLab server
- ▸ Creating a repository with GitLab
- ▸ Automating common tasks with Git hooks

Introduction

In this chapter, we will learn how to set up a popular version control system: Git. A version control system, also known as revision control system, can be thought of as a repository of files that record every single change in a file. Every update to a file or set of files is recorded as a new version, with some metadata about that specific modification. Metadata contains details of who made the change, a small comment explaining why the change was made, details on exactly what changed in each file, and a timestamp. You can easily switch back to an older version when needed.

Version control systems are generally used to track software source code, but they can be used with virtually any type of file. It is necessary for collaborative work where two or more people are working on the same file. Everyone maintains their own local copy of each file and works on them. When a person satisfactorily completes his work, he sends the updated file to the central repo. Others can synchronize their local copies with this central repo and receive any updates. If two people happen to modify the same file at the same time, they can choose what to keep and what to remove before sending updates to the central repository. If any issue happens with the latest updates, source code can be replaced with previous known-to-work versions. This allows you to track the changes over time and find the cause of the problem.

Over time, multiple version control systems have been developed; some are **centralized version control systems (CVCS)** and others are distributed version control systems. Centralized systems consist of a single central server that hosts all the versions and updates. Everyone sends new changes to the central server and gets updates from it. This makes it easy to administer the repository and enable fine-grained control, but it also becomes a candidate for a single point of failure. If a central server goes down, no one can push changes or get updates. CVS and Subversion are well known centralized version control systems.

Distributed version control systems, on the other hand, overcome this problem by distributing a full copy of the repository on each participating system. If a central server goes down, a copy from any client can be sent to the server to restore it. One can even choose to promote a client as a new server. Git, Mercurial, and Bazaar are examples of distributed version control systems. Bazaar is sponsored and developed by Canonical, the developer of Ubuntu. It is primarily focused on community-supported open source software development.

In this chapter, we will focus on Git, a popular version control system. It was primarily developed by Linus Torvalds to support the development of the Linux kernel. Git is influenced by the lessons learned from other version control systems. It was developed with the aim to support large projects, such as the Linux kernel, and the need for a fully distributed system and high speed. Later, GitHub, a social network for code and developers, ensured the widespread adoption of Git.

In this chapter, we will learn how to work with Git. Starting with the basics, such as installing Git and using it locally, we will also cover some advanced features of Git. We will also set up our own Git hosting with GitLab, an open source tool.

Installing Git

This recipe covers the installation of Git binaries on the Ubuntu server. As always, we will install the latest available Git package.

Getting ready

You will need access to a root account or an account with `sudo` privileges.

How to do it...

Git maintains a separate repository of the latest binaries on Launchpad. We will use PPA for this repository,to install the latest Git version:

1. Add PPA to the Ubuntu installation source:

   ```
   $ sudo add-apt-repository ppa:git-core/ppa
   ```

2. Update the `apt` repository cache:

   ```
   $ sudo apt-get update
   ```

3. Now, install Git with a simple `apt-get install git` command:

   ```
   $ sudo apt-get install git -y
   ```

4. Once installation completes, you can check the Git version with the following command. You can cross check the version with the official Git download page:

   ```
   $ git version
   ```

5. Now introduce yourself to Git by providing your name and email address. Git will add this information to every commit message made by you:

   ```
   $ git config --global user.name "Your Name"
   $ git config --global user.email "email@domain.com"
   ```

6. You can cross-check the configuration by using the `--list` parameter to `git config`:

   ```
   $ git config --list
   ```

7. Use `git help` to get a list of the basic daily use commands:

   ```
   $ git help
   ```

How it works...

Here, we have the installed the latest Git version from the repository maintained by Git developers. The Ubuntu default package repository contains the Git package, but often it is not updated. Ubuntu 14.04 still provides Git version 1.9.1.

Once the Git packages are installed, you need to identify yourself to Git. This information is used to tag the commits created by you. We have globally set the username and email with the `git config` command. Now, whenever you create a new commit in any repository on this system, the commit will get tagged with your username and email. This helps in tracking who did what, especially when you are working in a large group. You can get a list of configuration settings with the command `git config --list`, and the output should look something like the following:

```
$ git config --list
user.name=yourname
user.email=youremail@example.com
```

If you execute the same command from within a repository directory, the list will show some extra settings specific to that repository:

```
~/sample-repo$ git config --list
user.name=yourname
user.email=youremail@example.com
core.repositoryformatversion=0
core.filemode=true
core.bare=false
core.logallrefupdates=true
```

Now, if you are not already familiar with Git, you can make use of the `git help` command to get documentation and manual pages. The default help menu lists commonly used commands with a short description. You can get a list of all available commands with the same `git help` command and a flag, `-a`.

```
$ git help -a
```

Additionally, the installation contains some guides or manual pages to help you get started with Git. To get a list of the available guides, use:

```
$ git help -g
```

The common Git guides are as follows:

- `attributes`: Defines attributes per path
- `glossary`: A Git glossary
- `ignore`: Specifies intentionally untracked files to ignore

To open a particular guide, use the `git help guidename` or the `man git [guidename]` command:

```
$ git help everyday # or man giteveryday
```

There's more...

Git has become a mainstream version control system, especially after the rise of the social coding site **GitHub**. There are other well-known version control systems available, such as Subversion and Mercurial. Facebook uses a modified version of Mercurial for their internal code hosting. Bazaar is another distributed version control system sponsored and developed by Canonical, the force behind Ubuntu. Bazaar provides tight integration with Launchpad, a collaborative development platform by Canonical.

You can get more details about Bazaar on their official page at `http://bazaar. canonical.com/en/`.

See also

You can read more by following these links:

- **Git basics**: `https://git-scm.com/book/en/v2/Getting-Started-Git-Basics`
- **Git book**: `https://git-scm.com/book/en/v2`
- Check out the Git interactive tutorial at: `https://try.github.io` and `http://git.rocks/`
- **Launchpad**: `https://launchpad.net/`

Creating a local repository with Git CLI

Now that we have the Git binaries installed, let's take a step forward and create our first local Git repository.

Getting ready

Make sure that you have installed Git.

How to do it...

We will take a common path by starting a new pet project, where we will simply create a new local directory, add some files to it, and then realize, *Ohh I am gonna need a version control system*:

1. So, yes, quickly create your new project:

   ```
   $ mkdir mynewproject
   $ touch mynewproject /index.html
   $ touch mynewproject /main.js
   $ touch mynewproject/main.css
   ```

2. Add some sample content to these files by editing them:

   Now you need to create a Git repository for this project. Sure, Git covered you with the `git init` command.

3. Make sure you are in the project directory and then initialize a new repository, as follows:

   ```
   $ cd mynewproject
   $ git init
   ```

This will initialize a new empty repository under the project directory. A new hidden directory gets created with the name `.git`. This directory will contain all the metadata of your Git repository and all revisions of every single file tracked by Git.

How it works...

Here, we have used the `git init` command to initialize a new repository on our local system. The files created before initializing a repo are optional; you can always skip that step and directly use `git init` to create a new local repository. Later, when you need to push (synchronize) this repo with a remote hosted repository, you can simply use the `git remote add` command. We will see examples of `git remote add` in the next recipes.

With the `git init` command, you can also create a bare repository by using the `--bare` flag. The difference between a normal repository and a bare repository is that a **bare repository** does not have a working copy. You cannot use a bare repository directly to edit and commit files. Unlike a normal repository, where revision history, tags, and head information is stored in a separate .git directory, a bare repo stores all this data in the same directory. It is meant to be a central shared repository where multiple people can commit their changes. You need to clone these types of repositories to access and edit files. The changes can be pushed using the `git push` command from the cloned copy.

There's more...

You can also use `git clone` to clone existing repositories. The repository can be local or remote. The `clone` command will replicate the contents of a parent repository, including revision history and other details. We will see more details of `git clone` in the next recipes.

See also

You can read more by following these links:

- **Git init**: `https://git-scm.com/docs/git-init`
- **Git clone**: `https://git-scm.com/docs/git-clone`

Storing file revisions with Git commit

We have initialized a new repository for our project. Now we will learn how to store file modifications using `git add` and `git commit`.

Getting ready

Make sure you have initialized a new git repository and created sample files under your project directory. Follow the previous recipes to get more details.

How to do it...

Now that we have a new repo initialized for our project, let's go ahead and check in our files.

1. Before we add any files, simply check the current status of the repo with the `git status` command. This should list all the files under the `Untracked files` list, as follows:

    ```
    $ git status
    ```

```
ubuntu@ubuntu:~/mynewproject$ git status
On branch master

Initial commit

Untracked files:
  (use "git add <file>..." to include in what will be committed)

        index.html
        main.css
        main.js

nothing added to commit but untracked files present (use "git add" to track)
```

As shown by `git status`, none of our files are being tracked by `Git`. We need to add those files before Git tracks any changes to them.

2. Let's add all the files to the tracking list with `git add`:

   `$ git add .`

   This command does not create any output, but stages all untracked files to be added to the repo. The symbol (`.`) specifies the current directory and processes all files under the current directory. You can also specify file name(s) to add specific files.

3. Now check the git status again. This time, it will show newly added files marked by green text and a message saying `Changes to be committed`:

```
ubuntu@ubuntu:~/mynewproject$ git add .
ubuntu@ubuntu:~/mynewproject$ git status
On branch master

Initial commit

Changes to be committed:
  (use "git rm --cached <file>..." to unstage)

        new file:   index.html
        new file:   main.css
        new file:   main.js
```

4. Next, commit the current state of the files with the `git commit` command. Commit means asking Git to save the current state of staged files:

   `$ git commit -m "First commit"`

```
ubuntu@ubuntu:~/mynewproject$ git commit -m "First commit"
[master (root-commit) 4459fcc] First commit
 3 files changed, 0 insertions(+), 0 deletions(-)
 create mode 100644 index.html
 create mode 100644 main.css
 create mode 100644 main.js
ubuntu@ubuntu:~/mynewproject$
```

The `git commit` command will display details of updates to the repository, along with the commit ID (`4459fcc`). In this case, we have added three new files without any new insertion or deletion of contents.

5. Now if you check the `git status` again, it should show the `nothing to commit` message:

   ```
   $ git status
   On branch master
   nothing to commit, working directory clean
   ```

6. Next, make some changes in any file and check the repo status again. This time, it should show the modified files as follows:

   ```
   ubuntu@ubuntu:~/mynewproject$ git status
   On branch master
   Changes not staged for commit:
     (use "git add <file>..." to update what will be committed)
     (use "git checkout -- <file>..." to discard changes in working directory)

         modified:   index.html

   no changes added to commit (use "git add" and/or "git commit -a")
   ```

7. You can check the exact differences to the previous version and current modifications with the `git diff` command. Use `git diff` without any file name to get all modifications in all files, or use it with a file name to check specific files:

   ```
   $ git diff
   ```

   ```
   ubuntu@ubuntu:~/mynewproject$ git diff index.html
   diff --git a/index.html b/index.html
   index e69de29..398a696 100644
   --- a/index.html
   +++ b/index.html
   @@ -0,0 +1,9 @@
   +<!DOCTYPE html>
   +<html>
   +<head>
   +        <title>Git demo</title>
   +</head>
   +<body>
   +        <h2>My new project :)</h2>
   +</body>
   +</html>
   ```

8. Now you can repeat the add and commit process to store these changes. We have modified an existing file without creating new files. We can use the -a flag with git commit to stage changes and commit them in a single command, as follows:

```
$ git commit -a -m "index.html updated"
```

The -a flag will stage all modified files and commit will proceed with newly staged contents. Note that this only works with modified files. If you have created any new file, you need to use git add to stage them.

How it works...

This recipe uses two primary commands: git add and git commit. The first one stages the content for the next commit, and the second actually stores the current state of the content. The git add command is used to add new files, stage updates to existing files, and remove any entries of deleted files. All these modifications to the current working tree are staged for the next commit. The command can be used multiple times to stage multiple modifications. Additionally, you can stage all files under the current directory at once by adding a single file, naming it explicitly, or even choosing a single line from a bunch of updates in the single file.

Once the modifications are staged, you can use git commit to store the updates. When the changes are committed, Git stores the updates in the revision history and changes Git Head to point to the latest revision. All updated files are stored in the form of a **binary large object** (**blob**) as a new snapshot. The commit process also triggers some hooks or events that can be used to execute external scripts to carry out some additional functions. Later in this chapter, we will discuss Git hooks in more detail.

Other than git add and git commit, we have used git status and git diff commands. As the name suggests, git status shows the current status of the repository in question. It lists all files that have been modified after the last commit, newly created or deleted files, and any updates that have already been staged. The git diff command can be used to list all modifications to a given file. It compares the current state of a file against its last committed or indexed state. Note that you can use git diff before indexing any file with git add.

There's more...

Another useful command is git checkout. It can be used to discard any modifications and restore a file to its previous state, or restore the deleted file to its known revision.

Synchronizing the repository with a remote server

Up to now, we have learned how to create a local Git repository and add or update files to it. In this recipe, we will learn how to set up a remote repo and synchronize local code with it. We will be using GitHub to host our remote repository; feel free to choose any other code hosting service.

Getting ready

You will need a GitHub account. Sign up for a free account if you do not already have one.

How to do it...

To create a new repository on GitHub, log in to your GitHub account and create a new public repository:

1. Click the **Create repository** button. Make sure that the checkbox **Initialize this repository with a README** is unchecked. The new repository form should look something like this:

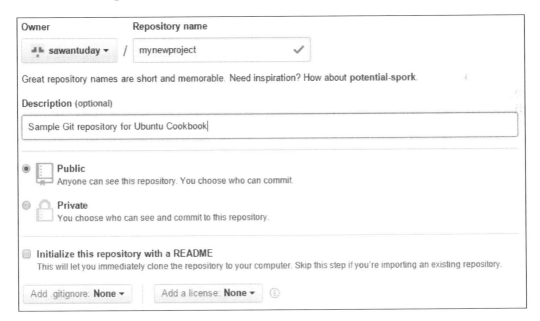

2. On the next page, you will be given an option to initialize this repository. We already have a local repository, so we will use the ... **or push an existing repository from the command line** option:

...or create a new repository on the command line

```
echo # mynewproject >> README.md
git init
git add README.md
git commit -m "first commit"
git remote add origin https://github.com/sawantuday/mynewproject.git
git push -u origin master
```

...or push an existing repository from the command line

```
git remote add origin https://github.com/sawantuday/mynewproject.git
git push -u origin master
```

---

3. Copy both commands and execute them on a local Git repository:

```
$ git remote add origin https://github.com/sawantuday/
mynewproject.git

$ git push -u origin master
```

The first command, `git remote`, adds a reference to the remote repository on GitHub and sets it as its origin. The next command, `git push`, synchronizes all local content with the remote repository. The `git push` command will show the details, as follows:

```
ubuntu@ubuntu:~/mynewproject$ git remote add origin https://github.com/sawantuda
y/mynewproject.git
ubuntu@ubuntu:~/mynewproject$ git push -u origin master
Username for 'https://github.com': sawantuday
Password for 'https://sawantuday@github.com':
Counting objects: 3, done.
Compressing objects: 100% (2/2), done.
Writing objects: 100% (3/3), 225 bytes | 0 bytes/s, done.
Total 3 (delta 0), reused 0 (delta 0)
To https://github.com/sawantuday/mynewproject.git
 * [new branch]      master -> master
Branch master set up to track remote branch master from origin.
```

4. You will be prompted to authenticate with your GitHub account from the command line. Enter your GitHub username and password. This ensures that you are allowed to push the changes to the repository. Alternatively, you can add your local SSH public key to your GitHub account to avoid manual authentication.

Now you can use your GitHub repository to share code with others or clone it to some other system. On the GitHub page, check the code tab to take a look at files in the repository.

How it works...

Local repositories are good for personal work. A single person can work with them easily. A centrally hosted repository is required when you need to share the code base with a group of people. Everyone can make a local copy of the central code base and send their changes back to the central copy. GitHub solves this problem by hosting repositories that are accessible over the Internet. You can simply create a free public repository and share its URL with colleagues. Through access control, you can select who can check in their code. You can also set up your own centrally hosted repository. All you need is a system accessible over your network or Internet.

Here, we have created a central shared repository on GitHub. GitHub provides various options to initialize a repository and add code to it. As we already have our local repository ready, we just need to add a reference to the remote repo and synchronize our changes with `git push`. The `git remote` command is used to add a reference to the remote repository. We have set the remote repository as **origin,** that is, the default remote repository. When using `git push` or `git pull` commands, if we do not specify any remote name it is assumed to be origin. Also, by default, Git marks the first remote as origin.

Next, we used Git push to push or synchronize our local contents to a remote copy. We have explicitly mentioned the remote name as origin and the remote branch as master. By default, Git always pushes to a remote named origin and branch master.

There's more...

You can create your own remote copy on a local shared server. All you need is a normal user account on that server.

Log in to the shared server and create a bare repository with the following command:

```
$ git init --bare shared_repo
```

This will create an empty bare repository under the `shared_repo` directory. If you check its contents, you will find all Git-specific files and directories.

Now you can clone this repo from your workstation or use the `git remote add` command to add a remote to your already initialized repository. Use the following command to clone the repo. Replace the username with the user account on a shared server:

```
$ git clone ssh://user@ server_ip_or_name/full/path/to/repo
```

This command will ask for the password of the user account you have used in the username. Additionally, you can remove the password prompt by setting key-based SSH authentication with a shared server.

GitHub pages

You can host your own simple static website with GitHub for free. All you need is a Git repository hosted on GitHub. Follow these steps to get your own GitHub page:

1. Create a new repository with the name `username.github.io`, where `username` should be your GitHub username.

2. Clone this repository to your local system. If you already have a project created on your local system, you can add this repository as a remote. Check this recipe for how to add a remote.

3. Create `index.html` if you do not have one. Add some content to `index.html`.

4. Stage all content, commit to the local repository, and then push to GitHub.

5. Next, point your browser to username.github.io. You should see the content of index.html.

GitHub pages works with websites generated using static website generators such as Jeykyll, Hugo, and Octopress. By default, you get a `github.io` sub-domain, but you can use your own domain name as well.

See also

Check the manual pages for git remote and git push with `man git-remote` and `man git-push` respectively:

▶ Read more about generating SSH keys: `https://help.github.com/articles/generating-ssh-keys/`

▶ Get free hosting for your static website at GitHub pages: `https://pages.github.com/`

Receiving updates with Git pull

In the last recipe, we learned how to set up a remote repository and send local changes to a remote using the `git push` command. The story is not complete yet. When the repository is shared by multiple people, everyone will push their own changes. The central repository will keep on updating. When you want to synchronize or push your changes to the central repo, you need to download any updates made by other users and then push your modifications on top of that. A git pull command will be used to pull down any updates to the remote central repository to your local repository.

This recipe covers the git pull command. We will use this command to resolve a rejected push, but it is generally used simply to update your local copy.

Getting ready

You will need one central remote repository; it may be hosted on GitHub or anywhere else.

Secondly, you will need two local copies of the central repo. Use the `git clone` command to create a local replica of the remote repository. These two copies are used for demonstration purposes; in the real world, you will already have multiple copies with different users of your repository:

```
$ git clone https://github.com/sawantuday/mynewproject.git local_copy_1
$ git clone https://github.com/sawantuday/mynewproject.git local_copy_2
```

Now enter `local_copy_1`, create a new file with random content and then commit and push the changes back to the remote repository:

```
$ cd local_copy_1
$ echo "// Modifications by user 1" >> index.php
$ git add .
$ git commit -m "Index.php created with comments"
$ git push origin master
```

Your push command should complete without any errors or warnings.

Next, enter `local_copy_2` and create a new file with random contents:

```
$ cd local_copy_2
$ echo "\\ Modifications by user 2" >> main.php
```

How to do it...

Suppose you are user two working on a copy, `local_copy_2`. You cloned the repository and started working with the code base. In the meantime, user one completed his work and pushed his changes back to the central repo. Now, after you have completed your work, you are ready to send updates to the remote repo:

1. Commit your modifications to the local repository:

   ```
   $ git add .
   ```

   ```
   $ git commit -m "main.php created with comments"
   ```

   ```
   ubuntu@ubuntu:~/local_copy_2$ git add .
   ubuntu@ubuntu:~/local_copy_2$ git commit -m "main.php created with comments"
   [master e84e941] main.php created with comments
    1 file changed, 1 insertion(+)
    create mode 100644 main.php
   ubuntu@ubuntu:~/local_copy_2$
   ```

2. Try to push your commit to the central repo:

   ```
   $ git push origin master
   ```

   This time, your push should fail, saying someone else had already updated the remote repository. Git will give you details of a rejected push, as follows:

   ```
   ubuntu@ubuntu:~/local_copy_2$ git push origin master
   Username for 'https://github.com': sawantuday
   Password for 'https://sawantuday@github.com':
   To https://github.com/sawantuday/mynewproject.git
    ! [rejected]        master -> master (fetch first)
   error: failed to push some refs to 'https://github.com/sawantuday/mynewproject.g
   it'
   hint: Updates were rejected because the remote contains work that you do
   hint: not have locally. This is usually caused by another repository pushing
   hint: to the same ref. You may want to first integrate the remote changes
   hint: (e.g., 'git pull ...') before pushing again.
   hint: See the 'Note about fast-forwards' in 'git push --help' for details.
   ```

3. Now you need to pull remote changes; first, with git pull, merge any potential conflicts, and then try to push again:

    ```
    $ git pull origin master
    ```

```
ubuntu@ubuntu:~/local_copy_2$ git pull origin master
remote: Counting objects: 3, done.
remote: Compressing objects: 100% (2/2), done.
remote: Total 3 (delta 0), reused 3 (delta 0), pack-reused 0
Unpacking objects: 100% (3/3), done.
From https://github.com/sawantuday/mynewproject
 * branch            master      -> FETCH_HEAD
   4459fcc..585f879  master      -> origin/master
Merge made by the 'recursive' strategy.
 index.php | 1 +
 1 file changed, 1 insertion(+)
 create mode 100644 index.php
```

4. You will be asked to enter a merge message in **nano** or a similar editor. Simply accept the pre-filled message and save the file by pressing *Ctrl + O*, then press *Enter* to save, and then *Ctrl + X* to exit.

5. Now try to push again. This time it should complete successfully:

    ```
    $ git push origin master
    ```

How it works...

As we saw in the previous example, git pull is used to pull the remote modifications to the local repository. It is a good idea to use git pull before starting your work on the local copy. This way you can be sure that you have all remote updates in your local repository, thus reducing the chances of a rejected push.

The git pull command can be used any time, even to simply update your local codebase with the remote copy. I have used it in a commit and push flow just to demonstrate the rejected push and merge scenario.

The example demonstrates the simple automated merge. It may happen that both user one and user two are working on the same file and incidentally modify the same part of the code. Git will report a Merge conflict, as follows:

```
Unpacking objects: 100% (3/3), done.
From https://github.com/sawantuday/mynewproject
 * branch            master      -> FETCH_HEAD
   e762fed..6e3e1f4  master      -> origin/master
Auto-merging index.php
CONFLICT (content): Merge conflict in index.php
Automatic merge failed; fix conflicts and then commit the result.
ubuntu@ubuntu:~/local_copy_2$
```

Now, in this case, Git may not be able to automatically merge both updates. It will combine both updates in single file and mark them in a special format, as follows:

```
<<<<<<< HEAD
// Modifications by user 2 index.php
// generating conflicts
=======
// Modifications by user 1 inde.php
>>>>>>> 6e3e1f4f6360d0b2a5f1eab6f8c1f1aedc2135d4
```

In this case, you need to decide what to keep and what to remove. Once you are done with solving conflicts, remove the special tags added by Git and commit the conflicting file. After that, you can push your updates along with the new commit for merging.

See also

You can read more by following these links:

- **Git pull**: https://git-scm.com/docs/git-pull
- **Git merge**: https://git-scm.com/docs/git-merge
- **Git fetch**: https://git-scm.com/docs/git-fetch

Creating repository clones

Git clone allows you to create a copy of your repository in a new directory or location. It can be used to replicate a remote repository on your local system or create a local clone to be shared over an intranet. This recipe covers the `git clone` command. We will learn to create a clone of a remote repository and then take a look at various transport protocols supported by Git for cloning.

Getting ready

You will need Git binaries installed on your local system, plus a remote repository. Note down the full path (clone URL) of the remote repository.

How to do it...

Create a clone of the repository with the `git clone` command, as follows:

```
$ git clone ssh://ubuntu@192.168.0.100:22/home/ubuntu/cookbook.git \
ubuntu_cookbook
```

You will be asked to enter a password for the user account `ubuntu`.

This command will create a new directory named `ubuntu_cookbook` and clone the repository cookbook.git into this directory.

How it works...

As seen in the previous example, the `git clone` command will create a new copy of an existing repository. The repository can be a local repository or one located on a remote server. Git supports various protocols to transfer the content between two systems. This includes well-known protocols such as SSH, HTTP/S, and rsync. In addition, Git provides a native transport protocol named Git. Note that the Git protocol does not require any authentication and should be used carefully. In the previous example, we have used the SSH protocol. When working with local repositories, you can use `file:///path/to/repo.git` or even an absolute path `/path/to/repo.git` format.

Cloning requires a single argument, which is the path of the repository to be cloned. You can skip the destination directory and Git will create a clone in a new directory named after the repository name.

You can also create a new **bare clone** with the `--bare` option of the `git clone` command. This is useful for creating a shared central clone that is used by a group of people.

Another important option is the **depth** clone. When cloning a large repository that contains years of work, and you do not really need the entire history of the repository, the option `--depth` can be used to copy only a specified number of revisions. This will help you in quickly downloading just the tip of an entire repository, and will save you some bandwidth by avoiding unnecessary downloads. The syntax for the `--depth` option is as follows:

```
git clone --depth 1 https://github.com/torvalds/linux.git mylinux
```

See also

You can read more by following these links:

  ▶ **Git clone**: `https://git-scm.com/docs/git-clone`

Installing GitLab, your own Git hosting

Up to now in this chapter, we have worked with the Git **command line interface** (**CLI**). It is a very flexible and powerful interface. This recipe covers the installation of a web interface for Git repositories. We will install GitLab, an open source self-hosted Git server. Through GitLab, you can do most administrative tasks, such as creating new repositories, managing access rights, and monitoring history. You can easily browse your files or code and quickly make small edits. GitLab is also adding support for collaboration tools.

Getting ready

You will need access to a root account or an account with `sudo` privileges

Make sure you check out the minimum requirements for installation. You can use a single core 1 GB server for an installation with less than 100 users. An server with 2 cores and 2 GB RAM is recommended.

Also check the available disk space. The installer itself takes around 400 MB of disk space.

How to do it...

We will use the recommended Omnibus Package Installer. It provides a .deb package for Debian/Ubuntu systems. Additionally, the omnibus installation takes care of housekeeping tasks such as restarting the worker process to maintain memory use. If you choose to follow the manual installation process, you can get the detailed installation guide from the GitLab documentation:

1. First, we will need to download the installer package. Download the latest installer package from the GitLab download page at `https://packages.gitlab.com/gitlab/gitlab-ce`:

    ```
    $ wget https://packages.gitlab.com/gitlab/gitlab-ce/packages/
    ubuntu/xenial/gitlab-ce_8.7.1-ce.1_amd64.deb/download
    ```

2. Once download completes, install GitLab using the `dpkg` command, as follows:

    ```
    $ sudo dpkg -i gitlab-ce_8.7.1-ce.1_amd64.deb
    ```

3. After installation, use the following command to configure GitLab:

    ```
    $ sudo gitlab-ctl reconfigure
    ```

4. Optionally, check the system status with the `gitlab-ctl status` command. It should return a list of processes and their respective PIDs, as follows:

```
ubuntu@ubuntu:~$ sudo gitlab-ctl status

[sudo] password for ubuntu:

run: gitlab-workhorse: (pid 806) 57803s; run: log: (pid 805)
57803s

run: logrotate: (pid 31438) 202s; run: log: (pid 810) 57803s

run: nginx: (pid 813) 57803s; run: log: (pid 812) 57803s

run: postgresql: (pid 817) 57803s; run: log: (pid 811) 57803s
```

5. Then, open your browser and point it to your server IP or hostname. You will be asked to set a new password for the administrator account. Once you set a new password, use `root` as the username and your password to login.

How it works...

GitLab is a Ruby-based web application that provides centralized hosting for your Git repositories. We have installed an open source community edition of GitLab using their Omnibus installer. It is an integrated installer package that combines all dependencies and default settings. The installer combines Nginx, Redis, Sidekiq, Unicorn, and PostgreSQL. Unfortunately, the community edition with the Omnibus installer does not support switching to the MySQL database server. To use MySQL, you need to follow the manual installation process and compile GitLab from source, along with other various dependencies.

The configuration file is located at `/etc/gitlab/gitlab.rb`. It is quite a lengthy file and contains numerous parameters, separated by each component. Some important settings to look at include `external_url`, where you can set your domain name, **database** settings, if you are planning to use external PostgreSQL setup, and **email** server settings, to set up your outgoing email server. If you choose to modify any settings, you will need to reconfigure the installation using the `gitlab-ctl reconfigure` command. You can get a list of enabled configurations using the `gitlab-ctl show-config` command.

The GitLab Omnibus package ships with some extra components: **GitLab CI,** a continuous integration service, and **GitLab mattermost**, an integrated installation of mattermost that provides an internal communication functionality with a chat server and file sharing. GitLab CI is enabled by default and can be accessed at `http://ci.your-gitlab-domain.com`. You can enable mattermost from the configuration file and then access it at `http://mattermost.your-gitlab-domain.com`.

There's more...

Git provides an inbuilt web interface to browse your repositories. All you need is a repository, web server, and the following command:

```
$ git instaweb --httpd apache2  # defaults to lighttpd
You can access the page at http://server-ip:1234
```

Check the GitWeb documentation for more details at `https://git-scm.com/docs/gitweb`.

See also

Check out the requirements for GitLab installation: `https://github.com/gitlabhq/gitlabhq/blob/master/doc/install/requirements.md`.

Adding users to the GitLab server

We have set up our own Git hosting server with GitLab, but it still contains a single admin user account. You can start using the setup and create a new repository with an admin account, but it is a good idea to set up a separate non-root account. In this recipe, we will cover the user management and access control features of the GitLab server.

Getting ready

Make sure you have followed the previous recipe and installed the GitLab server.

Login to GitLab with your root or admin account.

You will need to configure the email server before creating a user account. You can use an external email service, such as sendgrid or mailgun. Update your GitLab email server configuration and reconfigure the server for the changes to take effect.

How to do it...

The default landing page for GitLab is a projects page. The same page is listed even when you log in as root. To create a new user, we need to access the admin area:

1. To open the admin console, click on the admin area icon located at the top-right corner of the screen. Alternatively, you can add `/admin` to the base URL and access the admin area.

   The admin dashboard will greet you with details about your installation and the features and components list. The left-hand menu will list all available options.

2. Click on the **Users** menu to get user account-related options.

3. Next, click on the big green **New User** button to open a new user form.

    Now fill in the required details such as name, username, and email. The form should looks something like this:

New user

Account

Name	
	* required
Username	
	* required
Email	
	* required

4. You cannot set a password for a new user account on the create user form. The reset password link will be mailed to the user at a given email ID. A new user can set his password through that link:

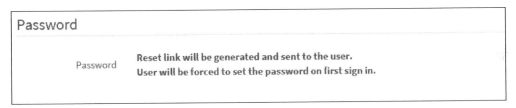

5. Under the **Access** section, you can mark this user as admin and set a limit on projects created by him:

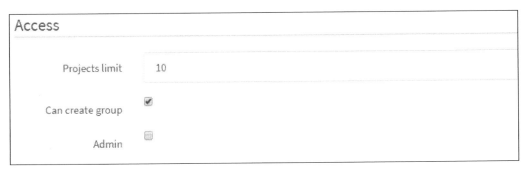

6. Next, under the profile section, you can add some more details for this user account.

7. Now, click on the **Create User** button at the bottom-left of the form. This will save the given details and trigger a password reset email. A screen will change to the **User Details** page where you can see the account details, groups, and projects of a given user, as well as other details. From the same page, you can block or remove the user account.

 A little workaround if you do not have email server set up is to click on the edit button on the user details page. This will open the same form as add new user, with the password fields enabled. Type in the new password, then confirm them, and click on the **Save changes** button. You have set the password for your new user without a reset email or the email server.

The new user account is ready to be used. Open the login page in a new window or private browser and use the email or username and newly set password to log in.

Creating a repository with GitLab

Now that we have set up our own Git hosting and created a new user account, we can start using our Git hosting by creating a new Git repository.

Getting ready

This recipe uses the GitLab setup. Make sure that you have followed the previous recipe and installed your GitLab server.

Log in with your user account on the GitLab server. You can choose the admin account, but a normal user account is recommended.

If you need to use SSH to clone and push to your repositories, you will need to set up your SSH key. From the dashboard, click on **Profile Settings** and then select **SSH Keys** to add a new SSH key. Check *Chapter 2, Networking*, for more details on how to create an SSH key.

How to do it...

In the previous recipe, we learned how to create a local repository and then push it to the remote. Here, we will first create a remote or hosted repository and then clone it to our local system:

1. Log in to your GitLab account. You will be greeted with the Welcome screen detailing your projects.

2. Click on the **NEW PROJECT** button to create a new repository:

3. On a new screen, enter the project or repository name in the project path field. Add an optional descriptive message and select the proper checkbox to make your repository public or private:

4. Next, click on the **Create Project** button to create a new repository. This will redirect you to the repository page.

A URL for your repository is listed, with some details on how to use your new repository. You can use HTTP URL if you have not set up SSH keys. Additionally, you may need to replace the hostname with the server IP from the repository URL:

5. Alternatively, you can create a readme file from the GitLab interface itself. Click on the **README** link to open a file editor in your browser.

When you clone the private repository using its HTTP URL, a local Git daemon will ask you for the username and password details for authentication.

Automating common tasks with Git hooks

One of the more interesting features of Git is hooks. With hooks, you can tie an arbitrary script to various Git events. Whenever a particular event, such as a `git commit` or `git push`, occurs, the script attached to that event gets executed.

Typically, an event consists of several steps, and a script can be attached to each of these steps. The most common steps are pre-event and post-event, with pre hooks executed before the event and post hooks after the event. A pre hook, such as pre-commit, is generally used to cross-check the updates and can approve or reject an actual event. A post hook is used to execute additional activities after an event, such as start a built process when a new push is received or a notification sent.

Every Git repository consists of a `.git/hooks` directory with sample scripts. You can start using those hooks by removing the `.sample` extension from the script name. Additionally, the hook scripts belong to a single repository instance and do not get copied with the repository clone. So, if you add some hooks to your local repository and then push changes to the remote, the hooks will not get replicated on the remote. You will need to manually copy those scripts on the remote system. Built-in sample hooks generally use the shell scripts, but you can use any scripting language, such as Python or even PHP.

In this recipe, we will learn how to use Git hooks. We will create our own post-commit hook that deploys to a local web server.

Getting ready

We will need a local web server installed. I have used an Apache installation; feel free to use your favorite server:

1. Set up a new virtual host under Apache and enable it:

   ```
   $ cd /var/www/
   $ sudo mkdir git-hooks-demo
   $ sudo chown ubuntu:ubuntu git-hooks-demo
   $ cd git-hooks-demo
   ```

2. Create `index.html` and add the following contents to it:

   ```
   $ vi index.html
   ```

   ```
   <!DOCTYPE html>
   <html>
   <head><title>Git hooks demo</title></head>
     <body>
       <h2>Deployed Manually </h2>
     </body>
   </html>
   ```

3. Create the virtual host configuration:

   ```
   $ cd /etc/apache2/sites-available
   $ sudo cp 000-default.conf git-hooks-demo.conf
   ```

4. Open the virtual host configuration, `git-hooks-demo.conf`, and replace its contents with following:

   ```
   <VirtualHost *:80>
      DocumentRoot /var/www/git-hooks-demo/html
   </VirtualHost>
   ```

5. Check the initial version by visiting your IP address in your browser.

6. Next, initialize a Git repository under the `home` directory:

   ```
   $ cd ~/
   $ mkdir git-hooks-repo
   $ cd git-hooks-repo
   $ git init
   ```

7. Copy `index.html` from the web root to the repository:

   ```
   $ cp /var/www/git-hooks-demo/index.html  .
   ```

Now we are equipped with the basic requirements to create our Git hook.

How to do it...

Git hooks are located under the `.git/hooks` directory. We will create a new post commit hook that deploys the latest commit to our local web server. We will be using a shell script to write our hook:

1. Create a new file under the `.git/hooks` directory of your repository:

   ```
   $ touch .git/hooks/post-commit
   ```

2. Add the following contents to our `post-commit` hook:

   ```
   #!/bin/bash
   echo "Post commit hook started"
   WEBROOT=/var/www/git-hooks-demo
   TARBALL=/tmp/myapp.tar
   echo "Exporting repository contents"
   git archive master --format=tar --output $TARBALL
   mkdir $WEBROOT/html_new
   tar -xf $TARBALL -C $WEBROOT/html_new --strip-components 1
   echo "Backup existing setup"
   mv $WEBROOT/html $WEBROOT/backups/html-'date +%Y-%m-%d-%T'
   echo "Deploying latest code"
   mv $WEBROOT/html_new $WEBROOT/html
   exit 0
   ```

3. We need to set executable permissions to a `post-commit` file so that Git can execute it:

   ```
   $ chmod +x .git/hooks/post-commit
   ```

4. Now, update the `index.html` content. Change the line `<h2>Deployed Manually </h2>` to `<h2>Deployed using Git Hooks </h2>`.

5. Commit the changes as usual. We have edited the existing file, so staging and committing can be done in a single command, as follows:

   ```
   $ git commit -a -m "deployed using hooks"
   ```

This time, the `git commit` result should output all echo statements from our `git hook`. It should look as follows:

```
ubuntu@ubuntu:~/git-hooks-repo/html$ git commit -a -m "deployed using hooks"
Post commit hook started
Exporting repository contents
"Backup existing setup"
"Deploying latest code"
[master 40b9322] deployed using hooks
 1 file changed, 1 insertion(+), 1 deletion(-)
```

You can check the latest deployed `index.html` by visiting the IP address of your system:

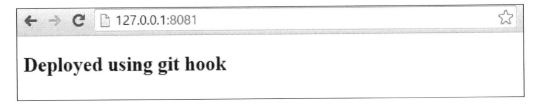

How it works...

We have created a simple post commit hook that exports all files from the Git repository, backs up the existing live site, and replaces it with new contents. This is a very simple shell script, set to execute after each commit event on the local repository. A script that starts with a hash bang signature defines that the script is expecting bash runtime. Later, we defined the WEBROOT and TARBALL variables, which contain the full path for the **web-root** directory and backup location respectively. Next, we created an archive of all the files with the `git archive` command. This command creates an archive of a named tree; a tree can be a specific commit ID or a branch. We have used a master branch for our export. The contents are exported in a tarball format with the export location set using the `--output` parameter. Once we have the tarball in place, we need to replace the live site with contents from the tarball. We have also taken a backup of the running site, just in case anything goes wrong.

This is a very primitive script and deploys only to the local server. To deploy on a remote server, you will need to use some synchronization tools such as **rsync** to update the content on a remote server. Make sure you are using an SSH connection for your deployments to live servers. Many blogs advise you to have a Git instance running on a live web server and setting it to deploy the live site using a `post-receive` hook. This can be an option for staging or a demo server, but on a live server I would try to avoid installing any tool other than a web server. Any additional packages will increase the effective attack surface and may compromise the security of your servers. Who knows whether Git contains some unknown shocks (remember shell shock?)

Note that we are creating a backup on each new commit. You may end up with an out of disk space error if your deployment is big or if you are doing frequent commits. That is not a big problem, though. The script can be easily modified to delete any directories created X days before. You can even choose to keep the last, say, 10 backups and delete others.

As we are deploying to a local web server, we have set the script to be a `post-commit` hook. If you choose to deploy it on a remote server, then make sure you set the script as a post receive or update script. We commit on a local repository and push updates to the remote server.

As we have seen, this is a plain shell script, and you can easily use any bash command in this script. Additionally, you can execute the script manually using the `sh script.sh` command or the short hand notation, `./script.sh`. This will help in debugging the script and monitoring the output without the need to create any Git commits. Also make sure that the script file is set as executable and that all directories you are working with are writable by your user account.

If you are using remote repositories hosted with GitHub or GitLab, they provide a webhook feature which works similar to Git hooks. You will need to set a script accessible over the Web through a URL. When a particular event happens, GitLab will make a `POST` request to a given URL with the relevant event data.

See also

- ▶ Read more about Git hooks at `https://git-scm.com/docs/githooks`
- ▶ Customizing Git hooks at `https://git-scm.com/book/en/v2/Customizing-Git-Git-Hooks`

12
Collaboration Tools

In this chapter, we will cover the following recipes:

- ▶ Installing the VNC Server
- ▶ Installing Hackpad, a collaborative document editor
- ▶ Installing Mattermost – a self-hosted slack alternative
- ▶ Installing OwnCloud, self-hosted cloud storage

Introduction

This chapter covers various collaboration tools. Collaboration enables people to share thoughts and solve problems collectively. With the help of the Internet, we can communicate quickly and more effectively. Tools such as WhatsApp and Slack have changed the way we communicate personally, as well as in corporate life. Services such as Google Docs hosts our documents in the cloud, which can then be shared with multiple people and simultaneously modified by them. Need a comment on your latest edit? Click that chat button and send your request. Need to discuss face to face? Click another button to start video call. Need to send a long detailed message? Yes, we've got e-mail services.

Most of these services are hosted by Internet giants and available as **SAAS (Software as a Service)** products. Simply choose subscription plans and start using them. Many of these services even offer free basic plans. The only problem with these services is you've got to trust a service provider with your data. All your messages, emails, photos, and important documents are hosted with some third party.

In this chapter, we will learn to how set up various open source tools on our own servers. We have already installed an email and instant messaging service, central Git hosting, and a file server. This chapter will focus on more advanced collaboration tools. We will cover the VNC server to share your desktop, the OwnCloud server for document and file sharing, and Mattermost, an open source Slack alternative.

Installing the VNC server

VNC (Virtual Network Computing) enables us to access the GUI of a remote system over a secured network. The VNC client installed on a local system captures the input events of a mouse and keyboard and transfers them to the remote VNC server. Those events are executed on a remote system and the output is sent back to the client. VNC is a desktop sharing tool and is generally used to access the desktop system for remote administration and technical support.

With Ubuntu server, we rarely need a desktop environment. However, if you are a newbie administrator or quite unfamiliar with the command line environment, then GUI becomes a handy tool for you. Plus, you may want to deploy a shared remote desktop environment where people can collaborate with each other. This recipe covers the installation of the VNC server on Ubuntu Server 14.04. We will install a GUI component that is required by VNC and then install and configure the VNC server.

Getting ready

You will need access to a root account or an account with sudo privileges.

How to do it...

The Ubuntu server and cloud editions generally ship with a minimal installation footprint and do not contain GUI components. We will use Gnome-core as our desktop component. Gnome-core is a part of an open source desktop environment.

1. Access the server shell and use the following command to install gnome-core:

   ```
   $ sudo apt-get update
   $ sudo apt-get install gnome-core -y
   ```

   This will take some time as the command needs to download a bunch of components and install them.

2. Once Gnome is installed, we can proceed with VNC server installation using the following command:

   ```
   $ sudo apt-get install vnc4server -y
   ```

3. When installation completes, start a new VNC session by using the following command:

   ```
   $ vncserver
   ```

As this is the first time we have started VNC, you will be prompted to set up a password. This session will also create a few configuration files required for VNC. Your screen should look similar to the screenshot below:

```
ubuntu@ubuntu:~$ vncserver

You will require a password to access your desktops.

Password:
Verify:

New 'ubuntu:1 (ubuntu)' desktop is ubuntu:1

Creating default startup script /home/ubuntu/.vnc/xstartup
Starting applications specified in /home/ubuntu/.vnc/xstartup
Log file is /home/ubuntu/.vnc/ubuntu:1.log
```

1. Next, we will edit the default configuration files created by our first session, kill the VNC process, and then edit the configuration file:

   ```
   $ vncserver -kill :1

   Killing Xvnc4 process ID 2118
   ```

2. Edit the default configuration file and set it to use the Gnome session. Open ~/.vnc/xstartup and uncomment or add the following line to it:

   ```
   $ nano ~/.vnc/xstartup
   #!/bin/sh


   # Uncomment the following two lines for normal desktop:
   unset SESSION_MANAGER
   # exec /etc/X11/xinit/xinitrc


   #[ -x /etc/vnc/xstartup ] && exec /etc/vnc/xstartup
   #[ -r $HOME/.Xresources ] && xrdb $HOME/.Xresources
   #xsetroot -solid grey
   #vncconfig -iconic &
   #x-terminal-emulator -geometry 80x24+10+10 -ls -title "$VNCDESKTOP
   Desktop" &
   #x-window-manager &
   metacity &
   gnome-settings-daemon &
   gnome-panel &
   ```

3. Optionally, disable the Gnome startup script. This will stop Gnome from starting with a system boot and you will see a CLI login instead of the new Gnome-based graphical login screen. Open `/etc/init/gdm.conf` and comment out the following lines:

```
$ sudo nano /etc/init/gdm.conf

#start on ((filesystem

#              and runlevel [!06]

#              and started dbus

#              and plymouth-ready)

#         or runlevel PREVLEVEL=S)
```

4. Save all modifications in configuration files and start a new VNC session. This time, we will add screen resolution and color depth options:

```
$ vncserver -geometry 1366x768 -depth 24
```

```
ubuntu@ubuntu:~$
ubuntu@ubuntu:~$ vncserver -geometry 1366x768 -depth 24

New 'ubuntu:1 (ubuntu)' desktop is ubuntu:1

Starting applications specified in /home/ubuntu/.vnc/xstartup
Log file is /home/ubuntu/.vnc/ubuntu:1.log
```

5. Next, from your local system, install the VNC client software and open it. I have used the TightVNC client. Enter your server IP address and a VNC desktop number to be connected. Here, we have created a single session to a sample IP address, which will be `192.168.0.1:1`:

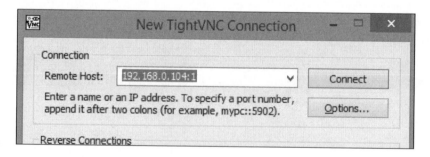

6. Click **Connect**; you will be prompted for a password to authenticate your session:

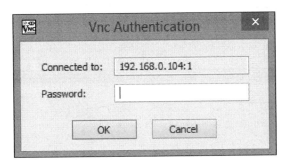

7. Enter the password that we created while starting the first session. You should see a desktop screen with a basic Gnome theme. The following is the scaled screenshot of the VNC viewer:

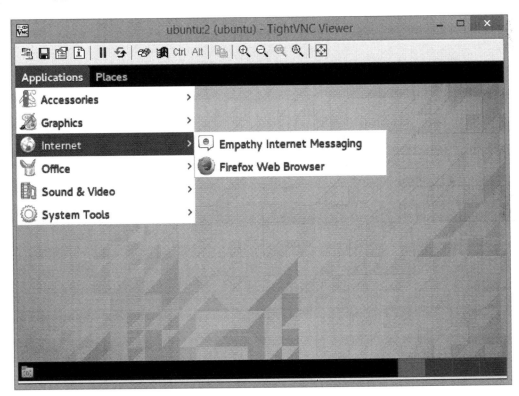

How it works...

VNC works with a client-server model. We have installed the VNC server daemon on our Ubuntu Server and a client on the local system. The server daemon communicates with the GUI buffer or frame buffer on the server side and transfers that buffer data to the client. The client renders that buffer in specially designed software called the VNC viewer. In addition to rendering the remote buffer, the VNC client or viewer captures mouse and keyboard (input) events happening over the client window. Those events are then sent to the VNC server, which applies them to the current graphics frame and any updates are sent back to client.

The pevious example uses simple Gnome-core components. This is a basic graphics suite which contains graphics drives, plus some other tools such as the Firefox browser and an instant messaging client. You can even choose to have a limited setup and install selective, required selected required Gnome packages as follows:

```
$ sudo apt-get install gnome-panel gnome-settings-daemon \
metacity nautilus gnome-terminal
```

This GUI does not match the one provided by Ubuntu Desktop. If you prefer to have the same experience as Ubuntu Desktop, you can separately install a package, ubuntu-desktop:

```
$ sudo apt-get install ubuntu-desktop
```

VNC does support multiple sessions to a single server. You may have noticed in the connection address used previously that we used **:1** to represent the first session or display. This is shorthand for the full port number, which is 5901 for the first session, 5092 for the second, and so on. You can use the full port or just the last digit to refer to a session. Notice the change in desktop number when we start multiple VNC sessions:

```
ubuntu@ubuntu:~$ vncserver -geometry 640x480 -depth 24

New 'ubuntu:1 (ubuntu)' desktop is ubuntu:1

Starting applications specified in /home/ubuntu/.vnc/xstartup
Log file is /home/ubuntu/.vnc/ubuntu:1.log

ubuntu@ubuntu:~$ vncserver -geometry 640x480 -depth 24

New 'ubuntu:2 (ubuntu)' desktop is ubuntu:2

Starting applications specified in /home/ubuntu/.vnc/xstartup
Log file is /home/ubuntu/.vnc/ubuntu:2.log
```

Additionally, you can start a new VNC session for different users with its own password. Simply log in or switch (su user1) to the user account, start vncserver, set the password, and you are done.

See also

▶ How VNC works on Stack Overflow - `http://stackoverflow.com/`
`questions/4833152/how-realvnc-works`

Installing Hackpad, a collaborative document editor

In this recipe, we will install a collaborative document editor, Hackpad. It is a document editor based on an open source editor, EtherPad. Hackpad was acquired by Dropbox, and in early 2015 they open sourced its code.

Getting ready

You will need a system with at least 2 GB of memory.

As always, you will need an account with super user privileges.

How to do it...

Hackpad is a web application based on Java. We will need to install the JDK; **Scala**, which is another programming language; and MySQL as a data store. We will start by installing dependencies and then cloning the Hackpad repository from GitHub.

1. Install JDK and Scala. The installation document mentions Sun JDK as a requirement but it works with Open JDK.

    ```
    $ sudo apt-get update
    $ sudo apt-get install openjdk-7-jdk scala -y
    ```

2. Install the MySQL server. You can get more details on MySQL installation in the chapter handling the database:

    ```
    $ sudo apt-get install mysql-server-5.6
    ```

3. Next, clone the Hackpad repository. You can choose not to install Git and download the ZIP archive of Hackpad from GitHub:

    ```
    $ git clone https://github.com/dropbox/hackpad.git
    ```

4. This will create a new directory, `hackpad`. Before we run the build script, we need to set some configuration parameters to match our environment. Change the directory to `hackpad` and edit the `bin/exports.sh` file as follows:

    ```
    export SCALA_HOME="/usr/share/java"
    export SCALA_LIBRARY_JAR="$SCALA_HOME/scala-library.jar"
    export JAVA_HOME="/usr/share/java"
    ```

5. Next, create a configuration file as a copy of the default configuration, as follows:

    ```
    $ cp etherpad/etc/etherpad.localdev-default.properties \
    etherpad/etc/etherpad.local.properties
    ```

6. Edit the newly created configuration, get the admin email address, and search for the following line in `etherpad/etc/etherpad.local.properties`:

    ```
    etherpad.superUserEmailAddresses =
    __email_addresses_with_admin_access__
    ```

    Replace it with:

    ```
    etherpad.superUserEmailAddresses = admin@yourdomain.tld
    ```

    Optionally, you can set the project to production mode by setting `isProduction` to `true`:

    ```
    devMode = false
    verbose = true
    etherpad.fakeProduction = false
    etherpad.isProduction = true
    ```

7. If you are using a domain name other than localhost, then configure the same with the following option:

    ```
    topdomains =yourdomain.tld,localhost
    ```

8. Set your email host settings. You will need an email address to receive your registration confirmation email. However, this is not a hard requirement for initial setup:

    ```
    smtpServer = Your SMTP server
    smtpUser = SMTP user
    smtpPass = SMTP password
    ```

9. Next, run a build script from the bin directory:

    ```
    $ ./bin/build.sh
    ```

10. Once the build completes, set up the MySQL database. The script will create a new database named `hackpad` and a MySQL user account. You will be asked to enter your MySQL root account password:

    ```
    $ ./contrib/scripts/setup-mysql-db.sh
    ```

```
ubuntu@ubuntu:~/hackpad$ ./contrib/scripts/setup-mysql-db.sh
Creating database hackpad...
Enter password:
Granting priviliges...
Enter password:
Success
ubuntu@ubuntu:~/hackpad$
```

11. Finally, you can start the server by executing `run.sh` from the bin directory:

    $ ./bin/run.sh

    This will take a few seconds to start the application. Once you see the HTTP server is listening to the line, you can access Hackpad at `http://yourdomain.tld:9000`:

```
ubuntu@ubuntu:~/hackpad$
ubuntu@ubuntu:~/hackpad$ ./bin/run.sh
./bin/run.sh: line 30: /home/ubuntu/hackpad/etherpad/data/etherpad.pid: No such
file or directory
Maximum ram: 1701M
Maximum thread count: 283
Using config file: ./etc/etherpad.local.properties
OpenJDK 64-Bit Server VM warning: Cannot open file ./data/logs/backend/jvm-gc.lo
g due to No such file or directory

Using mysql database type.
Establishing mysql connection (this may take a minute)...
mysql connection established.
Building cache for live migrations...
HTTP server listening on http://localhost:9000/
```

12. Access Hackpad and register with an email address that is used for an admin account. If you have set up an email server, you should receive a confirmation email containing a link to activate your account.

    If you have not set up email server access to the MySQL database to get your authentication token, open the MySQL client and use the following queries to get your token. The MySQL password for the Hackpad account is taken from the configuration file:

    ```
    $ mysql -h localhost -u hackpad -ppassword
    mysql> use hackpad;
    mysql> select * from email_signup;
    ```

```
mysql>
mysql> select * from hackpad.email_signup;
+--------------------+-----------------+------------------+--------------------+
| email              | passwordHash    | fullName | createdDate |
|         | token            |         |          |
+--------------------+-----------------+------------------+--------------------+
| admin@localhost.local | $2a$10$D61cP1yEInTmXPQbbG1cxuCGpvDLIvp1F9rW7WvoQtOyKat
NCqHOC | PgEJoGAiL3E2ZD12FqMc | admin    | 2016-01-08 11:54:13 |
+--------------------+-----------------+------------------+--------------------+
1 row in set (0.00 sec)
```

13. Select your token from the row matching your email address and replace it in the following URL. In this case, the auth toke is `PgEJoGAiL3E2ZDl2FqMc`:

    ```
    http://yourdomain.com:9000/ep/account/validate-
    email?email=user@youremail.com&token=your_auth_token_from_db
    ```

    The full auth URL for my admin account will look like this:

    ```
    http://localhost.local:9000/ep/account/validate-email?email=admin@
    localhost.local&token= PgEJoGAiL3E2ZDl2FqMc
    ```

14. Open this URL in the browser and your account registration will be confirmed. You will be logged in to your Hackpad account.

    Once you log in to your new account, Hackpad will start with a welcome screen listing all the default pads that looks something like the following:

You can click any of them and start editing or create a new document. When opened, you will get a full page to add contents, with basic text editing options in the top bar:

The document can be shared using the invite box or simply by sharing the URL.

How it works...

As mentioned before, Hackpad is a collaborative editor based on an open source project, EtherPad. It allows you to create online documents directly in your browser. In the same way as Google Docs, you can use Hackpad to create and store your documents in the cloud. Plus, you can access Hackpad from any device. All your documents will be rendered in a proper format suitable for your device.

When you log in for the first time, the home screen will greet you with stock pads. You can edit existing pads or start a new one from the top bar. An editor will give you a basic text editing setting, plus options to create lists and add comments. You can even add data in a tabular format. Click on the gear icon from the top bar and it will give you options to view document history, get an embedded link, or delete the document.

Every change in the document will be marked with your username, and if two or more people are working with the document at the same time, then the specific line being edited by each user is marked with the user's tag:

On the right-hand side of the document, you can see the options to invite your peers to collaborate on this document. You can invite people using their email address. Make sure that you have configured your email server before using this feature. Alternatively, the invites are also shown in a chat window with clickable links, as shown in the following screenshot:

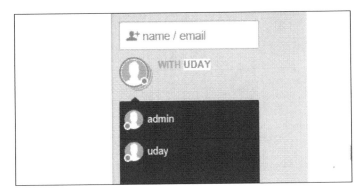

At the bottom of the document, you can find all activity logs about the new initiation and the editing of this document. There is an option to chat with participating people directly from the same window. It is located at the bottom corner of the right-hand side; it's the small bar with a chat icon named after your domain. This provides one-to-one chat, as well as a group chat:

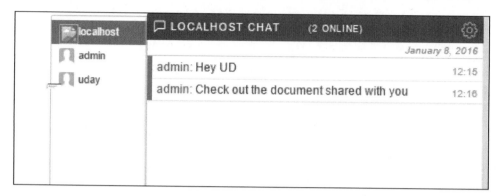

 Note that this setup does not work with IP addresses. You will need a domain name that maps to an IP address. You can set localhost files to set up local domain mappings, or use a local DNS server for your internal network.

There's more

Hackpad is a collaborative document editor. You can add snippets of code in a given document but not entire code files. To edit your code, you can use an open source Cloud IDE named Cloud 9 IDE. Check out the GitHub repo at https://github.com/c9/core/. Alternatively, you can get Docker images set up quickly and play around with the IDE.

Using Hackpad with Docker

The Hackpad setup contains a Docker file as well. If you have Docker installed, you can build a Docker image for Hackpad. Simply change your directory to Hackpad git repo and build a Docker image with the following command:

```
$ docker build -t hackpad
```

See also

Read more about Hackpad at the following links:

- Hackpad with Docker at `https://github.com/dropbox/hackpad/blob/master/DOCKER.md`
- Hackpad repo at `https://github.com/dropbox/hackpad`
- Etherpad at `http://etherpad.org/`
- Cloud 9 IDE at `https://c9.io/`

Installing Mattermost – a self-hosted slack alternative

This recipe covers another open source collaboration tool, Mattermost. **Mattermost** is a modern communication tool that includes one-to-one chat, group chat IRC-like channels, file sharing, and a super-fast search functionality. It can be thought of as a modern IRC tool. Mattermost is well known as an open source Slack alternative, but the Mattermost website says it is not limited to being a Slack alternative. You can find a list of features at `http://www.mattermost.org/features`.

The GitHub repository contains a step-by-step guide for installing Mattermost on production servers. We will use the same guide as our base.

Getting ready

You will need a 64-bit Ubuntu server and access to an account with sudo privileges. Mattermost prebuilt binaries are available only on a 64-bit platform. If you are running 32-bit Ubuntu, you will need to compile Mattermost from source. We will use MySQL as a database for Mattermost. I will use the same server for the database and Mattermost. You may want to separate these services on two different servers for better performance.

Create a separate MySQL user account and database for Mattermost. I will use the lowercase `mattermost` as a database name as well as a username.

Additionally, you will need a proxy if you are planning to load balance multiple Mattermost instances or have a secure setup with SSL enabled.

You will need a separate storage directory for shared multimedia contents. You should use a separate large volume specifically assigned for this purpose. Make sure that the directory is owned by the current user. To keep things simple, I will use a data directory under the current user's home, that is, `/home/ubuntu/mattermost-data`.

How to do it...

Mattermost is based on Golang as a backend and React, a JavaScript framework, for the frontend. Golang is capable of creating self-sufficient independent binaries. We will download the prebuilt package available on GitHub. As of writing this, the latest stable version is 1.3.0:

1. Download the Mattermost archive with the following command:

   ```
   $ wget
   https://github.com/mattermost/platform/releases/download/v1.3.
   0/mattermost.tar.gz
   ```

2. Extract content from the archive. This will create a new directory named `mattermost`:

   ```
   $ tar -xf mattermost.tar.gz
   ```

3. Next, edit the Mattermost configuration file located under the `config` directory:

   ```
   $ cd mattermost
   $ vi config/config.json
   ```

4. It is already configured to use MySQL as a data source. We need to set our username and password details for the database. Search for the SqlSettings section and replace the content of the `DataSource` parameter with the following line:

   ```
   "DataSource": "mattermost:
   password@tcp(localhost:3306)/mattermost?charset=utf8mb4,utf
   8"
   ```

5. Next, search for the FileSettings section and set the `Directory` parameter to the directory we created for multimedia content:

   ```
   "Directory":"/home/ubuntu/mattermost-data/"
   ```

6. Now, run the Mattermost server with the following command, and wait for the server to start listening:

   ```
   $./bin/platform
   ```

7. Now you can access the Mattermost service at the hostname of your server at `http://server_ip_or_host:8065`. However, the service is still running from the console and will be terminated when we close the terminal.

8. Terminate this process by pressing *Ctrl* + *C* and set a startup daemon so that we can start Mattermost in the backend and automatically start the service on system reboot.

9. Create a new upstart configuration under the `/etc/init` directory:

   ```
   $ sudo nano /etc/init/mattermost.conf
   ```

10. Add the following content to the newly created file:

    ```
    start on runlevel [2345]
    stop on runlevel [016]
    respawn
    chdir /home/ubuntu/mattermost
    setuid ubuntu
    exec bin/platform
    ```

11. Now you can start Mattermost with any of the following commands:

    ```
    $ sudo start mattermost
    ```

    Or

    ```
    $ sudo service mattermost start
    ```

    Optionally, if you want to load balance the Mattermost service using Nginx or HAProxy in front of it, please refer to *Chapter 3, Working with Web Servers,* for detail on how to do so. The use of a load balancer will also give you an option to enable SSL security for all communication.

12. Once you start the Mattermost service and access the homepage, you will be asked to sign up. Create an account with an email address and you can start using your own Mattermost instance. You can access the server at `http://yourserver:8065`.

How it works...

Mattermost is all about team communication and collaboration. When you access the Mattermost server for the first time and sign up with your email address, you will get an option to create a new team or join existing teams.:

To join an existing team, you need to submit your email address and Mattermost will reply with links to the team page where you are a member. If you have not yet created a team, simply proceed with signup. On signup, after you have entered your email address, you will be asked to select a team name and URI or a web address for your team page. Enter a good name for your team and click **Next**:

On the next page, you will be asked to choose a URL for your team page. The box should be pre-filled with a suggested URL. Feel free to change it if you have a better idea:

Once you are done with signup, you will be greeted with a welcome message and a simple walkthrough of the Mattermost service. Once you are done with the introduction, you will land on the Town Square channel. This is a prebuilt public channel accessible to all users. There's one more prebuilt channel named Off-Topic listed on the left side menu. You can create your own public channel, create a Private Group, or have a one-to-one chat through Direct Messages.

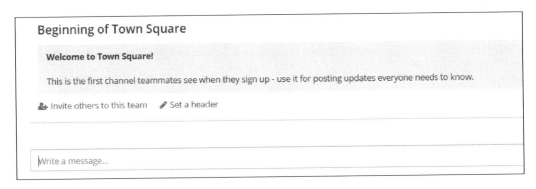

Before you start using the service, invite some more users to your team. Click on the **Invite others to this team** link or click on your username at the top left and then select the Invite New Member link. Here, you can enter the email and name of a single member to invite them. Optionally, you can get a team invite link, which can be shared with a group:

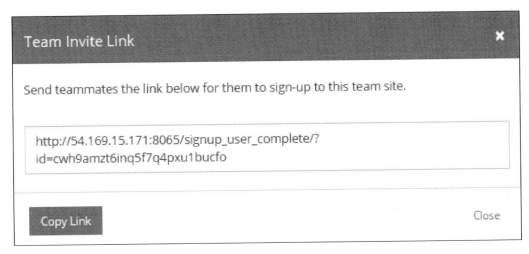

The username menu on the left gives you some more options. You can update team settings, manage team members, and even create a new team altogether. You will need to be a team admin to access these options. If you are part of multiple teams, then you can see an option to switch to a different team.

The team members will receive all communication in public channels. A user can decide to be a part of a channel or leave it and not receive any communication from a specific channel. Other options are Private group and Direct messages. In private groups, you can communicate and share with selected people and not the entire team, whereas in a direct message, as the name suggests, it is a one-to-one chat.

Every single message shared using Mattermost is archived and stored on the Mattermost server. Users can access their respective communication history and even search for a specific message, or documents from a specific user. Shared documents also become part of the archive and are available for later use. The search menu is available at the top-right corner of the screen.

The first user to sign up on Mattermost will get additional admin rights and can access the System Console (from the username menu) to configure system settings and set global defaults. Here, you can configure the database, set your email server and configure email notifications, configure default team settings, check system logs, and much more. When using Mattermost in production mode, make sure that you have configured the SMTP service under email settings and enabled email notifications. You can also enable email verification where account activation will need a user to verify their email address.

There's more ...

The Mattermost service provides an option to integrate with various other popular services. One such service we have worked with is the GitLab server. While working with Git, we have seen the installation process of the GitLab omnibus package. The omnibus package contains Mattermost as a configurable component. If you have GitLab installed through the Omnibus package, check its configuration to enable the Mattermost service. Alternatively, you can configure GitLab integration from the Mattermost settings as well.

From version 1.1, Mattermost added support for web hooks to integrate with external services. Mattermost supports both incoming and outgoing hooks. Incoming hooks can pull events from external services and vice versa. These hooks are compatible with Slack APIs and the tools developed to work with Slack should work with self-hosted Mattermost as well.

See also

Read more about Mattermost by following these resources:

- Mattermost features: `http://www.mattermost.org/features`
- Installation on Ubuntu: `http://docs.mattermost.com/install/prod-ubuntu.html`
- Mattermost Dockerfile: `https://hub.docker.com/r/mattermost/platform/`
- Mattermost web-hooks: `https://github.com/mattermost/platform/tree/master/doc/integrations/webhooks`
- Mattermost Source Code on GitHub: `https://github.com/mattermost/platform`

Installing OwnCloud, self-hosted cloud storage

OwnCloud is a self-hosted file storage and synchronization service. It provides client tools to upload and sync all your files to a central storage server. You can access all your data through a well-designed web interface, which can be accessed on any device of your choice. In addition to a simple contact service, OwnCloud supports contacts, email, and calendar synchronization. Plus, all your data is stored on your own server, making it a more secure option.

In this recipe, we will learn how to install the OwnCloud service on the Ubuntu server. We will be working with a basic OwnCloud setup that includes file sharing and storage. Later, you can add separate plugins to extend the capability of your OwnCloud installation.

Getting ready

You will need access to an account with sudo privileges.

How to do it...

OwnCloud is a PHP-based web application. Its dependencies include a web server, PHP runtime, and a database server. We will use the installation package provided by OwnCloud. The package takes care of all dependencies, plus it will help in updating our installation whenever a new version is available. We will install the latest stable version of OwnCloud. As of writing this, OwnCloud does not provide any packages for Ubuntu 16.04. I have used the package for Ubuntu 15.10:

1. Add the OwnCloud repository public key to your Ubuntu server:

    ```
    $ wget
    https://download.owncloud.org/download/repositories/stable/Ubu
    ntu_15.10/Release.key -O owncloud.key

    $ sudo apt-key add - < owncloud.key
    ```

2. Next, add the OwnCloud repository to installation sources. Create a new source list:

    ```
    $ sudo touch /etc/apt/sources.list.d/owncloud.list
    ```

3. Add an installation path to the newly created source list:

    ```
    $ sudo nano /etc/apt/sources.list.d/owncloud.list

    deb
    http://download.owncloud.org/download/repositories/stable/Ubun
    tu_15.10/ /
    ```

4. Update installation sources with the `apt-get update` command:

```
$ sudo apt-get update
```

5. Install the OwnCloud package. This will download and install all dependencies, download the OwnCloud package, and set up the Apache web server virtual host configuration. By default, OwnCloud use SQLite as a default database. This can be changed at the signup page:

```
$ sudo apt-get install owncloud
```

6. Once installed, you can access your OwnCloud installation at `http://your_server/owncloud`. This will open the registration page for an admin account. Enter the admin username and password for a new account. The first user to register will be marked as the admin of the OwnCloud instance.

> Your server may return a **Not Found** error for the preceding URL. In that case, you need to configure Apache and point it to the OwnCloud setup. Open the default virtual host file `/etc/apache2/sites-available/000-default.conf` and change `DocumentRoot` to match the following:
>
> `DocumentRoot /var/www/owncloud`
>
> Reload the Apache server for the changes to take effect. Now you should be able to access OwnCloud at `http://your_server`.

The same page contains a warning saying the default database is SQLite. Click the configure database link; this will show you the option to enter database connection details. Enter all the required details and click submit.

Once registration completes, you will be redirected to the OwnCloud homepage. If you need any help, this page contains the OwnCloud user manual. You can start uploading content or create new text files right from the homepage.

Optionally, install OwnCloud desktop and mobile applications to sync files across all your devices.

How it works...

OwnCloud is a web application that enables you to synchronize and share files across the web. Store a backup of all your files on a central OwnCloud server, or use it as a central place to send and receive files. OwnCloud also provides native applications for all platforms so that you can easily replicate the necessary data across all your devices. Once you have logged in to your account, OwnCloud will list the default directory structure with a PDF file for the user manual. The screen should look similar to the following:

With the recent updates, OwnCloud has removed various default packages and reduced the overall binary size. For now, the default installation contains a file browser, an activity monitor, and a gallery. The file browser supports the uploading, viewing, and sharing of files. You can create new text files and open PDF files right from the browser:

Default features can be extended from the **Apps** submenu accessible from the **Files** link at the top, left of the screen. It gives you a list of installed and enabled or disabled apps. Plus, you can search for apps across categories such as Multimedia, Productivity, Games, and Tools. Choose your desired category, scroll to the desired app and click enable to install a new component:

OwnCloud also allows flexible user management. When logged in as an admin user, you can access the Users menu from the top-right login section of the screen. Under users, you can create a new user, assign them to a group, create a new group, and even set the disk quota allowed:

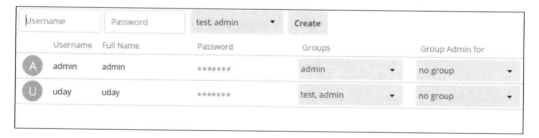

Next is the admin section, which is again accessible to users from the admin group at the top-right of the screen. This section lists all the administrative settings relating to the core OwnCloud setup, as well as for installed apps. Each section contains a link to detailed documentation. The important part of the settings is the email server setup. By default, OwnCloud uses default PHP-based emails. It is recommended you set up an SMTP service. You can use external SMTP service providers, such as MailChimp, or set up your own SMTP server. At the bottom of the admin settings page, you can see some links to improve your OwnCloud experience. This includes performance tuning the OwnCloud setup, security guidelines, theme support, and so on.

See also

- OwnCloud repositories: `https://download.owncloud.org/download/repositories/stable/owncloud/`

- OwnCloud admin manual: `https://doc.owncloud.org/server/8.2/admin_manual/`

13
Performance Monitoring

In this chapter, we will cover the following recipes:

- ▶ Monitoring the CPU
- ▶ Monitoring memory and swap
- ▶ Monitoring the network
- ▶ Monitoring storage
- ▶ Setting performance benchmarks

Introduction

When starting a new server, we tend to use stock images of the Ubuntu server and default installation process. The focus is on developing and improving the application code. The base operating system is not given much attention until we hit some performance issues. Once you reach the tip of application level optimizations and have collected all low-hanging fruit, the next obvious target is system monitoring and resource optimization. In this chapter, we will focus on various performance monitoring tools. We will learn to use various tools to track down the bottlenecks and then briefly look at possible solutions.

The chapter is separated in various recipes, and each covers the monitoring of a single system resource, such as the CPU and memory. At the end of the chapter, we will learn how to set up a performance baseline and use it to compare different configurations of system parameters.

Monitoring the CPU

Modern CPUs generally do not become bottlenecks for performance. The processing power is still far ahead of the data transfer speeds of I/O devices and networks. Generally, the CPU spends a big part of processing time waiting for synchronous IO to fetch data from the disk or from a network device. Tracking exact CPU usage is quite a confusing task. Most of the time, you will find higher CPU use, but in reality, the CPU is waiting for data to become available.

In this recipe, we will focus on tracking CPU performance. We will look at some common tools used to get CPU usage details.

Getting ready

You may need `sudo` privileges to execute some commands.

How to do it...

Let's start with the most commonly used monitoring command that is `top` command. The `top` command shows a summarized view of various resource utilization metrics. This includes CPU usage, memory and swap utilization, running processes, and their respective resource consumption, and so on. All metrics are updated at a predefined interval of three seconds.

Follow these steps to monitor the CPU:

1. To start top, simply type in `top` in your command prompt and press *Enter*:

    ```
    $ top
    ```

```
top - 20:22:53 up 10:53,  2 users,  load average: 0.25, 0.52, 0.53
Tasks: 107 total,   3 running, 102 sleeping,   2 stopped,   0 zombie
%Cpu(s):  9.1 us, 13.1 sy,  0.0 ni, 54.8 id,  0.0 wa,  0.0 hi, 22.9 si,  0.0 st
KiB Mem:   4047976 total,   657272 used,  3390704 free,    40836 buffers
KiB Swap:  1044476 total,        0 used,  1044476 free.   465296 cached Mem

  PID USER      PR  NI    VIRT    RES    SHR S  %CPU %MEM     TIME+ COMMAND
 8292 ubuntu    20   0   40016  12268   6448 R  80.8  0.3   1:44.48 python
    8 root      20   0       0      0      0 S  17.2  0.0   0:25.68 rcuos/0
    3 root      20   0       0      0      0 S   2.3  0.0   0:04.27 ksoftirqd/0
    7 root      20   0       0      0      0 S   1.3  0.0   0:18.50 rcu_sched
```

2. As you can see in the preceding screenshot, a single Python process is using 80% of CPU time. The CPU is still underutilized, with 58% time in idle processes:

   Optionally, you can use the `htop` command. This is the same process monitor as top, but a little easier to use, and it provides text graphs for CPU and memory utilization. You will need to install htop separately:

   ```
   $ sudo apt-get install htop     # one time command
   $ htop
   ```

   ```
   1  [||||||||||||||||              43.1%]   Tasks: 40, 29 thr; 1 running
   2  [|||||||||||||                 31.4%]   Load average: 0.14 0.25 0.15
   Mem[||||||||||            577/3953MB]   Uptime: 00:06:31
   Swp[                        0/1019MB]

     PID USER      PRI  NI  VIRT   RES   SHR S CPU% MEM%   TIME+  Command
    2171 ubuntu     20   0 40016 12240  6420 S 51.1  0.3  0:04.12 python -m SimpleH
    2172 ubuntu     20   0 25744  3568  3032 R  2.3  0.1  0:00.17 htop
     918 root       20   0  251M 15012 12492 S  0.8  0.4  0:01.26 /usr/bin/docker -
    1225 mysql      20   0 1108M  461M 13744 S  0.0 11.7  0:03.57 /usr/sbin/mysqld
   ```

3. While top is used to get an overview of all running processes, the command `pidstat` can be used to monitor CPU utilization by an individual process or program. Use the following command to monitor CPU consumed by MySQL (or any other task name):

   ```
   $ pidstat -C mysql
   ```

   ```
   ubuntu@ubuntu:~$ pidstat -C mysql
   Linux 3.16.0-30-generic (ubuntu)      01/16/2016      _x86_64_      (2 CPU)

   08:39:30 PM   UID       PID   %usr %system  %guest   %CPU   CPU  Command
   08:39:30 PM   105      8458   0.00    0.00    0.00   0.00     1  mysqld
   ubuntu@ubuntu:~$
   ```

4. With `pidstat`, you can also query statistics for a specific process by its process ID or PID, as follows:

   ```
   $ pidstat -p 1134
   ```

5. The other useful command is `vmstat`. This is primarily used to get details on virtual memory usages but also includes some CPU metrics similar to the `top` command:

```
ubuntu@ubuntu:~$ vmstat 1
procs -----------memory---------- ---swap-- -----io---- -system-- -------cpu-----
 r  b   swpd   free   buff  cache   si   so    bi    bo   in   cs us sy id wa st
 1  0      0 2933084  41284 466000    0    0     6     5   27   33  1  0 98  0
0
 0  0      0 2933068  41284 466000    0    0     0     0   40   77  0  1 99  0
0
 0  0      0 2933068  41284 466000    0    0     0     0   25   57  0  0 100  0
0
```

6. Another command for getting processor statistics is `mpstat`. This returns the same statistics as `top` or `vmstat` but is limited to CPU statistics. Mpstat is not a part of the default Ubuntu installation; you need to install the `sysstat` package to use the `mpstat` command:

```
$ sudo apt-get install sysstat -y
```

7. By default, `mpstat` returns combined averaged stats for all CPUs. Flag `-P` can be used to get details of specific CPUs. The following command will display statistics for processor one (0) and processor two (1), and update at an interval of 3 seconds:

```
$ mpstat -P 0,1 3
```

```
ubuntu@ubuntu:~$ mpstat -P 0,1
Linux 3.16.0-30-generic (ubuntu)        01/16/2016      _x86_64_        (2 CPU)

08:50:32 PM  CPU    %usr   %nice   %sys %iowait   %irq   %soft  %steal  %guest
   %gnice  %idle
08:50:32 PM    0    0.36    0.00    0.36    0.15    0.00    0.55    0.00    0.00
   0.00   98.58
08:50:32 PM    1    2.24    0.00    0.22    0.09    0.00    0.00    0.00    0.00
   0.00   97.45
```

8. One more command, `sar` (**System Activity Reporter**), gives details of system performance.

The following command will extract the CPU metrics recorded by `sar`. Flag `-u` will limit details to CPU only and `-P` will display data for all available CPUs separately. By default, the `sar` command will limit the output to CPU details only:

```
$ sar -u -p ALL
```

```
ubuntu@ubuntu:~$ sar -u -P ALL
Linux 3.16.0-30-generic (ubuntu)          01/23/2016        _x86_64_          (2 CPU)

08:34:56 AM        LINUX RESTART

08:35:01 AM        CPU     %user     %nice     %system     %iowait     %steal     %idle
08:45:01 AM        all      2.38      0.00        6.99        1.20       0.00      89.42
08:45:01 AM          0      1.32      0.00       10.16        1.35       0.00      87.17
08:45:01 AM          1      3.38      0.00        4.00        1.07       0.00      91.55

Average:           CPU     %user     %nice     %system     %iowait     %steal     %idle
Average:           all      2.38      0.00        6.99        1.20       0.00      89.42
Average:             0      1.32      0.00       10.16        1.35       0.00      87.17
Average:             1      3.38      0.00        4.00        1.07       0.00      91.55
```

9. To get current CPU utilization using `sar`, specify the interval, and optionally, counter values. The following command will output 5 records at an interval of 2 seconds:

    ```
    $ sar -u 2 5
    ```

```
ubuntu@ubuntu:~$ sar -u 2 5
Linux 3.16.0-30-generic (ubuntu)          01/23/2016        _x86_64_          (2 CPU)

08:49:30 AM        CPU     %user     %nice     %system     %iowait     %steal     %idle
08:49:32 AM        all      0.25      0.00        0.00        0.00       0.00      99.75
08:49:34 AM        all      0.00      0.00        0.25        0.00       0.00      99.75
08:49:36 AM        all      0.00      0.00        0.25        0.00       0.00      99.75
08:49:38 AM        all      0.00      0.00        0.00        0.00       0.00     100.00
08:49:40 AM        all      0.25      0.00        0.25        0.00       0.00      99.50
Average:           all      0.10      0.00        0.15        0.00       0.00      99.75
```

10. All this data can be stored in a file specified by the (-o) flag. The following command will create a file named `sarReport` in your current directory, with details of CPU utilization:

    ```
    $ sar -u -o sarReport 3 5
    ```

Other options include flag –u, to limit the counter to CPU, and flag A, to get system-wide counters that include network, disk, interrupts, and many more. Check `sar` manual (man `sar`) to get specific flags for your desired counters.

How it works...

This recipe covers some well known CPU monitoring tools, starting with the very commonly used command, `top`, to the background metric logging tool SAR.

In the preceding example, we used top to get a quick summarized view of the current state of the system. By default, top shows the average CPU usage. It is listed in the third row of top output. If you have more than one CPU, their usage is combined and displayed in one single column. You can press *1* when top is running to get details of all available CPUs. This should expand the CPU row to list all CPUs. The following screenshot shows two CPUs available on my virtual machine:

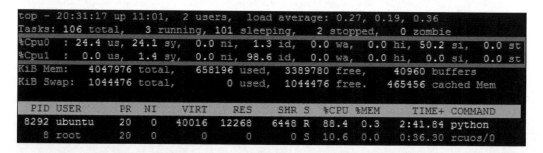

The CPU row shows various different categories of CPU utilization, and the following is a list of their brief descriptions:

- ► `us`: Time spent in running user space processes. This reflects the CPU consumption by your application.

- ► `sy`: Time taken by system processes. A higher number here can indicate too many processes, and the CPU is spending more time process scheduling.

- ► `ni`: Time spent with user space processes that are assigned with execution priority (nice value).

- ► `id`: Indicates the time spent in idle mode, where the CPU is doing nothing.

- ► `wa`: Waiting for IO. A higher value here means your CPU is spending too much time handling IO operations. Try improving IO performance or reducing IO at application level.

- ► `hi/si`: Time spent in hardware interrupts or software interrupts.

- ► `st`: Stolen CPU cycles. The hypervisor assigned these CPU cycles to another virtual machine. If you see a higher number in this field, try reducing the number of virtual machines from the host. If you are using a cloud service, try to get a new server, or change your service provider.

The second metric shown is the process level CPU utilization. This is listed in a tabular format under the column head, %CPU. This is the percentage of CPU utilization by each process. By default, the top output is automatically sorted in descending order of CPU utilization. Processes that are using higher CPU get listed at top. Another column, named TIME+, displays total CPU time used by each process. Check the processes section on the screen, which should be similar to the following screenshot:

PID	USER	PR	NI	VIRT	RES	SHR	S	%CPU	%MEM	TIME+	COMMAND
8292	ubuntu	20	0	40016	12268	6448	R	87.6	0.3	3:30.06	python
8	root	20	0	0	0	0	S	10.9	0.0	0:45.80	rcuos/0
3	root	20	0	0	0	0	S	1.3	0.0	0:06.15	ksoftirqd/0
7	root	20	0	0	0	0	S	0.3	0.0	0:25.41	rcu_sched
9	root	20	0	0	0	0	R	0.3	0.0	0:12.98	rcuos/1
1725	ubuntu	20	0	105744	4900	3824	S	0.3	0.1	0:04.17	sshd
8383	ubuntu	20	0	24828	2976	2540	R	0.3	0.1	0:00.35	top

If you have noticed the processes listed by top you should see that top itself is listed in the process list. Top is considered as a separate running process and also consumes CPU cycles.

To get help on the **top** screen, press *H*; this will show you various key combinations to modify top output. For additional details, check out the manual pages with the command, man top. When you are done with top, press *Q*, to exit or use the exit combination, *Ctrl + C*.

With top, you can get a list of processes or tasks that are consuming most of the CPU time. To get more details of these tasks, you can use the command, pidstat. By default, pidstat shows CPU statistics. It can be used with a process name or **process ID** (**pid**). With pidstat, you can also query memory usages, IO statistics, child processes, and various other process related details. Check the manual page for pidstat using the command man pidstat.

Both commands, top as well as pidstat, give a summarized view of CPU utilization. Top output is refreshed at a specific interval and you cannot extract utilization details over a specific time period. Here comes the other handy command that is vmstat. When run without any parameters, vmstat outputs a single line with memory and CPU utilization, but you can ask vmstat to run infinitely and update the latest metrics at specific intervals using the delay parameter. All the output lines are preserved and can be used to compare the system stats for a given period. The following command will render updated metrics every 5 seconds:

```
$ vmstat 5
```

Optionally, specify the count after delay parameter to close `vmstat` after specific repetitions. The following command will update the stats 5 times at 1 second intervals and then exit:

```
$ vmstat 1 5
```

The details provided by `vmstat` are quite useful for real-time monitoring. The tool `sar` helps you to store all this data in log files and then extract specific details whenever needed. **Sar** collects data from various internal counters maintained by the Linux kernel. It collects data over a period of time which can be extracted when required. Using `sar` without any parameters will show you the data extracted from the previously saved file. The data is collected in a binary format and is located at the `/var/log/sysstat` directory. You may need to enable data collection in the `/etc/default/sysstat` file. When the stats collection is enabled, `sar` automatically collects data every 10 minutes. Sar is again available from the package `sysstat`. Along with the `sar` package, `sysstat` combines two utilities: command `sa1` to record daily system activity data in a binary format, and command `sa2` to extract that data to a human readable format. All data collected by `sar` can be extracted in a human readable format using the `sa2` command. Check the manual pages for both commands to get more details.

There's more...

Similar to sar, one more well-known tool is **collectd**. It gathers and stores system statistics, which can later be used to plot graphs.

See also

▸ Get information on your system CPU with the following command:

```
$ less /proc/cpuinfo
```

▸ Details on `/proc` file system: http://tldp.org/LDP/Linux-Filesystem-Hierarchy/html/proc.html

Monitoring memory and swap

Memory is another important component of system performance. All files and data that are currently being used are kept in the system main memory for faster access. The CPU performance also depends on the availability of enough memory. Swap, on the other hand, is an extension to main memory. Swap is part of persistent storage, such as hard drives or solid state drives. It is utilized only when the system is low on main memory.

In this chapter, we will learn how to monitor system memory and swap utilization.

Getting ready

You may need `sudo` privileges for some commands.

How to do it...

In the last recipe, we used commands `top` and `vmstat` to monitor CPU utilization. These commands also provided details of memory usage. Let's start with the `top` command again:

1. Run the `top` command and check for the `Mem` and `Swap` rows:

```
top - 09:03:20 up 29 min,  2 users,  load average: 0.00, 0.01, 0.05
Tasks: 114 total,   1 running, 113 sleeping,   0 stopped,   0 zombie
%Cpu(s):   0.3 us,   0.2 sy,   0.0 ni, 99.5 id,   0.0 wa,   0.0 hi,   0.0 si,   0.0 st
KiB Mem:   4047976 total,   914372 used,   3133604 free,     26112 buffers
KiB Swap:  1044476 total,        0 used,   1044476 free.    297272 cached Mem
```

2. The **memory** line displays the size of total available memory, size of used memory, free memory, and the memory used for buffers and the file system cache. Similarly, **swap** row should display the allocated size of the swap if you have enabled the swapping. Along with these two lines, `top` shows per process memory utilization as well. The columns `VIRT`, `RES`, `SHR`, and `%MEM` all show different memory allocation for each process:

```
  PID USER      PR  NI    VIRT    RES    SHR S  %CPU %MEM     TIME+ COMMAND
 1225 mysql     20   0 1134984 473080  13744 S   0.7 11.7   0:08.93 mysqld
 2171 ubuntu    20   0   40016  12240   6420 S   0.3  0.3   1:06.74 python
 2374 ubuntu    20   0   24828   2972   2528 R   0.3  0.1   0:00.55 top
    1 root      20   0   33744   4316   2684 S   0.0  0.1   0:05.08 init
    2 root      20   0       0      0      0 S   0.0  0.0   0:00.01 kthreadd
    3 root      20   0       0      0      0 S   0.0  0.0   0:03.36 ksoftirqd/0
```

3. Similar to the `top` command, you can query memory statistics for a specific PID or program by using the `pidstat` command. By default, `pidstat` displays only CPU statistics for a given process. Use flag `-r` to query memory utilization and page faults:

```
$ pidstat -C mysql -r
```

4. Next, we will go through the `vmstat` command. This is an abbreviation of virtual memory statistics. Enter the command `vmstat` in your console and you should see output similar to the following screenshot:

```
ubuntu@ubuntu:~$ vmstat
procs -----------memory---------- ---swap-- -----io----- -system-- ------cpu-----
 r  b   swpd   free   buff  cache   si   so    bi    bo   in   cs us sy id wa st
 1  0      0 3133432  26204 297436    0    0    78    19  121  156  1  2 95  1
 0
```

Using `vmstat` without any option returns a single line report of `memory`, `swap`, `io`, and CPU utilization. Under the `memory` column, it shows the amount of swap, free memory, and the memory used for cache and buffers. It also display a separate `swap` column with **Swap In** (`si`) and **Swap Out** (`so`) details.

5. To get detailed statistics of memory and event counters, use flag `-s`. This should display a table, as follows:

```
$ vmstat -s
```

```
ubuntu@ubuntu:~$ vmstat -s
      4047976 K total memory
       915040 K used memory
       586468 K active memory
       251360 K inactive memory
      3132936 K free memory
        26288 K buffer memory
       297540 K swap cache
      1044476 K total swap
            0 K used swap
      1044476 K free swap
```

6. Another handy command is `free`, which displays the amount of used and available memory in the system. Use it as follows, with the `-h` flag to get human-friendly units:

```
$ free -h
```

```
ubuntu@ubuntu:~$ free -h
              total        used        free      shared  buff/cache   available
Mem:           992M         37M        708M        3.2M        245M        921M
Swap:          1.0G          0B        1.0G
ubuntu@ubuntu:~$
```

7. Finally, command `sar` can give you periodic reports of memory utilization. Simply enable `sar` to collect all reports and then extract memory reports from it or set a specific command to log only memory and swap details.

8. Finally, use `sar` to monitor current memory and swap utilizations. The following command will query the current memory (`-r`) and swap (`-S`) utilization:

   ```
   $ sar -rS 1 5
   ```

```
ubuntu@ubuntu:~$ sar -rS 1 5
Linux 3.16.0-30-generic (ubuntu)        01/23/2016      _x86_64_        (2 CPU)

09:19:16 AM kbmemfree kbmemused %memused kbbuffers  kbcached  kbcommit  %commi
t   kbactive    kbinact     kbdirty
09:19:17 AM   3132956    915020    22.60    26416    297676    910312      17.8
8    586880    251420       40


09:19:16 AM kbswpfree kbswpused  %swpused  kbswpcad  %swpcad
09:19:17 AM   1044476         0      0.00         0     0.00
```

9. For more details on using `sar`, check *Monitoring the CPU* recipe or read the manual pages using the `man sar` command. The command `sar` is available in the package `sysstat`; you will need to install it separately if not already installed.

10. All these tools show process-level memory statistics. If you are interested in memory allocation inside a particular process, then the command `pmap` can help you. It reports the memory mapping of a process, including details of any shared libraries in use and any program extensions with their respective memory consumptions. Use `pmap` along with the PID you want to monitor as follows:

    ```
    $ sudo pmap -x 1322
    ```

 All information displayed by `pmap` is read from a file named `maps` located in the `/proc/ file` system. You can directly read the file as follows:

```
$ sudo cat /proc/1322/maps
```

How it works...

System memory is the primary storage for processes in execution. It is the fastest available storage medium, but is volatile and limited in storage space. The limited storage is generally extended with the help of slower, disk-based Swap files. Processes that are not being actively executed are swapped to disk so that active processes get more space in the faster main memory. Similar to other operating systems, Ubuntu provides various tools to monitor system-wide memory utilization as well as memory uses by process. Commonly used tools include top, vmstat, and free.

We have used the `top` command to monitor CPU uses and know that top provides a summarized view of system resource utilization. Along with a CPU summary, top also provides the memory statistics. This includes overall memory utilization plus per process usage. The summary section in the `top` output displays the total available and used memory. It also contains a separate row for swap. By default, all Ubuntu systems enable the swap partition with nearly the same size as main memory. Some cloud service providers disable the cache for performance reasons.

The details section of top shows per process memory usage separated into multiple columns:

- Column `VIRT` shows the virtual memory assigned to a task or process; this includes memory assigned for program code, data, and shared libraries, plus memory that is assigned but not used.

- Column `RES` shows the non-swapped physical memory used by processes. Whereas column `SHR` shows the amount of shared memory, this is the memory that can be shared with other processes through shared libraries.

- The column `%MEM` shows the percentage of main memory assigned to a specific process. This is a percentage of `RES` memory available to task out of total available memory.

- By default, all memory values are shown in the lowest units, KB. This can be changed using the key combination, *Shift + E* for summary rows and *E* for process columns.

Similar to `top`, the command `ps` lists running processes but without refreshing the list. Without any options, `ps` shows the list of processes owned by the current user. Use it as follows to get a list of all running processes:

```
$ ps aux
```

> Sometimes it is useful to monitor a specific process over a period of time. Top shows you a list of all running processes and `ps` gives you a one-time list. The following command will help you monitor a single program within `top`:
>
> ```
> $ top -p $(pgrep process-name | head -20 | tr "\\n"
> "," | sed 's/,$//')
> ```

The command `vmstat` gives you overall detail regarding memory and swap utilization. The memory column shows the amount of available memory. Next to the memory column, the swap column indicates the amount of memory read from disk (`si`) or written to disk (`so`) per second. Any activity in the `si` and `so` columns indicates active swap utilization. In that case, you should either increase the physical memory of the system or reduce the number of processes running. Large numbers under the swap column may also indicate higher CPU utilization, where the CPU waits for IO operations (`wa`) to complete. As seen before, you can specify the delay and interval options to repeatedly query `vmstat` reports.

One more command, named `free`, shows the current state of system memory. This shows overall memory utilization in the first row and swap utilization in the second row. You may get confused by looking at the lower values in the `free` column and assume higher memory uses. Part of free memory is being used by Linux to improve file system performance by caching frequently used files. The memory used for file caching is reflected in the `buff/cache` column and is available to other programs when required. Check the last column, named `available`, for the actual free memory.

> If you are on Ubuntu 14.04 or lower, the output of the `free` command will contain three rows, with overall memory utilization in the first row, actual memory utilization with cache and buffer adjustments in the second, and swap listed in the third row.

The second row of `free` output displays the swap utilization. You may see swap being used under the `used` column. This is the amount of swap allocated but not effectively used. To check if your system is effectively swapping, use the command `vmstat 1` and monitor `si/so` columns for any swap activity.

System swapping behavior also depends on the value of the kernel parameter named `vm.swappiness`. Its value can range between `0` to `100`, where `0` configures the kernel to avoid swapping as much as possible and `100` sets it to swap aggressively. You can read the current `swappiness` value using the following command:

```
$ sudo sysctl vm.swappiness
vm.swappiness = 60
```

To modify the `swappiness` value for the current session, use the `sysctl` command with a new value, as follows. It is a good idea to use lower values and avoid swapping as much as possible:

```
$ sudo sysctl vm.swappiness=10
vm.swappiness = 10
```

To permanently set `swappiness`, you need to edit the `/etc/sysctl.conf` file and add or uncomment `vm.swappiness=10` to it. Once the file is updated, use the following command to read and set a new value from the configuration file:

```
$ sudo sysctl -p
```

Check the `swapon` and `swapoff` commands if you need to enable swapping or disable it.

There's more...

Most of these statistics are read from the `/proc` partition. The two main files listing details of memory and swap are `/proc/meminfo` and `/proc/swaps`.

The command `lshw` (list hardware) can give you the details of actual hardware. This includes the physical memory configuration, the firmware version, CPU details, such as clock speed, the cache, and various other hardware information. Use `lshw` as follows:

```
$ sudo lshw
```

See also

▶   Check the `swapon` and `swapoff` commands to enable or disable swap files:

```
$ man swapon
$ man swapoff
```

Monitoring the network

When we are talking about a server, its network is the most important resource. Especially in the cloud network, when it is the only communication channel to access the server and connect with other servers in the network. The network comes under an Input/Output device category. Networks are generally slow in performance and are an unreliable communication channel. You may lose some data while in transit, data may be exposed to external entities, or a malicious guy can update original data before it reaches you.

The Ubuntu server, as well as Linux in general, provides tons of utilities to ease network monitoring and administration. This recipe covers some inbuilt tools to monitor network traffic and its performance. We will also look at a few additional tools that are worth a space on your system.

Getting ready

Some commands may need `sudo` access.

You may need to install a few tools.

How to do it...

1. We will start with a commonly used command, that is, `ifconfig`. We mostly use this command to read the network configuration details such as the IP address. When called without any parameters, `ifconfig` displays details of all active network interfaces as follows:

```
ubuntu@ubuntu:~$ ifconfig
docker0   Link encap:Ethernet   HWaddr 56:84:7a:fe:97:99
          inet addr:172.17.42.1  Bcast:0.0.0.0  Mask:255.255.0.0
          UP BROADCAST MULTICAST  MTU:1500  Metric:1
          RX packets:0 errors:0 dropped:0 overruns:0 frame:0
          TX packets:0 errors:0 dropped:0 overruns:0 carrier:0
          collisions:0 txqueuelen:0
          RX bytes:0 (0.0 B)  TX bytes:0 (0.0 B)

eth0      Link encap:Ethernet   HWaddr 08:00:27:ea:fe:96
          inet addr:10.0.2.8  Bcast:10.0.2.255  Mask:255.255.255.0
```

2. These details contain the IP address assigned to each network interface, its hardware address, the **maximum packet size** (MTU) and basic statistics of **received** (RX) and **transmitted** (TX) packets, and the count of errors or dropped packets, and so on.

3. If you are only interested in quick network statistics, use `ifconfig` with flag `-s`, as follows:

```
ubuntu@ubuntu:~$ ifconfig -s
Iface   MTU Met   RX-OK RX-ERR RX-DRP RX-OVR   TX-OK TX-ERR TX-DRP TX-OVR Flg
docker0   1500 0       0      0      0 0           0      0      0      0 B
MU
eth0      1500 0  150716      0      0 0      151045      0      0      0 B
MRU
lo       65536 0      56      0      0 0          56      0      0      0 L
RU
```

4. If you do not see a specific network interface listed in the active list, then query for all available interfaces with the `-a` option to `ifconfig`.

5. Another commonly used command is `ping`. It sends ICMP requests to a specified host and waits for the reply. If you query for a host name, `ping` will get its IP address from DNS. This also gives you confirmation that the DNS is working properly. Ping also gives you the latency of your network interface. Check for the `time` values in the output of the `ping` command:

```
ubuntu@ubuntu:~$ ping www.google.com -c 4
PING www.google.com (74.125.200.99) 56(84) bytes of data.
64 bytes from sa-in-f99.1e100.net (74.125.200.99): icmp_seq=1 ttl=44 time=1011 m
s
64 bytes from sa-in-f99.1e100.net (74.125.200.99): icmp_seq=2 ttl=44 time=273 ms
64 bytes from sa-in-f99.1e100.net (74.125.200.99): icmp_seq=3 ttl=44 time=268 ms
64 bytes from sa-in-f99.1e100.net (74.125.200.99): icmp_seq=4 ttl=44 time=326 ms

--- www.google.com ping statistics ---
4 packets transmitted, 4 received, 0% packet loss, time 3012ms
rtt min/avg/max/mdev = 268.283/470.026/1011.957/313.726 ms, pipe 2
```

6. Next, comes `netstat`. It is mainly used to check network connections and routing tables on the system. The commonly used syntax is as follows:

```
$ sudo netstat -plutn
```

```
ubuntu@ubuntu:~$ sudo netstat -plutn
Active Internet connections (only servers)
Proto Recv-Q Send-Q Local Address          Foreign Address       State
PID/Program name
tcp        0      0 0.0.0.0:111            0.0.0.0:*             LISTEN
711/rpcbind
tcp        0      0 0.0.0.0:80             0.0.0.0:*             LISTEN
1487/nginx
tcp        0      0 0.0.0.0:38512          0.0.0.0:*             LISTEN
_
```

7. The preceding command should list all TCP (`-t`) / UDP (`-u`) connections, plus any ports that are actively listening (`-l`) for connection. The flag, `-p`, queries the program name responsible for a specified connection. Note that flag `-p` requires sudo privileges. Also check flag `-a` to get all listening as well as non-listening sockets, or query the routing table information with flag `-r` as follows:

```
$ netstat -r
```

```
ubuntu@ubuntu:~$ netstat -r
Kernel IP routing table
Destination     Gateway         Genmask         Flags   MSS Window  irtt Iface
default         10.0.2.1        0.0.0.0         UG        0 0          0 eth0
10.0.2.0        *               255.255.255.0   U         0 0          0 eth0
172.17.0.0      *               255.255.0.0     U         0 0          0 docker0
ubuntu@ubuntu:~$
```

8. You can also get protocol level network statistics using the `netstat` command as follows:

   `$ netstat -s`

```
ubuntu@ubuntu:~$ netstat -s
Ip:
    151192 total packets received
    0 forwarded
    0 incoming packets discarded
    151190 incoming packets delivered
    151392 requests sent out
    4 outgoing packets dropped
Icmp:
    38 ICMP messages received
    0 input ICMP message failed.
```

9. One more utility very similar to `netstat` is `ss`. It displays detailed TCP socket information. Use `ss` without any parameters to get a list of all the sockets with a state established.

10. Another command, `lsof`, gives you a list of all open files. It includes the files used for network connections or sockets. Use with flag `-i` to list all network files, as follows:

    `$ sudo lsof -i`

```
ubuntu@ubuntu:~$ sudo lsof -i
COMMAND     PID     USER     FD    TYPE DEVICE SIZE/OFF NODE NAME
rpcbind     711     root     6u    IPv4 10803      0t0  UDP *:sunrpc
rpcbind     711     root     7u    IPv4 10806      0t0  UDP *:858
rpcbind     711     root     8u    IPv4 10807      0t0  TCP *:sunrpc (LISTEN)
rpcbind     711     root     9u    IPv6 10808      0t0  UDP *:sunrpc
rpcbind     711     root    10u    IPv6 10809      0t0  UDP *:858
```

11. To filter output, use flag `-s` with protocol and `state` as filter options:

```
$ sudo lsof -iTCP -sTCP:LISTEN
```

12. Next, we will look at a well-known tool, `tcpdump`. It collects network traffic and displays it to a standard output or dump in a file system. You can dump the content of the packets for any network interface. When no interface is specified, `tcpdump` defaults to the first configured interface, which is generally `eth0`. Use it as follows to get a description of packets exchanged over `eth0`:

```
$ sudo tcpdump -i eth0
```

13. To log raw packets to a file, use flag `-w`. These logged packets can later be read with the `-r` flag. The following command will log `100` packets from the interface `eth0` to the file `tcpdump.log`:

```
$ sudo tcpdump -i eth0 -w tcpdump.log -c 100

$ tcpdump -r tcpdump.log
```

14. Next, to get statistics of network traffic, use the command `sar`. We have already used `sar` to get CPU and memory statistics. To simply extract all network statistics, use `sar` as follows:

```
$ sar -n ALL 1 5
```

```
ubuntu@ubuntu:~$ sar -n ALL 1 5
Linux 3.16.0-30-generic (ubuntu)        01/23/2016      x86_64          (2 CPU)

09:41:54 AM     IFACE   rxpck/s   txpck/s   rxkB/s    txkB/s    rxcmp/s   txcmp/
s    rxmcst/s    %ifutil
09:41:55 AM     eth0     0.00      0.00     0.00      0.00      0.00      0.0
0       0.00     0.00
09:41:55 AM     docker0  0.00      0.00     0.00      0.00      0.00      0.0
0       0.00     0.00
09:41:55 AM     lo       0.00      0.00     0.00      0.00      0.00       0.0
0       0.00     0.00
```

15. This will log all network statistics at an interval of `1` second. You can also enable periodic logging in the file `/etc/default/sysstat`. For network specific usage of `sar`, check flag `-n` in the man pages.

16. There is one more utility named `collectl` which is similar to `sar`. In the same way as `sar`, you will need to separately install this command as well:

```
$ sudo apt-get install collectl
```

17. Once installed, use `collectl` with the `-s` flag and value `sn` to get statistics about the network. Using it without any parameters gives you statistics for the CPU, disk, and network:

```
ubuntu@ubuntu:~$ collectl -s sn
defined(@array) is deprecated at /usr/share/collectl/formatit.ph line 3149.
        (Maybe you should just omit the defined()?)
waiting for 1 second sample...
#<-----------Network----------><-------Sockets----->
#  KBIn  PktIn  KBOut  PktOut  Tcp  Udp  Raw Frag
     0      6      0       0    71    0    0    0
     1     10      1       8    71    0    0    0
     0      8      0       3    71    0    0    0
```

How it works...

This recipe covers various network monitoring commands including the commonly used `ifconfig` and `ping`, `netstat`, `tcpdump`, and `collectl`.

If you have been working with Linux systems for a while, you should have already used the basic network commands, `ifconfig` and `ping`. **Ifconfig** is commonly used to read network configuration and get details of network interfaces. Apart from its basic use, `ifconfig` can also be used to configure the network interface. See *Chapter 2, Networking*, to get more details on network configuration. With `netstat`, you can get a list of all network sockets and their respective processes using those socket connections. With various parameters, you can easily separate active or listening connections and even separate connections with the protocol being used by the socket. Additionally, `netstat` provides details of routing table information and network statistics as well. The command `ss` provides similar details to netstat and adds some more information. You can use `ss` to get memory usages of socket (`-m`) and the process using that particular socket (`-p`). It also provides various filtering options to get the desired output. Check the manual pages of `ss` with the command, `man ss`.

There's more...

Following are some more commands that can be useful when monitoring network data. With a limit on page count, it is not possible to cover them all, so I am simply listing the relevant commands:

Many of these commands need to be installed separately. Simply type in the command if it's not available, and Ubuntu will help you with a command to install the respective package.

- ▶ `nethogs`: Monitors per process bandwidth utilization
- ▶ `ntop` / `iftop`: Top for network monitoring
- ▶ `iptraf`: Monitors network interface activity
- ▶ `vnstat`: Network traffic monitoring with logging
- ▶ `ethtool`: Queries and configures network interfaces
- ▶ `nicstat` / `ifstat` / `nstat`: Network interface statistics
- ▶ `tracepath`: Traces a network route to destination host

Monitoring storage

Storage is one of the slowest components in a server's system, but is still the most important component. Storage is mainly used as a persistence mechanism to store a large amount of processed/unprocessed data. A slow storage device generally results in heavy utilization of read write buffers and higher memory consumption. You will see higher CPU usage, but most of the CPU time is spent waiting for I/O requests.

The recent developments of the flash storage medium have vastly improved storage performance. Still, it's one of the slowest performing components and needs proper planning— I/O planning in the application code, plus enough main memory for read write buffers.

In this recipe, we will learn to monitor storage performance. The main focus will be on local storage devices rather than network storage.

Getting ready

As always, you will need `sudo` access for some commands.

Some of the commands many not be available by default. Using them will prompt you if the command is not available, along with the process necessary to install the required package.

Install the `sysstat` package as follows. We have already used it in previous recipes:

```
$ sudo apt get install sysstat
```

How to do it...

1. The first command we will look at is `vmstat`. Using `vmstat` without any option displays an `io` column with two sub entries: bytes in (`bi`) and bytes out (`bo`). Bytes in represents the number of bytes read in per second from the disk and bytes out represents the bytes written to the disk:

```
ubuntu@ubuntu:~$ vmstat
procs -----------memory---------- ---swap-- -----io---- -system-- -------cpu-----
 r  b   swpd    free   buff  cache   si   so    bi    bo    in   cs us sy id wa st
 1  0      0 3123824  27100 300008    0    0    35     9    66    94  1  1 98  1
 0
ubuntu@ubuntu:~$
```

2. Vmstat also provides two flags, `-d` and `-D`, to get disk statistics. Flag `-d` displays disk statistics and flag `-D` displays a summary view of disk activity:

```
ubuntu@ubuntu:~$ vmstat -D
        27 disks
         3 partitions
     18203 total reads
      4881 merged reads
   1232378 read sectors
   2471384 milli reading
      7315 writes
      3128 merged writes
```

3. There's one more option, `-p`, that displays partition-specific disk statistics. Use the command `lsblk` to get a list of available partitions and then use the `vmstat -p` partition:

```
ubuntu@ubuntu:~$ lsblk
NAME                        MAJ:MIN RM   SIZE RO TYPE MOUNTPOINT
sda                           8:0    0    20G  0 disk
 ├─sda1                       8:1    0   243M  0 part /boot
 ├─sda2                       8:2    0     1K  0 part
 └─sda5                       8:5    0  19.8G  0 part
   ├─ubuntu--vg-root (dm-0)  252:0   0  18.8G  0 lvm  /
   └─ubuntu--vg-swap_1 (dm-1) 252:1  0  1020M  0 lvm  [SWAP]
ubuntu@ubuntu:~$ vmstat -p sda5
sda5          reads    read sectors   writes   requested writes
               7098         625450      2026         168776
```

4. Another command, `dstat`, is a nice replacement for `vmstat`, especially for disk statistics reporting. Use it with flag `-d` to get disk read writes per seconds. If you have multiple disks, you can use `dstat` to list their stats separately:

```
$ dstat -d -D total,sda
```

5. Next, we will look at the command `iostat`. When used without any options, this command displays basic CPU utilization, along with read write statistics for each storage device:

```
ubuntu@ubuntu:~$ iostat
Linux 3.16.0-30-generic (ubuntu)          01/23/2016      _x86_64_        (2 CPU)

avg-cpu:  %user   %nice %system %iowait  %steal   %idle
           0.62    0.04    1.07    0.53    0.00   97.74

Device:            tps    kB_read/s    kB_wrtn/s    kB_read    kB_wrtn
sda               1.88        58.81        15.84     314884      84806
dm-0              3.14        58.23        15.84     311785      84800
dm-1              0.04         0.17         0.00        896          0
```

6. The column `tps` specifies the I/O requests sent to a device per second, and `kb_read/s` and `kb_wrtn/s` specifies per second blocks read and blocks written respectively. `kb_read` and `kb_wrtn` shows the total number of blocks read and written.

7. Some common options for `iostat` include `-d`, that displays disk only statistics, `-g` that displays statistics for a group of devices, flag `-p` to display partition specific stats, and `-x` to get extended statistics. Do not forget to check the manual entries for `iostat` to get more details.

8. You can also use the command `iotop`, which is very similar to the `top` command but it displays disk utilization and relevant processes.

9. The command `lsof` can display the list of all open files and respective processes using that file. Use `lsof` with the process name to get files opened by that process:

```
$ lsof -c sshd
```

```
ubuntu@ubuntu:~$ sudo lsof -c sshd
COMMAND   PID    USER    FD    TYPE      DEVICE SIZE/OFF    NODE NAME
sshd      1254   root    cwd   DIR       252,0     4096       2 /
sshd      1254   root    rtd   DIR       252,0     4096       2 /
sshd      1254   root    txt   REG       252,0   766784   11349 /usr/sbin/ssh
d
sshd      1254   root    mem   REG       252,0    47712  655587 /lib/x86_64-1
inux-gnu/libnss_files-2.19.so
```

10. To get a list of files opened by a specific PID, use the following command: $ lsof -p 1134. Or, to get a list of files opened by a specific user, use the $ lsof -u ubuntu command.

All these commands provide details on the read write performance of a storage device. Another important detail to know is the availability of free space. To get details of space utilization, you can use command df -h. This will list a partition-level summary of disk space utilization:

```
ubuntu@ubuntu:~$ df -h
Filesystem                    Size  Used Avail Use% Mounted on
/dev/mapper/ubuntu--vg-root    19G  2.8G   15G  16% /
none                          4.0K     0  4.0K   0% /sys/fs/cgroup
udev                          2.0G  4.0K  2.0G   1% /dev
tmpfs                         396M  604K  395M   1% /run
none                          5.0M     0  5.0M   0% /run/lock
none                          2.0G     0  2.0G   0% /run/shm
none                          100M     0  100M   0% /run/user
/dev/sda1                     236M   38M  186M  17% /boot
```

11. Finally, you can use the sar command to track disk performance over a period of time. To get real-time disk activity, use sar with the -d option, as follows:

```
$ sar -d 1
```

```
ubuntu@ubuntu:~$ sar -d 1
Linux 3.16.0-30-generic (ubuntu)        01/23/2016      _x86_64_        (2 CPU)

10:10:33 AM          DEV       tps   rd_sec/s   wr_sec/s   avgrq-sz   avgqu-sz      awai
t       svctm       %util
10:10:34 AM       dev8-0      0.00       0.00       0.00       0.00       0.00       0.0
0       0.00       0.00
10:10:34 AM     dev252-0      0.00       0.00       0.00       0.00       0.00       0.0
0       0.00       0.00
10:10:34 AM     dev252-1      0.00       0.00       0.00       0.00       0.00       0.0
0       0.00       0.00
```

12. Use flag -F to get details on file system utilization and flag -S to display swap utilization. You can also enable sar logging and then extract details from those logs. Check the previous recipes in this chapter for how to enable sar logging. Also check manual entries for sar to get details of various options.

Setting performance benchmarks

Until now, in this chapter we have learned about various performance monitoring tools and commands. This recipe covers a well-known performance benchmarking tool: **Sysbench**. The purpose of performance benchmarking is to get a sense of system configuration and the resulting performance. Sysbench is generally used to evaluate the performance of heavy load systems. If you read the Sysbench introduction, it says that Sysbench is a benchmarking tool to evaluate a system running database under intensive load. It is also being used as a tool to evaluate the performance of multiple cloud service providers.

The current version of Sysbench supports various benchmark tests including CPU, memory, IO system, and OLTP systems. We will primarily focus on CPU, memory, and IO benchmarks.

Getting ready

Before using Sysbench, we will need to install it. Sysbench is available in the Ubuntu package repository with a little older (0.4.12) version. We will use the latest version (0.5) from Percona Systems, available in their repo.

To install Sysbench from the Percona repo, we need to add the repo to our installation sources. Following are the entries for Ubuntu 14.04 (trusty). Create a new file under `/etc/apt/source.list.d` and add the following lines to it:

```
$ sudo vi /etc/apt/sources.list.d/percona.list
deb http://repo.percona.com/apt trusty main
deb-src http://repo.percona.com/apt trusty main
```

Next, add the PGP key for the preceding repo:

```
$ sudo apt-key adv --keyserver keys.gnupg.net --recv-keys
1C4CBDCDCD2EFD2A
```

Now we are ready to install the latest version of Sysbench from the Percona repo. Remember to update the `apt` cache before installation:

```
$ sudo apt-get update
$ sudo apt-get install sysbench
```

Once installed, you can check the installed version with the `--version` flag to `sysbench`:

```
$ sysbench --version
sysbench 0.5
```

How to do it...

Now that we have Sysbench installed, let's start with performance testing our system:

1. Sysbench provides a prime number generation test for CPU. You can set the number of primes to be generated with the option `--cpu-max-prime`. Also set the limit on threads with the `--num-threads` option. Set the number of threads equal to the amount of CPU cores available:

   ```
   $ sysbench --test=cpu --num-threads=4 \
   --cpu-max-prime=20000 run
   ```

2. The test should show output similar to the following screenshot:

```
Running the test with following options:
Number of threads: 4
Random number generator seed is 0 and will be ignored


Primer numbers limit: 20000

Threads started!


General statistics:
    total time:                          15.8695s
    total number of events:              10000
    total time taken by event execution: 63.4510s
    response time:
        min:                             2.72ms
        avg:                             6.35ms
        max:                             33.44ms
        approx.  95 percentile:          11.73ms
```

3. Following are the extracted parts of the result from multiple tests with a different thread count on a system with a dual core CPU. It is clear that using two threads give better results:

Threads	1	2	3	4
Total time	33.0697s	15.4335s	15.6258s	15.7778s

4. Next, we will run a test for main memory. The memory tests provides multiple options, such as block-size, total data transfer, type of memory operations, and access modes. Use the following command to run memory tests:

```
$ sysbench --test=memory --memory-block-size=1M \
--num-threads=2 \
--memory-total-size=100G --memory-oper=read run
```

5. Following is part of the output from the memory test:

```
Threads started!

Operations performed: 102400 (1663868.39 ops/sec)

102400.00 MB transferred (1663868.39 MB/sec)


General statistics:
    total time:                          0.0615s
    total number of events:              102400
    total time taken by event execution: 0.0569s
```

6. If you have enabled huge page support, set the memory test support allocation from the huge page pool with the parameter, `--memory-hugetlb`. By default, it's set to off.

7. Next comes the storage performance test. This test also provides you with a number of options to test disk read write speeds. Depending on your requirements, you can set parameters like block-size, random or sequential read writes, synchronous or asynchronous IO operations, and many more.

8. For the `fileio` test we need a few sample files to test with. Use the `sysbench` `prepare` command to create test files. Make sure to set a total file size greater than the size of memory to avoid caching effects. I am using a small 1GBnode with 20G disk space, so I am using 15 files of 1G each:

```
$ sysbench --test=fileio --file-total-size=15G \
--file-num=15 prepare
```

```
ubuntu@ubuntu:~$ sysbench --test=fileio --file-total-size=15G --file-num=15 prep
are
sysbench 0.5:  multi-threaded system evaluation benchmark

15 files, 1048576Kb each, 15360Mb total
Creating files for the test...
Extra file open flags: 0
Creating file test_file.0
Creating file test_file.1
```

9. Once the test preparation is complete, you can run the `fileio` test with different options, depending on what you want to test. The following command will perform random write operations for `60` seconds:

```
$ sysbench --test=fileio --file-total-size=15G \
--file-test-mode=rndwr --max-time=60 \
--file-block-size=4K --file-num=15 --num-threads=1 run
```

```
Operations performed:   0 reads, 10000 writes, 1500 Other = 11500 Total
Read 0b  Written 39.062Mb  Total transferred 39.062Mb  (1.2449Mb/sec)
  318.69 Requests/sec executed

General statistics:
    total time:                          31.3789s
    total number of events:              10000
    total time taken by event execution: 0.1245s
```

10. To perform random read operations, change `--file-test-mode` to `rndrd`, or to perform sequential read operations, use `seqrd`. You can also combine read write operations with `rndrw` or `seqrewr`. Check the help menu for more options.

> To get a full list of available options, enter the `sysbench` command without any parameter. You can also query details of a specific test with `sysbench --test=<name> help`. For example, to get help with I/O tests, use:
>
> ```
> $ sysbench --test=fileio help
> ```

11. When you are done with the `fileio` test, execute the `cleanup` command to delete all sample files:

```
$ sysbench --test=fileio cleanup
```

12. Once you have gathered various performance details, you can try updating various performance tuning parameters to boost performance. Make sure you repeat related tests after each change in parameter. Comparing results from multiple tests will help you to choose the required combination for best performance and a stable system.

There's more...

Sysbench also supports testing MySQL performance with various tests. In the same way as the `fileio` test, Sysbench takes care of setting a test environment by creating tables with data. When using Sysbench from the Percona repo, all OLTP test scripts are located at `/usr/share/doc/sysbench/tests/db/`. You will need to specify the full path when using these scripts. For example:

```
$ sysbench --test=oltp
```

The preceding command will change to the following:

```
$ sysbench --test=/usr/share/doc/sysbench/tests/db/olltp.lua
```

Graphing tools

Sysbench output can be hard to analyze and compare, especially with multiple runs. This is where graphs come in handy. You can try to set up your own graphing mechanism, or simply use prebuilt scripts to create graphs for you. A quick Google search gave me two good, looking options:

- ▸ A Python script to extract data from Sysbench logs: `https://github.com/tsuna/sysbench-tools`

- ▸ A shell script to extract Sysbench data to a CSV file, which can be converted to graphs: `http://openlife.cc/blogs/2011/august/one-liner-condensing-sysbench-output-csv-file`

More options

There are various other performance testing frameworks available. Phoronix Test Suite, Unixbench, and Perfkit by Google are some popular names. Phoronix Test Suite focuses on hardware performance and provides a wide range of performance analysis options, whereas Unixbench provides an option to test various Linux systems. Google open-sourced their performance toolkit with a benchmarker and explorer to evaluate various cloud systems.

See also

- ▶ Get more details on benchmarking with Sysbench at `https://wiki.mikejung.biz/Benchmarking`

- ▶ Sysbench documentation at `http://imysql.com/wp-content/uploads/2014/10/sysbench-manual.pdf`

- ▶ A sample script to run batch run multiple Sysbench tests at `https://gist.github.com/chetan/712484`

- ▶ Sysbench GitHub repo at `https://github.com/akopytov/sysbench`

- ▶ Linux performance analysis in 60 seconds. A good read for what to check when you are debugging a performance issue at `http://techblog.netflix.com/2015/11/linux-performance-analysis-in-60s.html`

14
Centralized Authentication Service

In this chapter, we will cover the following recipes:

- ▶ Installing OpenLDAP
- ▶ Installing phpLDAPadmin
- ▶ Ubuntu server logins with LDAP
- ▶ Authenticating Ejabberd users with LDAP

Introduction

When you have a large user base using multiple services across the organization, a centralized authentication service becomes a need rather than a luxury. It becomes necessary to quickly add new user accounts across multiple services when a new user comes in, and deactivate the respective access tokens when a user leaves the organization. A centralized authentication service enables you to quickly respond by updating the user database on a single central server.

Various different services are available to set up centralized authentication. In this chapter, we will learn how to set up a centralized authentication service using a **Lightweight Directory access Protocol** (**LDAP**). A directory is a special database designed specifically for high volume lookups. LDAP directories are tree-based data structures, also known as **Directory Information Trees** (**DIT**). Each node in a tree contains a unique entry with its own set of attributes.

LDAP is specifically designed for high volume read systems with limited write activities. These directories are commonly used for storing details of users with their respective access control lists. Some examples include shared address books, shared calendar services, centralized authentication for systems such as Samba, and storage DNS systems. LDAP provides lightweight access to the directory services over the TCP/IP stack. It is similar to the X.500 OSI directory service, but with limited features and limited resource requirements. For more details on LDAP, check out the OpenLDAP admin guide at `http://www.openldap.org/doc/admin24/intro.html`.

Installing OpenLDAP

This recipe covers the installation and initial configuration of LDAP. The Ubuntu package repository makes the installation easy by providing the required packages for the LDAP service.

Getting ready

You will need access to a root account or an account with `sudo` privileges.

How to do it...

Let's start with installing the LDAP package and helper utilities:

1. Update your repository using the `apt-get update` command and then install the OpenLDAP package, `slapd`:

    ```
    $ sudo apt-get update
    $ sudo apt-get install slapd ldap-utils
    ```

2. You will be asked to enter the admin password and to confirm it.

3. The installation process simply installs the package without any configuration. We need to start the actual configuration process with the reconfiguration of the `slapd` package. Use the following command to start the re-configuration process:

    ```
    $ sudo dpkg-reconfigure slapd
    ```

4. This command will ask you a series of questions including the domain name, admin account, password, database type, and others. Match your answers as follows:

    ❏   Omit LDAP server configuration – NO.

- DNS Domain name – Enter your domain name. You can use any domain name. For this setup, I will be using `example.com`. This domain name will determine the top structure of your directory:

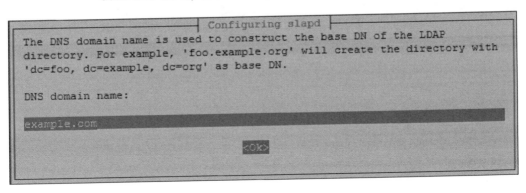

- Organization name – Enter your organization name. I am using `example` as my organization.
- Admin password – Enter a password for the admin account. It can be the same as the one entered during installation, or a totally different one. Make sure you note this password as it will be used to access the admin account.
- Database backend – HDB

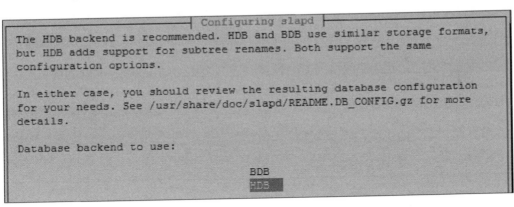

- Remove the database when `slapd` is purged - this is about removing the database in case you uninstall the `slapd` package. Choose NO as you don't want the database to be deleted:
- Move old database - YES

❑ Allow the LDAPv2 protocol - unless you are planning to use some old tools, choose NO:

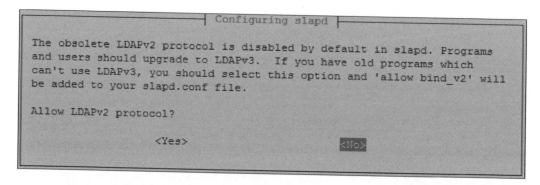

```
                      ┤ Configuring slapd ├

The obsolete LDAPv2 protocol is disabled by default in slapd. Programs
and users should upgrade to LDAPv3.  If you have old programs which
can't use LDAPv3, you should select this option and 'allow bind_v2' will
be added to your slapd.conf file.

Allow LDAPv2 protocol?

            <Yes>                              <No>
```

5. Once you have answered all the questions, the process will reconfigure the LDAP service. Now your LDAP service is installed and ready to use:

```
ubuntu@ubuntu:~$ sudo dpkg-reconfigure slapd
 * Stopping OpenLDAP slapd
   Moving old database directory to /var/backups:                    [ OK ]
   - directory unknown... done.
   Creating initial configuration... done.
   Creating LDAP directory... done.
 * Starting OpenLDAP slapd                                           [ OK ]
Processing triggers for libc-bin (2.19-0ubuntu6.6) ...
ubuntu@ubuntu:~$
```

6. Now you can use utility commands to query existing data. To test whether the LDAP service is installed and running properly, use the `ldapsearch -x` command. You should see output similar to following screenshot:

```
ubuntu@ubuntu:~$ ldapsearch -x
# extended LDIF
#
# LDAPv3
# base <> (default) with scope subtree
# filter: (objectclass=*)
# requesting: ALL
#
```

7. Use `ldapsearch` as follows to query our newly added domain, `example.com`:

   `$ ldapsearch -x -LLL -H ldap:/// -b dc=example,dc=com dn`

```
ubuntu@ubuntu:~$ ldapsearch -x -LLL -H ldap:/// -b dc=example,dc=com dn
dn: dc=example,dc=com

dn: cn=admin,dc=example,dc=com

ubuntu@ubuntu:~$
```

8. The following command will query the default content for `example.com`:

   `$ ldapsearch -x -LLL -b dc=example,dc=com`

```
ubuntu@ubuntu:~$ ldapsearch -x -LLL -b dc=example,dc=com
dn: dc=example,dc=com
objectClass: top
objectClass: dcObject
objectClass: organization
o: example
dc: example

dn: cn=admin,dc=example,dc=com
objectClass: simpleSecurityObject
objectClass: organizationalRole
cn: admin
description: LDAP administrator
```

The `ldap-utils` package also provides more commands to configure the LDAP service, but it is quite a lengthy and complex task. In the next recipe, we will learn how to set up a web-based admin interface that make things a little easier.

How it works...

With the respective packages available in the Ubuntu package repository, installing **OpenLDAP** is quite an easy task. All we have to do is install the required binaries and then configure the LDAP system to serve our desired domain. We have installed two packages: one is `slapd`, the LDAP daemon, and the other is `ldap-utils`, which provides various commands to work with the LDAP daemon. After installation is complete, we have re-configured LDAP to match our required directory setup. We have chosen to go with LDAPv3 API and disabled LDAPv2. If you have any older systems working with LDAPv2, then you will need to enable support for old APIs.

See also

- Open LDAP admin guide at `http://www.openldap.org/doc/admin24/intro.html`

- Ubuntu OpenLDAP guide at `https://help.ubuntu.com/lts/serverguide/openldap-server.html`

- LDAP protocol RFC at `http://www.rfc-editor.org/rfc/rfc2251.txt`

- LDAP protocol technical details at `http://www.rfc-editor.org/rfc/rfc3377.txt`

- Get more help with LDAP configuration using the `man ldap.conf` command.

Installing phpLDAPadmin

In the previous recipe, we installed the LDAP service, but working with LDAP using the command line interface is quite a complex and lengthy task. This recipe covers the installation of a user interface, phpLDAPadmin. The `phpldapadmin` package provides an easy-to-use web-based user interface for the LDAP service.

Getting ready

Make sure that you have the LDAP service installed and running.

How to do it...

Follow these steps to install phpLDAPadmin:

1. The Ubuntu package repository makes things easy again by providing the package for phpLDAPadmin. The web interface can be quickly installed in a single command as follows:

   ```
   $ sudo apt-get install phpldapadmin
   ```

2. The installation process takes care of installing all dependencies including PHP and the Apache web server. It also creates necessary configurations and sets up Apache with the required settings for phpLDAPadmin. Once installation is complete, you can access the admin interface at `http://youServerIP/phpldapadmin`.

3. Before we access the admin page, let's make some small changes in the configuration file. The file is located at /etc/phpldapadmin/config.php. By default, phpLDAPadmin shows warning messages for unused template files. These warning messages get shown in the main interface before the actual content. To hide them, search for hide_template_warning in the configuration file and set it to true. You will also need to uncomment the same line:

```
$config->custom->appearance['hide_template_warning'] =
true;
```

4. The other settings should have already been set by the installation process. You can cross-check the following settings:

```
$servers->setValue('server','host','127.0.0.1');

$servers->setValue(
    'login','bind_id',
    'cn=admin,dc=example,
    dc=com'
);
$servers->setValue(
    'server','base',array('dc=example,dc=com')
);
```

5. Once you are done with the configuration file changes, save and close it and then access the admin interface through your browser:

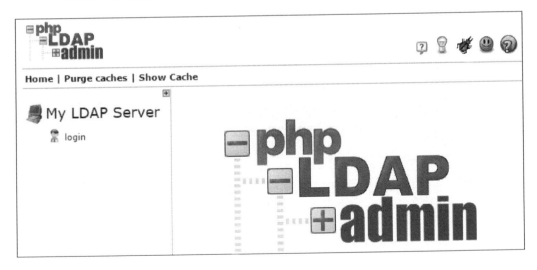

6. Click on the **login** link on the left of the page to get the login dialogue box. The username (**Login DN**) field is already filled with details for the admin account. Make sure the details match the domain you have set up. Enter the password for the admin account and click the **Authenticate** button:

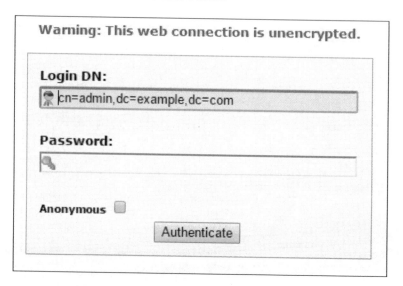

 You can also log in as an anonymous user. In the login box, do not enter a password, click to check the **Anonymous** checkbox, and then click the **Authenticate** button. This gives you a read-only view, which is quite useful when you just need to verify some details.

7. You should have noticed the warning on the login box saying the connection is unencrypted. This is just a reminder that you are using the admin console over a non-HTTPs connection. You can set up Apache with SSL certificates to get an encrypted, secure connection with your LDAP server. Check *Chapter 3, Working with Web Servers*, for more details on how to set up SSL certificates on the Apache web server.

8. Once you log in to phpLDAPadmin, you can see the domain listed in the left-hand side menu. Click on the domain link to view its details.

9. Next, click on the small plus link (**+**) to expand the domain link and see its children. With the default settings, it should show only the admin account:

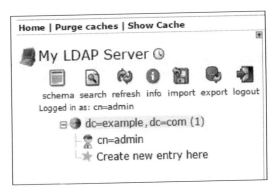

10. Along with the link for the admin account, you will see an option to create a new entry. Clicking on this link will show you a list of templates for the new entry:

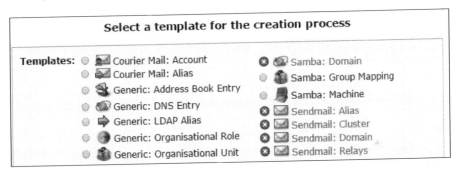

While clicking on some of these templates, for example *Generic: User Account*, you may notice a PHP error saying `Error trying to get non-existent value`. The form rendering fails and you cannot see the complete form the with submit button. This is a small bug and can be fixed with a small edit.

Open `/usr/share/phpldapadmin/lib/TemplateRender.php`.

Search for the following line:

```
$default = $this->getServer()
->getValue('appearance','password_hash');
```

Now update the preceding command as follows:

```
$default = $this->getServer()
->getValue('appearance','password_hash_custom');
```

Now you are ready to create groups and respective user accounts on your LDAP server.

How it works...

In this recipe, we have installed a web-based administration console for the LDAP server. The `ldap-utils` package provides various commands to work with the LDAP server, but it is quite a complex and lengthy task. A graphical user interface gives you a better listing of all options and existing configurations, making things a little easier.

The phpLDAPadmin package is a PHP/Apache-based web application that provides a graphical interface for the LDAP server. It displays all options and configurations in an easy-to-use graphical format and passes all user actions to LDAP APIs.

There's more...

Apache directory studio is another user interface for LDAP administration. It is a desktop application based on Java. You can get more details at `https://directory.apache.org/studio/`.

See also

▸ A StackOverflow answer for the phpLDAPadmin error message at `http://stackoverflow.com/a/21195761/1012809`

Ubuntu server logins with LDAP

So, we have installed and configured our own centralized auth server with LDAP. Now is the time to use LDAP to authenticate client logins. In this recipe, we will set up a separate Ubuntu server to use our LDAP server for authenticating users.

Getting ready

You will need a new Ubuntu server to be set as an LDAP client. Also, `sudo` privileges are needed for the initial setup.

Make sure you have followed the previous recipes and have set up your LDAP server.

How to do it...

1. We will need to install the LDAP client-side package on the client system. This package will install all the required tools to authenticate with the remote LDAP server:

    ```
    $ sudo apt-get update
    $ sudo apt-get install ldap-auth-client nscd
    ```

2. The installation process will ask you some questions regarding your LDAP server and its authentication details. Answer those questions as follows:

    ❏   `LDAP server URI`: `ldap://you-LDAP-server-IP`: Make sure you change the protocol line from `ldapi:///` to `ldap://`

    ❏   `Distinguished name of search base`: Match this to the domain set on the LDAP server in the format `dc=example,dc=com`

    ❏   `LDAP version to use`: 3

    ❏   `Make local root database admin`: Yes

    ❏   `Does LDAP database require login`: No

    ❏   `LDAP account for root`: `cn=admin,dc=example,dc=com`

    ❏   `LDAP root account password`: The password for the LDAP admin account

3. Next, we need to change the authentication configuration to check with the LDAP server. First, run the following command to set the **name service switch** file `/etc/nsswitch.conf`:

    ```
    $ sudo auth-client-config -t nss -p lac_ldap
    ```

4. This will change `/etc/nsswitch.conf` as follows:

```
# /etc/nsswitch.conf
#
# Example configuration of GNU Name Service Switch functionality.
# If you have the `glibc-doc-reference' and `info' packages installed, try:
# `info libc "Name Service Switch"' for information about this file.

# pre_auth-client-config # passwd:         compat
passwd: files ldap
# pre_auth-client-config # group:          compat
group: files ldap
# pre_auth-client-config # shadow:         compat
shadow: files ldap
```

5. Next, add the following line to `/etc/pam.d/common-session`. This will create a local home directory for LDAP users. Edit the `common-session` file and add the following line at the end of the file:

    ```
    session required          pam_mkhomedir.so umask=0022
    skel=/etc/skel
    ```

6. Now restart the `nscd` service with the following command:

    ```
    $ sudo /etc/init.d/nscd restart
    ```

    Now you should be able to log in with the user account created on your LDAP server. I have set up an **Organizational Unit** (**OU**) named **users** and created an admin user under it:

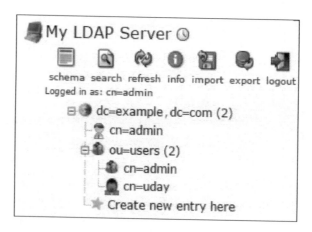

7. Next, change the login to the newly created LDAP user account with the `su username` command. You will need to enter a password that is configured on LDAP server. As this is a first-time login for this new user, our PAM settings have created a new home directory for him:

    ```
    ubuntu@ubuntu:~$ su uday
    Password:
    Creating directory '/home/users/uday'.
    $
    ```

This new user is a member of the admin group on the LDAP server, so he will get `sudo` privileges on the local server as well.

You can always use a default login prompt to log in with LDAP users, as well as local user accounts that already exist on the server.

How it works...

Here we have configured the Ubuntu server to authenticate with our centralized LDAP system. This is not limited to the Ubuntu server and you can configure the Ubuntu desktop in a similar way as well. Using a centralized authentication makes it easy to administer hundreds of user accounts from a single place. A user can still log in as a local user if he has any local credentials.

Using centralized authentication enables you to log in from any system. You will get the same access rights and permissions from any terminal. Additionally, if the LDAP configuration supports roaming profiles then all your data will be replicated to any new system you log in from. You may have noticed the home directory for the LDAP user account is located in the /home/users directory and not in /home. This separates your account from any local users.

Finally, the groups and roles configured on the LDAP server also apply on the system you are logging in from. So, if the user is assigned admin rights on the LDAP server, he will get admin rights, including sudo privileges, on the system he is logged in from. This is because Ubuntu contains a default group named admin with sudo privileges. When a user logs in with his LDAP account, the groups and roles assigned to his LDAP account are matched with local groups and roles. You can either disable such groups from any remote systems, or set the proper access rights on the LDAP server itself.

See also

- ▶ The Ubuntu community page for LDAP client authentication at
  https://help.ubuntu.com/community/LDAPClientAuthentication

Authenticating Ejabberd users with LDAP

In this recipe, we will learn to set up the Ejabberd server to authenticate the user with our LDAP server. Until now, we have set up the LDAP server and used it to log in to the Ubuntu server with a user account created on the LDAP server. This recipe covers the configuration of an external service to work with our LDAP installation.

The Ejabberd server provides built-in support for LDAP-based authentication. You can use LDAP for user authentication as well as vCard storage. As stated in the Ejabberd admin guide, Ejabberd use LDAP as a read-only data source. We cannot create new user accounts in the LDAP directory, but we can change passwords if the mod_register module is enabled.

Getting ready

You will need the Ejabberd service installed and running. Go through *Chapter 10, Communication Server with XMPP*, for details on the installation and configuration of the Ejabberd server.

Create a user account on the LDAP server to be used with Ejabberd.

How to do it...

As Ejabberd provides inbuilt support for LDAP-based authentication, we simply need to edit configurations and set the `auth` method to LDAP. If you have used a Debian package for the Ejabberd installation, your Ejabberd should be installed in `/opt/ejabberd-version` directory and the configuration can be found at `/etc/ejabberd-version/conf`. If you have installed Ejabberd from source, all configuration files are located in the `/etc/ejabberd` directory:

1. Open `ejabberd.yml` from your Ejabberd configuration directory and search for Authentication. With the default settings, it should contain the following line indicating internal authentication:

   ```
   auth_method: internal
   ```

2. Comment out that line by changing it as follows:

   ```
   ## auth_method: internal
   ```

3. Next, find Authentication using LDAP. This section contains a few parameters and configures communication with the LDAP server. Search and update the following parameters:

   ```
   ldap_servers:
     - "domain/IP of LDAP server"
   ldap_port: 389
   ldap_rootdn: "cn=admin,dc=example,dc=com"
   ldap_password: "password"
   ldap_base: "ou=ejabberd,dc=example,dc=com"
   ```

   I have used a default admin account to authenticate with the LDAP server itself. In a production environment, you should change it to a different account. With a default LDAP setup, you can skip the `ldap_rootdn` and `ldap_password` settings to enable anonymous connection.

4. Next, under the `ldap_base` parameter, I have restricted users to the Organizational Unit named `Ejabberd`. Only the user accounts that are configured under the `Ejabberd` unit can log in with the Ejabberd server.

5. Now, save the configuration file changes and close the file, and then restart the Ejabberd server with the following command:

```
$ sudo /opt/ejabberd-version/bin/ejabberdctl restart
```

6. If the server fails to restart, check the log files for any configuration errors. Alternatively, you can use the `reload_config` option to `ejabberdctl` to update the in-memory configuration without restarting:

```
$ sudo /opt/ejabberd-version/bin/ejabberdctl reload_config
```

7. Once the server has started, you can log in with your LDAP accounts. You will need a JID to log in with Ejabberd, which is a combination of a UID from the LDAP server and any host configured on Ejabberd, for instance, uday@cookbook.com, where uday is the **UID** on LDAP and cookbook.com is the **host** served by Ejabberd server. The domain entries on the LDAP server and Ejabberd need not match.

The following is the default host entry for my Ejabberd installation:

```
## hosts: Domains served by ejabberd.
## You can define one or several, for example:
## hosts:
##   - "example.net"
##   - "example.com"
##   - "example.org"
##
hosts:
  - "ubuntu"
```

8. Now you can log in to Ejabberd with your LDAP username. Here is the account set up in my chat client with the JID uday@ubuntu, where uday is my LDAP user and ubuntu is the Ejabberd host:

```
Account
  XMPP Address:  uday|@ubuntu
                 Example: juliet@capulet.com
  Password:      ••••••••                        [ Change... ]
```

Once all things are set up, you should be able to connect to the Ejabberd server using your LDAP user account.

How it works...

Here, we have set up Ejabberd as an example of LDAP-based authentication. Similar to Ejabberd, various other systems support centralized authentication through LDAP with either built-in support or with a plug-in module. Make sure that you create a proper directory structure with organizational units, roles, and separate users in proper groups. Also use a separate user account for authenticating with the LDAP server itself. You need to set the respective LDAP credentials in the Ejabberd configuration file. If somehow your Ejabberd server gets compromised, then the LDAP server credentials are readily available to an attacker. To limit the risk, using separate and limited accounts is a good idea. Ejabberd also supports anonymous authentication with the LDAP server and mostly uses it as a read-only database. So, even if you skip the authentication details (depending on the LDAP configuration), Ejabberd should work well and authenticate your users.

Ejabberd also provides good enough debug logging, where you can see the actual communication with the LDAP server. You will need to set logging to debug mode in the Ejabberd configuration. The log files are located in the `/opt/ejabberd-version/logs` directory or the `/var/log/ejabberd` directory, depending on the source of the Ejabberd installation.

See also

> ▸ Ejabberd docs LDAP section at `https://www.process-one.net/docs/ejabberd/guide_en.html#ldap`

Index

Made in the USA
Middletown, DE
28 May 2017